THEATERS of WAR: We Remember

Edited by
Wendy Phillips Lazar

Book design by John Wattai

Theaters of War: We Remember / edited by Wendy Phillips Lazar.

First Edition

Publisher's Cataloging-in-Publication

p. cm.

1. World War, 1939–1945—Personal narratives,
American. I. Lazar, Wendy

D811.5.T44 2001 940.54'8173'0922
QBI0I-700388

ISBN #0-9710246-9-3

Title page photo: Monument to a dead American soldier, Normandy

CONTENTS

General Dwight D. Eisenhower in England

FOREWORD

The stories contained in the following volume, *Theaters of War: We Remember*, provide a glimpse into the individual lives of those who fought the most all-encompassing and pivotal war in our nation's history. They bring an understanding of World War II from the personal perspective of those who actually lived through the experience. Although words will always fail to communicate the overwhelming and complex emotions felt by all Americans during the war years, these come close.

It is difficult to describe the depth of patriotism that was so pervasive in this country during the war years. Youth itself has a way of anesthetizing us against the full weight of our own thoughts and feelings. We couldn't wait to defend our country and our way of life against the dark forces of tyranny and oppression that were the Axis powers. All that national spirit and youthful exuberance blurred our vision of the reality that was to come.

When the basic training, pride in the new uniforms, and final good-byes faded, the youth of America found itself in foxholes, gun turrets, and aboard fighting ships facing a very real enemy bent on destroying them. No one who has not experienced the situation can ever truly understand it. Reading these stories may, however, help readers appreciate what these brave men and women suffered and sacrificed on their behalf.

All the proceeds from the sale of this book will help support the National World War II Memorial in Washington, DC…a lasting tribute to an extraordinary generation of Americans and a reminder to subsequent generations of the true cost of freedom.

Special thanks to Wendy Lazar, President of Glendale Industries, for her unselfish dedication and hard work to preserve the memory of patriots.

Sincerely,

Bob Dole

BOB DOLE

American soldiers entering a Belgian town

PREFACE

Sixteen million men and women served in our nation's armed forces during World War II. They fought in the service of our country united in a common cause. They left their families, uprooted their lives, endured endless hardships over months and years, gave all they had to give and still found the strength to give more, and saw the best and worst of human nature. Some of their stories are recounted within these pages. Some remember these events as if they happened only recently; others admit to the haze of dimmed memories over the extended passage of time. Many submitted old newspaper articles and photographs to verify events recalled.

The experiences took place in all theaters of operation, as combat regions are called, so the book's title *Theaters of War: We Remember* is, in one sense, obvious. But more than that, it refers to the veterans' experiences that contain everything dramatic theater offers—tragedy and comedy, pathos and passion, love and hate, good and evil. Theater is a playwright's interpretation of events either real or imagined. But war is real, all too real. In describing encounters with the enemy, one of the more frequent expressions used throughout this book is "all hell broke loose." Yet, according to O. B. Hill, chairman of the 508th Parachute Infantry Regiment Association, "War is not hell. It is worse than hell."

The reality of this war depended on where a soldier was stationed, when he served his time, and which branch of service he was in. Those in the infantry came face to face with the enemy; those in the air force did not. In the Pacific theater, there were palm trees and oppressive heat; in Europe, hedgerows and unbearable cold. Some served in forested mountain passes; others, on open ships in turbulent seas. Some suffered from jungle rot and malaria; for others, it was frostbite and dysentery. Food for most was canned C-rations, while some were forced to turn to cannibalism for survival. It was a horrific experience to be the target of enemy fire; it was far, far worse to be attacked by "friendly" fire from U.S. military personnel and equipment. One man's hell would be another's version of paradise; while paradise for another would be an end to the unbearable pain and suffering.

Many of the personal accounts that follow are being told for the first time for purposes of this book; several are excerpts taken from self-published memoirs; others are from pages written previously for the benefit of children and grandchildren. All were submitted to Glendale, an international catalog company that outfits military honor guards, color guards, and drill teams. As owner and president of Glendale, I compiled *Theaters of War: We Remember* because I felt a need to preserve the veterans' personal accounts as a tribute to their indomitable spirit, strong resilience, exceptional commitment, and willing sacrifices. In their honor, proceeds from this book will be donated to The National World War II Memorial in Washington, DC. The American Battle Monuments Commission, which is responsible for the design and creation of the memorial, has endorsed the project from its inception.

My own contribution to World War II was in 1942 when, as a child in Rochester, New York, I gave up my metal toys to answer the call for donations of metal salvage. Thousands upon thousands of men, women, and even children did whatever they could both at home and abroad to keep our American forces healthy, safe, and comfortable. Whether it was a child donating toys, women (my own mother included) who volunteered their services with the Civilian Defense Council—as technicians, typists, cooks, seamstresses, knitters, drivers, whatever their talents, and wherever they were needed—the men and women who built the equipment so heralded by our soldiers, the doctors and nurses who tended the sick and wounded, or those who maintained the stability of our country at home, we were all in this noble cause together. It was a proud period in our history.

I am grateful to the veterans and their families who contributed segments of these personal histories and feel privileged to be able to share these individual perspectives from the war years.

Special thanks also go to my own family and friends who have listened to me talk endlessly about this project for two years. My enthusiasm never waned, nor did their patience and encouragement.

Wendy Phillips Lazar

REFLECTIONS

Sign on Tarawa

Carter Strong

I still can't realize that I of all people have or will have served three years in the U.S. Army, my 19th, 20th, and 21st year. I feel so much older in a worldly or hard facts of life respect. Normally, I wouldn't have been in contact with so many things that have been unpleasant. I would have been able to enjoy a few more years of aloofness from many of the undesirable parts and people of the world. As it is now, I have seen everything evil thinkers can bring upon man, how crude much of the living is in the world. I've seen so much misery that life in the U.S. seems like a dream. I can't picture Grandmother pulling a cart full of manure or kindling logs down through the center of town, or Dad picking up cigarette butts as soldiers flick them into the gutter, or Joe hobbling down the street on crutches with two or three friends with him in the same condition.

Across the street is a large former department store that a few months ago was housing 1,400 people. Today there are still several hundred there. Whole families and more in one small room with no possessions except what they can carry. Some of those families are well educated; some were wealthy people, all coming from every part of Europe. They have nothing now. For some of them, good; others, I don't think they all deserved their present plight. No one can deny that there are some, maybe a few, good Germans. Those few are the ones I feel sorry for, and I can't help thinking what it might have been like if a similar thing had happened in America. Boy, the world is not a bed of roses, and I feel I have absorbed that fact more than anything else since being in the army.

In another way, I must be better off for knowing it now. Nothing will be beyond my comprehension in that line in the future, because I feel I can take anything after this. I'm sure every other GI feels somewhat the same and is much more appreciative of his own home and country than he ever was before.

Another angle is the millions of little children in this country. Never have I seen such large groups of kids, and the younger they are, the more there are of them. Many are without families and will be a state problem for a long time. Hitler said, "Give me five years and you won't recognize Germany." He was certainly right. He killed thousands of cripples, aged, and diseased, but gave the people in return hundreds of thousands of legless and armless young people. Oh, these people made such a mess for themselves.

Richard Bayman

War is a barbaric act of pitting the finest young men of a country against an enemy determined on destroying them, and the only way of survival is to kill or be killed. Rules of conduct do not exist on the battlefield, where survival depends on your killing the enemy any way you can before he kills you and then on to the next one and the next one until your luck runs out and you, too, become a statistic, whether dead or wounded.

The horror of war can be comprehended only by those who have actually experienced it, which brings out not only the worst in man but also the best in man as men sacrifice their own young lives to save those of their buddies. Heroism becomes a common virtue in the face of death.

Every day, as you became more weary, your attitude toward living and dying became more hardened, as the only way out of combat, short of the war ending, was to either be killed in action or wounded so badly you were no longer able to fight. Whether it was true or not, one GI who had been overseas in combat zones for a long time said he did not shoot to kill the Japs, but rather tried to shoot them in the stomach just to hear them scream.

It took great discipline to enter into combat with a fanatical enemy whose mindset was fight until death, never surrender under any circumstances, and who was deeply entrenched in well-fortified positions that had been prepared for several years. Our fighting men displayed great valor day after day as they continued to press on against deadly enemy fire. My thoughts were that death is everywhere. I can see it; I smell it; and, as I looked it in the eye, I wondered when it would be my turn.

Letter Home

Dear Mom and Dad,
The war is over now; my task at last is through.
But, Mom and Dad, there is something that I must ask of you.
I have a friend, oh, such a friend, he has no home you see;
So, Mom and Dad, I would like to bring him home with me.

My, son, of course we don't mind if someone comes back with you;
I'm sure he could stay with us for a day or so.

But, Mother, you don't understand what I'm trying to say,
I want him to live with us, as long as he can stay.
Mother, I must tell you something. Please don't be alarmed,
My friend, you see, in a battle, just happened to lose his arm.

My son, don't be ashamed to bring him home with you.
He could stay here and visit for a week, or even two.

But, Mother, he's not only a friend; he's like a brother.
That's why I want him to live with us, and he'd be like a son to you.
But before you give your answer, there's something I must say.
My friend fought in a battle in which he lost his leg.

My son, it hurts me to say this, but my answer must be no.
Your father and I would have no time for a boy who is crippled so.

Some months later, a letter came saying their son had died. When they read the cause of death, the letter said "suicide." When the casket arrived draped with our nation's flag, they saw their son lying there without an arm or leg.

Author Unknown

Joining Up!

Seymour Karpen.

U.S. Marine Raiders on Cape Totkina on Bougainville, Solomon Islands

C. Gordon Fletcher

pril 1940. Here I was standing before an officer of the Massachusetts National Guard, being sworn to protect my country, constitution, and state. For this I received a new uniform plus one dollar for showing up to duty one evening each week, payday being $12 every three months, and a serial number 20123441. I was 19 years old.

This was my indoctrination into the National Guard as a member of I Troop, 110th Cavalry, 26th Yankee Division, and a horse was assigned to me to ride every week. How did I get into such a predicament?

One friend, Harold Thayer, came over one day and said he had joined the National Guard and had a lot of fun horseback riding every week. Harold talked me into joining, so I told my mother what I was going to do. As mothers go, she didn't like the idea and said, "If you join you might have to go to war." So my answer, which I can remember as if it were yesterday, was "Oh Mom! There hasn't been a war for 20 years; there won't be one now." What a foolish statement! I wasn't reading much of what the newspapers and radio were saying about Hitler in Europe. I joined, and so did my cousin Bud Morton, both on the same day. I had never been on a horse.

So, here I was, in the cavalry. For three months we went to the Commonwealth Avenue Armory in Boston every Wednesday evening and rode. A lot of training took place, how to saddle a horse, learn the parts of a saddle, how to ride with saddle, and how to ride bareback. Then came riding in marching order two abreast, four abreast, and everything from a walk to a trot to a full gallop. These sessions lasted from two to five hours, and we would collapse into bed when we got home. The next morning, after riding, our legs ached and we could hardly get our knees together.

July 1940. Two weeks of maneuvers in Canton, New York, near the Saint Lawrence Seaway. This was to be all cavalry units, both infantry and artillery. We left from Boston by train with horses in front boxcars and arrived in late afternoon. Our first job was to set up tents and establish a picket line. A picket line is for the horses. Each end of the line is attached to a solid object, and from 40 to 50 horses are tied along it. Being in the cavalry means your horse comes first before yourself. You must feed and water him, currycomb him after every ride; then you can get yourself to the chow line. When at base camp there is a stable volunteer, so you don't have to shovel manure.

The first week was a disaster. Rain, rain, and more rain turned our camp into one large mud pond, but rain doesn't stop the training. The second week was good, and our big three-day battle was to take place the middle of the week. We would be away from base camp bivouacking in different locations.

Cavalry only rides into battle but always fights on foot. Second day out, I Troop, the Blue cavalry, was to keep control of the main road and not let the Red cavalry past. Another soldier and I were told to go up to a rise on the field and watch for enemy troops. We gave our horse to another and took a position behind some rocks a few hundred yards up on the rise.

Our troop left, and we stayed at our position for over an hour. Across the field came another soldier, also Blue, and we asked him what happened to I Troop. They had pulled out a half hour ago and, forgetting us, left us up on the hill. We walked to the road and headed in the direction I Troop was last seen headed. In two or three miles, we came to a crossroad where both Red and Blue prisoners were held, so we sat with them. Around 4 P.M. down the road came I Troop, along with my horse. I never did find out who won, Red or Blue.

Leaving the USA, we still didn't know where we were going, but found out that we were now Task Force 6814. Our 180th Field Artillery, 182nd Infantry, parts of 101st Infantry, and other units were taken out of the 26th Yankee Division and were now known as task force 6814. From the position of the sun, we knew we were heading south, but this January 23rd was cold as we stood out on deck watching the other ships and our escort destroyers. A blimp flying overhead watched for submarines. The Germans had submarines off our coast and had sunk a ship a short distance off New York harbor the week before we left.

A convoy goes only as fast as the slowest ship, and most of our convoy was older ships. We traveled slow and did a lot of zigzagging, our ship being the last one in the convoy. The second morning out, we woke to quiet, no motors turning. Up in a hurry, out to deck, we were all alone, broken down in the Atlantic somewhere off the Carolinas. This was a nervous time, and the guns were well manned; but what could we do like a sitting duck in a pond? By noon, the motors were going again, and shortly afterward a blimp came over us and followed us the rest of the day. By late afternoon we had caught up to the convoy and took our place in line.

The weather kept getting warmer, and nine days after leaving New York we arrived at the entrance to the Panama Canal. The *McAndrew* entered the canal about 9 A.M. With the other ships in front of us, it was a wonderful sight. The day was February 1st, and we knew we were not going to Europe. The trip through the canal was beautiful, and it took the whole day. It was interesting to watch us being pulled in and out of the locks by the little locomotives. Midday, when we were going through Gatun Lock, someone mentioned this was freshwater. There was a rush to the showers to have a freshwater shower, as all we had had over the last week was saltwater with saltwater soap. This was our last freshwater shower for over a month. Late afternoon we had gone through the last lock and were on the Pacific side, where we docked at Panama City. That evening we watched food and water being loaded on, and early the next morning we were headed west across the Pacific Ocean. Where were we going? How long would we be at sea? Were we going to the Philippines? These are some of the questions asked, but we got no answers.

We crossed the Pacific Ocean during the whole month of February, and it wasn't a pleasant cruise. The ATS *McAndrew* was a banana boat that now had more than 1,500 troops on board. Only two meals a day were served on army transport ships, and this one had only one kitchen deck below main deck and no dining room. After we got our food in our tin plate and coffee in our tin cup, we would come up to the main deck, then up one more deck, where we ate in the open. We ate here good or bad days, and if it was rough, much food got spilled before we reached the eating area. The mess lines were too long. If you got up early you could be near the beginning, but if you got in line by 9 A.M., you wouldn't eat for at least an hour. The supper line would start forming by 3 P.M.

There was no space on deck for any formation, so no exercising was ever done. I was assigned to the gun crew in the bow of the ship, and the weather was getting hotter every day. I spent many nights sleeping outside. This was great, as inside it was hot. C Battery quarters were on the main lounge off the main deck but loaded with tiers of bunks six to eight bunks high. I always grabbed the top bunk. In cases of seasickness it was best to be up top.

One mishap on our ship, which was sad—a soldier of an outfit below decks was killed. One soldier cleaning his rifle slid a shell into the rifle chamber and it went off. The bullet hit one of his buddies sitting across the room, killing him instantly. The funeral was held on deck by a captain, and the body, wrapped in cloth, was slid out from under the American flag into the Pacific Ocean. This got us all thinking and talking about how we didn't know what the future had in store for us.

Joe Hannan

The Dark Side of the Golden Door

In December 1941 my response to the bombing of Pearl Harbor was to join the U.S. Coast Guard. My choice was influenced by the vision of those beautiful white cutters I saw when my father took me fishing out of Hoboken, New Jersey. But by the time I was called to active duty on January 10, 1942, the U.S. Coast Guard had joined the U.S. Navy, and all those white cutters were painted battleship gray. That was the first shock.

We were sworn in at the barge office on the Battery in Manhattan. My father came to see me off and then went home and gave away my fishing rod, my ice skates, and all of my clothes. I guess he didn't expect me back.

All of us 18 year olds knew that if you joined the army, you first went to Fort Dix and then to basic training. A few may have known about navy training facilities in Newport, Rhode Island. Nobody, but nobody, had the vaguest notion of where you went to become a coast guardsman.

We who joined the U.S. Coast Guard in New York were the sailors quickest to find a swaying deck beneath our feet. Ten minutes after the ceremony we were herded (too soon to be marched) aboard a ferry. Ten minutes later we went ashore on Ellis Island.

I don't remember anyone having the temerity to ask why we were there, but it soon became clear when a cadre of nasty little petty officers took charge. We were in something the coast guard and the navy call "boot camp." It was eight weeks of hell designed to make men of us, to make sailors of us, to make us wish that we'd waited to be drafted, to help us over our homesickness by ensuring complete exhaustion every night.

That didn't work too well for many "boots" on Ellis Island. If you were from Brooklyn, there it was off to the right (starboard). Manhattan was off to the left (port), and New Jersey was just back (aft) of the drill field. I could spit on it, but I couldn't go visit.

Our section of the island (it's really two islands) was crowded. Packed. In prewar days the "boots" had a drill shed for use in bad weather. Now the drill shed was a dormitory with bunks stacked three (or was it four?) high. We did our drilling on the narrow paved area in front of the Great Hall formerly used for the Immigration and Naturalization Service to process new arrivals from Europe.

There were always intertwined lines of scared-looking sailors snaking though the buildings. We stood in line for shots, for medical checks, for food, and when things really got crowded, for showers. What we didn't get in line for was uniforms.

My purpose for enlisting so early, aside from helping to win the war, was to get one of those keen-looking uniforms with the bell-bottomed trousers and little white hats. But the coast guard, like the rest of the armed forces, hadn't expected a war quite so soon. For 14 days I wandered around in my fashionable fingertip corduroy-reversible jacket trying to look military.

As soon as we could recite the General Duties of a Sentry from memory—and to make us feel responsible for the security of our nation—we were assigned seawall watches. At the beginning of the watch we were issued a Springfield 30-03 rifle, a web belt complete with bayonet, and one clip of ammunition. The 03 stood for 1903, the year that rifle was accepted for use by our armed forces. A gunner's mate showed us how to load the clip but threatened us with death if we ever did so.

So there I was: a web belt buckled around my fingertip-reversible, carrying an ancient rifle that I was forbidden to load and I didn't know how to fire anyway. No one told me what I was guarding. I assumed I was there to keep dastardly German U-boat crews from boarding our island and sweeping into New York harbor. It never occurred to me that we might have been placed there to keep people in. No one had mentioned it.

I didn't find out about the rest of the island's residents until my next duty assignment. It was midnight, and this time I was issued not a rifle but a nightstick. The petty officer of the guard marched us through seemingly endless corridors relieving each sentry along the way. My post was a short, dead-end corridor with large doors on either side. My instructions were simple: "Don't let them mingle or communicate." "Who are they?" I asked. "Enemy aliens!" he said and then marched off with the rest of his contingent. There they were—the enemy! And all I had to protect myself with was a nightstick. I eased it out of its holster and cautiously approached one of the doors, ready for an attack.

I looked in. All men and boys here. Funny, those who weren't asleep looked like my neighbors from Paterson—the baker, the shoemaker, the street sweeper. The large room, bunks three high, smelled of poorly aired bedding, unwashed bodies, and oranges. I'll always remember the oranges. I crossed to the other door. All women and girls. Being 18, I was interested in girls. They sure didn't look like enemies either. They looked like girls. A lot of the women wore headscarves and dark dresses, but the girls were in bobby socks, saddle shoes, and skirts. Were they really dangerous? I put my weapon back into its holster. What were these very American-looking people doing locked up on Ellis Island? As the officer of the guard said, they were enemy aliens, mostly German or Italian nationals. Later, during day-time watches, I got to talk to them.

After the war I did some research. I found from my reading that many had been in the country for years but had never bothered to get citizenship papers. So they, along with their American-born children, were deemed potential threats to our national security. One of the most famous of these "enemy aliens" was Ezio Pinza, star of the Metropolitan Opera. He was four months away from citizenship when the FBI picked him up for sending coded messages from the stage of the Met. After a court battle he was released on June 10, 1942. I guess it's possible that I was one of his guards.

Eventually I completed my training and left Ellis Island for various assignments, none of which had to do with guarding the coast of the United States.

(Printed in *The Record*, 1986, and in *The Quarterdeck Log*, the voice of the USCG Combat Veterans Assn., July 1999)

George Dawson

When I joined the navy shortly after Pearl Harbor, I was hoping for duty on a destroyer. I didn't get it. After graduating from radio school as an RM Third Class I was sent to an army camp (Camp Crowder, Missouri) along with about two hundred other navy men. In addition to the radio operators, there were men who could speak various foreign languages, such as French or Spanish. There were also many navy officers. We had no idea why we had been sent to an army facility. We were given much the same training that many Army Signal Corps men received.

Equipped with rifles, gas masks, helmets, and army-type clothing, we were considered ready for some sort of action. When we asked for explanations we were told only that "when you come back, if you come back, you will be covered with medals." We thought we would be invading Spain and that our task would be to go ashore with the invading force and set up field radio stations to communicate with ships off shore, with our Allies, and possibly with underground freedom fighters.

When the Rock of Gibraltar came into view, we were convinced that, indeed, an invasion of Spain was imminent. We passed right by the rock, however, and ended somewhere off the coast of North Africa. The ship anchored way off shore one night, and we navy men were ordered to go ashore in landing craft. As I climbed down the rope ladder, the landing craft was plunging up and down violently, and I lost my helmet overboard. It was a long trip to the beach, and we maneuvered in and around the masts of sunken ships. We landed without incident and awaited the arrival of our officers, but then were told that the officers would not come in until the next morning.

We did not know where we were or what we were supposed to do, so we scouted around until we found a spot that seemed to be safe, secure, and quiet. We dined on K-rations; sentries were posted, and then we huddled together in our little tents. We tried to sleep. In the morning, we awoke and started to examine our surroundings in the daylight. To our great discomfort, we found that we had settled down in a French Navy ammunition depot. There were huge shells and cases of gunpowder all around. We were at least grateful that our efforts to start small fires the night before had failed. We quickly moved to another neighborhood!

(From *White Hats of the Navy* by George Sharrow)

Raymond Barker

Jefferson Barracks

Two weeks of my military life spawned more vivid memories than any other two-week period in my life. It started when we arrived at about 6 or 7 A.M. The train pulled up right next to a large mess hall on the edge of the base. We immediately went in and had a huge breakfast. After breakfast, still in our civilian clothes and carrying suitcases, we marched in a ragged formation a mile or two to our tenting area. All along the route, we were taunted by GIs chanting, "You won't like it here; you won't like it here." This is the only base I was at that we heard such remarks. Actually, as it turned out, they were right. It was a terrible place. Even Brigadier General Nathaniel Lyon, the first Union general to fall in the field of battle on August 10, 1861, at the battle of Wilson's Creek near Springfield, Missouri, had a like opinion. He declared Jefferson Barracks "a most unhealthy place, and the quarters are shockingly out of repair." Things hadn't improved much in more than 80 years.

After arriving at our camping area, we were issued the usual army clothes. It was cold this time of year even this far south, so we got heavy woolen long winter underwear that itched like crazy. There were also woolen pants, shirts, a heavy jacket, as well as a long heavy woolen overcoat. Also we got big army boots and, since it was muddy in places, big four-buckle overshoes. We were pretty weighted down just with clothes. This was all topped off by a woolen stocking cap beneath a helmet.

The huts were sided with boards, and they had canvas roofs. There was a tiny stove in the center that burned soft coal, so you can imagine the black smoke coming from hundreds of tents in the area. It was difficult to control the fire so we were either way too hot or too cold. The smell of burning coal along with our wet woolen clothing drying out, as well as the stench from the mess-hall garbage, left an unforgettable odor throughout the camp.

About the first time we left our area we had gone for some distance when the head of the column turned into a building. We were ordered to take off our coats and shirts and enter a room. It wasn't till then that we saw what was up. There were four medics, two on each side. As each guy went between the first pair, he was slammed in both arms at once with big, long, dull, seemingly rusty needles. Three more feet and the other two medics bore in with their needles. More than one guy fainted to the floor. To this day I can't stand to get a shot for any reason, and I think of that horrible day so many years ago.

Another day we marched to an old wooden theater building and got a lecture along with graphic slides about venereal diseases. There again a bunch of guys fainted and were taken out of the room by men in white coats.

This was at best a difficult sloping area to learn how to march. Among our squadron was a guy who simply could not march in step. He had absolutely no rhythm in his body. Our drillmaster, Sergeant White, quickly found this out and singled him out for personal instruction. Sarge even locked his arm with this unfortunate victim and shouted into his ear—hup, hoop, heep, hore. It did no good. Finally, he got behind and grabbed the guy around his waist, yelling and kicking the backs of his legs but to no avail. The poor guy simply couldn't do it. Sergeant White then began to call him, "Route-step Charlie." (Route-step is a command to march along not in any particular step, just any old which way.)

Edward K. Fox

Five weeks after the attack on Pearl Harbor, I enlisted in the Army Air Force. On the evening of February 17, 1942, loaded with gear, we walked a gangplank into the side of a huge troop transport ship in Boston Harbor. It was the *Queen Mary*, and we were the first American troops she carried during the war. We sailed the South Atlantic along the coast of South America to Rio de Janeiro, crossed over to Capetown, South Africa, and on to Freemantle on the west coast of Australia. We arrived at our destination, Sydney, Australia, after 40 days at sea.

Four of us were assigned to the ground forces of the 39th Fighter Squadron of the Fifth Air Force. We became fast friends—one a car salesman from Kentucky, two farm boys from Iowa and Kansas, and a kid just out of school from Idaho. We four stayed together all three years of our overseas time. We still keep in touch with each other and enjoy seeing each other at the 39th Squadron reunions.

Arthur Zirul

I Get Drafted

I was inducted into the U.S. Army February 22, 1943, in midtown Manhattan, in a building called Grand Central Palace. The name conjures up images of trains and old grandeur, but it had nothing to do with trains and certainly not with grandeur. It was a building near Grand Central Station that had a ground floor large enough to handle the inductees from a city of eight million. They were very efficiently organized. Hundreds of men were run through there every day, including holidays. In fact, the day I reported was Washington's Birthday (in those days a major holiday), and they were going full blast.

Perhaps the most memorable part of the day was the vision of a vast space filled with naked men protected only by shoes and socks, a manila folder, and an iodine identification mark painted on their shoulders. The manila folder held the beginnings of a file that was to follow me all through army life. To this day I wonder what impatient examiners who devoted less than a minute per interview per man scribbled in it.

I remember my interview with the psychiatrist. It lasted perhaps 30 seconds. "Do you like girls?" he asked. "I probably would," I answered, "if I knew any." The humor went right past him. I don't think he was paying attention anyway. I was just another virginal, pimply faced adolescent trying not to look embarrassed while hiding naked behind a manila folder.

The most memorable encounter of the day, however, occurred toward the end when I received my first short-arm examination. There was a line of men in front of me that decreased as each man made a right turn into a little cubicle where he was hidden from view. When my turn came I made my turn and found myself facing a sad-faced little sergeant seated at a wooden table. When I handed him my manila folder he glanced up only long enough to peer at my midsection and command: "All right, milk it down."

"Milk what down?" I asked. I was truly mystified.

"Your pecker," he replied.

"My what?" I asked, even more mystified. In those days I was considered an intellectual scholar; today I would be called a geek.

"Your pecker," he said. "Your Peter, your Johnny. What do you call it, your penis?"

"I don't call it anything," I said. "I hardly ever even speak to it."

I can still see the look on that sergeant's face as he sent me on my way. For most of the day I was prodded, poked, and invaded by a horde of doctors, dentists, and God knows who else. A deranged sex offender could have gotten in among us and no one would have noticed his presence. We were given meal tickets to buy the lunch of our choice and a half hour to eat it in. Not surprisingly most of us chose to eat in the in-house cafeteria. I had a carton of milk and a sandwich of some kind. I think it was cheese. Not that I don't remember; it was just that the material between the Wonder-bread slices was indescribable.

The examination process ended late in the afternoon at the selection tables. There were three tables, each with a representative of one of the military branches seated behind it—the army, the navy, and the marines. "What branch of the services would you like to be in?" one of them asked me.

I considered my options. I weighed about 150 pounds in those days. I was all bones, bad skin, and poor posture. I couldn't swim, so the navy was out. I had no death wish, so the marines were out.

"The army," I squeaked.

"Thank God!" the marine muttered in a loud aside to the navy man.

The last function of that day was the actual swearing-in ceremony. I entered Grand Central Palace Mr. Arthur Zirul, a skinny civilian, and I came out Private Arthur Zirul, a skinny soldier. I was given subway fare to get home and seven days to clean up my affairs before reporting for duty. Since my affairs consisted mainly of finding a hiding place for my collection of spicy detective stories I had little to do but wait.

It was 5 A.M. March 1, 1943, and very dark outside when my father accompanied me to the selective service board office in our Brooklyn neighborhood. I joined a bunch of other scared teenagers milling around in the predawn gloom. We were put on a school bus and transported to Pennsylvania station in Manhattan.

A crowd of parents and well-wishers had gathered at the station to see us off. Imagine my surprise to see all my friends there waving and whistling. I was the first one of my group to be drafted, and they wanted to give me a big send-off. Their being there came as a big surprise, but I certainly appreciated seeing all those smiling faces.

For some reason I was appointed custodian of the records. I was handed a canvas bag filled with manila folders, and I dragged it with me onto the train. If I knew then what I know now, I could have escaped into the crowd with that bag and set us all free. It was in the days before computers, and there was no backup to those records. It would have taken the army months, if ever, to reassemble the information.

Railroad rolling stock was in short supply in 1943 so the army was using "summer cars" to transport us. They had open slat sides and wooden seats, not very practical for a cold winter day. I sat on one of those hard benches clutching my canvas bag to me as the cold wind whistled through the car. We were on our way to Fort Dix in New Jersey and the start of a great adventure.

Irvin Blumberg

I served in the U.S. Army from January 1, 1944, to December 31, 1945. I was married in April 1943 and supported my wife, mother, and grandfather. I could have avoided the draft; however, when I was called, I signed up. Why?

I had been affiliated with the new antidefamation unit of B'nai Brith as an undercover person attending the meetings of the German-American Bund and those of Joe McWilliams, Father Coughlin, and other anti-Semitic groups. From what I had seen, heard, and learned, and being Jewish, I felt so strongly against Germans and Germany. Should Germany conquer Europe and with my experience with Germans here in the States, I felt my family, friends, and all Jewish people would not survive in the States.

My basic training was at Camp Croft in Spartanburg, South Carolina. Most of the recruits were from the South. There were only two Jews in our barracks. Did I encounter anti-Semitism? Very quickly. The first week, the sergeant in charge of our group held a meeting and told all of us recruits that any beer cans were not to be left in the barracks but to be returned to the canteen. The following week prior to lights out, he came into our barracks and found quite a few empty beer cans. He called me and gruffly told me to take them all to the canteen. I told him I do not drink beer and in accordance with his instructions, I should not take the cans to the canteen and for him to find the person responsible for the empty cans. The next morning, at roll call, we were all lined up and he called me out and then ordered me to put on a fully loaded knapsack and to run around the field until he told me to stop. I was doing this for more than 30 minutes when a lieutenant came up to me and asked me why the punishment. I told him to call the sergeant, then I would explain in front of him. He did, and when he heard my story, sent me back to the barracks.

Basic training was no problem for me. I was young, strong, and had a goal. I never concerned myself with conditions, food, or anything but to get in good physical condition and to learn to use all types of weapons, which I did. I was sent overseas immediately after basic training to a replacement camp in England.

One day I learned that an old friend of mine from the States was an officer at this same camp and went to see him. When I returned to my barracks late in the afternoon, I found the barracks empty. Everyone was gone. I immediately went to headquarters and was told that all of the men, including me, had been assigned and transferred to the 82nd Airborne in Scotland. I was told to stay put until I was reassigned. Within a week, I was assigned to the 2nd Infantry Division, which landed on Omaha Beach. I was in active combat throughout Normandy.

After the conquest of Normandy, our division was sent to Brest. I recall living in a foxhole under lots of shellfire, and one day I woke up to find myself on a ship going back to England. I was in the hospital. While there, I learned that the 82nd Airborne made an air drop at Antwerp, Belgium, and sustained 75 percent casualties. That's the unit I had originally been assigned to. Somebody up there was looking out for me.

Dawn Was Breaking: Pearl Harbor

USS Shaw *exploding during Japanese attack on Pearl Harbor*

Japanese raid on Pearl Harbor.

December 7, 1941

Notes from Battery F, 251st CA (AA)

6 A.M.

It has often been said that getting drunk could be the death of one, but never that it could save a life. Strange, but that is exactly what happened to Joe Jenny, Battery F. It all started when his best friend, Bill Graves, made corporal during the first part of November. He sent home for some money to take his friends out for a night on the town. The money arrived, and it was decided that the next leave night they would spend it. A trip to a local liquor store netted a quart of bourbon and a case of beer, and off to the baseball field they went, where they concocted "boilermakers" until all the liquids were gone. Joe didn't remember much of what happened after that, as he didn't drink the hard stuff very often or to any great amount. The one thing that he recalled was that he was in his bed and having difficulty keeping it on even keel. It pitched and rolled like a small boat in a rough sea.

Several of the men had formed a little flying club, and they would go to John Rodgers Airfield and rent Piper Cubs about once a month. They would fly across the island, land at the old landing field, have breakfast, take a swim, and then fly around for a while until their hour was almost up, then return to Rodgers Field and land.

At about 6 A.M. on the morning of December 7th, Joe was awakened by Clyde Brown and Henry Blackwell, also members of the flying club, as it was time to go to the airport. Since Joe was having a great deal of difficulty in keeping his bed from throwing him out, he begged off and went back to sleep. One other man, Warren Rasmussen, was found and off to the airport they went.

7 A.M.

Kitchen crews hard at work. Breakfast usually served about 7:45 A.M. The meal for the day was pancakes and sausages; most all batteries had the same meal (the army way). About 7:30 A.M. Joe Jenny woke up hungry and went to the mess hall, where after four or five cups of battery acid (coffee), he was able to eat. A cook brought him a large plate of food, and he had just started in when the roof of the mess hall was stitched by machine-gun fire from a Jap plane. For some reason, he still doesn't know why, he stuffed all the pancakes into one pocket of his fatigues and the sausages in the other.

About 7:40 or so, the plane with Brown, Blackwell, and Rasmussen was shot down by the incoming Japs. Only a small portion of the plane was found, and it was presumed that they were killed. It is thought that these men from Battery F, 251st CA (AA) were the first army casualties of the war. Their names are on the plaque in Pearl Harbor.

8 A.M.

Wetzel Sanders was just going to sleep because he was leave truck driver on December 6th. But the Japs came and his sleep-in was out that morning. He went to the motor pool to get his truck so the unit could move into Pearl Harbor.

Hobart Crabtree remembers the staccato of the Japanese guns on Japanese planes firing on our encampment, then the 16-inch guns of Fort Barrett with their unmistakable boom. They could have been firing at one of the small subs off coast. Hobart was able to fire at the planes at treetop level, and he never missed. Then, there was the ride in the back of a 1936 Chevy truck loading ammunition in belts, while pulling our 37mm antiaircraft gun. Then Sergeant Don Masters getting out on the running board with his .45 pointed at the head of a Japanese man who would not let us pass. We passed as he took off for the bushes. On to Pearl Harbor where the ferry was not running. We opened the gates to the Navy Recreation Center overlooking the harbor. We saw burning ships in the harbor—the *Arizona* and *Vestal* were just below.

Frank Wright woke with a terrible hangover since he was in town the night before with another hillbilly talking about Kentucky and drinking cheap bourbon. He had been scheduled for KP that day, but the Japs settled that for him when they strafed the camp. He felt that they did one poor GI a favor when they got him off KP.

Warren Hutchens was at breakfast with his unit, Battery G, when they heard explosions but didn't know what they were. After coming out of the mess hall, they looked toward Pearl Harbor and saw "ack-ack" exploding. We all thought at first it was a maneuver until the Jap planes started to strafe our camp, wounding some soldiers. Warren was the battery bugler, so he started running messages from the colonel to the captain. He had to stop at the latrine on the way. While he was sitting on the commode, the planes strafed through the roof, cutting in half the commode next to him, which was 18 inches away.

Bob Byer was near the beach by Pearl Harbor when the Japanese struck. He had gone to the sidewalk on the strand for a short walk. An enemy airplane pilot saw him and came down to strafe him with two machine guns going. He escaped at high speed and luckily was not injured.

Gordon Wilkinson had just gone off guard duty and was relaxing until breakfast time with another soldier when he heard the machine gun go off. The soldier who took over Wilkinson's gun was known to be notorious for freezing on the trigger and firing 250 rounds by accident. "I said, there he goes again." And when the bugle started to blow, Wilkinson said, "We don't have to go to fire call; we just got off duty." Then a Japanese plane strafed the barracks, and suddenly he and his buddy were looking at daylight through the walls. The two soldiers headed out the door, but Wilkinson had to run back for his gas mask. "I came back, and they got him [his buddy] in the throat and chest. Either one of the bullets would have killed him; he was sent back and had a platinum throat put in." After seeing to his buddy, he went and took the gun away from the trigger-happy soldier. "The first thing I got on was my old standby, the .30-caliber machine gun, and in just about 15 minutes it cost the Japanese government about $40,000 in plane and one less pilot. He went over my head only about 50 yards and banked, so I had a perfect side shot. Boy, when you hit the tank or oil line, they sure do burn up." Asked if he could see the pilot he shot down, he said, "He was smiling. That's how close he was."

Kenneth Little was in bed, half awake, barely conscious of large cannon firing to the south of Camp Malakole. Why, he wondered, is the navy having target practice on a Sunday morning? Next, he heard machine-gun fire, and one of the senior sergeants in the opposite end of the building screamed out in surprise and pain. He was a casualty of the first of many strafings from Japanese aircraft. Although an antiaircraft (AA) regiment, our main guns were in traveling position and could not be fired. Some machine guns were set up and fired at the aircraft. Most got off a few shots from their 1903 rifles.

George Baude stated that he had been on the firing range, and when he completed that exercise there were thousands of rounds of ammunition in a state of readiness to be used in the guns, all belted up and ready to go. Hawaiian Department rules required, however, that all unused ammunition in belts be removed and stored in boxes. In the army, regulations are regulations and are inflexible. To violate them can result in a court martial, regardless of the circumstances. No one would risk disregarding that order. Taking .50-caliber machine-gun ammunition belts apart is hard work, so when the Japanese hit us on December 7th, we still had some ammunition belted up—not nearly enough but it was better than none at all. So there we were firing our machine guns at the attacking planes and loading the belts as fast as we could, but a gun uses up ammunition 15 to 20 times as fast as we could load the belt links. The gunners had to stand there helplessly while more ammunition was linked up. Before the attack, the international situation had been very touchy, but the only preparation that was evident was that one battery in every artillery regiment, or one company in the infantry regiments, had to remain on the post on weekends as the "alert" battery or company. What good this would do is hard to figure, as we had very little in the way of any defense ready. My battery was the alert battery that weekend, so I was in camp when the attack occurred. I had gotten up late that Sunday morning, and I was just coming back from washing up when a number of strange planes buzzed the camp and I heard that unmistakable rat-ta-tat-tat of .30-caliber machine-gun fire. That big red ball on the wings of the plane told me quickly who they were, too. Oddly, my first thought was "Damn! Now I won't get any breakfast." We could see the attack on the naval vessels at Pearl Harbor; the smoke was blackening the sky, and we could see the planes dive-bombing them. Their attack on Camp Malakole was just a nuisance raid to cause some confusion. I doubt that the Japanese even had us on their charts. They must have seen us from the air as they came in, but they really worked over the important installations like Pearl Harbor, Hickam Field, Ford Island, and Schofield Barracks.

Joe Swider, Battery C, states that he and his fellow servicemen were getting ready to hit the beach and enjoy a day of sun and surfing when suddenly, at about 8 A.M., disaster struck. "We all had our trucks loaded with surfboards in front of the mess hall and were all ready to go to Waikiki for the day," recalled Joe, who had enlisted just six months before the attack. "Then suddenly, we heard a lot of bombs being dropped; we were about five miles away from Pearl Harbor. Just as I got down to the mess-hall stairs, the Japanese planes came in and strafed us with machine-gun fire. The bullets were hitting right at my feet." Members of his unit raided the gun-supply shed, despite the protests of the supply sergeant, and set up an air defense to stave off Japanese bombers attacking their camp. The outfit was credited with shooting down two planes.

(Submitted by Leonard Owczarzak)

Task Group 38.3 in the Philippines

Jonathan J. Morrow

It was 2 A.M., and I was fast asleep on the top bunk. Our bunks were stacked six beds high. Just prior to retiring for the night, my buddies and I were happily celebrating the birthday of one of our new fellow mates. I was suddenly awakened when I was thrown from my top bunk to the floor. Our carrier had just been torpedoed by a German U-boat. Within half an hour, our carrier was sunk. The crew of 500 servicemen were all fighting for their lives, trying to stay above water.

For nine hours I struggled with a mere life vest around my waist and a prayer. Together with a pal from Alabama, we waited in the chilly waters of the English Channel. All sorts of thoughts and visions ran through our minds; at one point, I could swear I saw God.

Close to being godlike, an English ship, the HMS *Beagle*, stopped and picked us up. Of the original 500, only about 40 of us survived. It did not turn out to be a very happy birthday for my buddy; he wasn't one of the survivors.

The first thing the English soldiers did for us was to wrap us in blankets and give us shots of rum. They brought us to an English naval base and outfitted us in English naval uniforms. We stayed with the English for about a month. They kept us busy doing light duties, such as keeping guard duty.

We finally left the English headed for the Fargo Building in Boston aboard the USS *West Point*. As a reward for our survival, we were dressed with a Purple Heart and a month of leave. When I returned to the service, I finished my time as a pharmacist mate, third class, attached to the marines. For the next few years, I was stationed at numerous places overseas, including Guadalcanal, Guam, Okinawa, and China.

I left the service on June 6, 1946, yet those hours spent in the water have stayed with me every day of my life. From the fall off the top bunk, I received damage to my wrist, which has left me with an uncontrollable tremor. I also wound up with shrapnel in my leg from the ship, not to mention the loss of friends and comrades. Despite the losses, I am lucky to have survived and am more appreciative of how precious life is.

George E. Miller

Our shakedown cruise on the LCI(L)1023 amounted to a voyage to San Diego, California. Our only problem occurred when we crossed the mouth of the bay at Los Angeles on an outgoing tide. This 152-foot-long and 36-foot-wide vessel bobbled like a cork in the ocean, costing all of us our lunch.

From San Diego we were sent to Pearl Harbor. We were converted from an LCI(L) to an LCI(M). This was basically removing the troop landing ramps from either side of the ship and welding three 4.2 mortars to the deck. It also included assigning an army lieutenant to the complement. It was his responsibility to train and supervise the crew on the firing of the mortars.

After months of practice landings, the task force was formed and sailed westward, ending up at Iwo Jima. The day after our arrival, we were ordered to proceed to within about 150 yards of the coastline and to lob mortar shells onto the beach. Not long after the beginning of the shelling, LCVPs carrying the landing force passed by. We shelled for several days, increasing the range as the marines inched their way forward. We were at Iwo Jima several weeks and were then sent to the Philippines.

In the Philippines, we were formed into another task force that on April 1st led the invasion force landing on Okinawa. Compared with Iwo Jima, the Okinawa landing seemed quite mild. However, little did we know the Japanese planned to use the kamikaze to try to destroy the fleet. We were assigned to lay smoke around the ships in Naha Harbor. So much smoke was being made that we did not realize that we had sailed close to a battleship when it let loose with its 16-inch guns. I thought our welded plates surely would come apart. Several weeks prior to the end of the Pacific war we were ordered back to Pearl Harbor. Many of our sister ships had blown their engines, and the serviceable ships were assigned the task of towing the crippled ones. We blew our engines on the way to Pearl and wound up being towed ourselves. Approaching the harbor at Pearl, our radioman reported that the Japanese had surrendered.

George Billias

Merchant Marine

Escape

Out on the ocean, sailing alone at eight knots was worrisome. The crew of the *Mississippi* was delighted to hear that, after loading cargo at Aruba for the port of Mariel, Cuba, they were to join a convoy with armed escorts. Armed escorts! A great relief.

About 25 ships, mostly tankers, lay at anchor in the port of Aruba at dawn in August 1942. The sun rose in the form of a tropical gift as the ships, one by one, steamed out into the Caribbean toward Windward Passage, each to be dropped off at its port of destination by the three armed escort vessels. After the convoy was formed into a rough square, the destroyer escort took its place, zigzagging at the head of the pack, and the two corvettes stationed themselves, one on the port, the other on the starboard side of the convoy. They herded the ships into position like sheep dogs. The commodore vessel, a freighter, which was in charge of giving orders by flags or blinker, was in the first line across with two ships on either side, and the *Mississippi* was two rows behind, smack in the center of the entire convoy. The sea was as smooth as blue paint, and Walter Ivers, first mate, went to bed that night feeling totally secure. It was daybreak when the first great fiery explosion eliminated the destroyer escort and shook the *Mississippi* from keel to truck. Walter had rolled out of his bunk, totally naked, and was out on deck when the commodore ship rumbled, its smokestack collapsed, and it rolled over on its port side, sinking unbelievably swiftly and silently below the surface. The remaining two corvettes darted about launching depth charges, and explosions continued to quake the *Mississippi*. Men on the poop deck saw two torpedoes miss her stern by a few short feet and continue on to hit vessels behind her and to her port side. There were flames from burning tankers in competition with the fiery sunrise, and many men were in the water. It sounded as though they were all wailing in unison.

On the morning after the savage submarine attack, the convoy was clearing Windward Passage between Cuba and Haiti. The predators had not gone away. The explosions began anew, and before the attack subsided, many more ships would be hit. The corvettes advised the vessel to make port the best way it could. The two escorts twisted here and there before exiting the area, dropping depth charges until they had no more. The surviving ships from the convoy dispersed. The *Mississippi* hugged the north coast of Cuba and ran westward with engines beating loudly, smokestack spewing black smoke, lifeboats swung out on the davits, and life jackets at arm's length. Each man waited tensely for the torpedo to strike. It never did. The *Mississippi* arrived at the Mariel sea buoy, but no pilot was there to take the ship in. The captain inched the ship into the harbor before anyone would venture aboard.

Joseph V. James

Merchant Marine

I was age 20 when I was drafted into World War II. I still have my original draft card. I remember seeing Uncle Sam's big finger pointing right at us: We Want You. His picture was posted on buses and walls all over. To me it was an honor to serve a country that gave me its soul—not by birth but by adoption. I was born in the Republic of Panama, and I became a United States adopted son in 1939.

Aboard ship, I remember hearing bombs falling, so I got up and ran to my gun station. Unfortunately, I fell down over the deck cargo and punctured my left lung during the struggle to get my gunner. I was treated for my injuries after the German raid, then taken to England and to the Panama Canal Zone. I was glad when they brought me back to New York City.

JOSEPH V. JAMES

To you who answered the call of your country and served in its Merchant Marine to bring about the total defeat of the enemy, I extend the heartfelt thanks of the Nation. You undertook a most severe task—one which called for courage and fortitude. Because you demonstrated the resourcefulness and calm judgment necessary to carry out that task, we now look to you for leadership and example in further serving our country in peace.

Harry S Truman

War is not a pretty sight. Even though we fought for a cause, we left with our hearts broken. After the destruction of lives on both sides of the fences, bombs took lives and left human misery and hunger and homeless veterans. It still tears my heart to see my fellow comrades living on these streets today forgotten by the system.

Dr. Albert J. Kubany

The Coffin Corner

I was 17 and just out of high school in 1943 when I enlisted in the U.S. Maritime Service as an apprentice seaman. I passed the qualifying tests for radio school, graduated in January 1944 with Platoon R-49, and shipped out of Brooklyn, New York, on a Liberty ship, the SS *James McHenry,* in a 106-ship convoy bound for the Mediterranean. Just 18 years old, I was the youngest officer on the ship.

From Gibraltar, German spies could count the number of ships from Franco's Spain. Nothing could hide coming through that narrow strait. High-level German bombers hit the convoy. Two planes were shot down. One ship was seen burning out of control and floated away from the rest of the convoy.

After shuttling cargo from Oran and Algiers, North Africa, and Naples, Italy, we carried troops and cargo to the invasion beachhead of southern France. The year 1944 was an interesting one in Mediterranean geology. We observed Vesuvius erupting, as well as Mt. Etna, and really flaming and boiling Stromboli. These were awesome sights. We sat at anchor in the Bay of Naples for over a month while ships were unloaded and assembled. During that time, a severe storm arose and some ships were blown around dragging anchor. Ships were helpless, since their boilers were down. One ship kept coming closer, slid along our starboard and ripped away the lifeboats on that side. During wartime, lifeboats were fixed outside the hull ready to drop to the sea. We spent the rest of the voyage with only half our lifeboats.

We returned to New York in September 1944, and after a few weeks on the beach, I took the SS *Cyrus T. Brady* out of Philadelphia. After assembling at Hampton Roads, Virginia, 94 ships sailed in convoy toward Gibraltar. We carried supplies for the Russians via the Persian Gulf. We were placed in the coffin corner of the convoy. Our cargo was high explosives and toxics. If we were torpedoed and exploded, we were expected to float away without endangering the rest of the convoy.

While going through the Suez Canal, we had an experience that caused some official anxiety. Our ship lost steering while the third engineer was relieving the first engineer for dinner. It was due to a faulty steam-reducing valve. We went aground and glanced off the side of the canal. We were soon righted, but the canal pilot was suspicious. We were suspected of attempting to sabotage the canal. This was critical since Rommel's Afrika Corps wished to do the same thing, but they failed. When we reached the southern end of the canal at the city of Suez, our officers had to answer for the incident.

Vane S. Scott

President, USS *Radford* DD/DDE 446 Association

On a serious note: Our ship was the first in history to shoot down an enemy plane while the guns were all under radar control. It was the ship's first action during Guadalcanal. Up until then the young crew was all happy-go-lucky, that is, until the skipper ordered the two dead airmen hauled aboard, laid out, and stripped on the after deck. With their brains frying on the hot steel deck, he then ordered every man on board to file past and take a good look. From that day on, they became, in the words of the skipper, "An absolute killing machine!"

They went on to shoot down eight enemy planes, sink three submarines. Later, while rescuing 468 men from the torpedoed cruiser USS *Helena* in the pitch black of night, they sank two enemy destroyers and a cruiser, while firing over the heads of those being rescued.

Under the category of seriously funny, the torpedo crew accidentally fired one of our own torpedoes through our No. 1 stack. Needless to say, it was scary at the time. Now we laugh because the engineering officer saw it and fainted.

Jack R. McKinzie

I was an electrician's mate 3/c stationed onboard the USS LST P69, which was the only USCG manned LST in that flotilla. The rest were navy. On Saturday May 20, 1944, we were listening to Tokyo Rose, and she announced that the sailors who were headed for Saipan were in for a great surprise. We had just returned from maneuvers in the waters off Maui. The LST flotilla came into Pearl Harbor, and the ships were tied side-to-side to the dock in the north shore of West Loch, Pearl Harbor. The LST P69 was either the fourth or fifth ship from the dock, and two or three more were tied outboard from our LST. They were all loaded, and it was rumored that we were headed for Saipan. The next morning, Sunday, May 21, 1944, the officer of the day logged that two oriental welders crossed our deck from the dockside to the LST outboard from us. Within 15 minutes from that time, a fire broke out on the last LST in the line and began to spread through all the inboard LSTs through the gasoline drums and explosives. Our captain called out over the loudspeakers, "Everybody to their mooring stations. We are getting out of here." My station was the aft steering post on the bottom under the crews' quarters. While I was down there with my headphones in place, I waited for the engines to start. I never heard them start, and all I could hear was muffled explosions. I don't know how long I was down there, but it must not have been very long when the chief machinist mate, thinking someone may be in the engine room, called out. But I was the only one who heard his call to "Abandon ship!" over the earphones.

I came up through the crews' quarters and nobody was present, but the life preservers and helmets were still there. I began looking for mine, but after a few seconds, I asked myself, "What are you doing?" so I put on the first vest life preserver and helmet I came to and went out the port side door. I looked toward the bow and all I could see was fire and smoke, so I made my way to the stern and still didn't see a person aboard. I started to climb over the rail to jump, but at that time the whole center of the ship exploded, and I hit my knees on something and then I was bounced around like a ball in a washing machine.

The next thing I knew, I was in the water with my life vest but not my helmet. I tried to swim to the shore, which was about 100 to 150 yards away. When I tried to kick with my feet, my knees wouldn't work and they just hung down; so I tried to use my arms to swim, but I couldn't get my arms over my shoulders, and I felt like a truck had hit me in the back. I finally made it to the shore by dog paddling with my hands, but the shrapnel kept falling around me and burned my head and my life jacket. Each time this happened, I ducked under the water to put out the fire. Finally, I reached the shore and the cane fields. I started to run away from the ships but my legs folded up under me and I stumbled. Then half crawling and half stumbling, I finally reached a place where the fire didn't reach me anymore. I collapsed in one of the field roads.

I don't know how long I lay there, but I felt someone lift me up and lay me on the floor of a flatbed truck or pickup. I don't know which. I don't know where I was taken or how long I was taken care of, but I woke up at the naval sick bay. My body felt like I'd been run over by a truck, and my head was burning. A medic told me that the life vest saved my back from burns. He had counted over 100 burn holes, some as large as small marbles, but the vest, soaked with water, stopped them from reaching my skin. The aide told me that they had removed a lot of small pieces of metal from my head. For the next couple of days, I was picking little bits of metal from my hair. I stayed there for a while until my strength allowed me to walk around by myself. All of this—the LST's explosions, my injuries by the explosions, and my treatment—was never recorded in my medical records. WHY???

By the way, the exact cause of the explosion has remained unknown, although careless handling and a defective fuse of a mortar shell have been considered. We who were serving on the LST believe this fire was an act of sabotage.

Herbert W. Church

Shipmates Never Forget

On June 26, 1944, during the invasion of Saipan Island in the Pacific Mariana Islands, there was a serious accident. At 8:45 A.M. Seaman Second Class Bobby Noel Burdette was killed when caught underneath a cargo elevator aboard ship. After an investigation was conducted, we prepared him for burial at sea. Bobby Burdette had reported aboard ship on April 25,

1944, while I reported aboard on May 9, 1944. We were both 17 years old, just out of boot camp, and both seaman second class. He never had a chance to enjoy life.

One shipmate aboard the LST 240, Homer Inman, remarked at a reunion in 1993 that all these years he was bothered with trying to save the life of a shipmate who was injured aboard ship in Saipan in 1944. He inquired about his name and where he came from. I had a copy of the ship's log, which had records indicating that this shipmate came from Huntington, West Virginia. Homer stated that some day he would try to contact the family of our shipmate and tell them the story of how their son or brother had died.

While in Huntington in August 1993, he contacted the local Veterans of Foreign Wars post, the American Red Cross Chapter, and, finally, a local barber shop, where they found in the telephone book the name of James Burdette, an older brother of Bobby. When Homer called the brother, he said, "Stay right where you are so I can meet you." During lunch, Homer explained in detail the death of his younger brother almost 50 years ago. His brother stated that he was very appreciative of his visit and to think that some one off the LST 240 would take the time and money to contact the family after all these years.

This is an example of a real true shipmate and shows that men serving aboard ship become as close as brothers and remain so to the present day.

Clarence Shapiro

Sea Stories

In February 1943 I was transferred to the Air Operational Training Command in Jacksonville, Florida. My first job was to ferry yachts the navy commandeered. I took them from Long Island, New York, to Jacksonville, Florida, where they were supposed to be crash rescue boats. I made several trips and, when these vessels proved worthless, I was given command of a real crash boat. A crash boat is like a PT but does not have torpedoes. It has one officer and six enlisted men. It can go 50 miles per hour. We would patrol the sea over which fliers were taking operational training, in radio contact in order to rescue them if they crashed, and we had many crashes. We would pick up these beautiful young men—dead. We would lose our officers to depression after they served for six months or so. After six months, I was taken off the boat and put on the admiral's staff. As the lowest-ranking member, my job was to carry out special missions for the command—ferrying vessels to and from the command's 14 air stations in the Southeast and Gulf of Mexico states. It was very exciting, and I can truly say that I have been to every town on the U.S. coast from Rio Grande to New York.

When you are promoted, you are transferred. I was slated to become a lieutenant (JG) in April 1944. I was tired of small vessels, eating out of a frying pan, and so on. My idea was to get on the *Bon Homme Richard* being built in Philadelphia. A JG would have been second in command of the soda fountain—no responsibility and lots of amenities. The admiral's assistant told me that I could have anything I wanted when they were ready to release me. In May 1944 they sent me to Washington to select my new duty. When I got to navy personnel, they could not find my file. We finally discovered that the day before I had been assigned to the amphibian's force. This was the last place I wanted to be. I was ordered to report to the amphibian-training base at Little Creek, Virginia, for training. Before reporting, I detoured to New York for a couple of days. While there I met a young lady on June 6th, and we were married on September 10th of that year. I reported to Little Creek and was classified as a PCO (Potential Commanding Officer of an LSM). The LSM was a newly designed ship built to overcome the deficiencies that existed at Normandy. We needed a fast and maneuverable landing ship that could load tanks and their crews thousands of miles away from the point of embarkation and carry it all to the beach. The LSM, 200 feet long and 2000 tons, met these tests. We had a navy crew of 55 enlisted men and 5 officers. We had accommodations for a full platoon of Sherman tanks, its supply train, and 60 army personnel. We could stay at sea for three months. The accommodations were clean and airy. Of course it had a flat bottom, and in a rough sea it was like riding a bronco.

On the first day at Little Creek we formed our crew and went to school together for 12 weeks learning how to operate an LSM. At the end of our training, we were ordered to the Charleston, South Carolina, navy yard where they were building our ship. We were assigned the US LSM 172, a commissioned ship of the U.S. Navy, and I was given a "spot" promotion to lieutenant (SG) because that was the rank the job called for.

All this was a major miracle. Here I was a 21-year old from Brooklyn, a married man, a lieutenant (SG) USNR, and CO of a commissioned vessel of the U.S. Navy with a crew of 60 men and officers. It was scary.

For the next six months we sailed to Norfolk, Panama Canal, San Diego, and Pearl Harbor. In all cases we sailed without any escort. Our armament was two 40mms, four 20mms, and four .50-calibers—totally inadequate against a sub. Our greatest defense asset was that no self-respecting sub commander would waste a torpedo on us.

On each of our voyages we sailed in groups of three to six LSMs. Because I was senior CO (by date of rank), I was in command. The orders on sighting a sub were to close and ram. Fortunately, we never saw one. At each of our ports of call, we trained and conducted landing exercises so that by March of 1945 we were pretty good seamen and fighters for a bunch of former landlubbers. As a 17-year-old member of my crew said recently: "Can you imagine sailing around half the world on a 200-foot, flat-bottom ship with 55 17-year olds and a 21-year-old accountant." Great sport!

We arrived at Pearl Harbor and soon were advised that an invasion was imminent. We loaded our tanks and army crew and set sail for Okinawa as part of the 5th Fleet. On April 2, 1945, we anchored at Kerama Reto, a small island near Okinawa. Our primary mission was to transport the 1st

Platoon of Company A, 713th Flame Throwing Battalion to Okinawa, landing there at southern Nogushi Beach. This we did on April 5, 1945. After landing our cargo and guests, our duties were:

1. Lighterage:
   The supply ships would anchor offshore. We would go alongside and take on their supplies and carry them to the beach.
2. Make smoke as protection:
   The transports and cargo ships were anchored offshore. We would be anchored upwind and we would make smoke to cover them during air raids. They were covered; we were open. Air raids with kamikazes happened at least four times a day.
3. Protecting the fleet:
   We would ring the anchorage to absorb the torpedo attacks by the Japanese.
4. Picket duty:
   The navy had picket stations between Okinawa and Japan. A picket station was usually three or four small vessels, which would be attacked before the Japanese descended on the main fleet. We were highly expendable.

In war, it is better to be lucky than good. One night we were making smoke for the freighters when a kamikaze came over the mountain and came at us. The plane was so low that we could not depress our guns on it. I was on the flying bridge just stupefied by him as he approached. I can still remember my thoughts. Here I was a newly married man and all was going to go up in smoke. When he was about 50 yards from us, for some unknown reason, he rose. We brought our guns to bear and destroyed him. I think about him. He was probably my age, someone's son, someone's father, someone's brother. Luck is the fortune of war. He was unlucky.

I loved being at sea, the daily routine of celestial shots at sunrise and sunset, and the competition about who got the best positions. I had my own cabin and spent much of the day reading (we had an extensive library) and writing letters.

At the Admiralty we received orders to go to Cebu, Philippines, to load the Americal Division to invade Japan. It was all very distressing. In the first invasion, we were lucky. No one was hurt although we had a few close ones with kamikazes. Japan, thus, was going to be tough. We departed, three ships. I was the leader. At the officer's club on the Admiralty, I was moaning and groaning about my job. Here I was, married for about a year. I had spent less then three months with my bride, and the odds were that we would not survive this one. My hosts told me to cheer up. They had the word that the United States had a secret weapon that would end it all.

Three days at sea, we received word that the atomic bomb was dropped. The ships went wild. They lowered the U.S. flag and hoisted "Jolly Rogers"; all guns were shot. It was a wild celebration.

We arrived in Cebu, took on our guests, and set out to occupy Japan. We landed the army in Tokyo Bay. While at anchor, a typhoon came up and winds were 190 miles per hour. They sent us out to sea to return to Manila. The only way we could go was downwind. If we went into the wind, we would break apart. If we went crosswind, we would capsize. The rudders were useless; we had to steer with engines. It was ferocious. We heard over the radio that destroyers capsized and giant aircraft carriers had their decks warped. We survived and, after nine days, steamed into Manila Harbor. I had gotten sick a day or two out and lost 30 pounds. I was taken off the ship and sent to the hospital in an ambulance. After several weeks, I was well, and the navy had an oversupply of lieutenant (SGs) who were only qualified to be COs of LSMs, so they sent me home and released me to inactive duty.

Jim Stuart

Saving Seaman Stuart

The Great Depression was almost over as our country looked across the Atlantic and Pacific oceans in disbelief as another major war unfolded on the world stage. Here I was at age 15 when the United States declared war on Nazi Germany and the Empire of Japan. I now believe that my terrible destiny with the ship USS *Franklin* in 1945 was set at that very time by the dastardly attack on our ships in Pearl Harbor. The radio hammered the news into my head hourly, and I remember feeling already connected into the global showdown called World War II.

My name is Jim Stuart, and I will be telling this story with authority, as I was there. I was saved four times and lived to tell about it! Here are the highlights.

Suddenly, a single Japanese Judy dive-bomber screamed out of a low winter cloud and sped for my ship, the USS *Franklin*. The "Judy," as we called this Japanese aircraft, had shaken one of our Hellcat fighters and now reached its release point and dropped one 500-pound bomb on the flight deck, then returned a second time and dropped another. The first bomb struck the flight deck and ripped below, igniting gasoline and ordnance in a flash of flame and concussion and blowing the 32-ton aircraft elevator into the air. It fell back into the holocaust. Sailors were incinerated where they stood in chow line, while others were blown out the hanger doors into the sea. The two blasts drove the 21,000-ton ship out of the water and whipped her to the right. She began to settle into a 13-degree starboard list.

That morning I was just too exhausted to have breakfast, even though I had not eaten for almost two days. That could have saved my life, as many buddies were lost in the chow line when the bombs hit. I was stretched out on two chairs in the library trying to rest when the ship shuddered and frightening explosions threw me across the room against the bulkhead, leaving me crumpled on the deck for a few moments. All of us in the library jumped up and headed for our battle stations. On the way out, I grabbed a towel and soaked it in the water cooler and urged others to get something wet. We rushed out but didn't get far because of the intense heat and black smoke. There were 25 of us groping in the smoke-filled hallway, then we descended two decks trying to find a way out of the smoke, and finally we worked our way onto the fantail deck where we could see daylight.

The conditions here were unbelievably horrible. Smoke and fire were everywhere, 40mm ammunition was exploding above us on a gun mount, and our own rockets from the burning planes were soaring up and down the deck. Men were on fire; others had limbs torn or shredded, and ghastly things like faces were gone or heads blown off. An explosion ripped off one side of my life preserver, and shrapnel creased my battle helmet and burned the right side of my face. A piece of metal imbedded in my hand. But this was the second time I had been saved from this holocaust. The ship began settling and listing, then secondary explosions slapped us down again. It was time to leave! By now, there were only six men left alive in my location and three of us left by climbing down a rope, then falling the remaining 40 feet into the burning, turbulent ocean. The three sounds I remember at this moment were the Japanese warplanes buzzing around eager to join in the finale, the plopping and splashing of shells and bullets in the sea, and the roar of gunfire. I did not think that the ship or we would survive the fall of night.

When I hit the water from that distance, my torn life preserver tangled in the battle helmet and was choking me. I nearly drowned right where I jumped! Underwater, I pushed off the helmet, kicked off my shoes, and followed the torn preserver to the surface for a desperate breath. For the third time, my life was spared for a while longer. At that frightening moment, I stared at the ship watching her float rapidly away, listing ominously and trailing smoke. It was like seeing my companion and my security moving quickly away; I wanted to reach out and pull her back to me like a toy sailboat.

Being in the sea with ships passing me by, oil fires blazing, bodies and body parts floating along, with everything imaginable bobbing up and down was absolutely frightening, and I was losing my optimism as the fatigue factor worsened. Maybe, I should have stayed with the ship. Then, I started to worry about not making it, instead of fighting the circumstances. Two heavy cruisers, the *Pittsburgh* and the *Santa Fe,* passed me by while I waved desperately using precious stamina. I knew I was only 60 miles off the coast of Japan and the thought of being picked up by an enemy boat leading to torture and imprisonment spanned the gamut of my chilling thoughts. At this point, I was 90 percent gone, and I knew that. Would I get a fourth chance to live?

Then, as if a dream could come true, the destroyer *Hickox* steamed over into our area, her guns blazing away. I tried to wave my presence, but could not muster the strength. This was my last chance. The crew spotted me and threw things to latch onto. I was no help to my rescuers and could not have survived many more minutes in the water. The *Hickox* made only one rescue pass, then steamed back to her battle position and resumed the raucous firing of her cannons and rapid-fire antiaircraft guns. The noise on this small ship was deafening, but she was my new home, and I loved her for the relative security she offered my worn-out body. The *Hickox* zigged and zagged, took several cannon hits, but she and I made it to nightfall. I had been saved for the fourth and final time!

I learned later that the *Hickox* rescued 400 sailors from the stricken *Franklin*. A residual *Franklin* crew put out the fires, recovered some power, and made their own way back to Hawaii, then eventually to the U.S.A. I joined other *Franklin* survivors at Ulithi Atoll and we, along with some marine survivors from Iwo Jima, made it to Pearl Harbor by troopship.

(Submitted by his brother, Curtiss N. Stuart)

Lyle R. Radeleff

Tank Crewman, A Company, 3rd Tank Battalion

The Untold Story of LST 477

On February 18, 1945, all hands were at general quarters due to possible submarine contact. The following day LST 477 was in the area of Iwo Jima, developed steering trouble, and dropped astern until control could be regained. There was no indication that at 1718 hours that day the crew of LST 477 and the 3rd Tank Battalion were to be severely tested.

It was a low overcast day as five suicide planes came in low from astern. One banked to the right, then made a low left bank into LST 477. The red, round (meatball) Japanese ensign on the wings could plainly be seen, as were the two Japanese pilots in the plane just before crashing into the starboard side forward. In the surprise attack, they went after the last ship astern. A great thunderous explosion from the two bombs on the aircraft took place with the elevator, debris, and smoke going up over a hundred feet into the air. The five-ton elevator came back down, slamming itself edgewise into the elevator opening. Ready ammunition for the 40mm and 20mm guns began to explode from the fire. Marines helped with the guns, working as loaders, fighting fires, and throwing hot ready ammunition overboard. On the starboard side, a flaming Japanese aircraft went down, crashing into the side of the AKN *Keokuk*. Quickly, crewmen used emergency fire pumps, drawing water from lines thrown over the side.

The gun crews remained at their stations despite the fires and exploding ammunition with shell fragments flying around. Power was out due to the blast, and the fire was nearing the forward magazine. The fire hoses were temporarily useless; only a few emergency pumps worked. LST 477 was dead in the water with the convoy moving ahead. Throughout the air attack and fire that followed, the marines of the 3rd Tank Battalion fought side by side with the ship's company, manning guns and fire hoses, heaving hot ammunition over the side, and helping care for the wounded.

There actually was a Japanese pilot who jumped out in a parachute when his plane was shot down. Watching the parachute astern on the starboard side slowly drop into the water some crewmen standing next to a marine remarked, "I bet if we gave a rifle to one of these marines he would shoot the bastard before he hits the water." A ship's officer issued orders that there would be no firing upon the Japanese pilot in the water. No attempt was seen to pick him up. Five aircraft had attacked the convoy and no aircraft survived.

With LST 477 dead in the water with no electric power, Motor Machinist Mate, 2/c Blaine Heinze fought his way through the fire over hot ammunition to an escape trunk leading down to the fourth deck emergency pump room. In the darkness and partially flooded space he succeeded in starting the pump and remained with it until pressure was restored in the fire mains. He remained at this station until all pressure was restored. With all this, to one marine looking for the rest of the convoy, the ships seemed to him to be miles ahead, ready to disappear in the distance. Many waist-type life vests had been inflated by the small pressurized bottle and could be heard going "pooch."

The ship's commanding officer, Charles T. Hazelrigg, U.S.N.R., was determined to beach and unload the cargo. Debris littered the shrapnel-riddled tank deck, and the five-ton elevator was hanging sidewise into the opening so that it blocked the tank-deck ramp. Two compartments forward were punctured through the bottom and water jetted in faster than the pumps could remove it, adding weight to the ship's bow down far below proper draft for beaching. Cargo was shifted aft as aft fuel and water tanks were filled to the limit. Men entered the bottom forward tanks and actually bailed out water to get the last gallons.

The attack upon LST 477 by Japanese kamikaze aircraft was part of a 50-enemy plane group to stage a three-hour attack against U.S. ships off Iwo Jima. Thirty miles from where LST 477 was attacked, the *Bismark Sea* was also sunk. The *Saratoga* was badly damaged, and the *Lunga Point* was also damaged. The Japanese kamikaze aircraft were from the 2nd Mitate Special Attack Unit from Katori Air base on Honshu. There were no survivors from this group.

Philip A. Mione

Before the Red Freeze

When I left Philadelphia as radio operator aboard the SS *Rheinhold Richter* in early March 1945, I had no idea that we were headed for the Black Sea until I met our five Russian passengers. They were engineers in various fields who had been sent to the United States to study American methods of mass production.

Since the *Richter* was a 10-knot Liberty ship, it required 27 days to deliver its estimated $1 million cargo of medicines, food, vehicles, and explosives over 6,000 miles of water to Novorossiysk. Our predawn arrival made it necessary to anchor outside a breakwater pending the arrival of a tug and pilot. Meanwhile, many of the crew had gone to sleep. Shortly afterward, a party of Soviet officials and their interpreter awakened me, explaining to Captain Herbert that it was necessary for his group to inspect our cabins. When they came to my quarters, the interpreter began to thumb through all my books and magazines, while the others searched my personal belongings. One of the periodicals contained a picture story of the leading figures of both sides of the warring nations. Rip! Out came a picture of Adolf Hitler. "*Niet*!" warned one of the party. It was at best a crude attempt at censorship. Soon they escorted me to the radio shack, where they placed a seal on my transmitters before continuing their inspection of the remainder of the vessel. Unloading activities were to begin late in the afternoon once we were secured to a dock and proceeded slowly over the next three weeks.

Ashore I was to see the beginnings of the Iron Curtain in the late Premier Stalin's own native Soviet Georgia. But first I had to find a place to dispose of the 60 rubles given me by the local representatives of the Soviet government. It was a gesture of gratitude on their part and was extended to all incoming American merchant sailors. If the Russians created goodwill in that manner, they destroyed it in other ways.

Walking through Novorossiyk was indeed depressing. More than 95 percent of the city had been destroyed in the war. Empty shells and pockmarked remains of buildings lay heaped along sections of the main road. Few civilians survived the German land and air assaults, and few German soldiers lived through the Russian counterattacks.

Nevertheless, some old farmers could be seen in the fields outside the gutted city using the crudest of implements to plow the earth, which held claim to the thousands of decaying bodies.

Steaming Nightmares: Guadalcanal, Guam, Bougainville, Iwo Jima

U.S. Marine on Peleliu Island

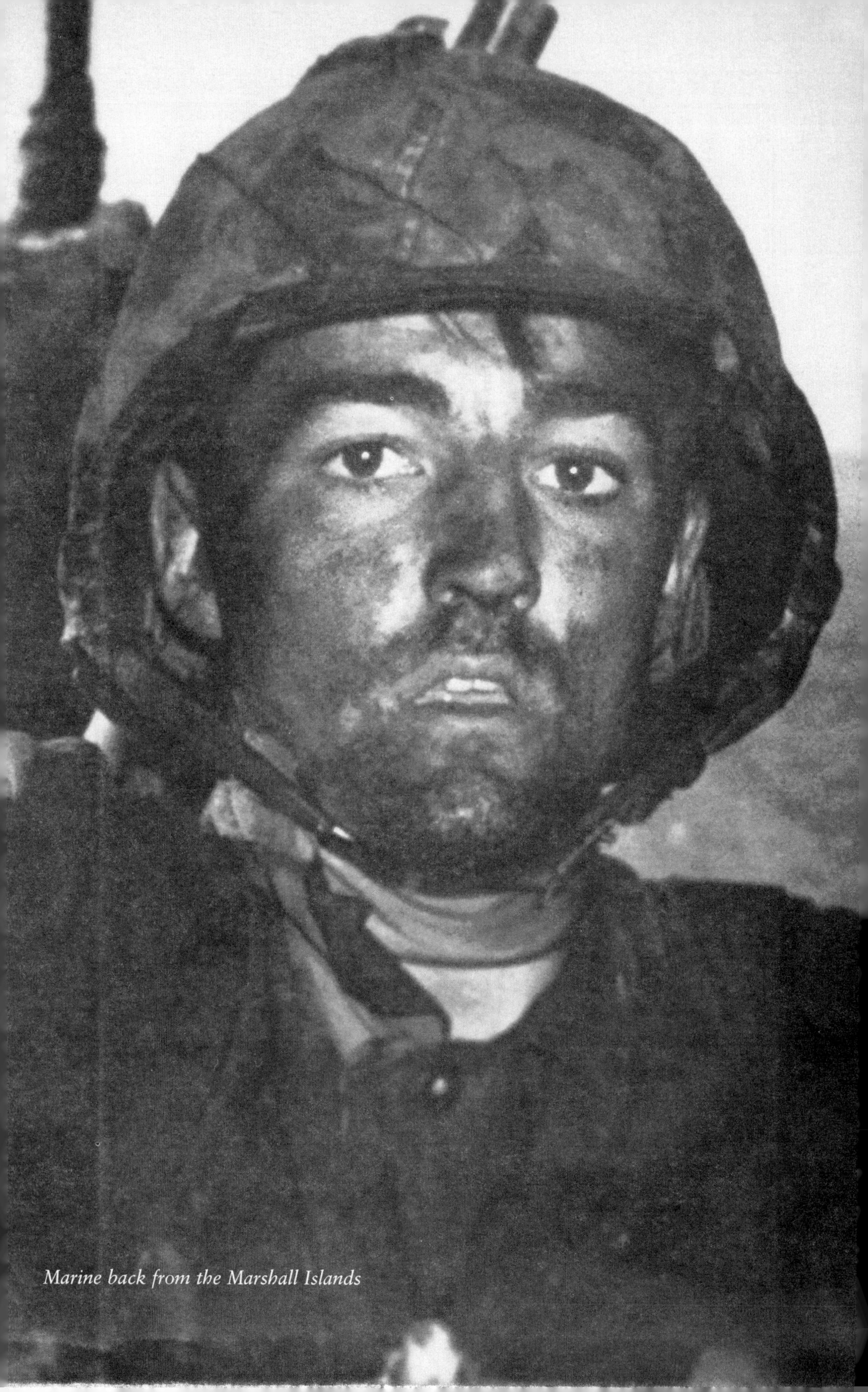

Marine back from the Marshall Islands

Leo Solomon

The Herd Instinct

Someone had to man the other end of the foxhole. I gave up trying to get cooperation. So stooped, I shuffled the 20 feet to the other end, then rested to catch my breath and to think. I had no idea how I could protect that entrance. All I had was my navy-issue pocketknife. The blade was three inches long and fairly dull. I never knew why the navy felt compelled to issue a knife that couldn't do more than sharpen a pencil.

The image of a Jap crawling on his belly to our foxhole, pulling the pin on a grenade, and rolling it into the opening was perfectly clear to me; I had seen it done many times in movies. If that happened, perhaps I'd be quick enough to grab the grenade and toss it back outside. I remained crouched at the entrance. Perhaps five minutes later—it was too dark to read my watch—I heard the sound of cracking underbrush. Slowly the sound came closer. Then I heard the sound of metal against metal.

I was alone. It was unnerving not being able to see what was coming toward me. I took my helmet off and, holding it in my hand, I extended it up over the edge of the foxhole hoping to trick the enemy to attack it. They didn't. Eventually my arm got tired. The sounds were getting closer and louder. I was getting more and more tense, and I couldn't stand the uncertainty any longer. I opened my knife. Slowly I raised my head to look in the direction of the sounds. In front of me, in the faint moonlight, I could just make out a native cow, wearing a makeshift bell consisting of two metal plates on a rope, casually strolling through the field in my direction.

There was a difference between being bombed and being shelled. It was only when a bomb left the plane and gained momentum as it hurtled downward that we began to hear it tearing the air apart. Then came the explosion when it hit.

Shelling was different. We'd hear a boom off in the distance. A soft whistle growing in intensity would alert us to a shell on its way, then, when the shell hit, the explosion. The length of time it took from the noise of a shell fired from a cannon traveling and then exploding when it hit was much longer than the noise of a bomb, making our anxiety longer. The old saying, "You never hear the one that gets you," wasn't much consolation.

On September 1, 1942, my outfit, the 6th Seabee Battalion, reinforced the 1st Marine Division on Guadalcanal. Our job was to convert the dirt landing strip there into a giant all weather airfield. Henderson Airfield was to be the key to the allied offensive in the Pacific.

Four of us were assigned to a captured Jap power plant not far from the airstrip. Our job was to get the equipment operating to send electricity to the airfield. The Japanese generating equipment, marked "Westinghouse," was housed in a flimsy two-story structure. The walls were covered with paper-thin wood that protected the equipment only from rain. Shrapnel or bullets would go completely through the building. We had four cots in a small room on the second floor.

There weren't any streets or roads on Guadalcanal. To make paths or roads, all we did was shove the underbrush, made up mostly of decaying coconut fronds, aside. Because there were no lights, we'd usually turn in at dusk. We'd sit on our cots smoking and shooting the breeze. Being thousands of miles from home, any topic was possible. All bull sessions eventually ended with talk of girls. There was a dreamlike quality in our conversations as though girls were on another planet. That lulled us to sleep.

Occasionally when I got bored with our usual night routine, I'd stroll over to Company B of the 1st Marine encampment. The marines would greet me with, "Here comes a swab jockey, a feather merchant." I'd answer, "Any seagoing bellhops around?" "You got any pogey bait, swabbie?" a marine asked. "Trade you guys some for Jap cigarettes." "You got a deal swabbie."

"What's on the radio tonight?" I asked. "You missed the Kate Smith hour. Fred Waring's Orchestra is on right now. Tonight we can get most anything clear from the West Coast. In about ten minutes, we should be able to bring in our old friend, Tokyo Rose. She'll play nice music for a while. Then she'll go into her bullshit." "It's time for Tokyo Rose," someone yelled. Another marine turned the dial and said loudly, "Here she is, everyone's sweetheart, Tokyo Rose."

Tokyo Rose was an American woman who collaborated with the Japanese. Her job was to undermine our morale. "Hello out there. This is your friend, Rose, with all the news about home. Almost all the American marines on Guadalcanal were killed by our heroic forces. The few Americans remaining are hiding out in the hills or caves. Marines, while you are away from home, men back in the United States are making love to your sweethearts and wives."

We would mimic her: "There are no more Americans on Guadalcanal." That's right, we're a mirage. We knew she constantly lied, but it was unsettling hearing her words come from the radio at night. After we assured one another we were still alive, I'd carefully make my way back with only the moon to light the way. No long bull sessions on those nights.

Sleep

The long, loud mournful wail of the siren on Guadalcanal broke the silence of the night: CONDITION RED. Four of us navy Seabees, who were asleep on the second floor of the former Jap power plant, were jarred awake. We never knew if the siren sounded because a Japanese warship was preparing to shell us, if an attack by enemy troops was imminent, or if a flight of Mitsubishi bombers was on its way.

Two of my buddies pulled on their navy denims. Another left in his skivvies. I always washed my denims the day before so I could use them as pajamas. This way I was prepared to leap out of bed and immediately leave.

My denims had been washed so many times they'd become thin and soft. My high-top shoes were alongside my cot, so in the dark I was able to slip them on quickly. My rifle was leaning against the wall close by, so there was no fumbling when I went for it. Then I joined the others in dashing toward the large foxhole. As we ran, the crackle of the underbrush seemed so loud I was concerned the enemy, two hundred yards away, would hear. It had taken us less than a minute to arrive at the nearest entrance of our shelter. One by one we crammed into the opening of the long, covered foxhole. We were quiet, fearing that the sound of our talking, amplified by the night, might carry to the enemy. In the dark, I could barely make out each of my buddies, but I could sense the tension they felt.

The foxhole was perpendicular to the power plant. It was deep enough for the previous occupants, the Japs, to walk through, but we had to stoop as we moved in. It was 5 feet wide and 20 feet long with an "L" entrance at each end to reduce concussion in the event of a near hit. Its entire length was covered with coconut logs, topped with half-inch steel plating and covered with sandbags. It was excellent protection from everything but a direct hit.

I took out a crumpled pack of Jap cigarettes. Even though we were under cover, I automatically cupped my left hand around the lighter as I thumbed it. I could always manage to scrounge a thimbleful of high-octane fuel to fill my Zippo. I inhaled a deep drag and gagged at the taste. "Watch that cigarette!" said an angry voice out of the dark. I continued to move toward the far entrance keeping my left hand cupped around the lit tip. There was an eerie silence as I peeked out the far-end opening. The moonlight on the swaying coconut fronds cast ominous, dancing shadows.

In a minute, the silence was broken by the sound of a plane. Because of this nightly visitor's engine's sound, we named him "Washing Machine Charlie." Charlie would shut his motor and glide in over us, and then he'd turn his ignition on and zoom back up. With his motor off, there was no fiery exhaust for our marine gunners to aim at. Charlie repeated this again and again until he felt he had awakened everyone. On his final run, he'd climb high, shut his motor, glide in over us, release his bombs, restart his motor, and leave for the night. Hidden in the hills was an English coast watcher who tracked Charlie by his exhaust on his way back to Rabaul. When the watcher was certain the plane wasn't returning, he'd radio headquarters, which would then, if all other conditions warranted it, sound the more pleasant ALL-CLEAR siren.

"You know fellas," I said, "This running back and forth to the foxhole is getting to be one big pain in the ass. What do you think of moving our cots into the foxhole?" "No one's ever done that before," Mike said. Then the rest joined in. "Yeah, never heard of nobody doing that," George said. We walked back to the power plant, now all fully awake.

The next day the clouds opened up and the ground couldn't absorb the rain fast enough. There was a layer of water all over. The mess sent a lunch truck that spun its wheels in the mud, sliding all the way. We sloshed out in the rain to be served. The menu was the chef's special: fried Spam, scrambled powdered eggs, damp bread, and something hot and black we called coffee. We held our food-filled aluminum mess kits under our ponchos and rushed back to the power plant. After eating we went back to work.

"One good thing about the rain, it's unlikely Tojo will send bombers over," Ed said. The rain continued. Then, at four o'clock, it stopped as suddenly as it had begun. The sun came out with a vengeance and turned the island into a muddy, hot, and steamy encampment. Our clothes stayed damp from the humidity. We kept working at the power plant long after five and wondered how chow would get to us as the roads continued to worsen. What poor roads we had became quagmires.

"I'll be a son of a bitch," Ed said. "There's a damn tank coming." A light alligator tank clanged up to the front of our plant. A marine stuck his head out and, smiling, said, "We deliver." We'd already cleared the area in front of the power plant, so we were able to walk to the tank without getting muddy. "Broiled Spam tonight! What imagination! My compliments to the chef!"

I said, "Who the hell makes up these menus?" We knew little food was arriving, but we bitched anyway. The coffee had its usual green cast from being brewed in galvanized garbage cans.

Daylight was fading, so it was impossible to continue work on the large diesel generator. Using any kind of light was certain to draw enemy fire. "How long do you think the war will last?" George asked.

"The Golden Gate in '58," Ed, the group comedian, replied.

"That's 16 years away," I said, "God, I hope not. Can you imagine being stuck in this hell hole for 16 more years and not seeing a girl all that time?" The way the war was going, 16 years didn't sound impossible.

Dusk descended spreading a gray cast through the sky. "We might as well turn in. Can't see much any more," Gus said.

"Do you guys really think the war can last 16 years more?" I asked. The conversations continued as it grew darker. When anyone had a thought he just threw it out for discussion; nothing was taboo. One by one the guys dropped out of the conversation. By ten we were all asleep.

During the night, explosions shocked us awake. Then came the long mournful wail of the siren, announcing CONDITION RED. The warning siren sounding after the bombs exploded confused me. That had never happened before. Groggy and in total darkness, I tried to get off the wrong side of my cot, but there was an obstruction. I pushed hard, forcing the cot to slide back. I stood between the wall and my cot, and then I dropped to my knees and crawled under. By then I was fully awake and was aware of what I'd done. I grabbed my rifle and sprinted to the foxhole. I'd run farther than the distance we'd cleared. When I stepped into mud. The rich, gooey, adhesive muck sucked my shoe off, and my foot landed in the ooze. I pulled my work shoe free, then hobbled to the foxhole carrying the muddy shoe in one hand and my rifle in the other. "That settles it," I said, "Tomorrow I'm moving my cot into the hole!" After a few minutes, the ALL CLEAR sounded so we went back to the plant. I wiped the mud from my foot, then went back to sleep.

The following morning I took my cot apart and carried it into the foxhole. I welcomed the damp, sour odor of the earth walls and floor, as though the smell were an additional barrier, insulating me from the hostile world outside. As dark descended, we sat outside the power plant talking of politics, home, and girls. All our conversations had an unreal quality, as though we were speaking about another life, another world. We'd gotten used to not seeing any females or other semblances of civilization, so the war became our reality.

"It's getting dark, fellas," George said. So they left and went inside the plant. I lowered myself into the foxhole and went to my cot. In the middle of the night, CONDITION RED sounded. In less then a minute my three buddies arrived. They sat on the dirt floor while I lay on my cot. For three minutes nothing happened, so I whispered, "Probably a false alarm," rolled over and went back to sleep.

"Leo, get up."

"What's the matter?" I said, still groggy.

"'Washing Machine Charlie' is overhead, and he's ready to bomb us."

"What the hell am I supposed to do about that; why didn't you let me sleep? If I awoke in the morning, I'd have lived through the bombing; and if I didn't wake up, I wouldn't have known the difference."

Standing near the entrance, Gus said, "Listen!" Being ten feet from the opening I didn't hear anything. Then I heard a faint hum. The sound died and a few moments later it started again. The plane's engine was being turned on and off. This was vintage "Washing Machine Charlie." He wanted everyone's sleep disturbed. The bombs left the plane and began their downward rush. From a whisper that began like a distant locomotive speeding toward us bombs tore the air apart—louder and louder as they came closer. Then the explosions; then quiet. Charlie had glided in over us, dropped his bombs, restarted his engine, and zoomed away. No ALL CLEAR had sounded, so everyone remained in the shelter. After a few minutes, I rolled over and fell asleep again. When I woke, I could see light at the opening. I needed to wash and pee. I walked stooped over to the entrance. My eyes took a moment to adjust to the brightness of the morning. There were my buddies sitting on the ground, their faces drawn with bloodshot eyes.

"What the hell happened to you guys?" I said.

"You lucky son of a bitch," George said. "After 'Washing Machine Charlie' bombed us, no ALL CLEAR sounded because a Jap battleship was approaching. It stayed out at sea and shelled us all night. And you slept through the whole fucking thing!"

Raymond G. Davis

Guadalcanal

After a year of basic school, a year-plus of sea duty, and a year with the 1st Marine Division in Cuba, Quantico, and Camp Lejeune, I was finally going off to combat. I would get to see whether the doctrine, tactics, techniques, and equipment taught in the Marine Corps schools, by the U.S. Navy at sea, and by the Fleet Marine Force (FMF) in Cuba and stateside were actually going to work. (Marine combat units are all assigned to the Fleet Marine Force.)

On December 7, 1941, Japan launched its Pacific offensive by attacking the U.S. Fleet at Pearl Harbor. Rapid advances against British, Dutch, and U.S. possessions brought Japanese forces to a position that threatened Australia. The Japanese were building an airfield in the Solomon Islands on Guadalcanal from which they could attack shipping lanes into New Zealand. It was to become our task to block their effort.

As a battery commander sailing for combat with the 1st Marine Division, I was launching the building of what I hoped would be a distinguished record during operations in the Pacific. At the same time, some of my less fortunate Quantico classmates sat out the war either as prisoners of the Japanese or in the drudgery of defending various pieces of real estate on small Pacific isles.

I landed on Guadalcanal D-Day, 7 August 1942, an hour and a half after the first wave of assault troops. Essentially, it became an "administrative landing" in that the Japanese did not defend at the beaches, but chose to fight the attacking troops inland. As we loaded into boats and were heading for shore, however, a formation of Japanese torpedo bombers attacked us. This was the first engagement for these American ships, and shot and shell were flying—it seemed as if everybody was shooting at everything and everybody. The sky was full, just full, of bullets.

By nightfall, the 1st Marine Division had captured the Japanese airstrip there, which became Henderson Field. It was to become the target of Japanese land, sea, and air forces for the remainder of the campaign.

My primary mission was antiaircraft defense of Henderson Field. I had a challenging experience in that my command post was sited just 100 feet off the edge of the airstrip, which was being expanded closer and closer to me. Remember that this strip was the main target of the Japanese for the next six months. Enemy troops were trying to capture that airstrip by attacking overland. They also sent airplanes over every day and sailed warships down to shell us. As I recall, we were the first American troops in history to ever be heavily shelled by enemy battleships. During the month of October, there were 31 consecutive days during which we were bombed from overhead with the "Betty" bombers every day at noon. Also, we were shelled at night, every night, from the battleships, cruisers, and destroyers offshore. It was a very busy time.

In the hurry to get the airfield in operation, one of the first things I recall is that ordnance hauled in several airplane and shiploads of bombs and scattered them in the high grass around Henderson Field. No attempt was made to build bunkers for the ammo, just hurry the bombs in. The kunai grass grows very tall, and it was a serious fire hazard. The first few times the Betty bombers flew over, they set fire to the grass after the bombs had fallen. Being the local commander, I would rush my troops out in order to extinguish the fires. On one occasion I lost a boot while running toward the fire. Minutes later I found myself standing with one shoe on and one bare foot on top of a 500-pound bomb, beating out fire around it to keep the fire off the bomb. Those were just the kinds of exciting times we had in the early days of Guadalcanal.

How did all this look from the marine aviator's point of view? Major John L. Smith, a fighter squadron commander and subsequently a Medal of Honor recipient, told me one day of the way his squadron operated. Every day at noon the Japanese would come over and drop bombs. The scheme of the fighter squadron was to climb to maximum altitude just before noon to wait for the Betty bombers, and, as the bombers came by, the marine fighters would dive through the formation. Because the marines were few in number, they always targeted the bomber on the left wing of the formation. Every day, day after day after day, they would shoot down the guy on the left wing of the bomber formation, which would eventually cause a shortage of volunteers to fly out there, it would appear. The result was, Smith told me, it began to break up the formation. The guy on the left wing would get so nervous coming in that he'd fly erratically and maybe peel off to hide among the other bombers, causing the whole formation to be rattled.

As this bombardment continued, we, of course, kept digging our holes deeper and deeper in the ground. We had a rule that there would be two men in a foxhole. In a deep, narrow foxhole there would be two guys, so a direct hit would never get more than two marines. This tactic really paid off.

Another lesson learned by the entire 1st Marine Division: During those first nights ashore, troops will shoot at shadows, noises, or ghosts all night long. A sergeant of mine sitting in my command post raised up to shoot an approaching enemy in the darkness. I managed to knock his Tommy gun up just in the nick of time as I recognized our Battalion Commander, Bob Luckey. (Luckey was lucky!)

When I'm asked if my guns ever shot down any Japanese aircraft, my answer is that we claimed some. The Zeros would come around every now and then and swoop down over the strip to see what was going on. Two or three were shot down, and of course my guys claimed them. One thing is for sure—my guys enthusiastically shot any Japanese who might have been in range.

Every day at noon those Betty bombers would come over, and we got so salty that we would wait until the bomb bays opened at a certain point in the sky before we got into our holes. Colonel Cliff Cates located his infantry regimental headquarters nearby, just across the runway. He had a little scheme going. If people didn't get low enough in their holes during an air raid, he'd shoot toward them with his pistol. A few rounds came over my way, and as soon as that stick of bombs went by and the dust was still up, I went tearing across that runway to straighten out whoever the hell it was shooting at me with his pistol. I ran headlong into Clifton Bledsoe Cates for the first time! He told me exactly what was going on. In short, if I'd been in my hole, there would've been no chance of my getting shot. I said "Aye, aye, sir!" to the future Commandant of the Marine Corps and moved out smartly.

One night the password was something or other, and the response (from the incoming man) was "Hallelujah!" To be sure that he is heard by the defending marine, the man returning to the lines shouted loud and clear so as not to be fired on. The result of that, of course, was that the entire night was filled with endless shooting and shouts of Hallelujah; it sounded like a Holy Roller meeting on the 4th of July!

As a follow-up to this, one of my drivers killed three cows, which he claimed was a squad of Japs moving toward his night position. After struggling to bury them (this was his punishment) he decided to burn them. Result? A major grass fire threatened a key ammo dump.

The Division Commander, Major General A. A. Vandegrift (the next commandant), soon stopped the night firing by requiring that weapons be unloaded and bayonets fixed at nightfall. This became a pattern in the subsequent landings in which I participated.

There were many problems other than that of live firing. For example, I was sent for by the Division G-4 (the Supply/Logistics Officer), a colonel named Stan Fellers. He was upset and accused my outfit of stealing jeeps. I wasn't aware of this, so I went back to investigate. It seems that my troops had become so hardened to the bombers' air raids that after awhile when others abandoned jeeps in the area in response to early warning and got into holes, my men would get the abandoned jeeps and haul them off to nearby woods, where they would paint out the numbers and unit symbols. Not surprisingly, we did have extra jeeps, but I noted that they were always army jeeps; marines would not "steal" from brother marines. The variations in paint made it easy to spot the four extras and send them back to the army.

Then there were problems with chow and health. After the Japs drove our navy off, we had few rations, and Japanese rice with raisins (to camouflage the bugs!) became the staple diet at times. Finally, some brave California fishing boats brought some supplies in to us. As a division, our health deteriorated mostly from malaria and dysentery—our medical supply ship had been lost. Later, we found the Japanese quinine supplies, which helped to keep malaria under control. Hundreds of enemy corpses multiplied the fly population, even though we soon learned to bury corpses quickly.

A final note from the campaign at Guadalcanal: I saw Chesty Puller several times, but we had enough problems to solve and we didn't get much talking done. However, let me point out that Chesty, at Guadalcanal, was the commander of the 1st Battalion, 7th Marine Regiment, the same unit that I would later command in the Inchon-Seoul and Chosin Reservoir Campaigns in Korea.

Good fortune found me fishing with a great marine, Walter McIlhenny, who became known worldwide for his Tabasco sauce and known to every marine as a principal founder of the Marine Military Academy.

When Guadalcanal was over for my men and me, we next moved to Australia to resupply and recover. While there, in May 1943, I would become commanding officer of the 1st Special Weapons Battalion and prepare for further operations against the Japanese in New Guinea and Cape Gloucester.

Peleliu

At Peleliu, I really joined the infantry! The citation for the Navy Cross, our nation's second highest award for valor in combat, was recommended by none other than Colonel Chesty Puller, himself no stranger to this navy blue-and-white ribboned medal, with a record five of them!

I once made a key statement, after surviving three wars (World War II, Korea, Vietnam), that to me Peleliu was the most difficult assignment I have encountered. So, when asked specifically about this, I wrote that Peleliu was tough because we never found a way to get the enemy out of his defensive situation. The Japs were in deep caves, had small holes for fixed machine-gun fire, etc. Consequently, we were being hit from all sides with no way to get at them.

Yet the 1st Marine Division was well prepared for this amphibious assault. I took the battalion over to Pavuvu, a muddy, palm-covered little island where we went on some hikes, had equipment inspections, and so forth. We seemed to be in good shape because most of the key people had been through both Guadalcanal and Gloucester. We immediately started training for Peleliu in an area where we could assault four or five positions with total freedom of action. We employed mortars overhead with live ammo, plus rockets and flame-throwers in assault teams. It was the best assault team training I ever witnessed and totally realistic. It was dangerous, but we were going into a very dangerous situation.

These were innovative tactics, because captured documents had given all of us an indication of the heavy fortifications we would face at Peleliu. The small-unit commanders knew the lives of their men were at stake, and they really went at it with the training. We built Japanese-style bunkers, then assigned a squad of marines, with satchel charges, flame-throwers, and rockets/bazookas the task of taking the bunker.

It was on the second day ashore that I (now commander of the 1st Battalion) connected with Captain George Hunt. His company had become isolated and was under great pressure as he later described in *Life* magazine (he became a senior editor). My battalion moved into a large gap to ease pressure on Hunt's company.

In many respects, it became the most hotly contested and brutal campaign of World War II. A figure I'm not proud of is the fact that my battalion had 71 percent casualties including me, and the whole regiment was almost as bad. The enemy had tunneled back under the coral ridge lines, sometimes 100 to 200 feet, and they would lay a machine gun to shoot out of a distant hole, with deadly crossfire from well dug-in and fight-to-the-death defensive positions. We were withdrawn within three weeks, because we had just been expended. My Charlie Company commander, Captain Everett Pope, a 25-year-old Massachusetts native, was to receive the Medal of Honor. The deepest penetration the 1st Marines made on the 19th was achieved by C Company. At about noon Captain Pope was ordered to seize Hill 100, a steep, apparently isolated knob, which dominated the east road and the swampy low ground to the battalion's right front.

Already reduced by casualties to just 90 men, C Company was in as good a shape for the mission as any of the depleted rifle companies. The marines approached Hill 100, known as Walt Ridge, through a swamp filtering forward past shell-torn tree trunks, which jutted skyward like broken fingers. Reaching the road at the base of the height, they found and attacked two large pillboxes but were almost immediately pinned down by machine fire from the right. Firing from only 50 yards away, the Japanese machine gunner was situated on the other side of a pond where the marines could not get to him. Unable to move forward and taking heavy casualties from the fire, Pope requested permission to pull back, pass to the left of the main swamp area, and push up the road with tank support. The road here angled abruptly east, crossing the swamp over the narrow causeway. The single-track crossing was located along the mouth of a wide draw, later known as "the Horseshoe." It then skirted the base of Pope's objective and angled northeast.

Pope extricated his men, but it was late afternoon before C Company was able to renew the push. The tank support did not live up to hopes. Trying to negotiate the causeway, the first tank slipped over the edge and stalled. A second tank ventured out to extricate the first and slipped over the other side, blocking the causeway to any more armored support.

Leaving the tanks behind, the marines rushed across the causeway by squads, paused briefly at the foot of the hill, then started the steep scramble up, backed by mortars and machine guns. Here and there a blasted tree, stripped of its branches, jutted skyward, but there was little cover for the approach. Among the casualties were two marines killed by U.S. tank fire as they tried to knock out an enemy machine gun.

Enemy fire from Hill 100 and surrounding heights took a heavy toll of the attacking marines, but by sliding around to the right, some two dozen survivors made it to the summit. There, to their consternation, they found the maps were wrong. Hill 100 was not an isolated knob; it was merely the nose of a long ridge dominated by a higher knob only 50 yards to their front. Pope did not need his Phi Beta Kappa key from Bowdoin College to understand he now had a major problem on his hands. Exposed to fire from the high ground to their front, as well as crossfire from a parallel ridge to the west, he was in a very precarious position.

As twilight fell, the marines took what cover they could among the jumbled rocks. Their perimeter was very compressed—about the size of a tennis court by Pope's reckoning—perched on the edge of the cliffs. They had no real ground contact with the rear and only what ammunition they had been able to carry up in the initial assault. Noted the C Company war diary, "The line is flimsy as hell, and it is getting dark. We have no wires and need grenades badly."

At 1700, a machine-gun crew supporting C Company saw six men moving toward Japanese lines. Challenged, the strangers merely crouched down in the road. One of the machine gunners walked over to them, a belt of ammo in his hands. He was on top of the men before he realized they were Japanese. Slapping the lead Japanese in the face with the ammo belt, the marine knocked him cold. The next Japanese fired at him but missed, his bullet striking an unlucky marine lieutenant in the jaw and exiting through the back of the officer's head. The machine gunner shot the six Japanese, but the lieutenant was dead. The Japanese went for Pope's men after dark, and they kept coming. At first, they tried to infiltrate the marine perimeter; then they commenced a series of counterattacks, each made up of 20 to 25 men. How many there were and how often they came soon dissolved into a confused blur to the marines.

Most of the thrusts came down the ridge. Pope had some radio contact with battalion and received some illumination. What he really needed was artillery support, but he was too closely engaged to call in fire from the big guns.

Back at a company command post, Private Russell Davis listened to the fighting over the radio. The front-line marines were screaming for illumination or for corpsmen; men were crying and pleading for help, but there was nothing anybody could do to help them. In the CP, Davis's company commander listened to the whimpering calls from the hills, cursing monotonously and helplessly, his head down between his knees.

Up on the ridge, two Japanese suddenly materialized near the position defended by Lieutenant Francis Burke of Scranton, Pennsylvania, and Sergeant James P. McAlarnis of Kentucky. One of the Japanese ran a bayonet into Burke's leg. Burke tore into his attacker, beating him senseless with his fists. McAlarnis, meanwhile, went to work on the second Japanese with his rifle butt. They tossed the bodies over the precipice.

Pope's marines managed to throw back the Japanese attacks, but as dawn streaked the sky, they were running perilously low on ammunition. "We used rocks," recalled Pope, "not so much to try to hit them with rocks . . . but you throw a rock and they wouldn't know if it was a grenade or not and they'd wait a minute to see if it was going to explode. Throw three rocks and then one of your remaining grenades and slow them down a bit."

As the fighting became hand-to-hand, the marines pitched some of their attackers bodily over the steep cliffs. Spotting two enemy soldiers climbing the slope to his position, a sergeant heaved an empty grenade box at them, then opened up with his rifle. Private First Class Philip Collins of Gardiner, Massachusetts, picked up Japanese grenades before they exploded and tossed them back. "He did that until one exploded in his hand," reported Pope. "Then he picked up a rifle and used that until he was too weak to load the weapon."

Much of the enemy fire focused on the light machine gun, which was taken over by the assistant after the gunner was hit. The gun began jamming after a couple of hours of constant firing, and the gunner had to clear it by hand, exposing himself to enemy fire. "Every time he went up, they threw grenades," recalled a witness. The gun was finally blown off its tripod, but the gunner kept it in action until he was wounded and unable to continue.

By daylight, down to about a dozen men and out of ammunition, Pope received orders to withdraw. The order came just as the last Japanese assault began to sweep the survivors off the ridge anyway. There was little order. Those who could scrambled down the slope as fast as they could. There had been no question of sparing able-bodied men to evacuate the wounded during the night. Anyone who could not get out on his own was doomed.

Making their way through the light scrub at the base of the hill, the marines dodged streams of enemy tracers whipping through the brush. Pope's radioman was killed by his side as he talked on the phone. Japanese infantry could be seen against the skyline where the marines had been only moments before. Another enemy group came around to the right, where a couple of them proceeded to set up a light machine gun, much to Pope's discomfiture as he suddenly realized that they had singled him out personally for their attention. He kept moving fast until he and the other survivors found cover behind a stone wall near the causeway below.

Of the two dozen or so men Pope had brought up the hill, only nine made it down safely. Of these, many were wounded, including Pope himself. Sometime during the fighting, he had taken a spray of shrapnel in his legs and thighs, an injury he dismissed as "not consequential." He picked the metal fragments out with a pair of pliers at the infirmary a couple of days later. He walked off Peleliu, the only company commander in the 1st Battalion to retain his post through the entire operation.

Pope's survivors were still pulling themselves together at 1630 when the company received orders to attack up a ravine along the ridge they had just lost. Pope contacted regiment and reported that he had only 15 men and 2 officers able to attack. The order was rescinded.

It was five months before fresh units could secure that island. They did it eventually by building what they called a "moving sandbag wall." They would inch these sandbag walls forward until they could get close enough to dig out the Japanese. But the great sorrow to me of this operation was that the lessons learned were not adequately exposed to the marines going to hit

Iwo Jima some weeks later. What we had learned was somehow not communicated to them, and they paid in blood for this mistake. They went into Iwo in a similar situation, but were not fully prepared for it.

When people ask me about my own personal decorations, the Navy Cross and the Purple Heart, I tell them that I never felt I fully deserved the Navy Cross because of all the hurt that my battalion endured. But in retrospect, we probably got more done for the cost than other units. To show you how bad it was, even though we came ashore "in reserve"—probably because our commander had been relieved, and I was the newest battalion commander—the second day ashore I was assigned a mission of the central thrust up to the north of the island in the worst of the defended territory, and we went to work on it. One historian said we expended more 11-inch battleship shells in one night than ever were expended before trying to break up this enemy defensive system and keep them off us during the night. After three days of this deadly fighting, we had enough success to please Chesty Puller as he came forward. He then recommended me for the Navy Cross.

Puller was impressed as he was carried up there on his stretcher—he had a flareup of a bad wound he sustained as Commander of 7th Regiment's 1st Battalion on Guadalcanal and could not walk—and he could see that this was a nearly untenable position with fire coming from three directions, but one where we salvaged our gains. The situation was desperate, and we held on. While he was there, Puller saw the bandage on my knee; he pulled it off and told me that it was not bad enough to be evacuated. He was aware that they had wanted to haul me off to the hospital ship, but that I wouldn't go. He almost smiled at that.

Let me offer a little glance into the Japanese character: We had just been assigned a couple of war dogs, with their handlers, as we captured a large enemy shop area near the airfield. I used one of these heavily reinforced concrete buildings for my communications center and sick bay. My command post was outside in some holes in the ground. That night, one of the dogs yelped, a couple of shots were fired, somebody yelled, and I went to investigate. An enemy soldier, wearing nothing but a loincloth, armed only with a bayonet, had been sent to toss a grenade into the aid station. Seems that the dog fell asleep, was frightened by the shots when his handler shot the Japanese, so he yelped. As happened more than once, the lone enemy soldier, if not shot to death, would try to stick himself with the bayonet after he had tossed the grenade into the group of wounded marines. He'd commit suicide after accomplishing this mission—and that was characteristic of the people we were fighting against.

Orders for me arrived soon thereafter when my battalion and I returned to Pavuvu and I got ordered home. Yet the real climax of my Pacific War is best described by my wife, Knox: " We were married when Ray was a captain. We weren't married but a few months; Ray went to war; I had our son Gilbert; we struggled; Ray was gone three long years!"

(Excerpts from his memoirs, *The Story of Ray Davis*)

William Marshal Chaney, Sr.

Company B, 147th RCT

Upon reaching the high seas, each individual soldier was issued a copy of the following form letter from the President of the United States:

> TO MEMBERS OF THE UNITED STATES ARMY EXPEDITIONARY FORCES:
>
> You are a soldier of the United States Army. You have embarked for distant places where the war is being fought. Upon the outcome depends the freedom of your lives: the freedom of the lives of those you love—your fellow citizens—your people. Never were the enemies of freedom more tyrannical, more arrogant, more brutal. Yours is a God-fearing, proud courageous people, which, throughout its history, has put its freedom under God before all other purposes. We who stay at home have our duties to perform—duties owed in many parts to you. You will be supported by the whole force and power of this Nation. The victory you win will be a victory of all the people—common to them all. You bear with you the hope, the confidence, the gratitude and the prayers of your family, your fellow citizens and your President.
>
> Franklin D. Roosevelt

We young GIs, who were venturing out on the war-torn seas for our first voyage with thoughts of home and the loved ones we were leaving behind, found the President's letter very comforting, and it instilled in us a sense of purpose.

On October 20, 1942, the 1st Battalion, 147th Infantry boarded the USS *Neville* and sailed via the New Hebrides, landing at daybreak on November 4, 1942, at Aola Bay, Guadalcanal. We were an element of a task force consisting of a battery from the 246th Field Artillery Battalion, the 5th Marine Defense Battalion, the 14th Naval Construction Battalion, and the 2nd Marine (Gung Ho) Raider Battalion, under command of Colonel Evans F. Carlson. Lieutenant Colonel James "Jimmy" Roosevelt (F.D.R.'s eldest son) made an appearance at the landing site. During the landing, American fighter planes and Jap Zeros were dog fighting overhead; otherwise, the landing was unopposed. The combat units moved inland and established a perimeter defense, with the reserve units participating in securing rations and supplies as they were delivered from the ships to the beach. The temperature was always hot and the humidity high, and it rained often, even occasionally when the sun was shining. The mud and swamps were everywhere, as were the insects and anopheles mosquitoes. We GIs were assured if the Nips didn't get us, the mosquitoes would. Our rations were of poor quality, and our diet reminded me of a neighbor back in southeastern Kentucky wintering his horses on corn-fodder. Within a week after the landing, an army of insects had invaded our dried beans, soup, and cereal. Initially, we tried to sort the bugs out as we ate, but their colors blended in with our food. In disgust we gave up, consoling ourselves with the thought that nature had provided us with meat to spice our dried milk, dehydrated eggs, and other goodies, such as GI's chocolate bars (which were as scarce as hen's teeth).

Patrols operated daily in front of the perimeter, and the 2nd Marine Raider Battalion penetrated deep into the interior northwestward of Aola Bay, making sporadic contact with the enemy. Shortly after the landing, a group of natives informed our headquarters that several Nips were bivouacking in a village some ten miles or so northwest of our perimeter and inland some distance from the coast. A patrol from B Company, 147th Infantry and a detachment of marines made a daylight attack on the village, killing all the Japs but one. The native guides lashed the Jap's hands and legs together, strung him on a pole, and carried him into the 147th Infantry 1st Battalion Headquarters. He was interrogated by a Japanese-speaking American soldier and then sent to the island stockade.

On December 9, 1942, Major General Alexander M. Patch, United States Army, assumed command of all combat operations on Guadalcanal. In early January 1943, General Patch called on the Nips to surrender by having thousands upon thousands of planes drop pamphlets over the Japanese-held section of the island, which the Japs ignored. The general then launched an all-out campaign to secure the island, contending there wasn't room for both the Americans and the Japs, too.

After arriving at Kokumbona on or near January 24, 1943, and remaining in reserve briefly, the 147th Infantry was chosen by the 14th Corps Commander to continue the attack and pursuit of the enemy.

On January 30, 1943, as the regiment advanced through a coconut grove running parallel with the coast and on approaching the east banks of the Bonegi River, all hell broke loose. The fight developed into a full-scale battle. Artillery fire was stepped up, and the navy and air arms were called upon for support. Three destroyers were sent up from Henderson to shell the Japs on the west bank of the river, and they were strafed by several planes. Halftracks were brought up to reinforce the 1st Battalion sector; it was a hell of a fight. B Company earned more Purple Hearts on January 30, 1943, than at any time during their long stay on Guadalcanal. Two sergeants were awarded the Silver Star Medal for gallantry in action.

When daylight broke on the morning of January 31st, it was hard to tell where the frontlines were. The Japs had infiltrated through the openings in our lines and had taken positions in the coconut palms and the jungle covered foothills to our rear. When our machine guns and mortars opened up, we drew fire from Hill 124 and the jungle to our immediate front. The Sixth Marines of the CAM Division were in reserve, and they were brought forward to clear the Nips from our rear. As they delivered volley after volley of sweeping fire on the well-hidden Japs, the bullets showered and came close over the occupants on Hill 118.

We were in unsettled primitive land. The only signs of civilization were the presence of the Japs and us Americans, and we were trying to kill each other, as well as Lever Brothers' Coconut Groves in the coastal area. However, about 500 yards to our right front through an opening in the jungle, a buddy and I sighted a well-constructed framed bungalow. It looked to be a story and a half. Two uniformed Japs walked out of the front of the house. One of them sat down at the base of a tree, and the other stuck out his hand and braced himself against the tree. They both looked toward our position on Hill 118. I fired a couple of rounds at them. Captain Rosskopf sent a runner down with orders for me to cease firing and advised that we had troops in that vicinity. Was this well-concealed house General Hyakutake's General Headquarters? We later learned that the foothills west of the Bonegi River and slightly west of where the house was sighted were honeycombed with dugouts by the hundreds. Did the Japs expect that we Americans would land on the coast west of the Bonegi and move south through the flat coastal coconut groves?

About February 1, 1943, a small terrier-type dog, white with black spots, appeared at the jungle's edge. The dog sat down on his haunches and took a friendly look at us and then suddenly returned to the jungle from whence he came. I scratched my head and wondered if this four-footed Jap K-9 was later a veteran of the Peleliu Campaign. Perhaps the Japs had a corps of these K-9s. Anyway, that is how it was as the curtain went down on the final phase of the Guadalcanal Campaign. It was from Hill 118 that Company B observed the sinking of the USS *DeHaven*.

Guadalcanal to the American military and naval service is a "Monument to Victory." We Americans, with a handful of service people from Australia and New Zealand plus a few local native scouts, landed at Guadalcanal August 7, 1942, exactly eight months to a day after Pearl Harbor. American marines, airmen, navy, and coast guard members, plus two U.S. Army Infantry divisions and a Regimental Combat Team, with token Allied support, met the Japanese on their chosen fields of battle, and they were ours. It took six months and two days to secure the Island—from August 7, 1942, to February 9, 1943.

Guadalcanal was the first land victory for America and her allies in the Asiatic-Pacific Theater. America and her Allies never lost another campaign all the way through to Tokyo Bay and September 2, 1945, including the campaigns in both the subtheaters of the Western Pacific and the Central Pacific. Yes, Guadalcanal stands out like a bandage on a sore thumb among the Asiatic-Pacific veterans of World War II. The Japs remember Guadalcanal as "Starvation Island" and "The Island of Death." As we Americans "Remember Pearl Harbor," the Japs took one hell of a beating at Guadalcanal.

The 1st Battalion, 147th Infantry boarded the SS *Mormac Wren*, a merchant marine troop transport, for British Samoa via American Samoa on May 11, 1943, and got underway on May 12th. As the *Mormac Wren* sailed out of the harbor, through Indispensable Strait into the high seas, this writer looked back from the ship's stern upon the green stagnated, malaria-infested hellhole of Guadalcanal. I asked myself, "What price glory, what price victory?" I thought about those American marines, sailors, and soldiers with their crude crosses that we were leaving in the American Military Cemetery near Henderson Field. Some of them were members of the 147th Infantry. I thought about the hundreds of sailors who went down with their ships in "Iron Bottom Sound." And there were the heavy bombers and their crews, escorted by fighters from Henderson Field, who went out daily in groups so large they cast shadows upon the earth as they passed overhead to attack targets in the upper Solomons and elsewhere, with many of the crews not returning.

Leonard M. Owczarzak

Christmas 1943

Christmas Eve 1943 found our antiaircraft unit on Bougainville Island in the Solomons. For many of us 18 and 19 year olds, it would be our first Christmas away from home and loved ones. The prospect of having a merry Christmas on an embattled jungle island over 9,000 miles from home seemed very dim.

The Japanese, from their base on Rabaul, began their bombing runs early Christmas Eve and continued them throughout the night. At 4 A.M. Christmas morning they finally left, and we all dropped exhausted into our bunks. At 5 A.M. we were rudely awakened by a violent earthquake that was heaving and shaking Bougainville's crust. Fleeing our tents, we found the ground so unstable that we were hardly able to stand. Nearby jungle trees were swaying as if some giant wind were blowing into them. A two-and-a-half-ton truck had rolled across the area and came to a halt in the middle of the mess tent. Every piece of our equipment was knocked off level.

While relevelling our guns and radar, a Jeep carrying a Salvation Army officer pulled into our area. He approached and handed each of us a small Christmas gift package containing candy, gum, cigarettes, and toilet articles. With a hearty "Merry Christmas and God bless you" he departed. The surviving members of our unit will never forget those 24 hours of Christmas 1943 during which they experienced enemy attack, Mother Nature's power, and Christian charity!

Frank "Blackie" Hall

Tales of My Youth

It is dusk on a hot December evening in 1943, and we are settling down for the night in our foxhole. We are settling down because once it is dark, we do not light a match, we do not talk above a whisper, and we positively do not leave our foxholes. Anyone walking around after dark gets shot because he will be Japanese. They get very brave at night and try to infiltrate our lines and quietly cut a few throats. This evening, I'm very happy we have that rule.

We are in a foxhole because we took this piece of land away from the Japanese a few days ago, which makes them very unhappy, and they wish to take it back. If you see this piece of land, you will wonder why anyone wants it because it is a swamp full of mosquitoes, other pesky creatures, and, most of all, mud. This does not, however, deter the Seabees who are busy building an airstrip inside our lines. In six weeks, starting with a swamp, they have B-24 navy bombers landing and taking off. It is our job to land on the beach, push inland to form a semicircle about ten miles deep, then make sure the Japanese keep off the Seabees' backs. This we do. The day we come off the front lines to leave the island, we cannot believe what we see—a miracle, a gigantic airstrip built on crushed coral piled about six or eight feet above the level of the swamp.

Our foxhole is not really a foxhole; it is an "acting" foxhole. Since we are in a swamp, we cannot dig down; we must build up. We outline what would be our foxhole and use tree branches and mud to build a little log cabin with walls about a foot and a half to two feet high. Then we stretch our shelter halves over the top to keep out the rain. It does a pretty good job keeping out the rain, but I am not so sure if will keep out the shrapnel if the Japs attack with their mortars.

About dawn this morning we wake with a shake; the ground is moving around and the trees are swaying. We decide it must be an earthquake. Now we have a problem. Do we stay in our foxhole and maybe have a tree fall on our roof and bury us, or do we jump out and maybe get shot by a Jap prowling around? The shaking stops before we can make up our minds. A few trees do fall, but not on us. They are already weakened by all the mortar firing when we take over. As the daylight gets brighter and we can see across to the mountains about ten miles away, we see the biggest one has smoke coming out of it. We get a little spooked, what with the jungle, the earthquake, and now a volcano. All we need is King Kong to show up.

Most of the Japanese are on the other side of those mountains and they have a big problem trying to get their artillery and other heavy equipment on to our side of the island. In fact, for three or four days, we have a forward observer from the 12th Marines, our artillery regiment, way up a tall banyan tree right near our foxhole. He has a pair of field glasses and is watching some Japs about seven miles away carrying a big artillery gun through a mountain pass on their backs. The gun is broken down into several pieces. We hear him on his field telephone reporting their progress. Finally, on the third day we hear him say, "They are digging in and assembling the gun," and he gives their map coordinates.

The next day, just as the Japs are about ready to load the gun and start firing, our guy in the tree says, "Fire one." Then, "Fire two." After he sees where his 155mm shells land, he gives new coordinates, then hollers, "Fire for effect." We hear the whomp, whomp of about ten shells exploding, then he cheers and reports they blew up the gun. We all cheer, and when he climbs down, we tell him we like the way he waits until the Japs do all that work before he destroys the gun. We invite him to come back any time.

Now the reason most of the Japanese are on the other side of the island is because just before we land, they send about two divisions out of the four that were in this swamp over to Choiseul Island in response to a feint by Admiral "Bull" Halsey. He lands a battalion (about 1,000) marine paratroopers on Choiseul Island, which is nearby and has few Japanese defenders.

The paratroopers dash in, make a lot of noise, shoot up the Jap camps, and generally make a nuisance of themselves. Then they leave. The Japanese believe this is our real target and send a couple of divisions over from Bougainville to help out. Since they have troops all over Bougainville, they pull their divisions out of the least desirable part of the island, the Empress Augusta Bay swamp area, figuring if we do invade Bougainville, we will never invade the swamp.

Bougainville is the northernmost of the Solomon Islands, about 500 miles northwest of Guadalcanal. It is about 200 miles long by about 50 miles wide with a chain of mountains running lengthwise. If we build an airfield here, our bombers can reach into many Japanese strongholds and can have fighter planes along to help. They can support MacArthur over in New Guinea and also hit north to Rabaul in New Britain and Kaviang in New Ireland.

So the Japanese have about 40,000 troops on Bougainville to make sure we do not proceed any farther. It seems they do not wish us to build any more airfields. We have the 3rd Marine Division of about 20,000, not counting a battalion of Seabees who can also fight when they have to.

As soon as the lap troops land on Choiseul, Halsey moves the navy in to make sure they stay there. Then we land on Bougainville. First the Raiders land on a small island, which is only a half a mile or so off the coast. After a severe battle, they secure the island, and the main force, the 3rd and 9th Marine Regiments, land on Bougainville. There is another battle, and then the troops start moving inland and also in both directions along the beach to expand the beachhead.

We (the 21st Marines) do not land until later. It is November 11, 1943. We come up from Guadalcanal in old fourstack destroyers. Ours is the *John Walker*. Like some of our rations, it was made for World War I. How we go from the beach to our foxhole is another story.

Earlier today, while we are out on patrol, a tree falls down and lands on top of our foxhole. When we return, we cannot find our foxhole, and at first we are upset, but quickly change our minds. It does not hurt our walls, and since we can still see out the front, we are happy, because we are now well camouflaged.

Every day we go out on a five- or six-man reconnaissance patrol to cover the jungle right in front of our position to make sure the Japanese are not massing for a surprise attack. Our colonel does not like surprises.

Since I am a first scout, I lead the way while we look for Japs. We hike out two or three miles in one direction, take a left turn for another couple of miles, then left again to return. We make a big triangle using a compass and make notes as to where we locate Japanese. We do not attack; we reconnoiter. We come across small groups at times, but they do not see us. I hear other patrols are ambushed, but we are lucky; we always see them before they spot us.

This morning, after we recover from our earthquake, wash up a little out of our steel helmets, have a cup of "Joe" and some C-rations, we take off for our patrol. Today, our sergeant tells us we must hike three miles out toward the mountains. We each have a compass so, in case we get in a firefight and get separated, we can find our way back. As usual, we are looking for any large groups of Japs to see if they are gathering for a surprise attack. We climb through the barbed wire and go down the hill and walk in single file through the jungle. All we have to do is stay close enough to see the guy in front and far enough so we do not get hit by the same Nambu machine gun or grenade.

I line up my compass for 95 degrees and draw a bead on a tall tree about 100 yards away and start heading toward it. There is a patch of thick underbrush about 20 feet high between me and the tree, so I have to very quietly ease my way through and around wait-a-minute vines, small trees, bamboo, and all kinds of bushes, keeping an eye on where I last see the tree. Meanwhile, I watch for possible ambush sites. It will be a lot easier to follow a trail, and the other guys let me know this after our first patrol. But after they hear our buddies in E Company and G Company get all shot up when they follow the trails, they do not complain. I see my job as finding out where the Japs are and not letting them see us so we get back alive.

So we never follow a trail. The Japs love to wait alongside trails wherever there is a sharp bend, a small hill to climb, or a little stream to cross—any kind of natural barrier, which will distract us while we walk around it—so they can surprise us while we are not looking.

I walk silently, keeping about 10 to 20 yards away from any trail. Nobody in the patrol says anything. We use hand signals. When I reach the big tree, I take out my compass and do the same thing again. Mike double-checks with his. He delegates Gunner to count paces so we have an idea when we go three miles. Now, the jungle is pretty thick, and what with weaving around trees and bushes and over dead tree logs, it is not easy to keep track of our direction or the distance we travel.

I have my machete in my left hand, and a Browning automatic rifle (BAR) in my right. I am supposed to carry an M-1 rifle, but I soon learn that being out in front and having an automatic weapon that can get off 20 rounds in a hurry is much better insurance against a surprise ambush than an 8-shot semiautomatic M-1. So after we land in combat, I pick up the nearest BAR that is no longer needed by the original owner. One problem that tends to discourage such trade-ins is that the BAR weighs 18 pounds, while the M-1 weighs about 9 pounds. Except for the BAR, today we are traveling light. All I have with me is my cartridge belt with two canteens of water and a first aid kit, a bandolier with six magazines of ammunition, and a couple of grenades. Oh yes, I also have a D-ration in my pocket. It looks sort of like a chocolate bar, but it will never melt. It is not exactly homemade chocolate and does not taste very good, but I survive on it.

After about two hours, we reach the three-mile point and we take ten. Mike and I very quietly discuss the new 350-degree direction. We no sooner start forward than we come to a stream and I see what might be a good spot for an ambush about 30 yards upstream. On our side a path meets the stream and a big tree is lying in the water blocking the way. The path continues on the other side and passes right by a little hill covered with very dense underbrush.

I motion for our guys to hold up, and Louie and I go downstream so we can cross out of sight of anybody who might be waiting for us at the log. We make a big circle and come up beside the path as it continues toward the mountains. Sure enough, we hear a low murmur, and, as we sneak a little closer, we see two Japs peering over a mound watching the tree trunk in the stream, while about 15 more are on the reverse side of the little hill and only about five feet off the path, lounging around eating their fish heads. We cannot be sure of the exact number because of the density of the bushes, but 15 are enough for us. We know they do not plan an attack on our front lines today; they just want to pick off a patrol or two.

Louie and I very cautiously sneak away and rejoin the rest of the guys. We explain what we see, and Mike marks the spot on his map. We go around the ambush and continue on our course. Nothing much happens during the rest of the patrol, but in a couple of places we spot evidence of recent Japanese occupation by 40 or 50 soldiers. Today we can be sure they do not plan a big attack because for a big attack they will need at least a division and a couple of days or so to get organized. Our patrols keep them off balance.

After we leave the island and the Americal Division of the U.S. Army takes over, we find out later that their patrols do not do their job. They walk out only 100 yards or so into the jungle until they are out of sight of the front lines, then sit down and hang around all day. When they come back later, they report they see no enemy. After a few days of this, the Japanese catch on. They bring in a couple of divisions from over the mountains, get organized, and catch the army by surprise at dawn and overrun our old foxholes. The navy has to call in some marine reserves to protect the airfield and take back the lost ground.

So in the daytime, we stalk the Japanese. At night, they stalk us. We have what we call a double-apron barbed-wire fence zigzagging along our front line. The land drops off about 30 feet or so in front of the barbed wire, so to surprise us, the Japs must climb a steep hill, then get across the wire. It is called a double apron because if you look at it from the end, it is shaped like a pup tent. And it zigzags so we can have machine guns aimed lengthwise down the zig in one direction, and up the zag in the other. We are prepared for a night attack but can be surprised by one man.

The Japanese try to sneak up on us, but they run into the barbed wire. We tie empty C-ration cans containing a few pebbles on the wire, so when the Jap touches the wire, we hear him. Then the Japs shake the wire to try to panic us into firing our machine guns so they can spot them and call in their mortars. We do not bite. Not even when they holler insults about Babe Ruth. We toss a few hand grenades, and that usually quiets them down. Every night they play these games, so by dawn we are more than somewhat annoyed and cannot wait to get at them.

Every time I ask myself what am I doing strolling through the jungle carrying a rifle and hunting for Japs, a little voice in my head asks: "Did you not rush over to 299 Broadway in New York City to sign up soon after the Japanese bombed Pearl Harbor?" I always answer yes, but it is all Red Meany's and Goldie's fault. They decide they want to join the marines and talk me into going with them. They both fail the physical, but I do not, and I wind up a marine. Red is now in the air corps learning how to fly a plane, and Goldie is in the Seabees eating all that good chow, while I am looking for Japanese behind every bush.

All at once, I see a tank come out of nowhere from behind us and immediately get bogged down in the mud. A Japanese officer comes running up to the front of the tank and starts to slash at it with his sword. We stand there with our mouths open as he tries to slay the tank with his saber. Some more Japs come running up, but they have a magnetic antitank mine, which they try to stick on the side of the tank to blow a hole in it. We open fire and finish them off. The tank commander comes out and thanks us, then calls for a tow.

Somehow I do not think these tanks are made for this swamp. Later, I see why this Jap thinks he can cut open our tank; even though our tanks are so old they must be left over from World War I, Japanese tanks are like sardine cans on tracks. The metal on the sides is not much stronger than stiff canvas.

We continue on. There is much noise of machine guns, rifles, grenades, and hollering coming from our left; then all is quiet. G Company runs into the Jap stronghold and, after a couple of hours, wipes it out. They pass the word, the battle is over, and we get orders to dig in for the night.

Our sergeant says we must look around out front of our lines. We spot a Jap rifle leaning against a tree, and everybody wants to pick it up as a souvenir. Our training film about booby traps comes to mind where it shows how the Japanese love to leave something around for us and booby trap it with a grenade. So Louie gingerly ties a string around the barrel, then we get about 20 feet away, hit the deck, and pull the string. Nothing happens. It seems they are in a hurry today and do not have time to booby trap this one. So Louie has a souvenir. Seeing no other signs of Japanese, we go back to our lines where we dig our three-man foxholes for the night. Actually, we dig the mud around the foxhole and pile up little walls around us.

Tonight turns out to be the spookiest night I ever have. Our battalion forms a big circle in the jungle, like pioneers circling their wagon train when they stop for the night as they cross the prairie. Everybody is on the front line in three-man foxholes. We take turns keeping watch, but no one sleeps. We can see nothing, we hear all kinds of strange sounds, birds, bugs, and swear it is the Japanese signaling to each other. It is pitch black; there is no moon tonight, and we are sure every sound is a Jap sneaking up to cut our throats. This makes the guys edgy, so all along the line people are opening up with rifles, BARs, and even machine guns. Every time someone opens up, we think the Japs are attacking. One section spooks the next and around and around it goes. We spend the whole night like this, shooting at every sound. If we were not marines, I would say we were scared silly. But of course we are, so we are not. I am sure I see a whole platoon of Japs marching up and down in front of my foxhole. It seems every spooky movie I ever see becomes real tonight. I swear if I ever get out of this, I will never go see another one.

Finally, when we think the night will never end, it does. The sun decides we've had enough and comes up. We all decided we had enough about 10:00 last night. There is not a Jap body in sight, so what with some thousand guys shooting at shadows all night, that is all it is—shadows. All the guys are very angry and can't wait to find some Japs.

We find out later that every unit goes through something like this their first night in combat in the jungle. We never do that again, but later, on other nights, we hear sounds of much shooting in the distance, and shake our heads in scorn and say, "Boots." We are now truly salty. But the nights remain spooky until we leave this island.

It is Thanksgiving, and they tell us that the President orders that all troops should have a traditional Thanksgiving dinner of fresh roasted turkey, mashed potatoes, gravy, vegetables, the works. What the President does not know is we do not have our mess gear. How are we going to hold those mashed potatoes with all that gravy? Now, a lot of people went to a lot of trouble to bring the turkey over to these islands, to cook it, then to get it up to the front lines through all that mud. And we have nothing to put it on.

[After an eight-day battle] we are without our packs, ponchos, shelter halves, mess gear, and toilet articles like toothbrushes, soap, and razors. We do not really miss the mess gear, because we do not have any mess. We survive on D-rations, which are unmeltable, tasteless chocolate bars, and C-rations, which are little cans of stew or something.

About this time, we invent instant coffee; well at least we make the instant mean instant. It seems we must take the tracer bullets out of the BAR and machine gun ammunition because when we fire them, we do not wish the Japanese to know where the fire is coming from. So when it comes time to heat up some coffee, we open up the tracer bullets and after we find a dry spot, pour the powder out in a spiral like the burner in an electric stove. Then we light the powder at one end and hold the canteen cup full of water over the trail of burning powder. Presto, boiling water in about 60 seconds; then you add the coffee.

But now we miss our mess gear. Whoever expects to have a real meal here? Frenchy Godier, a very resourceful guy, shows us how we can have our Thanksgiving dinner and eat it too. He takes a banana leaf, which is about three feet long, and shapes it into a plate. We scramble to get banana leaves just in time for the cook, who shows up for the first time since we leave him at the beach, to ladle it out to us as we hold out our banana leaves. For silverware, we use our bayonets. We must take turns leaving our foxholes to get the turkey, then return, and, keeping one eye out for Japanese, we go to work on the meal.

This is truly a Thanksgiving dinner, one that I always remember. We are thankful to be alive, and after a couple of weeks of D-rations, no meal ever tastes better. Even on Guadalcanal where we trained, we did not have fresh meat. Back there on our day off, we hitchhiked on the back of a truck for 20 miles to buy a Spam sandwich at the USO tent. We have not had a square meal since leaving our friends in New Zealand last June. And we do not have another for a long, long time.

Yesterday we land and fight our way up the cliffs. We spent last night in foxholes across a saddle along the top of these cliffs. Our front line follows the line of the cliffs, going up and down with the topography. Just to our left is a little hill where one of our guys is sitting with an '03 rifle (bolt action Springfield, but very accurate), which has a telescopic sight. He is leisurely firing one shot at a time for about 15 minutes. When I go over to see what this is all about, it turns out that from his position he can see a bunch of Japanese about 1,000 yards away, milling around having a conference. He is slowly picking them off one by one, and they cannot figure out what is happening because they are so far away they do not even hear the sound of the rifle.

Over on our right is a little hill where the guys in E Company are dug in. We do not see much action, but all night long there is a terrible commotion in front of E Company. It seems they take a little hill about 100 yards in front of their main position, and the Japanese spend the night playing king of the hill with them, trying to knock them off. E Company has a lot of trouble, and not only from the Japanese. The captain calls for some artillery fire from a destroyer assigned to support our battalion and a few rounds fall short and kill a few marines.

The fierce battle rages back and forth all night, and we do not know who is left on top when daylight comes. Finally, when it is light enough, I see a

Japanese officer climb up from behind the hill and stand on top with his hands on his hips, and I nail him with one shot from my BAR. I think I have it on automatic, but when I squeeze the trigger, only one shot fires. It is enough. It is a tracer, so I see it hit him right in the stomach and he topples over. Then I attach a rifle grenade and fire a grenade over the top of the hill in case he has any buddies dug in. The grenade works perfectly, just like in practice, and it explodes about five feet above the ground, so whoever is there gets hit even if dug in.

A little later, our sergeant takes us around a bigger hill to our left to fill in a gap by the road, which runs along the top of the cliffs. The road has dirt embankments on each side, which remind me of roads back home when they plow after a heavy snowfall. We're assigned to some foxholes, which are already dug into the back of the embankment. We can see that something terrible already happened here because some of the holes contain bodies of dead marines, while the others are empty except for a little blood where obviously people were wounded then evacuated.

What I am doing floating through the air is more than I can say because I never floated before, and it can be hazardous to the health to be floating around up in the air, especially here at the top of the cliffs on Guam where the Japanese are gathered to protest our arrival. When the Japanese are looking for easy targets and shooting at everything in sight as they do all morning, I find it much more convenient to stay below ground and try to draw a bead on any Jap I spot.

Besides, just one second ago I was lying three feet below the ground in the bottom of my foxhole, which I just dug. I hear a couple of booms, then a real loud one, and the next thing I know I'm floating and thinking, "All that work, and they still blow me right out of the hole." Actually, I find myself standing right beside my foxhole in a daze wondering what happened. My arm is bleeding a little and so is my leg, but they both still work, so I feel okay.

But Tony and Gunner are not so lucky. Tony's foxhole is right beside mine, about two feet away, and Gunner's is about two feet on the other side of Tony's. Something lands right between their foxholes and kills them both. I am horrified by what it does to them. A corpsman (navy medic) grabs me and asks me if I can climb down the cliff on a rope, and I do. I see seriously wounded guys being carried down by corpsmen who hold them between their legs while they climb down the rope, hand over hand. They save their lives by getting them to the hospital ship. These cliffs are pretty high and remind me of the Palisades by Route 9W along the Hudson River.

Since they cannot get a stretcher down the cliffs, some guys hit bad enough to need one die of exposure in the hot sun, despite the best and sometimes heroic efforts of the corpsmen. They are being shot at while trying to save these guys. Later, I find that my good buddy, Hunky Kazarick, died because they couldn't get him down. I see the Seabees working like beavers while under fire from the Japanese, building a road right up the cliff, which they finish the next day. If you tell me that 50 years from now it takes more than a year to repave a five-mile stretch of a superhighway, I will call you liar. In the next few weeks, the Seabees build a highway along the beach at a rate of one mile per hour per lane. That's starting from scratch, laying a foundation of crushed coral, and right through to paving with asphalt.

Anyway, I climb down the rope, and some corpsmen take a look and send me to the beach where a boat takes me to one of the transports that is serving as a hospital ship. They patch me up, but tell me they decide to leave a piece of shrapnel in my leg and that it will probably work its way out some day.

Now we find out what happened to the guys we replaced. It turns out that the something that hit us and killed my two buddies was a 77mm (about 3 inches) shell from a Japanese mountain gun, which was on a little hill about 50 yards to our left. The Japs hid the gun in a cave, then wheeled it out and fired it right down the line, raising the elevation one click each time. They got about six rounds off and killed and wounded a number of our guys before the carrier planes, called in by our captain, came zooming down on them to try to blow them up. But they pulled the cannon back into the cave and the planes went away.

During the time we are replacing the dead guys in the foxholes, they are hiding in the cave. One pilot, however, stays up above in a cloud, so the Japs do not see him. When they haul the cannon out to fire at us, they get only three rounds off before the Corsair comes screaming down and blows them up. The third round, however, is the one that gets Tony and Gunner. But the pilot saves the lives of a lot of guys to my right where the next three or four rounds would have landed.

Two days ago, some 200 guys climbed down that cargo net on the ship, and after the ferocious night battle, we wound up with 23. Not all were killed, of course, most were wounded and some 30 or so had only minor injuries and rejoined the company within a few days (like me) or a few weeks.

We ride the landing craft until we get to the coral reef, then we climb into amphibious tanks, which then crawl over the reef and head for the beach. Amphibious tanks are armored on the sides, but they have no roof. It is like sitting in a very slow open boat driven by tracks instead of a propeller. As we watch, the Japs are dropping 90mm mortars all around us. One lands in the tank next to ours and makes an awful mess of the guys. Everything seems like it is in slow motion except for the shells.

Once our tank crawls up on the beach, we cannot wait to get out and run to our designated positions and get organized. We are the third wave, and in a few minutes, we must pass through the first wave and cross the coconut to the base of the cliffs and start climbing.

As I am lying in a little shell hole waiting for the signal to move out, I'm watching the rest of the landing. It seems unreal, like I'm watching a newsreel of a battle. It is very noisy what with explosions here and there where the Jap mortar and artillery shells land; guys are running and collapsing as they get hit; tanks are being hit; and more guys keep coming ashore. It is a movie, right?

Even while climbing the cliff with Japs popping out of caves shooting at us, and others rolling hand grenades down at us from the top, it still seems unreal. Leal gets shot, and his buddy, Griffith, takes his BAR and charges into the cave and wipes out all five Japs in it; then he is killed as he comes out. Now here's a guy we all think is an eight ball with two left feet, and he turns out to be the bravest of us all.

It does not become real to me until that shell explodes next to me and blows me out of my foxhole. Now I realize this is not a newsreel, and a guy could get killed if he is not careful and sometimes even if he is.

Frank Witek

None but the Bravest

Guam was a weird and ghastly invasion for the marines—a nightmare of steaming jungle and mad banzai charges by hordes of Japs crazed with dope and sake. From their first encounter with the insane spectacle of a Jap banzai charge, Americans had wondered what made the fierce little samurai tick. Were they religious fanatics, eager to get to Shinto heaven? Were they doped? Were they drunk? Surely no rational man would rush, screaming, to seek death!

On Guam, the 3rd Marine Division found part of the answer—liquor, in huge quantities, and some dope. A few prisoners were taken alive, too drunk to walk. Dead Nipponese reeked of alcohol, and their canteens were half full of assorted sake and imitation whiskey. Assembly areas from which banzai charges had erupted were littered with empty bottles.

Frank Witek's outfit had suffered badly even before the invasion assault. His battalion had started for Guam on a packed assault transport. Anyone who has spent one day at sea in the tropics on a combat-loaded attack transport knows what sheer misery can be. For 50 days, the ship steamed aimlessly in circles under a broiling sun. A Jap task force had been spotted not far beyond Guam. To invade risking counterattack by enemy warships and carriers would have been suicide. So the American assault force waited, one steaming day after another.

On board, heat rash, dysentery, and every other kind of physical misery plagued the tense, crowded group of men. Bleak boredom and dwindling supplies of food and cigarettes weighed down their spirits. As weeks of aimless sweating went by, the men began to get weak and sickly. Witek was no "company comedian," nor was he a professional soldier. He was a serious-minded, sober young fellow. Clear-eyed, open-faced, and friendly, he talked with a direct honesty and amiable frankness that won the respect of his buddies. He suffered like all the rest, but he stayed cheerful and reasonable. While other men grew short-tempered and nasty in their misery, he kept a sense of balance and of humor.

"You guys never had it so good," Witek said. "Here we are on a cruise of the romantic South Seas, at government expense. Nothing to do but take it easy. Pretty good deal, if you look at it right. Cut the griping and enjoy it." Then he'd grin and return to his automatic rifle.

It doesn't sound like much, telling it now. But it told a lot about Frank Witek. It explained his character. While other men griped, swore, and quarreled among themselves, he kept a sane, levelheaded sense of balance. He was good for his outfit in the time of waiting and boredom. He was to be good for it in the fiery test of battle.

On 21st July, the assault of Guam began. Amphitracks packed with helmeted marines churned toward the beaches. To the weary leathernecks it was actually a relief just to be doing something. Even an invasion assault was better than the misery of the sweltering troopship.

The 9th Marines stormed ashore at Agana Bay and drove across the beaches toward the hills above. First Battalion led the way. Witek was just one of the running, panting men, weakened by the long inactivity aboard ship. Heart pounding and lungs gasping for air in the blazing heat, he ran, dove down, and dashed forward again with his mates. From the hills beyond, enemy machine guns spat and rattled venomously. Artillery boomed and cracked, sending geysers of flame, steel, and sand spouting among the running Yanks. Mortars coughed wickedly, their deadly bursts tearing gaps in the oncoming lines.

Marines spun, fell, and slumped down heavily on the red-spotted beaches. Huddled figures, still, with the unmistakable motionlessness of death dotted the wide band of sand. But Witek and his mates kept moving into the scrubby jungle that fringed the bay. Then once into some cover, Witek's BAR and the rifles and machine guns of his buddies began to snap and stutter. Raking, searching fire defiantly spat back at the Japanese.

With the skill of long training and the aggressive determination that marks the men of the Marine Corps, the 9th Marines moved forward. They were badly out of condition after their enervating stay aboard ship. Straining, sweating, and laboring, they kept moving. By late afternoon, they had reached the top of the ridgeline dominating the landing beaches. They had taken Asan Point, at the corner of the bay, and had secured the crucial right flank.

All this had been done in the face of murderous fire from skillfully hidden, long-prepared defensive positions. Witek and the others had faced, with horrified amazement, the first of many banzai charges. Wild yelling, screaming, whistles, and bugle calls sounded in the matted jungle undergrowth. The Japs were working themselves up for the mad assault. Startled marines, unable to see more than a few yards ahead in the thick brush, looked at each other in puzzled uncertainty. The noise was like the howling of an insane asylum. Then one Yank yelled, suddenly, "Here they come!" Out of the half-light, half-dark jungle, a weird sight appeared. A wave of little men led by sword-swinging officers came crashing and leaping toward the waiting Yanks. It was a banzai charge. Faces contorted with drunken excitement, eyes glaring with stupid ferocity, mouths open with hysterical, frenzied screams, the Japs came plunging forward.

Witek's BAR stuttered and then settled into a steady staccato beat: bub-bubbubbubbub. As calmly as though on the firing range, he aimed and fired, sweeping smoothly from one clump of Japs to the next. Then he reloaded swiftly and fired again. All the while, streams of bullets from the oncoming Japs snapped and hissed overhead. All up and down the marine line, rifles and BARs whanged and cracked in a steady roar.

Japs fell like wheat cut down by a scythe. But in their places came more, leaping and yelling in an ecstasy of drunken hysteria. Here and there, a marine pitched forward, too, cut down by the hail of bullets fired by the crushing Japanese.

Witek was reloading when the Nipponese reached the American position. He looked up just in time to see a Jap officer, samurai sword raised high, poised to slash an American's head off. As the sword started down, Witek fired pointblank. The howling officer stopped as though he had run into a steel wall. Smashed back by the burst of bullets, he fell dead right in front of Witek's gun muzzle. His chest and stomach were a gory horror. The marine paused only for a second. Then he raised his gun again, picked another target, and opened fire.

Witek killed about 20 enemy soldiers in that wild melee. But that was still not why the M/H [Medal of Honor] stands after his name. The final act, the last scene in the drama, was yet to come.

It came on the 3rd of August, only a few days after the landing. It came after endless 9th Marines—artillery, mortars, machine guns, tanks, flares, and high-explosives. On the night of the 2nd of August, Witek helped to beat off a particularly crazy charge. For ten minutes, the Japs had been screaming and yelling in a patch of jungle, while the marines waited beyond an open area, a clearing covered with kunai grass. Flares arched into the black sky, bathing the scene in sudden light. A nightmare picture appeared. Japs, too drunk to run straight, were reeling and staggering forward, tossing grenades and firing guns aimlessly, laughing crazily and yelling like maniacs. A savage, brutal slaughter took place, ending with hand-to-hand struggles of gun butt against sword and machete. Afterwards, the American artillery pouring into the jungle-patch area made horrible mincemeat of the retreating Nipponese. Howling in drunken terror, the Japs fled back, while arms, legs, and heads flew through the air, thrown high by the crashing shells.

That was the terrible prelude to Witek's last day. The 9th Marines had passed Tiyan Airstrip by then and were nearing the tiny village of Fingayan. Off to their right, the Army's 77th Infantry Division was having a tough time of its own at Mt. Barrigada. The tempo of the marines' advance was speeding up as they neared Fingayan, but the patches of jungle and open areas of grass made a series of perfect ambush positions for the Japs.

Witek was very tired by this time, like all the men of 1st Battalion. Sheer willpower kept his feet moving through the dense, low jungle and hip-high grass, as tough and sharp as bamboo. Enemy snipers lurked in trees and behind bushes, forcing the tired Yanks to remain ever wary. Witek was still cheerful, despite his fatigue and despite hundred-degree heat. "If we keep moving," he said to a buddy, "they won't able to set up a solid defense. Maybe we can get this over with pretty soon."

That, too, was a remark characteristic of American fighting men. A battle to them, fundamentally, was just a tough nasty job of work—a job to be done and finished as quickly as possible. Witek took no pleasure in his deadly prowess. He got no joy from killing. It was a matter of duty. So his squad moved warily forward in the blazing heat. Carrying more weight than most, what with his heavy BAR and extra ammunition, Witek had it just a bit tougher than most. But no man in his platoon ever heard him whine. He griped a little about the heat and fatigue, as did the others. But there was no "quit" in him. He kept moving. Not far from Fingayan, his squad made contact with the main Jap defense line in a sudden blaze of action. Moving through a patch of jungle, his platoon was met by a sudden storm of fire from the front and from both flanks. Hundreds of Japs, hidden in camouflaged positions, opened up on the advancing point platoon. Then, with fiendish yells, about 60 Japs came charging at the lead squad—Witek's squad.

Most of the Americans dove to earth. They were in a death trap, nearly surrounded and terribly outnumbered. The approaching Japs would swarm over them in seconds. Pinned down, the Americans couldn't see to shoot through the thick growth. That was when Frank Witek won his Medal of Honor.

Someone had to hold off the Japs. The platoon was doomed, unless someone could save it at once. There was someone—Frank Witek.

With bullets clipping twigs all around him, he leaped upright in full view of the onrushing enemy. Point blank he fired his big BAR, full automatic, sweeping the line of screeching Japanese with a spray of lead. Eight Japs spun and fell under his blast. The rest, startled by the sheer effrontery of the one-man reception, halted and took cover. Witek kept shouting for the platoon to move back to a spot where they could take cover. His BAR chattered again and again as he stood erect, a solitary figure of defiance.

Covered by Witek, the platoon fell back, calling him to come too. He began to back away. Halfway back, he passed a wounded buddy lying alone. Somehow he could not leave his friend. Again he stopped. Again his gun chattered protectively, while buddies rushed to the wounded man and dragged him to safety. Then Witek started backing away again, his BAR snarling defiance at the enemy.

Back in the relative safety of a small draw, the shaken marines regrouped. They knew that the Japs must not be allowed to solidify a defense line. Once dug in again, the enemy would be very hard to push out. There were far too many for one weakened platoon to handle. The call went back for tanks.

Half an hour later, three light tanks came crashing and clanking up to join them. Meanwhile, the growing racket of machine-gun fire up ahead told of a buildup of enemy defenses. The situation was bad, and getting worse. Unless the three tanks and one platoon could break it up, the Jap defense line would grow into a wall of fierce resistance. The marines started forward again.

"Let's go, you guys!" Witek shouted. The tanks, each accompanied by a squad, ground and snorted toward the waiting Jap line. Enemy machine guns sprayed the oncoming iron machines, forcing the foot soldiers down to earth—all but Witek.

In the midst of the hail of bullets, he kept on moving. Without men nearby to protect their sides, the tanks were half-blind and easy prey. One machine-gun nest in particular was raking the tanks, keeping their vital riflemen away and down—all but Witek.

As though unaware of the bullets snapping all around him, Witek plunged toward the machine-gun nest. Standing hardly five yards from it, he fired a burst into it, just as its muzzle swung around toward his chest. Eight Japs were in the hole, eight dead Japs, when Witek's gun stopped chattering. Then, through the uproar, Witek's voice was heard: "Come on, you marines! Let's go!" Those were the last words Frank Witek ever uttered. As the marines leaped forward in a charge that was to break the Japanese line, Frank Witek fell dead. An enemy bullet at last had found him. His great heart was stopped. He fell with his face toward the foe, leading his buddies in a surge of fierce gallantry, inspiring them to an irrepressible charge. So died Frank Witek. For this epic heroism, Frank Witek was awarded the Medal of Honor posthumously.

It does seem that one main idea emerges from the story of how Frank Witek won the "Blue Ribbon" of gallantry, a simple thing to say in words. Just this: He fought for the team. His own safety was forgotten, while he risked his life for his squad, for his platoon, for his outfit. And his outfit, in the last analysis, was the nation.

Perhaps that is the real secret of the Medal of Honor—gallantry that is forgetful of self, that dares death for the nation.

(Written by George T. Calahan for the June 1958 issue of *Battle Cry*. Submitted by Jean Witek Christy, sister of Frank Witek)

Howell Heflin

Bougainville

I was among the marines who landed on the island of Bougainville, about 600 miles northwest of Guadalcanal at the west end of the Solomon

Islands in November 1943. Guadalcanal is the easternmost island in the chain. Bougainville was a big island. It was fortified by the Japanese, but it was big enough that a landing place could be selected where not too much resistance could be anticipated. There would eventually be trouble, however. There was sure to be a battle later over the beachhead, which had been established.

The idea of a beachhead was to move inland far enough that enemy artillery couldn't hit ships and couldn't hit the beaches. Usually a beachhead would give you protection for a radius of 15 miles or so. The range of the Japanese artillery determined the size. We wanted to be able to land safely and protect the beach as supplies came in. Our particular mission was to take an area where the Seabees could put in a landing strip for our aircraft. This would advance our forward base several hundred miles from Guadalcanal.

We landed at Princess Augustus Bay and had very little resistance. There was a small group of Japanese nearby, but they had anticipated a landing some other place. So we landed and moved forward.

There's a humorous story a buddy likes to tell. He claims that I held up the invasion of Bougainville. After we'd moved in several hundred yards and secured our objective area, we were relaxing. The island was muddy, and when you hit the beaches you got sand and mud all over everything. I went back to take off my shoes and wash out my socks and pants. I put my shoes down and a big wave took them out to sea. I had a duffle bag with another pair of shoes on the ship we came from. They had to radio and have somebody go down in the hold of the ship, get the shoes out of my duffle bag, and bring them to me. I held up the invasion of Bougainville until I could get my size twelve-and-a-halves.

There was a scary experience in Bougainville that didn't involve the Japanese. I've never been fond of snakes, and I woke up one night with a snake wrapped around my leg. I grabbed hold of it and threw it outside the foxhole. It was dark, and I don't know what type snake it was. It didn't bite me. Many years later I went down to Opp, Alabama, just before they were going to have their rattlesnake roundup. They wanted to wrap this rattlesnake around my neck and take promotional pictures for the roundup. They claimed several other people in public life had done it. [Howell Heflin is a former U.S. Senator from Alabama.] I said, "Not me. You can hold him over there and put three people between us."

By the fourth or fifth day, the marines had moved well toward their objective of securing the beachhead. We were three or four miles in, close to the apex of the beachhead and we were moving on up. We had dug foxholes, and a redheaded marine was at the forward part of our perimeter. We were in the front line, and every now or then a Japanese sniper would fire. Well, the redhead developed diarrhea one night. There were no toilets, and you had to use your helmet as a pot. His area was fairly clear, without too much jungle, and the tropical moon was shining down. As he did his business, the white, pink skin of his exposed extremities was showing in the tropical moonlight. Some Japanese sniper spotted it and fired, and the bullet went in and out both cheeks. It made four holes. Red was a humorous sort of fellow, and the next day he said, "I want to put in for four Purple Hearts."

When people had diarrhea or something like that, they couldn't get up and wander around. We were on the front lines, and there were Japanese snipers and patrols out there. The next morning, they'd find some water or something and clean the helmets out.

By Thanksgiving Day we had moved pretty well along and thought we were fine. Some way or other the cooks had gotten a turkey from the ship, and they were going to fix turkey and dressing. Well, about the time we were getting ready to sit down to eat, word came to move out to a battle at Piva Forks. We had to leave our turkey dinner. In two or three hours, we got to the battle location. As we moved forward, we saw that the Japanese had dug in, and this was a battle line where they wanted to fight.

We started moving up this hill. There were surrounding hills, but this was the highest. The Japanese were there, and we were at close range. It was thick jungle with vegetation and, even when we were close to the top of the hill, we couldn't see them. When we stood up, they could spot us, but we couldn't spot them. They waited until we got nearly to the top of the hill and opened fire on us with machine guns and everything else.

It later became known as Grenade Hill because you were close enough to throw grenades and hit the Japanese. This was all in the jungle, with these big banyan trees. My sergeant, Harvey Carbaugh, and I and the others were pinned down. We were throwing grenades, but when we'd fire bullets they'd go up the hill and over the line of fire. When you're going up a hill, you've got an incline, and the bullets weren't hitting anything. The only way we could be effective was to get on the level where we could spray them.

Carbaugh and I decided that he would create a diversion, and I would take a BAR and stand up to fire. If you didn't have some diversion and you moved, they'd fire their machine guns at you. His people threw hand grenades and attracted their attention, and I got up with a BAR and sprayed the area. The next day when we charged up the hill, we found we had destroyed several machine gun nests and quite a large number of Japanese soldiers.

I got some hand-grenade fragments, but I wasn't hurt enough to go to sickbay. I just picked them out, because they were just skin deep. That was a major battle in Bougainville called the Battle of Piva Forks, but our outfit always called it Grenade Hill.

After Bougainville was secured, the 3rd Marine Division went back to Guadalcanal and continued to train. By this time, a grand strategy in the Pacific was being followed, both by Admiral Nimitz, who had command in the northern part of the battle area, and General MacArthur, who was in command in the south. The strategy was to island hop in a large movement northward and westward, and to pick and choose carefully, using surprise when possible. This strategy was working. It not only saved American lives, it stranded thousands of Japanese soldiers on isolated islands. Large air bases were established as the Americans went along.

After Bougainville, my unit returned to Guadalcanal for more training. When we got back, I had lost about 50 pounds and was down to something like a 30-pant size. The C-rations were terrible; the only decent meal we would have had was that Thanksgiving dinner we didn't get to eat. It was the end of the year, and the New Zealanders we'd known before were there. They invited us to come over and celebrate New Year's Eve with them.

After a few weeks, the division was loaded on another ship. At the time, American forces were in the battles for Saipan and Tinian. A lot of resistance was encountered on Saipan, and leaders thought they might have to deploy the 3rd Marine Division there. The division was held in reserve for 62 days, and the men stayed onboard the ship.

It was confining on the ship, particularly for the enlisted men. They were down in the hole with layer after layer of hanging cots. There wasn't much exercise. We finally went ashore at Kwajalein and Eniwetok and certain places where they got some exercise. Being confined was a terrible thing, and a lot of people got seasick.

The leaders finally decided to have the 3rd Division go ahead with its regular mission of landing on Guam, which was some 1,500 miles north of Bougainville in the Mariana Islands. When Guam was invaded in July of 1944, Americans had driven the Japanese back all across the Pacific and were preparing to launch an attack on Japan. The first step was to get air bases close enough for bombing. Japanese troops were still fighting desperately and ferociously, but there was no question that Japan faced certain defeat.

The Japanese knew we would try to liberate Guam, because it had been American territory, and they fortified it pretty well. Guam was the first American territory liberated in the Pacific. We had acquired Guam at the end of the Spanish-American War and it was a focal point in the trans-Pacific trade. We had airfields and some naval bases there before the Japanese took it.

The strategic plan was to use Guam, Saipan, and Tinian to launch bombing raids against mainland Japan. The long-range bombers sometimes had difficulty going the distance from these locations to Japan and returning. Iwo Jima was close enough that they could bomb and return, and it also provided a place for planes from Guam or one of the other places to land if they got into trouble.

My outfit was to land on Guam at a designated area, and we would be among the first to hit the beach. On the day we were to land, our company commander called a meeting and then had to leave for a few minutes. One of the lieutenants had a bandolier of hand grenades. He was throwing it over his shoulders, and one fell out and the pin broke. We were in a stateroom, which is what they called a sleeping room for officers. The thing went off.

There must have been four or five of us in that room, but not a single one got hurt. It was remarkable. Some way or another the Lord must have been taking care of us.

Guam was a much bigger operation than Bougainville. On Guam, our mission was to recapture the whole island. The landing was pretty heavily opposed. Again it was the idea of taking a beachhead and moving inland. The Japanese were well fortified and were firing artillery. They knew pretty well where we would land, and their artillery hit the shore and sank some of the landing craft in the harbor and on the beaches. We had to move forward and get to high ground as fast as we could.

We got over the first hill, and there was another hill up ahead. I got hit in the hand going up the next hill. The bullet went through my thumb. They fused it later, and I've still got a stiff thumb. I kept going. A short time later, I was hit in the leg. I was pretty well immobile, but I could still move forward. We got to the top of that hill, which was the immediate objective. From there, we could move up our mortars and begin to blow up some of their artillery. Our planes hit them, and there was some naval gunfire.

I was placed on the hospital ship, USS *Solace* and shipped with a lot of other casualties to Aiea Heights Naval Hospital in Hawaii, where I stayed about a month. The bone in the leg was chipped, and the bullet was still there. They put a cast on my right hand, and I remember I'd salute left-handed. Everybody would look at me and wonder what I was doing, but that was a way of doing things rather than not saluting.

When I was at Aiea Heights in Hawaii, this fellow Shockley shows up. He was not wounded but was covered with jungle rot, a fungus growth that was just like athlete's feet. It was all over his whole body. Imagine having that all over your body. Oh Lord! He was in terrible itching pain. I never saw anybody with so much fungus growth all over him.

(Adapted from a draft of his biography written by John Hayman)

Joseph N. DuCanto

H&S Company, 3rd Pioneer Battalion, 3rd Marine Division

Parris Island Boot Camp

Upon arriving at boot camp and going through the processing program, I, together with my mates, was given the option to accept or reject the $10,000 GI life insurance policy that cost something like $3.60 a month deducted from our $50-per-month paychecks. Since I was an orphan, I declined to be covered, since I had no one in particular that I wished to benefit one cent from my early demise. I was soon approached by Sergeant Peterson seeking an explanation for this deviant behavior, since a $10,000 payout (equivalent to $100,000 today) was a hefty chunk of change not to go to somebody if I bought the farm. After listening to me for a very brief time, he asked me point-blank, "Do you know what a point man is?" To which I replied, "No, sir," and he then proceeded to explain as follows: "A point man is sent out 20 to 30 yards or more ahead of the platoon to seek out possible enemy contact and/or ambush. When the shooting starts, he is usually among the first to get it! Do you know, Boot, who we designate as point man?" Really a rhetorical question, to which I quickly replied, "No, sir," with his rejoinder, "The guy without GI insurance." Suffice it to say that since nobody had ever explained it to me that way before, I very quickly signed the authorization card.

Romping and Stomping

It was quite evident that our weeks at sea in a cramped tub and overcome by boredom had produced a surly and quite unruly group of marines. The commander of the group, recognizing the foregoing, decided he had to do something. That something was to design a spot-training mission for us: humping the atoll. Humping the atoll consisted of our putting together all of our gear and 65-pound packs, going over the side and practice landings, being ferried into shore and various atolls, none of which rose more than two or three feet from their surrounding expanse of the Pacific blue. Weak from inactivity, surly by disposition, we had as I recall an absolutely miserable two days. But for me it was very close to being a very short exercise, as I nearly went under the waves, never to come up again! I stepped off the stern into seven or eight feet of water in full combat gear. I did not panic because I knew the craft was a small one and that if I could move forward only 30 or 40 feet I would be close to the beach and up for air. Fortunately, a fellow marine from Texas, all 6'2" of him, turned around, saw this helmet bobbing below the waves, and reached down and grabbed me and pulled me up for air and shore. I was coughing up so much water and cursing so loudly that I never did get his name, but wherever you are I am deeply grateful.

We proceeded to march from atoll to atoll, sometimes with a strip no wider than a few yards connecting one island from another, as the wind, rain, and waves washed over us, making us absolutely miserable. One of the islands we crossed has become a household word even as it no longer exists, having been obliterated by testing of the hydrogen bomb—Bikini Atoll. I was never certain as to whether all this romping and stomping made us any better marines than we would have been without it, but I am certain that it made us painfully aware of the psychic and physical cost of going soft.

With a large bit of pain, there did come some pleasure—namely, our later transport to a rec area where we each received two warm beers, a hamburger or equivalent, and an opportunity to swim and loll in the sun without getting our asses kicked. I have always enjoyed swimming, and of course engaged in doing so without being warned of the perils of swimming on or off a live reef. I stepped off the reef from a very shallow edge to deep water and was enjoying my swim until I sought to return and found that the coral edges of the reef were extremely sharp and made razor-like slashes on my lower legs as I exited the water. They were tiny cuts, and I thought nothing of them until a day or two later, when my legs swelled as if I had contracted elephantiasis. As it turned out, I had something somewhat more curable, but painful nonetheless: coral poisoning. Coral, as I discovered, is a living and growing organism that embedded itself in the razorlike cuts I had received and began to multiply much to my discomfort, requiring painful cleansing over a period of several weeks in order to eliminate this threat to the system. Surprisingly, there had been no prewarning to the troops so far as I was aware.

Rifle Inspection

Back aboard the ship we met the inevitable order, "Rifle inspection in 30 minutes." Needless to say, after two days and nights of sand, wind, rain, and saltwater we were filthy, and our weapons even more so. Nevertheless, in 30 minutes the platoon was lined up on deck between the hatches and the gunwale of the ship, a very narrow space to line three ranks of men. Lieutenant Angelo Bertelli, first inspecting the rank closest to the gunwale, began reaming everyone out, when he approached the young marine standing next to me. Lieutenant Bertelli went ballistic, yelling and screaming about the dismal shape of the weapon handed him, concluding, as he shoved the weapon back to the marine, "If I had a rifle that looked like this piece of shit, I'd throw it overboard!" The kid accepted the rifle, shrugged, and threw it overboard! I was so surprised I nearly dropped my rifle as I came up to "inspection arms," but not nearly as surprised as was Lieutenant Bertelli, who halted the inspection and called the officer of the deck to carry the young marine off somewhere. I never saw him again. There were, however, unconfirmed reports that the ship's company had a mysterious disappearance in mid ocean.

Boy Warriors

As I was coming up the ship's ladder one day, Lieutenant Bertelli braced me and told me that he had heard a rumor that there was an underage youngster in his platoon. He demanded to know if it was me, since I obviously looked like "the chicken," a name appended to all childlike marines. I assured him that it was not me because by this time I was "legal," having turned 17, and therefore out of danger of discharge. I became curious and went looking for the culprit and ultimately found him. He was a hulk of a man, 6 feet something, a throwaway kid of the depression years. Being unusually large for his age, he successfully enlisted in the merchant marines at age 12 and made two round trips between Murmansk and Archangel, Russia, and New York City. This was during the height of the U-boat sinkings in the North Atlantic, where the chances of even one successful sail and return was 50 percent or less, leaving out the fact that he had made two of them. He was then 15 years of age and loved the corps and planned to make it a career. Of course, I knew right away that he was slightly retarded, as indeed he was, but that did not diminish his avowed love for his marine corps and his wish to serve it well. Serve it well he did. After Iwo I went looking for him at his new unit and was told that he did not make it. Boy soldiers, as Colonel David H. Hackworth, a well-known military commentator, constantly emphasized, are the best, since they fear nothing, have no concept of future, and lack the quantitative and qualitative judgmental concerns that older warriors constantly exercise. I do not remember this kid's name, but I will never forget his looks, demeanor, and placidity.

Guam

Guam was truly a tropical paradise in many ways. Its beauty was captivating, and every stroll in the jungle brought some new marvel to my attention, particularly the wide and abundant range of birds. Cargo traffic, both ships and planes, evidently introduced on Guam a nonpoisonous but ravenous snake, which encountered no natural enemies on the island. Consequently, the snake has infested all areas of the island and has practically totally eliminated the native bird population. What a modern-day tragedy!

As the island became secure, the decision was made to set up a durable camp area and to move Fleet Headquarters from Hawaii to Guam. All of us were engaged in clearing the jungle and setting up a divisional base for ourselves in a semiremote corner of Guam. One of the details I worked on would take brush and debris to a spot overlooking a cliff where the material, together with the usual debris of camp life, bottles, cans, and waste of various kinds, would be pitched out and dropped 60-some feet below. Gasoline would then be thrown over the side and set afire to reduce the buildup of this dumping area.

One fateful day as I was pushing stuff out of the back of a cargo truck, I slipped and fell, going down the chute, falling 60-plus feet through the air and landing buried to the hips in brush that had been newly ignited. I remember saying to myself, "I've got to get the hell out of here!" I am told, although I do not remember, that I began piston-rodding my feet, virtually taking off over the top of this burning mound of stuff, ultimately collapsing outside the reach of the fire. It is fortunate I did so, since it took nearly half an hour before medics could reach me and rush a badly burned youngster to the field hospital. After being cleaned up and receiving lots of morphine, I found myself in a field hospital with some newly wounded, other accident victims, some heavy cases of fever, and even a circumcision case!

I knew I was badly burned, and I could feel my head and my ears to be about the size of a basketball and asked the corpsmen for a mirror, which they refused to provide me on the basis that I didn't need to shave. A day or so later, Gunnery Sergeant Van Guilder of my company came, bringing with him some of my personal kit, including my shaving gear. My recollection of that meeting was that there seemed to be a question as to whether I should be court-martialed for being so derelict as to become injured and losing duty time. Fortunately for me, this soon passed over. After Gunnery Sergeant Van Guilder left, I eagerly grabbed my shaving mirror, looked at my injuries, and was horrified to see this monster staring back at me! I thought I was disfigured for life, relieved only as the healing process took hold and the new pink skin began to replace the terrible crusting that accompanies a bad body burn. Indeed, my buds back at the company took great pleasure in telling me I was better looking after I came back from the hospital than I was before I entered.

Subsequent to settling in our new camp area, we began a training regimen, which emphasized attacking heavily fortified bunkers and the use of demolition, flamethrowers, and Bangalor torpedoes. Accompanying these were, of course, the full field pack marches and conditioning hikes for mile after mile until we all became numb. It wasn't all work, however, since we had open-air movie theaters and first-run movies, heavily peppered with wartime propaganda and made more exciting occasionally by finding a Jap straggler enjoying the movie along with his nemesis—the U.S. Marines. There were episodic reports of straggling Japanese soldiers showing up at twilight in lengthy chow lines, and it seemed that every time a leaf was turned over we captured yet another one. I can remember a near riot when Betty Hutton showed up in our camp area on the arms of two bird colonels! The USO, Bob Hope, Betty Grable, and those long, slender legs and back shot of her in a bathing suit seemingly were posted on every jungle trail. Cigarettes were either free or, at most, five cents a pack, but what did we not have? We did not have booze, liberty, and girls! And for a long time, no fresh chow!

The Buglers

During these World War II years, all company business was accompanied by bugle calls. Reveille, assembly, mail call, mess call, taps, and other special calls were routinely blasted by each company's permanently assigned bugler. Since there are four companies within a battalion and within easy hearing range, there would often be a coincidental cacophony of calls at the same time or within brief periods and intervals. My company, however, had one of the best! Our bugler was the only marine during my career that I can remember who was smaller than I was. He was a wisp of a guy but had a powerful pair of lungs and simply beautiful technique. Inevitably, when taps went down, everyone in the battalion waited for our bugler to truly end the day. We thus would lie in our sacks listening to three other buglers do their duty, to be followed by our company's send-off. He was terrific, and everyone from other companies who likewise waited and listened and heard him never challenged his primacy. He clearly imprinted his heart on every evening call, and I still sometimes hear it ringing in moments of reverie.

USS Indianapolis

In early July 1945, an older brother of a friend of mine had taken the trouble to look me up. His ship, the battle cruiser *Indianapolis*, had just completed a record run from Hawaii to Tinian where it had offloaded a mysterious cargo of extraordinary weight, which had made the ship tilt dockside. The ship then proceeded a short distance to Guam, which was by this time headquarters for the Pacific Fleet.

The *Indianapolis* was at the time one of the fastest ships of the fleet, with flank speed approaching 30 knots. She left Guam for the Philippine islands under strict radio silence and was never heard from again. Several days out of Guam, the *Indianapolis* passed within torpedo range of one of the few remaining, very slow, Japanese submarines. The submarine captain exploited this providential appearance and sank the *Indianapolis* with three torpedo hits, including one on the magazine, and sent her like a stone to a watery grave. Eleven hundred men went into the water and fewer than 300 would later be saved. Damnably, radio silence worked to doom a large number of these sailors, since a search for survivors did not commence for several days after the actual sinking and the onset of concern for the ship's nonappearance at its designated rendezvous. Unfortunately, my hometown acquaintance was not among those saved.

It is an irony of fate that the Japanese submarine caught the *Indianapolis* west of the Mariannas rather than east. On her trip from Honolulu the *Indianapolis* carried the bombs of Nagasaki and Hiroshima, and had the ship gone down before making delivery, most assuredly the assault on the homeland would have taken place as scheduled, and the war would have proceeded for many more months with untold numbers of casualties.

Subsequent to the end of World War II, the captain of the *Indianapolis*, Commander McVeigh, was court-martialed for failing to set a proper zigzag course then required of naval vessels, relying instead on the incredible speed of the *Indianapolis* to outrun any possible enemy. In another ironic twist, the Japanese commander of the U-boat that sank the *Indianapolis* was called upon to testify at Commander McVeigh's court-martial, attesting to the commander's failure to follow standing operational orders.

(Excerpts from his memoirs, *Sea Stories*)

Louis G. Dooley

My first reaction to marine corps behavior was astonishment, disbelief, and utter dismay. I just couldn't believe what seemed to be a totality of sheer stupidity and useless crudity. I thought the drill instructor's usual behavior was either insanity or he was abjectly moronic. I had joined the corps in good spirit, had expected to be trained in the use of weapons, in fighting, in "arts" of war, and was totally committed to this. I didn't need all the nonsense and abuse the drill instructor was deluging us with and felt deeply insulted by it all. On the first day I was already seriously wondering what I had gotten myself into and considering what I could and would do about it. I decided the only course was to nominally submit to it and get it over with; it just had to get better eventually, as there was no farther downhill.

Normal boot training would have been for three months, but cannon fodder was badly needed in the Pacific, so we were on an expedited six-week training schedule. The physical training was grueling, and at times I felt I might not make it but always did. We went through all the usual types of training one might see portrayed in movies: calisthenics, marching, judo-type hand-to-hand fighting, marching, bayonet fighting, marching, obstacle courses, marching, rifle firing, marching, grenade throwing, marching, automatic-rifle firing, and still more aimless marching. I concluded we did so much marching and drilling because our masters were not very inventive about teaching us useful skills of warfare, or else didn't know much about it. I got through all the qualification tests okay, neither at the bottom nor at the top of the heap.

The "exercise" that brought me closest to my limit was having to give other random platoon members a "fireman's carry" over the shoulder over a prescribed distance. Depending on the partner I wound up with, the task was reasonably doable, very difficult, or on the limit of impossible. A frame of 5'6" and 135 pounds carrying one of 6'5" and 200 pounds is a challenging exercise.

The frills of military life were a bore—making the bed a certain way, endless polishing of dress shoes, ironing of khaki uniforms, sprucing up for inspections, etc., but I grudgingly went through it all. I got into a minor problem about the second week, and the drill instructor (DI) in the evening took me out to the sandiest part of the drill field to subject me to his routine punishment for recalcitrant recruits. The theory was that he would run me around the field until I dropped; that would teach me not to be a smartass! Well, it didn't quite work out that way. I was always a good runner and was used to walking many miles a day. Bicycling all over Brevard County, Florida, had further strengthened me. Boot training additionally helped. I started running around and around the field; the DI yelling faster, faster, each time I passed him. I would very slightly speed up, then slacken off in the far turn. I don't know how many times around the field I loped, but I wasn't about to let this idiot grind me down. I was panting but had good wind then and, like the Energizer Bunny, just kept going and going and going. It got dark, and he finally tired of his sport and sent me back to quarters.

On the final day of our boot training the platoon leader lined us all up in formation for inspection. He gave us some general information about getting our new assignments the next day and then started down the line inspecting each of us. He stopped in front of me, told me he'd be getting his new assignment too, that I'd better hope we weren't assigned to the same outfit, and then irrationally added, "A bullet hole in the back of the head is not a pretty sight." I was somewhat startled, but couldn't let this challenge pass; I very politely, in a neutral tone replied, "Sir, what makes you think you can shoot straighter than I can?" The sergeant was accompanying him down the line, so he didn't continue the challenge, and that was the end of that. I hadn't realized before that I had been such a needle in his flesh.

I received my new assignment after boot training with some dismay. I expected to be shipped out with most of the others to combat units to fight in the Pacific. This was what I had joined for. Instead, still at Parris Island, I had been assigned to Field Music School for three months of training as a "field music." Someone had checked my background and, misreading that I had been somewhat of a musician for many years, had decided that this was the most appropriate assignment for me. And we were fighting a desperate war in the Pacific Ocean?

Field Music is an antiquated tradition, but military traditions die hard, and the Marine Corps perhaps is more tradition-bound than the other services. Bugles and drums and bagpipes lead men into battle (quiet death is never as "glorious" as that accompanied by bugle, drum, fife, and pipes!) and mark passing phases and events of the military day. We had three months to learn and memorize about 97 bugle calls, a dozen or so snare-drum ruffles and beats, and a number of marching songs on the single-valve horn. There were also special braids to learn to dress up the uniform, special flourishes to make with drumsticks and bugles, and so on. As an aid to memorizing the bugle calls, there were informal words to go along with each call; these were all coarse and obscene with a total absence of any cleverness or ingenuity.

Life was much easier in Field Music School. We moved into regular barracks, had more evening freedom, and had frequent weekend passes. Much of the day was spent in practice learning the bugle calls. The racket of all of us in one small hall practicing different bugle calls is unimaginable. In other locations, some practicing could be accomplished using only the removable mouthpiece. Drum practice was easier on the ears, since the actual drumhead wasn't needed; all one needed was a surface on which to practice with the drumsticks. There was also considerable drilling and marching, with classier formations and styles than in boot training and with fancy flourishes with the instruments from the bottom of which hung cloth marine logos. We were issued our full complement of summer (khaki) and winter (green wool) uniforms. The dress-blue uniforms were not required for our purposes, being reserved for shipboard, headquarters, embassy, and ceremonial duty stations. We were on tap for eventual combat unit assignment someday, not ceremonial duty.

On entering Field Music School, my basic weapon was changed from the standard M-1 rifle to a lighter .30-caliber carbine, and I was retrained with this. I liked the feel of the carbine; it seemed to fit better, and firing it was easier. The M-1 rifle had seemed somewhat cumbersome and awkward. There were three grades of shooting prowess: marksman, sharpshooter, and expert. I believe I was a sharpshooter, just slightly above average. I also had a Riesling submachine gun in reserve; this was a small hand-held machine gun. Only the officers had pistols—.45-caliber automatics. My salary as a private was about $60 per month; I signed a permanent continuing allotment for all but $15 of this to be sent home to Mom. I kept this arrangement throughout my tour in the corps. I used the $15 for PX purchases—candy, snacks, and eventually for beer, cigarettes, and other small items. It was all the money I needed in the Pacific.

Camp LeJeune is a major Marine Corps base, and, as a Field Music, I frequently had to stand special duty at the main headquarters. This involved sounding about half a dozen bugle calls throughout the day, e.g., reveille, morning colors, chow call, evening colors, tattoo, taps, etc. I also had to sound off the time each half hour by striking the correct number of peals on the station bell. The Marine Corps and navy are closely associated in some traditions. Aboard ship, time used to be announced every half hour by striking the ship's bell a certain number of times. ("Eight bells and all's well!") I had to be very careful about the exact time and number of strikes of the bell or I'd be in trouble. Some member of the headquarters command would have noticed any error. Bugle blowing was semimodernized—I raced by jeep to half a dozen public-address microphones in different locations and blew my calls at the microphones feeding loudspeakers. (Looked at honestly, I was an expensive replacement for an inexpensive clock mechanism and vinyl record and record player.)

My next destination after the additional Camp LeJeune training, though none of us knew it at the start of the trip, was Hawaii, the big island, not Oahu, though we would pass through Honolulu on the way to our base on the island of Hawaii. A troop train was formed to carry the battalion west to California where we would board our ship for Hawaii. I don't think there was ever a more miserable train trip taken by anyone across the continent, not even in the Wild West days. The trip took five days. We had railcars with hard wooden seats and no sleepers; we slept where we sat. The train used coal-burning locomotives the entire way, and, of course, the cars were not air conditioned, so we traveled mostly with the windows open. When the train approached a tunnel, we were supposed to close the windows, or the smoke would pour back into the cars. In open country, we were already getting sooty from the engine smoke, and several times when the windows were not closed in time, the soot just rolled in.

We were dirty, hungry, and thirsty the entire trip. The train picked up food along the way, supplied by the nearest bases or depots. I suppose someone had worked out a schedule in advance and decided at what stations and when there should be food waiting for us along the route. Such a theoretical plan could not work; U.S. peacetime train schedules were not even this precise. Several days, at least, we had to be on only two skimpy meals; even three meals were very skimpy rations.

Often the train would stop for 10 or 15 minutes at a station, but never near the terminal, for train refueling or perhaps a crew change or on a siding to let another train pass. We would wait eagerly for these opportunities and pour off the train, hunting for vending machines or any other facility that might have food, then race back to the train to catch it before it resumed the trip. There were regulations against this, but our commanders had enough sense not to enforce them. We lost several people along the way who didn't get back to the train in time. San Francisco was the train's destination.

Getting aboard the ship was a tricky undertaking: We had to climb from the heaving launch up a cargo net on the side of the ship to the ship's rail and then onto the deck. We had previous training on climbing up a rope cargo net with full pack and weapons but not also with sea bags. We had to improvise on this, and each of us devised our own solution. I don't recall what mine was, but I know I felt I needed three hands to do the climbing and also hold onto the sea bag.

The base site [in Hawaii] had been chosen for its isolation. We could fire our big guns in the general direction of Mauna Kea without danger to anyone. There were no cattle nearby, but in the distance we could occasionally glimpse herds of wild horses. In the distance towered Mauna Kea, the tallest mountain in Hawaii, and off to the left, slightly further away, was Mauna Loa, an occasionally active volcano. For some months during the winter, Mauna Kea was covered with snow.

The days generally were warm and hot, but the nights were cold because of the 8000-foot altitude and the cold winds sweeping down from Mauna Kea. We had a normal issue of two blankets; two additional blankets were issued. Many nights I used all four to stay warm. Each of our tents housed four to six men on canvas cots. I don't remember my tent mates and made no strong attachments to any of them. I scrounged a wooden crate for my writing and studying desk. At night there was not much for us to do, and I wrote many letters back home to various family members. I was also studying to finish the fourth year of high school. I had run out when I joined the Marine Corps.

The corps offered a correspondence-course program through the Marine Corps Institute, through which all personnel were eligible to take various study courses. In North Carolina I had signed up to complete the fourth year of high school. On completion, they were to send my grades to my local high school in Cocoa, Florida, and Cocoa High School would then issue the diploma. This was a good program. The Institute sent the textbooks one by one, a series of lessons and quizzes, which I returned by mail and then got back a grade. By the end of my tour, I had completed all the necessary courses, and when I finally got back to Cocoa, the principal of Cocoa High handed me my diploma.

Guam had been retaken from the Japanese not too many months before we arrived, and there were still stray Japanese soldiers hiding in the jungles. In general, they had not taken the suicidal path of the Japanese on Saipan. These were individuals who'd been separated from their units and were now merely trying to survive; they were not a threat to us, though we did maintain night guards around our base as a precaution. Occasionally, one would be rounded up accidentally in the course of our activities and turned over to the MPs. Some of the stories they would tell were interesting and ironically humorous, like sneaking past our guards at night to steal food, or moving up close at night to watch movies undetected. These strays were a hardy lot.

In Hawaii and in Guam we were rationed to two cans of beer per day, and that was enough for me. By the time we got to Guam, I learned a trick other guys played. Instead of buying the two-can ration every day, we were allowed to save up the daily ration and then, when we had a case saved up, buy the full case. This was useful for several purposes. We could sell off what we did not want to the heavy drinkers, and also, if we wanted to get drunk, we had enough to do it on, or we could throw a party for our friends.

The major problem with the beer was that we had no ice or iceboxes to cool it in. We had to learn to drink it the way the English do—warm. We experimented with various ways of trying to cool the cans of beer. We had no cool springs or flowing streams of water to soak it in. The most effective way to cool it was by rapid evaporation of gasoline. Put a couple of cans in a helmet, fill the helmet with gasoline from a vehicle, jeep, or 6-by, and then run the air pressure hose on the 6-by through the gasoline. This took only a few minutes and did a reasonably good job of cooling the beer, but was a bit wasteful of gasoline, and we couldn't use this method often. A backup method was to bury the cans in the dirt and then start a fire on the dirt surface saturated with any liquid that would burn readily—diesel fuel, kerosene, gasoline, etc., then dig up the cans when the fire went out. This worked too, but not as well. The easiest recourse was to learn to drink warm beer, which I did.

Frequently, we had rifle inspections by our local officers, and in these, for about a month, we had been having problems. Beginning in boot training, marines are taught to clean their rifle every day, very thoroughly, and we pretty much always did so. But in the routine rifle inspections, one or several of the guys each time were cited for having a dirty barrel—sighting down the end of the barrel, with the thumbnail in the breech reflecting light up through the barrel, light was not transmitted up the barrel. The offenders always swore they had cleaned the barrel. Someone quickly noticed what the problem was. On recleaning the rifle, a small, neatly cut circular portion of green leaf was discovered. How it got there was a mystery at first; blame being put on some unknown joker in the platoon, and suspicions of the culprit were bandied about. One day, by chance timing, the mystery was solved when one guy saw a wasplike insect flying near his rifle with a bit of leaf in its mouth and saw the insect fly into the barrel and fly out again without the leaf fragment. Even we did not at first believe his story, and it took longer to convince the sergeant that nature had been doing us in, but finally more witnesses were able to carry the case. Nature's adaptation to mankind is truly remarkable and often surprising. Suddenly these solitary wasp insects had been blessed with the presence of thousands of potential new homes, our rifle barrels, for their nests, and they took advantage of this new bounty. Our recourse was to check our rifle barrels just prior to inspection.

We landed and made camp on Guam on February 8, 1945. On May 8, 1945, we received word of our victory in Europe, but the war against Japan continued, and plans were pressed forward for the invasion of the Japanese homeland; our field training exercises were intensified. Unknown to all of us at the time was that scientific genius, diabolically applied, would intervene, making invasion of Japan unnecessary and thereby preserving many thousands of our lives. We listened in stunned silence to the radio announcement of the atomic bomb drops on Hiroshima and Nagasaki and quietly talked about it wonderingly in small groups.

We did not immediately realize the effect this would have on us and on our future until August 15, 1945, at 0900 Guam time when President Truman announced the surrender of Japan. This momentous news was received somewhat quietly and did not sink in fully until several days after the announcement. Then the joy and exhilaration rapidly began building and pragmatic questions like, "When do we go home?" began. Of course, no one had the answer yet, but we knew it had to be soon. Our only means of celebration was a bit more beer drinking, more happy camaraderie, and more lively accordion polkas.

World War II effectively was over, we thought, and we began seeing newsreels of celebrations at home, like we had seen for V-E day (victory in Europe). Our initial exuberance at the surrender of Japan began to pale as the weeks passed into months and we still sat on Guam. Disgruntlement set in as we continued to receive no word on when we would be sent back to the U.S.

An official statement was released saying that there were no ships available to take us back. We grumbled about this and doubted its veracity (what ships would have taken us ashore on the Japanese islands?), but gradually we settled down for the long wait before we would be able to go home. We were still a military outfit, and routine duties still ground along on their own momentum. Field exercises slacked off, and we had more off-duty time but not a great amount of things to do with it. I finished my correspondence lessons for high school graduation, and my name was listed back at Cocoa High School as a member of the current graduating class, all the others of that class, I'm sure, wondering who I was.

All the events of the six months or so we waited on Guam after Japanese surrender for ships to take us back to the U.S. are somewhat hazy in memory. After several months it became clear that we would not be returning as an outfit. Personnel lists began to be made up; some personnel would be returned before others, based on how long they had already been overseas, family status, and other reasonable factors. We saw no injustice in this, and individuals began calculating their personal overseas credits to see where they might stand on the priority lists for being returned. I was fairly near the bottom.

While waiting for ships to take us back to the U.S., disposal, dismantling, and packing activities gradually began. Most of my duties were still primarily headquarters oriented, and I was not directly involved in any of these activities, but I soon began hearing horror stories. Trucks jammed full of radio gear, weapons, munitions, cloth blankets, and field food rations were being driven off the piers in Agana Harbor and sunk in deep water, vehicles and all.

The claim was that the government had an unofficial, unpublicized agreement with our corporate and industry moguls that military gear was not to be taken back to the mainland to flood the markets and thus dampen profits of our industries and corporations. All goods were to be destroyed; also not to be left behind in a condition for use by the islanders. I saw trucks loaded with all kinds of gear I would dearly have loved to have. I had become attached to the jeep and wished I could have one of these back home. But into the deep waters it and many other vehicles all went, in perfect condition.

Eventually, about six months after the Japanese surrender, I was aboard ship, ready to return. Our camp was still functioning when I left, but many tents were fully or partially empty, so I don't know what their eventual disposition was. The tents and the temporary buildings would have been very useful to the natives, but I doubt they were left standing in usable shape. Field food rations also would have been useful to them, rather than being dumped under many fathoms of water in the harbor. (I would even have welcomed them aboard ship on the journey home.)

The ship was a wartime-built troopship designed for amphibious landings, rather than for ocean crossing; it was sensitive to every wavelet, continuously listing from port to starboard and bucking fore and aft. It was slow and relatively small and crowded. Hammocks five deep were our beds, and again I had a ship's loudspeaker too near my sensitive ears. One message I will never forget: first the bosun's shrill pipe and then the message, "Now hear this, now hear this—sweepers man your brooms, clean sweep down fore and aft," interminably throughout the day. We had been assigned duties while aboard the ship—sweeping the decks, chipping paint, galley duty, etc. From Guam to San Francisco, it was a long, dreary voyage of about 40 days, probably slower than Magellan centuries earlier. The only positive aspect was that we were, generally, sailing east rather than west.

The food situation was very inadequate; we had only two meals per day, and these were eaten only because we were ravenous. (I dreamed of all the food rations left behind and thrown away on Guam!) As soon as we approached the circular companionway downward into the eating area, the noisome stench of steam and food nearly overwhelmed us. Once below, we ate standing at swaying tables suspended by chains from beams above. One had to learn to sway with the table, rather than to lean against the sway of the ship. I won't describe the toilet facilities and conditions we had. We had, of course, no PX and no beer aboard the ship. Probably about midway of the voyage we stopped for part of one day at a fleet recreation site. Here we were able to swim at the beach and get beer, on the house. The beer storage area was a heavily guarded underground facility. An assigned work detail was allowed in to requisition a small truckload of beer, which we drank on the beach.

We were traveling alone now, rather than in convoy. One reason the voyage took so long was that we were sort of zigzagging around the Pacific rescuing small units marooned on various small islands and other isolated outposts. We had one major event on the voyage—a bit of mutiny. The navy has long traditions about special initiations for persons crossing the equator and the International Date Line. As we approached one of these events (probably the equator bit), the ship's crew began building gear on the fantail, and we began hearing unofficially about the coming initiation. We were a morose bunch of marines, and we just wanted to get home; we weren't interested in navy sport.

We talked it over, then sent word to the ship's captain through our sergeant that he call off the planned initiation. When this seemed to have no effect (work continued on the stage, on the fantail, etc.), we sent a small team out at night to dump it all overboard, and the next day we appeared nonchalantly on deck, all sharpening our bayonets. The captain got the message finally and about midmorning came the bosun's shrill piping and a special message from the captain over the PA system. He was rather distraught that we were so uncooperative and unwilling to uphold ancient naval tradition. He went on for about 15 minutes in a pained tone, but concluded by announcing, regretfully, that there would be no initiation ceremonies on the morrow. King Neptune and his Merry Crew had lost a round.

Dan Moriarty

Corporal 3rd. JASCO, 3rd Marine Division

The Last Marine To Die

July 1944

It was a glorious morning, the day after the end of the Battle of Guam. For four weeks our outfit had struggled to stay alive. Some didn't, but I did—surprisingly, since I volunteered three times to replace infantry radiomen who had been knocked out.

Yesterday, when Lieutenant Colonel Williams, 1st Battalion, 21st Marines had reached the north end of the island, he had me—the radioman in his five-man outpost group—contact the regimental command post. He proudly announced that the Island of Guam was secured. The battle was over, but it hadn't been easy, particularly the last two days. The enemy had fought hard.

For example, the battalion had moved through blasted enemy tanks that had held up our advance for a day. Their camouflaged, dug-in tanks had been "killed" by a night artillery attack that had sent shells screaming over our heads at treetop level. After that barrage, the enemy escaped to their caves overlooking the end of the island. So, yesterday, the enemy resistance had been light, as our outpost group and an infantry platoon scrambled down a steep cliff to the seacoast.

Today was nice. As I crawled out from my lean-to of palm branches cut with my machete, I spotted the colonel standing down by the beach. Everyone else was stretching and scratching. And there was a new sound: laughter. We were alive! And our stomachs began to loosen up as we sat eating the last of our rations.

Suddenly, an enemy machine gun cut the comedy. Three guys dropped over, one dead and two others clutching their throats. The two wounded men thrashed about until their buddies came to their aid. Through it all, Lieutenant Colonel Williams stood ramrod stiff, shouting orders that dispatched a patrol to seek and destroy the enemy. Then he turned his attention to the wounded. It was immediately apparent that they'd need more help than the corpsman could provide.

That meant shipping them out as soon as possible. But how? It was one thing to slip and slide down the steep cliff; it was quite another thing to haul two wounded men up on stretchers. That's when I spotted a U.S. Navy LCI cutting the water around the tip of the bay. I rushed to Lieutenant Colonel Williams and suggested taking the wounded out by sea. "How can we contact the ship?" he asked.

"That's a problem, sir," I responded. "We can't use the radio; I don't know the ship's frequency, but I may be able to attract their attention with signal flags."

"Okay, do it!" he ordered. As I raced toward the beach, I remembered that I had no signal flags. I'd have to use my hands or something. I noticed a marine with his rifle slung over his shoulder standing near the coral reef where I was headed, so I sidestepped around him.

Instantly, the marine shouted, "HALT!" I dug my heels into the sand and turned to face an M-l pointed at my guts. "What do you think you're doing?" the tough-looking marine snarled. "See what I'm standing next to?" he pointed. It was the glass top of a Japanese land mine. "You just ran over that thing! You could have blown us both to bits!" "Sorry, Mac! I didn't see what you were doing. I'm supposed to be signaling that LCI out there, so I'd better get going." With that, I whirled and proceeded more cautiously on to the coral reef jutting out from the beach. Once there, I took off my dungaree jacket—or what was left of it—for the back had been worn off from rot and the radio. I waved the jacket until I saw a navy signalman using flags, but he was too far away to read without field glasses. I wigwagged, "Two wounded, need boat to pick up, can't read flags."

A signal light gave me an "R" for Roger; they understood. A long pause followed, as the ship steamed down the coast toward our position, but well out beyond the reef. Then their light flashed a whole series of stuff, much too fast for me to read.

"What'd they say?" asked Lieutenant Colonel Williams, who startled me by being at my side. "I don't know, sir. It was too fast for me. I'll have to tell them to send one word at a time." The colonel's face said he didn't like my answer, but he realized nobody else could do the job. I signaled to slow down. Painstakingly, the navy light man blinked one word, then waited for my "Roger," then another, until the message was clear: "Sending small boat, have wounded at shore." After I sounded out the first three words, the colonel took off.

By this time the shoreline was filled with marines watching the rescue mission. They could see the small dinghy being put over the side and two sailors boarding it to row in. The sailors picked their way carefully through the coral reef, then paddled in quickly. Cheers went up as they beached and helped place the wounded men in the small boat. The sailors jumped back in and headed for their ship. We all held our breath as the dinghy bobbed about in the rough surf. Another cheer went up when the boat reached calmer water. Finally, when the wounded were lifted aboard the LCI, I signaled "Thanks!" "R" came back.

It was now time for the last detail: Bury the dead marine. A grave had been dug just in from the beach wall under a palm tree. The body was placed in a shallow hole, covered with his poncho. About six of his buddies shoveled dirt in with their short trenching tools. Finally, his rifle was stuck bayonet first in the ground as a marker, and a friend hung the one remaining dog tag on the trigger.

After that, we hitched up our gear and passed single file by the last marine to die in the Battle of Guam. All I could think was, "This wasn't supposed to happen! The battle was over!" I looked at the faces of my mates. They suddenly looked like old men. Their eyes had aged from seeing too much death.

As the line slowly headed toward the menacing cliff, there wasn't a sound. The morning's laughter had been buried in the sand behind.

(Excerpt from his memoirs, *Grandpa Stories for Young and Old*)

Pacific Tides

Wounded Marines on Iwo Jima

Flag raising on Iwo Jima

F. Joe Hoban

Battle of Iwo Jima—What's Real

Iwo Jima was a unique operation even by marine standards. From the first day to the last, there was no place like it. The contradictions in many events would be considered strange in an insane asylum. War, in and by itself, is irrational, so I found it hard to condemn the actions of the unfortunate people whose lives are only the pawns in the obscene chess game being conducted.

The instances of attempts at maintaining personal relationships that would be acts of insanity under normal conditions must be given their due consideration in that light of retrospection.

Laughter is one of the strongest indicators of a sound or normal mind. The context for that statement must always be kept in focus. If taken out of the narrow confines of thousands of men doing their best to kill one another on an ugly piece of land no one would want as a gift and placed against the fabric of any other battle, it would be easy to see the complete utter madness that had engulfed us all. We weren't mad and we were determined that the conditions would not force us to become so. We wished desperately to survive and still do what was necessary to get to the other side of the island. The Japanese were stopping us from doing our job faster than we or anybody else had planned. Patience comes hard to young men. Death was sudden and appeared too often to allow it to be too far removed from our minds.

We intercepted the full impact of the reality of where we were and what we were doing from crushing us with the only weapons youth could muster. We whistled as we walked in a graveyard. We often would gain on our shadows as we ran like jackrabbits in the low-lying shrubs you might see around any municipal airfield. Walking and running in a straight line was most dangerous on Iwo. Never being out of range of a mortar and knowing we were being watched at all times during the day took a great deal of discipline to ignore and carry out our assignments.

There were the alive and the wounded. There were the dead and the ones that would die. There was no escape from that reality. We didn't want to earn medals. We wanted to live, and we prayed often that we would have the will, skill, and the good fortune to do our job. We were forced to go beyond reason to accomplish our goal. We were forced to do these things simply because we were there with our buddies. The choice was clear.

It was down to the basics. It was them or us. That was the reality. Fear was part of that reality. The acceptance of that fear as a reality would be the thing that would take a great deal of maturity. We didn't have the years to mature naturally. Circumstances had placed the pressure on us like nature to create a diamond. Each man had to resolve this problem with himself. The ways could be different, but the result must be similar if we were to succeed as a group. It was one of those times we had all heard or read about. It was us on center stage and as young as we were, we knew it to be so, if even by some primal instinct. We could not fail, no matter if any of us lived. That was the reality.

(Excerpt from his memoirs, *Marines Don't Cry*)

Elwood Linton

When I graduated from high school at age 17, World War II was in full swing. My older brothers were already in service, one in the air force, the other in the infantry, and later on my two younger brothers would also join the air force.

I joined the navy in 1944, and, after completing boot training at Camp Perry, Virginia, I was very happy to be assigned to the U.S.S. *Nevada*, a battleship that had survived Pearl Harbor, action in the Aleutian Islands, and Atlantic Ocean convoy duty. On June 6, 1944, she was at the invasion of Normandy, then went on to the Battle of Cherbourg. The *Nevada* was the flagship for the Iwo Jima invasion and fired the first shot on February 16, 1945. I was still only 18 years old.

During this heated battle, the *Nevada* headed full speed straight toward Mt. Suribachi, coming within 500 yards of the island. Many of our LCIs were destroyed and damaged, claiming many victims, including one sailor on the LCI next to our ship seated at his gun mount with half his face blown away. It was during this battle that the *Nevada* shot down her first Jap plane since Pearl Harbor.

The constant noise and the continuous shelling went on for several days. Adding to this, the horrible sights of my wounded and dead shipmates and the lack of sleep have combined to haunt my days and nightmares for 55 years.

After Iwo Jima, it was back to Ulithi to enjoy a bit of peace and quiet with other ships and sailors. Watching a movie one night on deck, the film machine broke down and at that very moment, two Jap planes flew directly over us in the dark and crashed into the flight deck of the USS *Randolph*, destroying many of her planes, killing 19 men, and wounding many others.

On Easter Sunday, April 1, 1945, the land invasion began. Two days later, a Jap bomber narrowly missed us, crashing into the sea. Two pilots survived the crash, were picked up by a destroyer, and then were transferred to our ship where they were tossed into the brig. By April 7th, 125 Jap planes had been shot down and at least 13 American ships sunk. One ammo ship was hit just off our starboard beam, and it looked like a gigantic fireworks display as the fire spread and ignited the ammunition. Our ship was too close and had to move out of harm's way.

When the war was over our ship was then used for its best job—bringing our troops back home. I made six of these trips and then was ordered to the Brooklyn Navy Yard for my honorable discharge. The trip across country was made by bus—quite different from a battleship—but a much happier "cruise" with a far better ending.

Jim Headley

"Dog" Battery, 2nd Battalion, 12th Marines, 3rd Marine Div.

November 1943, Bougainville

An island, half-again as large as Guadalcanal, with thick, twisted jungle—bottomless mangrove swamps and crocodile-infested rivers with lots of insects. The island was the worst rain forest in the Pacific, with a wild uncultured race of people, reputed to be headhunters, plus about 40,000 Japanese. We were told that the other side of the island was a virtual paradise, but we never got to see it.

The initial landing was almost uneventful and nearly a surprise to the 40,000 Japanese on the island. We were immediately confronted with mangrove swamps, jungle, and mud. In fact, it was eight days before I removed my shoes, socks, and leggings because, had I done so before that, I would not have been able to put them back on, they were so wet. My feet were a dull shade of blue, and that was the beginning of "jungle rot" and jungle ulcers, which would show up later.

My job was that of a wireman and forward observer for the artillery. At one point during the 30 days we spent on Bougainville, we had to lay a line through a swamp. The water was up to our waist, and we tied the line or wire to available trees and bushes in the swamp. There were times that we laid the lines on trails, then vehicles would tear them up. Since we had our hands full, the infantry would send riflemen with us to protect against snipers.

Early in the morning one day after our troops spent a wet night in a clearing, we were awakened by a rumbling and shaking. We thought it was caused by our trucks running around, but it was an earthquake. The island had an active volcano, Bogana, and it was acting up. Our trucks were bouncing around, and the trees were dancing. Didn't know whether to get out of the foxhole and be hit by a tree or stay in my foxhole and have the ground open up, so I had one leg in and one leg out.

Another day while on phone duty on a forward slope of a hill and with about 20 skittish Raiders who were slated to leave for the States, shells started to crash all around. We all tried to jump into one foxhole—mine! I grabbed the phone, got the FDC, and yelled for them to stop firing. We did not know whose artillery, the Japanese or ours, was firing. A major answered and asked me just who I was. I told him, never mind, just stop all firing! Thank goodness he did, and sure enough, it was ours! No one was hurt, but to a man the Raiders thanked me, even though I was only doing my job. By the way, I was scared, too!

At the end of our 30-day tour, we were waiting to embark for our base camp in Guadalcanal when we were privileged to observe the natives, mainly women and children (women had their teeth filed to a point), and they were going through stacks of C-rations. They seemed to know just the rations that had the "three hard candies" in them. They were very happy, like children, and were not the least bit afraid of us. We were their friends. The natives didn't feel that way toward the Japanese; in fact, some Japanese, if caught out alone, ended up without a head. The Japanese had stolen some of the young native girls, and the natives didn't take a good view of that.

July 1944, Guam

One morning, needing to respond to the call of nature, I walked down a ridge about 300 feet with only my .45-caliber pistol in a shoulder holster. The time was first dawn and kinda' foggy from the ocean. I began to have the feeling someone else was close by and looking at me. I stopped, looked closely ahead of me, and then, about ten feet in front, lay a Jap soldier in one-and-a-half-foot-high weeds, flat on his back, looking right at me. He had a helmet on, uniform, and with both hands in his pockets. Of course, this startled me, and I flipped out my .45, as I could just imagine him having a grenade in his pocket. He had no other weapon on him.

I can remember that his eyes were big as he looked at me. Don't know which one of us was more frightened! The Japanese soldier got up and walked in front of me until I turned him over to our intelligence officer. The officer told me later that the Jap soldier had gotten lost during the night, that he was cold, and he had his hands in his pockets to keep warm. Also, I received some good info as to troop movement. I know he was treated well in POW camp and have often wondered what he told his family when he arrived home in Japan. The boys asked me if I finished what I started out to do. I couldn't remember!

As we were advancing across the high ground, two brothers and a sister approached us and had a conversation with our officers. The three of the Chamanos disappeared into a deep ravine or gully covered by dense brush and trees. In a few minutes, we heard sounds of voices and laughter. Out of the gully came older men, women, children, and women with babies. They had one cow for milk to feed the babies. The people had been hiding in the ravine from the Japanese and from our gunfire. These people were very hungry, so we gave them most of our rations. There wasn't a dry eye among our boys. This was a true liberation. Even today and every July 21st, Guam celebrates Liberation Day.

John Lane

The Solomon Islands were very hot and humid to the extent that our clothing rotted off our bodies. Guadalcanal was overrun with rats when we got there, but a contest with a prize of a case of beer for the most rats solved that problem. I have since read that those islands were rife with poisonous snakes and salt-water crocs, but in eleven months on Guadalcanal and Bougainville, I saw no crocs and one snake.

Guam was different—hot but not as humid, by far. The jungle was not as thick, and there was a lot of open space, which made fighting a lot easier. The flies were so bad that eating, for instance, was a two-handed operation—one hand constantly waving the flies away from the mess kit, and the other trying to eat the food before the flies did. Some aerial spraying helped a lot; it didn't get rid of them entirely, but it was better. The mosquitoes had the nighttime hours and the flies the daylight with about a 15-minute respite at dawn and sundown. They probably had a union.

Preparing for Iwo Jima we were issued combat jackets and, of all things, Chapstick. Now where are they sending us? When we got there, the "why?" of the jackets and the Chapstick were made apparent to us. It was cold. What they should have given us was tick repellant. "Try to stay away from vegetation," we were told, "you might get ticks." This was probably the understatement of the campaign. If you were lucky enough to survive the night's activities, the first order of business was to divest yourself of ticks. It was not uncommon to find six or eight of the little devils, and one lucky fellow had over 30 one morning. Thankfully, we had a naval corpsman that was very adept at removing them.

Russell J. Lacher

I was a U.S. Marine in the 3rd Marine Division when we had orders to invade and capture Iwo Jima. My job was to be the mess sergeant for Fox Battery, 12th Regiment. My part of loading for this invasion was very simple—take no cooking gear along, only things to fight with. On Iwo Jima my job was to see that the men all got their packets of combat rations. My cooks had other duties.

I had some free time one day and went down to the beach. There I found a bale of new shiny 20-gallon garbage cans. These were what we always made coffee in. I liberated one and carried it back to our gun position for when we would be issued coffee grounds again. In a few days, we were. This mess sergeant was ready. I pounded three empty 75mm shell casings into the ground to fit the bottom of the coffee can. Then, under the center of the coffee can, I set on fire a ration can with sand and diesel fuel. There were lots of small bags of extra gunpowder by our artillery pieces. Toss one of these bags close to the little can of burning oil and "whoosh," a white-hot flame enveloped the coffee can for a short time. Then toss in another until the water was boiling. Add the dry coffee grounds to the water and very soon we were drinking hot coffee.

Now I had to figure out how to cook chow, two meals per day, for our 175 men. Down at our truck park were some men who knew how to cut up empty fuel barrels with cutting torches. I told them just what I needed. Each 50-gallon steel barrel would make me a stove and pot to cook in. A shallow pan inverted over the open top of the stove made a good pancake griddle. Burn some sugar in one of the pans a bit, add water and more new sugar, and we soon had syrup for pancakes.

The shells for our 75mm guns came in wooden crates so we had plenty of nice dry wood. The only place I was allowed to set up my kitchens was in front of these 75s. Every time they fired, the dust rolled all around us cooks. As we stirred a pan of food, the sand just grated in the inside of every pan.

The boys ate this food and sand, and we helped win the battle of Iwo Jima.

Hershel Woodrow Williams

Hershel Woodrow ("Woody") Williams's baptism by fire came swift and sudden in the invasion of Guam—as soon as he and his buddies of the 1st Battalion piled out of their landing craft in the first wave of the marine landing party on Guam. Their orders had been to grab a hunk of beach and "dig in." Keep moving ahead, because there was nothing to go back to. And that's the way it went for eight straight days. Duck in a foxhole, and crouch and hope, and then move ahead into another hole. How did he feel when he spotted a yellow face looking down and one slant eye squinted along a Jap rifle? How did he feel when the Japs tried their banzai suicide charges? One charge after the other, until, in Woody's own words, "You wondered why and how they kept coming and if there would ever be any end to them. We just had to keep firing and killing them until we had killed enough of them to break their main resistance."

Was he scared? Sure, he was scared at first! After that, you don't care any more. You don't give a darn whether you get hit or not. Just keep moving . . . or rather stumbling forward . . . sometimes it seemed as if you'd be better off if you did get hit. Then it would be all over with.

You wouldn't have to swelter through any more heat that drenched you to the skin with sweat or suffer sand that was scorching hot. No more filth and discomfort and boredom, the kind of boredom that drove you to read the labels on the C-ration tins. Anything just to be reading. Those C-rations glorified pork and beans—in olive drab. No more sweating out those shells marked "To whom it may concern" or praying in-between artillery barrages or wiggling your little finger just to see it move and know that you were still alive.

As Woody said, "I suppose the only thing that kept us going was the incentive to avenge the loss of our buddies that were killed. After a while you'd feel there was only one thing you wanted to do in the world—to get the guy that got your buddy."

During the training period on Guam, Woody had a chance to observe this typical coral island a little more closely than he had had while peering at it from a foxhole during the course of the invasion. The impressions he formed of the island, or "rock," as it was called by the men stationed there, didn't exactly coincide with the movie version. Instead of the enchanted South Sea island pictured on the screen, with its balmy breezes and glistening white sandy beaches and Tahitian maidens, there was heat and rain and aggravating humidity and sharp jagged coral rock in the water along the shore that cut and scratched your skin when you tried to go swimming and took weeks to heal.

There was "jungle rot," which was like athlete's feet, only ten times more infectious and irritating. There was dysentery, and insects, flies that came in droves, and mosquitoes that brought malaria, unless you took the necessary precautions, covered with netting at night, and took your daily Atabrine pills, which turned your skin a yellowish color. And then there was the tiresome monotony of the dull calm tropics—all this, and the Japs, too. When the annals of World War II are written, the Battle of Iwo Jima will no doubt be inscribed with a bloody finger that will be approached only by that of Okinawa.

Because of the Japs' strongly entrenched positions in concrete pillboxes on the slopes overlooking the beach at Iwo, advance was difficult—so, for that matter, was survival. Even nature seemed an enemy. The black volcanic sand with its gritty irritating granules got in your eyes and nose and smudged your face and body black with grime. The heat increased the stench from sweating or the rotting bodies of dead Japs.

When his outfit hit Iwo on February 21st, 1945, Woody was still a corporal but had been made acting sergeant of C Company's demolition squad. On the 23rd, word came back to the command post that the tanks had been stopped dead in their tracks in an effort to open a lane for the infantry through a barrier of concrete pillboxes and buried land mines.

Corporal Williams was at the command post. He was told that the six men in his squad were all casualties—one killed and five wounded. The situation was bad. They would be pinned down until those fanatically defended strong points were knocked out. Artillery bombardment had proved ineffective. The shells hitting against these structures, which were reinforced with sand, would just throw up more sand on top of them.

The only way to put them out of action was with a flamethrower. But how? A guy wouldn't stand a chance in a thousand of reaching those pillboxes nearly a mile away with the Japs peppering away at him with machine guns. But Woody decided to take that chance, and in his quiet, slow-speaking sort of way, he told his CO, "I'll see what I can do." It took a lot of nerve, or bravery, call it what you may, to make a decision like that, but somewhere deep in his soul he found an unutterable courage that ignored self and sustained him. Perhaps Woody was inspired by his comrades who had fallen, for how can one American watch another die by his side in his cause without realizing that that cause must be worthwhile, and therefore must be pursued to a victorious end, whatever the cost. Whatever the motive, Woody's rise above the call of duty served another purpose, for it inspired others to follow.

With the tanks of his flamethrower strapped firmly to his back, the nozzle grasped in his right hand, and charges of TNT in his left, Woody went forward alone in the face of withering fire from an enemy determined that he would never reach his objectives. But Woody had a couple of extra weapons that the Nips didn't see—luck and courage. By degrees he inched his way up to the first box and skirted around behind it, then heaved the pole charge of TNT through the opening. Smoke and dust billowed out. Just to make sure the job was complete, Woody mounted the pillbox and sent a stream of intense fire from the flamethrower searing into the Japs inside, whose bodies flared up like pieces of celluloid as soon as it touched them. Although Woody was under terrific small-arms fire, he was covered by four riflemen from his company and for four grueling hours continued to reduce the other positions. His flamethrowers had a life of only eight to ten seconds unless fired in short bursts. His demolition charges could be used only once. Four times during those four hours he returned to the command post to get new flamethrowers and to obtain fresh TNT charges and struggle back to the Jap lines.

On the thirteenth day of the Iwo campaign, Woody's luck ran out. He was wounded in the knee by shrapnel but went on fighting, because the outfit was low on reinforcements and every available man, even rear-echelon men—cooks, bakers, clerks—were thrown into the front lines to strengthen their position.

Woody's heroic accomplishment made possible an advance that materially aided in the final hard-won victory on Iwo Jima that culminated in the planting of the "Stars and Stripes" atop Mount Suribachi, the volcano!

On Oct. 5, 1945, Woody stood on the White House lawn for his Commander-in-Chief, President Harry S Truman, to place the pale-blue star-spangled ribbon of the Medal of Honor around his neck. He received it for his daring actions, unyielding determination, and extraordinary heroism in the face of ruthless enemy resistance on Iwo Jima where he knocked out seven Japanese pillboxes with a flamethrower and was credited with killing 21 enemy soldiers. He was told by the President, "I'd rather have this medal than be President."

Peter A. Walters

In January 1943, our regiment boarded the SS *Lurline*, which had been the flagship of the Matson Lines and was now a troopship. At sunset the only light in the troop quarters was a single weak bulb in the head. Each night a dedicated group of marines sat on the floor of the head playing heavy games of poker. The toilet bowls and urinal were not always working and the floor was something to behold, but never once did it stop our poker players.

My unit, the 2nd Battalion, 21st Marine Regiment, landed on the beach off Empress of Augusta Bay on November 11th, 1943. We encountered thick jungle and swamps immediately off the beach.

An element of surprise accounted for our landing on this side of Bougainville. We learned later that the Japanese had positioned their forces on the other side expecting our forces to land there on the fine, sandy beaches. So our landings were unopposed. But the interlude was brief as the Japanese moved their troops to our side in a matter of a few days.

During the first one or two days, many of the small tanks that we had brought on other ships sank immediately in the swamps. They were useless and never saw action. The thickness of the swamps was unbelievable. We were issued machetes to hack away the vines to allow us to walk slowly, very slowly, through the jungle. We didn't make but a few yards from the beach during the first few days. I recall looking up one day as a Japanese Zero plane passed low over our heads. The pilot leaned out of the cockpit grinning at us. He passed over and out to sea.

Navy Seabees in tractors and graders were busy carving a new airfield near the beach. Japanese planes would come over, strafing our nearby positions. The Seabees never once stopped their work. In the early days of the campaign, Major Fissell was killed by a Japanese sniper who tied himself in the ball of a palm tree over the trail and killed the major. The Japanese was, of course, immediately killed by a volley of fire.

During the campaign, we encountered many Japanese who would tie themselves in the trees to kill a marine, knowing that they would be immediately killed. For this reason some of us, including me, were issued .45-caliber Thompson submachine guns. A 50-round drum was attached. We could spot a sniper and with one squeeze pulverize him and part of the tree. Unfortunately, the Thompsons quickly rusted in the equatorial climate. The bluing on the guns was too thin to counter the rusting, so the Thompsons were quickly withdrawn.

Finding words to describe the conditions is hard. We were in swamps each day in mud and water to our knees or higher. As we were still on or close to the equator, the heat and humidity, particularly in the confines of the thick jungle, made our lives much more difficult. Many marines, including me, had ugly sores on their legs and arms, which we called "jungle rot." The corpsmen told us to sprinkle sulphur powder in the sores from the small bags attached to our ammunition belts.

One evening, as it was getting dark, word was passed that Japanese troops were only a few yards from our position. The thickness of the jungle prevented any sightings, but we knew they were there, and they knew we were there. So they passed orders that no one would leave their holes that night under any condition.

Jerry Lomurno and I had been together since we landed on the island. Jerry and I dug our hole, and we crawled in for the night. A heavy rain came on, and its intensity increased as the night passed. Our hole filled up to our chests. Jerry developed dysentery during the night and became very ill. As he was evacuating frequently, he begged me to allow him to leave the hole. I physically restrained him, knowing he'd be killed by marines in nearby holes if he did. Word had been passed to shoot anyone moving outside the holes. Two marines were killed that night by other marines as they left their holes.

The night passed. Jerry Lomurno received treatment from a corpsman in the morning and gradually got better.

Then came the most terrifying incident. Our company had stopped for the night in the deepest part of the jungle. As we dug in our holes for the night, we heard the chatter of the Japanese troops, who were probably within 30 or 40 yards from our positions. As night closed in, we were ordered to remain in our holes for the night. We also learned that, somehow, the Japanese had captured one of our second lieutenants and that he was being held just yards away. Later in the night we began to hear screaming. Our lieutenant was being tortured. The Japanese started to yell at us. In very broken English they taunted us to come and rescue our officer. Stern orders were passed for us to remain in our positions. Apparently those in command had reason to believe that a much larger force of Japanese were involved than we had in our company. The screaming went on for hours. At dawn we cautiously advanced through the jungle. Word had been passed that the Japanese had moved out during the night. We found our lieutenant's body. He had been tortured all night with a bayonet being inserted slowly but gradually into his rectum.

During what proved to be our final days on Bougainville, another episode occurred that was quite frightening. We had retired for the night, if you can call it that, in a jungle clearing. I remember being posted on guard duty during the night. I was relieved sometime after midnight and returned to my hole for some sleep. We kept our dungaree pants on as well as our boots. Usually we wore nothing above the waist. Just before I went to sleep, I noticed a movement to my left. Seconds later a black snake slithered right over the hole and me and departed. I have often looked back, particularly in the many dreams I've had of this incident, and wondered what would have happened if I had dug my hole deeper. As it was, my body was almost even to the ground, which allowed the snake to move right across my body as if it were the ground. If I had dug my hole deeper, the snake might have fallen in with me. Of course, in the years following, depending upon the audience, the story varies as to the length of the snake, from three- to twelve-feet long, and the time it took to cross my body, a few seconds to a few minutes. But the crossing of that snake did indeed occur.

The time on Guadalcanal was not well spent. We knew we'd be going somewhere on our second campaign, but not knowing where or when was frustrating. Soon after my regiment was settled down in our near luxurious pyramidal tents, an order came one day for the entire regiment to assemble on a large clearing. We stood in strict formation. The commanding colonel of the regiment read a declaration to us. He read an order that he had just received from Marine Headquarters, Washington, D.C. In a loud, stern voice, he read that they reprimanded the regiment for leaving government property on Bougainville. We had indeed left numerous articles of clothing in our holes on the island, such as jackets, canteens, etc. They did not tell us that we had vanquished the enemy or that several thousand of us were casualties. No, only that Headquarters was very upset over the loss of government property.

Jerry Lomurno and I shared a tent on Guadalcanal for several months. Every once in awhile we would hear an armed forces radio program. Musical celebrities would entertain us from the States on shortwave radio. One night Dick Haymes sang " Stella by Starlight." Jerry's girl friend back home was Stella. He lay on his cot covered by mosquito netting and cried, listening to the song. Later that night and for many nights after that, he would plead with me to sing "Stella by Starlight" for him.

One day I piled my dirty underwear, tee shirts, and socks in a bag and took them down to a nearby creek. Several natives, who had survived the recent wars, were laundering their clothes by beating them on rocks in the water. Having no soap I figured this was the only way for me to proceed. I then made the very bad mistake of removing my tee shirt, my bare back exposed to the equatorial sun. I came back to our tent with my clothes. But I have no memory of the next two or three days. I awoke in a field hospital sometime later. My back was a complete blister. I was running a high fever. I was a very sick young man. I learned that severe sunstroke fell into the category of a preventable ailment such as a social disease. During war, incurring a preventable ailment subjected one to a dishonorable discharge due to loss of duty. Fortunately, I was able to avoid such a happening. I recovered in about a week and returned to duty.

While onboard ship and headed for Guam, a small group of us, possibly six or eight, noticed that an approximate two-foot gap was present between the steel deck and the ship's side. By lying down on the deck and lowering your arm through the gap, you would feel wooden railings. We learned that these were called sweat boards. Their purpose was to create a barrier to keep the cargo away from the side of the ship. I remember that our little group spent quite some time perusing this discovery, when one of us remembered that hundreds of cases of beer were stored somewhere down in the hold. The image of being able to retrieve some beer became overpowering. We came up with a fine idea. One of us would squeeze through the opening and see if he could climb down in the hold if the sweat boards provided a possible ladder. One brave soul volunteered. Not I. We found some empty sandbags and tied a rope line to a bag. Our volunteer was able to climb down the side of the ship carrying the empty bag, which was attached to the long line up on deck. Discipline was loose on our ship, so we could start this adventure in the dead of night shielded by the large anchor bastion. We each carried a large knife on our ammunition belt in addition to our .30-caliber carbines. The knives were just right for cutting into the cardboard beer cases! When the man holding the line on deck felt a few tugs on the line, he pulled up the bag filled with cans of beer. Our man climbed up on the boards, and we all drank one or two cans of very warm beer. This marvelous mission continued for several nights. I climbed down one or two times. On probably the fourth or fifth night, we began to hear ominous creaking noises from the hold. By that time we had emptied quite a few cardboard cases and the cases on the top were settling down! It dawned on us that anytime soon the man down below could meet an unfortunate death. Reluctantly, we called off our adventure. When we landed on Guam, there was much consternation by some officers when discovery disclosed several empty beer cases.

While several hundred marines were killed on Guam and a few thousand wounded, the campaign didn't seem to be as bloody as Bougainville. There, the jungle and the swamps added a dimension that was not present on Guam.

During the first week of February 1945, an unusual event unfolded. One battalion after another of the 21st Regiment, including my Headquarters Company, was assembled on a long, sandy beach on Guam. Fifty-gallon drums stretched down the beach. Fires were burning under the drums, which were filled with a mixture of creosote and oil. We had been told to bring an extra set of camouflage jackets and trousers with us. Groups of us gathered around the boiling drums, and, using long poles, we shoved the clothes into the oil, pulled them out, and laid them on the hot sand to dry. We were told to pack them later in our backpacks. Following all this, we were told that our next mission, as yet unidentified, would place us on an island that naval intelligence learned was infested with dangerous insects, also unidentified. Therefore, we would wear this clothing when we invaded the island.

None of this made us feel very well. On the other hand, we knew we were combat-tested marines. We had already completed two years in the Pacific, and we had survived two victorious campaigns. We were a proud bunch, so most of us figured some insects would not bother us too much.

In February 1945, lying off Iwo Jima, there were three reinforced marine divisions totaling some 61,000 troops. As the 3rd Division was being held temporarily in reserve, the 4th and 5th Divisions landed on Iwo Jima on February 17th from landing craft known as Higgins boats. From the rail of our ship, we watched the invasion. We were too far away to observe what was taking place when they hit the beaches. We felt at that point that some 40,000 marines would easily subdue this small rock in a matter of days. After all the shelling and bombing we felt sure that enemy resistance would be nil.

Then on the early morning of February 20th, orders were passed that the 3rd Division would climb down our nets into landing craft and join the Iwo invasion. We heard much later that both the 4th and 5th Divisions had suffered thousands of marines killed and wounded on just the first day of their landing. So enemy resistance far exceeded the original estimates and the 3rd Division was ordered into action on D-Day plus 3.

We grudgingly donned our foul smelling dungaree jackets and pants. Climbing down the landing nets with 50-pound backpacks, we took off for the beach in our Higgins boats. The temperature was in the sixties or seventies and we were downright cool. We had been living in steamy tropical climates for two years. As we neared the beach, sharp explosions were heard overhead. The Japanese were firing artillery, which used shells with timing. They were exploding over our heads and all the shrapnel fell down on some of our boats. Some marines were killed or wounded before they reached the beach.

Looking up from our landing craft, we saw that we would be landing on a beach right under the small mountain called Mt. Suribachi. Then our boat stopped alongside many dozens of landing boats, which had been hit by enemy fire. They were a sorry sight, half submerged. We were still about 50 yards from the beach but our boat couldn't proceed further. We were ordered to climb out of the boat and make our way to the beach by climbing over the wrecked boats. Japanese artilleries with the timed fuses were still exploding over the area. Nothing like this had happened in our landings on Bougainville or Guam.

We made the beach and were confronted with a sight that I've never forgotten. One of the few tanks that had made it to the beach had carved out a protective wall of black sand just a few yards from the water's edge. A group of marines was piling dead marines like you would stack firewood: four bodies one way, then four bodies on top facing the other way. They were throwing the bodies in piles as high as possible. All the bodies had been wrapped in each man's poncho that he carried in his backpack. The poncho had two purposes: to guard you from rain and also to wrap you when dead. There were many dozens of these rows of dead marines.

It was still early morning. By the end of the day we had advanced probably a hundred yards from the beach. Heavy mortar fire, machine-gun fire, and artillery fire from Mt. Suribachi and from other sections of the small island continued day and night. At nightfall we were ordered to dig in for the night. We found that the black sand was so loose we could hardly cover our bodies. During that first day we discovered that the only insects or animals on this godforsaken place were flies, millions of them. We shed our smelly jackets and pants and put on the replacement clothes from our packs with many choice words for naval intelligence.

By the second night my headquarters company found themselves under a small rise on top of which was Motoyama Airfield #1. The Japanese had completed this airfield. While the surface was rough compared with our standards, it was long enough to allow our B-29s to land—and thus the reason why three marine divisions invaded this miserable island. Iwo Jima was a strategic spot for refuge for aircraft crippled in bombing runs over the Japanese mainland and also as a base for aircraft engaged in searching for B-29s that were reported missing after bombing runs.

To call it just miserable was an understatement. There was no water on the island. The Japanese had operated sulphur mines, which were located throughout the island. Sulphuric steam rose continuously in clouds from the mines. The odor was nauseating. There were no trees, only bare stretches of dirt, sand, and rocks. There were literally no places to hide from the constant shelling.

Before I get back to that second night, I want to add more about conditions on Iwo. Bear in mind that by D-Day-plus 3, 61,000 marines were on the island. Our only water supply was in our canteens strapped to our belts. Eventually, a large canvas tank was erected filled with rejuvenated seawater. We were allowed to fill our canteens with this flat, smelly water. But it was water. Bathing was out of the question. After a few weeks we all smelled the same so it wasn't too noticeable. The sulphur fumes probably counteracted our odors.

Now back to that second night. By unwritten law we always paired up with another marine when time came to bunker down for the night. That night "Shorty" Reynolds and I dug our shallow hole in the sand on a near flat surface. We had wanted to dig our hole against the 20- or 30-foot wall of dirt and sand that led up to the airfield. Most of the shelling was coming down from the northern section of the island. So the marines who had dug themselves in against that wall figured that they were protected from direct hits. But as the area at the wall began filling up with holes, Shorty and I had to remain in our hole on the flat area just below the wall. Sometime later the shelling intensified and exploding shells were raining down on our positions. We learned the next day that the Japanese were attempting to hit our ammunition dump, which was located a few yards away. But they had miscalculated the location of the dump and the shells were landing literally on the area where Shorty and I lay in our hole. Then we heard the screams from wounded marines coming from their holes on the wall. The shrapnel from the shells landing on the flat area cascaded up against the wall killing and wounding many marines that night. Chance had it; Shorty and I survived, as only a direct hit would have killed us.

The shelling went on for hours. Then suddenly a marine clutching his head appeared standing on the edge of our hole. Blood was pouring from his head. He was screaming from pain and saying that he was blind. Shorty Reynolds stood up in the hole and told me that he would take this unknown marine down to the beach and find a corpsman station. I remember telling Shorty that we had to wait until the shelling stopped, saying that the two of them would never make it. Shorty turned to me and said, "I've got to take him down." And with that, he reached up, and, taking the marine by the arm, he turned and led him down toward the beach. I was positive that I would not see the two of them again. I have to truly admit that I would not have left that hole. Period. The shelling went on unabated. Probably a good hour later Shorty appeared at the hole. He lay down and said something to the effect that he found a corpsman and turned the wounded marine over to him. I have never in my life before or after Iwo Jima seen a person exhibit such courage to help save a stranger's life. I have told this story to probably hundreds of people, often with tears in my eyes.

It was probably only a few days later that I found myself standing on Motoyama Airfield #1. Above the airfield loomed Mt. Suribachi. I noticed some marines pointing to the top of the mountain. A large American flag had just been flown from a tall pole. I remember crying at the sight. It was only long after we left Iwo Jima that the news came to us of the famous flag-raising photograph on Mt. Suribachi.

Men from the 25th Regiment of the 5th Division had fought up the mountain taking many casualties before they reached the top. The end of Japanese artillery and mortar shelling from the mountain was one of the big turning points in the campaign.

Then my memory centers on an event a few days later. We had been on Iwo probably two weeks. Standing on a small rise a jeep came up alongside me. Driving the jeep was my old friend Jerry Lomurno. I had not seen Jerry since our times on Bougainville. He had remained in the 2nd Battalion while they had transferred me to Headquarters Company of the 21st. I yelled something to him in greeting, but I remember he looked at me with pure fear on his face. His only words were, "Pete, I've got to get off this rock. I'm not going to make it," or words to that effect.

While there was always shelling coming down from the Japanese positions in the northern sections, none were landing close to our area at that time. So I told Jerry to hang in, not to worry, and so forth. Without replying, Jerry drove away. Somehow, and I've forgotten how, word reached me a day or two later that a direct mortar hit exploded on Jerry and his jeep probably moments after he had left me. Jerry's death has preyed on my mind during the 50-plus years since Iwo Jima.

On the morning of my departure, I walked through the thousands of white crosses looking for Jerry Lomurno's grave. By sheer chance I found it! I remember standing by his grave saying some words for my dear friend Jerry. I've never forgotten him.

(Excerpts from his personal memoirs, *Once a Marine*)

Burns W. Lee

The Flag Raising . . . and More

The famous Iwo Jima flag-raising picture was only one of many factors that brought the Battle of Iwo Jima and the marines who fought there to the attention of the American people.

The horrors of the battle (February-March 1945) in which more than 6,000 were killed and 20,000 injured in the three marine divisions were reported in detail by veteran newsmen who had enlisted in the Marine Corps as combat correspondents, as well as by civilian correspondents who endangered their own lives throughout the four plus weeks of combat.

Personally, as public relations officer (first lieutenant) for the 5th Marine Division, I was the officer-in-charge of our 12 combat correspondents, as well as being responsible for providing major assistance to the 25 civilian war correspondents and photographers who, representing the Associated Press, United Press, *New York Times*, *Chicago Daily News*, *Washington Post*, CBS, etc., came ashore at one time or another.

Very early on D-Day, our marine combat correspondents began coming ashore with their assigned units under heavy mortar and artillery fire, but several were able to write stories on that day that were later put on a press boat that delivered them to the command ship for the daily press plane to Honolulu. Each man carried in his backpack a supply of paper adequate for immediate needs, along with a portable typewriter.

Included among our combat correspondents were prewar news writers, photographers, and radio broadcasters from the nation's leading news media. A total of more than 700 stories plus numerous radio interviews—many about the heroic front-line actions of "Joe Blows"—were produced by them during the battle.

Our radio team (two men with professional broadcasting experience) recorded the action on D-Day, and for several days, from a vantage point on a tank-carrying LSM (also carrying yours truly) as it came ashore.

Our own headquarters proved also to be a focal point for the civilians throughout the operation. For the first week that was merely a series of foxholes, but after that a blackout tent in one big foxhole became the workplace for both civilians and marines. During the first two weeks, it was necessary for everyone to eat field rations prepared individually. This proved to be a surprise for the civilians, who had expected our combat correspondents to cook for them! Most, also, came ashore without overnight bedding, and so it was necessary for us to share our scarce blankets!

Among the civilians who came ashore was Joe Rosenthal of AP Photos, who took the famous picture on the fourth day of the battle. Earlier that day, knowing that a flag had already been raised, Rosenthal had to be persuaded to make the hazardous climb up rock-strewn Mt. Suribachi when it was decided that the first flag was too small to be seen by the men from any distance. The second flag had to be raised by a group of five men in a big hurry so that it would be a simultaneous raising and lowering of flags (never two flags up at the same time).

So Joe, with camera in hand, quickly scrambled up a bunch of adjoining hard rocks, turned, and instantly snapped the picture! Two weeks later, when we first heard that a picture by Rosenthal had made front pages all over America, he thought it was one he had taken of a completely different battle scene!

Bill Nolte

Random Thoughts of Iwo Jima

Hit beach, hard to run on lava sand with flamethrower, stopped at cover on edge of Motoyama #1 airfield, ran across airfield with people dropping around me. Found cover on other side with heart pumping like hell.

Attacked first pillbox with cover fire from fire team—used only part of tank. Hit two more targets with cover from same fire team less one KIA. Burned a charging Jap from cave—went up like a ball of flame.

Night banzai attack while back at Company CP. Mortar crew shooting flare shells for visibility. Used machete and carbine. Horrible hand-to-hand fighting mostly using machete and Kabar knife; lost carbine somewhere. Found one later after fight was over. Around daybreak, on checking the casualties, found a badly wounded Jap. Group formed around him discussing what to do with him. Got too much so I shot him in the head. Got shoved by Sarge McCarthy, who cursed me out, and said I would be court-martialed. Heard nothing more about it.

Mile working our way up a hill to get to a big cave; the guy leading me was hit in the head by a sniper. I can still see him falling with his helmet cover waving in the air. We hit the deck; I flipped off the flamethrower and grabbed my .45 automatic. We located him and killed him. We were then above the cave entrance, which was big enough to drive a Jeep into. Inside was a Jap heavy-machine-gun crew. I couldn't work my way in position to shoot the napalm in, so we tried to bounce grenades in. Meanwhile, the Japs were throwing grenades out and up in the air. Finally, got a satchel charge and tied some rope to it. Managed to swing it into the mouth of the cave. The entire crew and gun were blown to hell. We found seven bodies and a case of sake. Our patrol stayed there for the night eating Jap cans of fish and sake wine.

Under a barrage of knee mortar shells, several of us were in a shell hole for protection. We were near the top of the hole when a shell landed a foot in front of me and another guy. It was a dud and just stuck there in front of us. The guy next to me was out of it. They tagged him and took him back. All he did was stare.

First hot food arrived and, when I took my mess kit out, I found a bullet hole through it. Don't remember when it happened, but the guys got a good laugh with lots of jokes.

Bill Crowthers and I went after three or four caves that were holding up A Company's advance. We had two fire teams' support. I hit the first two caves, and Bill went after the other one with a satchel charge. I grabbed an M-1 from the ground and killed three Japs coming out of Bill's cave. Found that the three caves were connected. Fifteen dead were inside including two officers.

In foxhole one night, it was raining real bad. Used two men to a hole. Standing orders were one man awake at all times. I was guarding, covered with a poncho with my .45 under poncho. No one was to be out of hole. During the night I either sensed or saw someone at edge of hole. I shot at the form and in the morning saw it was a damn Jap with his head smashed with a grenade where he fell. My bullet caught him under the chin and blew his skull off.

In the middle of a firefight, I noticed a flag flying on Suribachi. We were laughing about it and joking that the island was secured and we could go back to Guam, all the while continuing to fight. An hour or two later the flag was down, and we feared the Japs had won the top. Next somebody yelled, "We got it back." I wish that I could have seen it go up. It was the one that is now so famous.

One day my entire company was pulled off the line and replaced by a fresh company. We weren't pulled out for a break but were ordered to change our clothes into newly supplied ones and to wash up and shave. The reason, we later found out, was to give the appearance that we were new troops newly landed to lower the morale of the Japs. Needless to say, we thought somebody in charge had flipped. While washing and shaving using my helmet as a basin, the water was leaking out. I checked it out and found a bullet had creased the top and put a hole in it. I had no idea when it happened. Damn close!

Got pulled off line to get Japs who had attacked ground crew by Motoyama #2. They had tunnels going from our front to our rear. The air force had run like hell even though they were armed with M-4 grease guns. The bastards dropped the guns and ran. First time I saw an M-4, took one with me back to the lines. Luckily no casualties, and we got them all. I got four.

One of the guys spotted a Jap in a spider hole. He saw the cover move up and emptied his carbine into him. Before I could stop him he started to drag the dead Jap out of the hole. The Jap had booby trapped himself. Lucky the guy didn't get hurt much but was covered with Jap body parts—souvenir hunting.

Near the end we were in the north end of the island when six or seven Japs came charging out of a cave. They had only swords and were drunk as skunks. They came right at another guy and myself, screaming. We both had carbines and started to pop them off. We got them all. One of them had an officer's sword, which I confiscated.

Shot plain gasoline into a cave but matches on flamethrower didn't light. Threw a phosphorus grenade into cave from about 30 feet away and blew the cave to hell. Some of the phosphorus hit me in the wrist and burned like hell. Had scar for many years afterward.

Told by a damn 2nd Louie [second lieutenant] to defuse a 16" navy dud. Told him I didn't have the tools to do it and didn't know how to do it. He started to rant and rave, and I gave it right back to him. He calmed down. Finally got the okay to blow it up with some TNT. The lieutenant got killed later. He was a pretty good guy though.

Saw Webster being carried away on a stretcher. Talked to him a few minutes. Saw no blood, and he said he was OK. Gave him a cigarette and said *adios*. Found out later he died aboard the hospital ship. He had a small piece of shrapnel in the base of his spine.

Lying with my face in the lava sand because of machine-gun fire I saw a flower, a small blue one and the only one I saw on the island. I picked it and put it in my helmet so it would be safe??? Wished I hadn't lost it.

In slit trench one rainy night, had something tap my helmet. I swung my arm and hit a land crab. It flew up in the air and landed on top of a guy in a nearby foxhole. He started shooting and pretty soon everyone was shooting. Everybody caught hell the next morning. No one ever admitted starting the Land Crab Battle.

Killed a Jap officer during a banzai attack. Found maps and other information that looked important. Also took his Nambu pistol. Turned maps and info over to G-2. Got citation for it later on Guam.

During a lull in the fighting, I was heating a canteen cup of coffee. My buddy yelled, "Look out!" I ducked and a sword blade bounced off my helmet. Three of us opened up and made Swiss cheese out of my attacker. If I hadn't ducked in time, he would have chopped my head off. Couldn't figure out how he got so close—maybe a spider trap. The sword broke when it hit my helmet.

Of the platoon I was in when we landed with 30 men, total dead was 14, almost half. Can't believe it when I write it down.

After Iwo was secured, they set up a movie screen to amuse us until we shipped back. Army troops were also brought in for occupation. While walking back from the movie, a damn army machine-gun squad opened up on us and a few guys got hit, no KIAs though. Damn fools!

(Written February 21, 1995, on the 50th anniversary of the Iwo Jima invasion. These memories came to mind because of the extensive media coverage commemorating this historic event. The preceding flashbacks occurred at random, and I felt they should be documented.)

George J. Green, CW04

E Battery, 2nd Battalion Tenth Marines

Battle of Iwo Jima—Volcano Islands

ONE DAY IN THE BATTLE FOR IWO JIMA FEBRUARY 23 . . . "D" + 5

Good night's sleep—woke up only once during the air raid. Mortars hit the company area last night but none of my FO team was hit—several casualties in K Company.

It was still dark, but dawn was beginning to break when we crawled into the Jap pillbox that Lieutenant Colonel W. Duplantis, CO, 3rd Battalion, was using as his battalion command post. I know we reviewed the situation and what we were supposed to do, but the only specific thing I remember him saying is, "We have got to get the airfield today."

We started the attack this morning with about 220 men, and before we got back in reserve, K Company had around 90 men left. We were to pass through the lines of the 1st Battalion, continue the attack, and get to Airfield #2. We moved into position and took off right behind a rolling barrage. The first thing I noticed was a group of Japs in a low trench. Someone got them with a flamethrower, and they were still burning. Next, on this bright morning, I saw a wounded marine walking calmly back to the rear, the white bandages and crimson red of his blood standing out over his dirty dungarees. We were with Captain R. L. Heinze and his headquarters. We moved up to the runway, and I kept the team spread out and in the foxholes. We were doing pretty well on communications, as we were in touch with Lieutenant Pottinger at battalion. He wanted to know why we were not doing any firing; told him I could not see anything to shoot at, and troops were moving up fast. He said to pick out some prominent landmark and fire away. I set up a fire mission on the high ground where the runways cross and fired one round of smoke. Just as it hit, Captain Heinze yelled that they were going across the runway and heading for the high ground. I called off the fire mission, having fired only one shell. Captain Heinze, sitting on the edge of the runway about ten feet up from where I was, asked for my compass, as he had lost his. As I got ready to toss it up to him, he yelled for me to look out. And as I turned around, there was a Nip grenade sputtering about three feet in front of me. I sat in a small shell hole about two feet deep, looking at the grenade as it exploded. Instinctively I ducked my head, then looked back up and started to aim my carbine in the direction the grenade came from. As I aimed, I saw another one come flying toward me from some bushes. It landed just about the same place as the other one did. This time I got to duck my head before it went off. Captain Heinze came sliding down the slope of the runway with his pistol out, holding his right leg. He got a good size piece of one of those grenades in his right thigh on the inside; we helped him back to a deep shell hole. I tried to get a BAR man to spray the bushes, but he walked up to them and toppled over—the Nip shot him in the stomach. Now I could see the Nip in a foxhole with a top that he moved up and down like a spider trap. We got a fire team directed at him, and they dropped a few grenades into his hole. The next time I looked at him, we were moving up again, and he was plastered to one side of the hole. Looking back to our rear, I saw all these 4.5 rockets coming down at us. They were easy to see, as there were so many of them and they were making such a loud racket. From a good deep shell hole, we sat helpless watching those rockets creeping up on us and exploding on our rear troops. Finally they stopped, the last one about ten feet behind us. Lieutenant R. Archambault, K Company came up to take Captain Heinze's place.

We moved up along the slope of the runway, and one by one we rushed across that flat strip of land. I couldn't get over the amount of steel fragments from shells lying on the runway. As we were moving up along the slopes, I saw two marines helping a third, who was a victim of combat fatigue. He got loose of their grip and fell down on his knees, beating the ground with his fists and crying.

Our team all got across the runway safely, and we dug in next to Lieutenant Archambault's CP. A few yards to our rear there was a Sherman tank that had been knocked out by the Japs. One marine was lying underneath it. A corpsman was working him over and giving him something out of a bottle. I saw him change in color from very pale to a more natural look. I never did see what finally happened to him. We were all pinned down there by a heavy mortar barrage and could do practically nothing except dig a little deeper. Early in the evening, elements of the 2nd Battalion came up to fill in the gap on our left. It seems that Y and I Companies were the only ones to get across the runway.

How he did it I don't know, but after dark we heard a tractor coming, and sure enough, there was a guy driving that thing in the pitch-black night, pulling a trailer with food, water, and ammo. To this day, I don't know how he knew where he was going. It looked as if he aimed his Cat toward the front lines and kept going until he found someone. This guy had guts.

FEBRUARY 24 . . . "D" + 6

We got the word that we were to be relieved by the 9th Marines at 0830 and about this time the Japs opened up and pinned us down. We couldn't move back, nor could the company relieving us get to us. At about 1030 enough of the relieving company was in position to take over, and we started back the way we came—running across the runway.

We finally got back to our reserve position and proceeded to find holes to occupy. It's a funny thing, all during field problems we had to dig our own holes, but I never dug one on Iwo Jima. There were always plenty of them from previous occupants, Japs included, and various size shell holes. Our forward observer team was scattered about in one- and two-man holes and just behind a rather large shell crater, which was occupied by a considerable number of the company. All at once, the Japs let go a mortar barrage and it landed right on top of us. The first shell hit right smack into that large shell crater and did a lot of damage. While we were sitting around here in the same position, one man suddenly grabbed his chest, and we saw a bullet fall into his lap. A Jap bullet very near the end of its flight struck him smack in the middle of his chest but was not going fast enough to penetrate his clothing or skin.

FEBRUARY 25 . . . "D" + 7

We moved up into the 9th Marines' positions, and I took up an OP with naval gunfire.

When the time came for the attack, the men got out of their holes and craters and took off on the double behind the artillery falling about 200 yards ahead. Never in my life will I forget how these infantrymen just got up and took off into nothing. We saw no Japs. We just ran on a compass reading and didn't stop until we were out of breath. This attack and the one on D + 5 that enabled K Company to get across Airfield #2 are two days that will live with me forever and give me respect for the infantrymen.

We began to get a lot of small-arms fire where as before it was mostly artillery and mortars. When a man was hit earlier in the battle it was usually from a fragment, but now it was from bullets. We continued forward and came to a rise or hill in which it was necessary to go over the top. As you approached the summit, you could tell the Nips had it zeroed in by the sounds of the bullets. They had already got a couple of our men. I passed the word around to the team to dive over the top and not to stop. Over we went, one at a time. No sooner did we get over the hill then about 50 feet in front of us were several Jap tanks dug into the ground with only the turret exposed. The artillery barrage knocked off their camouflage. One was burning and a couple of Japs were trying to get out; they didn't get too far. All of a sudden the other tank began to shake along with its dirt and rock covering and proceeded to pull out of its dug-in position. With everyone shooting at it, it noisily clanked out of its hole and turned to our right and down behind some rocks to safety.

Now I ended up in another rather large shell crater and was lying to the right of a radio operator when we started to get bullets from our rear. The radio operator was shot in the ankle. We got him patched up and off to the rear. Then a rather heavy-set marine jumped into our hole. He was splattered with blood and pretty well shaken up. He was a combat photographer and told me he was taking movies next to this marine—and he pointed to one lying down next to a bluff to our left rear—when all of a sudden this marine got hit with something heavy that sprayed the blood all over the place, and when he saw there was nothing he could do, he took off for our hole.

We were to stay here for the night. Once again the 3rd Battalion, 21st Marines had made substantial gains with their attack. We in I Company were the farthest unit into the Jap positions, and we had been getting fire from both of our flanks and had to keep pretty well to our holes. Tonight most of us enjoyed the first hot meal since leaving the ship, because all we had to do was bury our C-rations about a foot in the ground, as we were in the middle of a sulphur mine. The ground is hot. Out of the shell hole we were in, we each scraped a niche to use as a bed, but you couldn't spend more than half an hour in the hole because you began to cook regardless of how you arranged your body. We didn't get much sleep that night.

FEBRUARY 26 . . . "D" + 8

We were moving along a path between jagged rocks about five paces apart when all of a sudden a white phosphorus shell exploded spreading its phosphorus all over the place. Luckily missing me and the men of my FO team but it got on several of the men from I Company. I sent them to the rear to get medical attention. I'm sure this was one of our shells because, as we advanced on the double, I glanced to my right rear and my eyes caught sight of an artillery shell arching down from the sky. I watched it sail down about 15 feet from where I was in a crouched position. I was so amazed at seeing this projectile; I watched it explode. The air sang with its fragments flying, but not a mark on me or any of the other men close to me. The going got tougher, both from the Japs and the lay of the land. Along with those two shells and some other heavy stuff falling I began to feel we had gone too far to our right, and the 4th Division was not to the right of us, but behind us and attacking us. There was a navy TBF bomber flying overhead. I assumed it was an observer, as he made several passes over our positions. As he came in right in front of us, I saw another artillery shell hit the plane just behind the lower turret knocking a big hole in the lower part of the fuselage, which caused the plane to go into a dive to his left. I could see the pilot's reaction. As the plane made an attempt to straighten out to level flight, the whole tail assembly fell off and he started spinning down to our left rear and crashed. I wondered if those fellows got out of that crash alive. Later I heard that several of them were thrown clear of the plane but no one got to them because of the heat of the battle. I'm sure this fellow was aware that when artillery was firing he was to stay above a specified altitude and probably, being pressed by someone for the positions of our front lines, came down low to see if we were marines or Nips.

After one more move we stopped; the small-arms firing and mortars probably mixed in with some of our own artillery pinned us down. We were unable to keep our wire in spite of the heroic efforts of Privates First Class Jundro and Dutton, who were constantly running out to see if they could find the break and repair it—this all under very heavy fire. Each time they went out I wondered if they would come back. I found a nice flat spot behind some rocks at the bottom of a hill and put Cooperman there with the radio. He had radio contact with battalion, and they advised me we were to attack again at 1600. I found Captain Stevenson and told him the news; he hadn't received the word from 3rd Battalion yet and doubted if we could be ready by then, as we were getting hit pretty hard. I'll be darned if I could see any live Japs. I found an observation spot on top of the hill in front of the radio position and started to register in for the barrage. This required me to spot the round, run down to the radio, give the correction, and run back up the hill to see where the shell landed. I could tell that some Nip was shooting at me whenever I appeared, as the bullets would be zipping past. After observing one spot, I started down the hill on the double, and about halfway down something hit my left arm just below the shoulder, spun me around, knocking me over. When I got to the radio position, I looked to see what had happened. A bullet pierced my utility jacket and field jacket, going in one side and coming out the other, but just touching my arm and giving me only a red spot. I had four holes in the two jackets. No matter how hard I tried I couldn't find our shell. It seems as if everybody was firing in front of us, so I gave battalion our position and told them to do the best they could.

Fight for Airfield No. 2

[This is an excerpt from an article on the Battle of Iwo Jima by Brigadier General Wendell Duplantis USMC (Ret). It was published in the *Battle Creek Enquirer and News* February 21, 1965, and submitted by George J. Green. It offers a different perspective of the battle above from the commanding officer's point of view.]

The Fourth and Fifth Divisions were now up against the main zone of resistance. Our regiment, the 21st Marines, was attached to the 4th Division. The orders were simple; pass through the battered 23rd Marines, take the "sag" out of the line, and break through the main zone of resistance.

The following morning (Feb. 22) the 1st and 2nd Battalions jumped off in the assault, the 1st Battalion on the right. Progress was slow and extremely difficult as they engaged the mutually supporting positions arranged somewhat like checkers at the start of the game. While limited advances were made on the right and left, the "sag" was still there. No one could cross the end of the airfield and live. By dark both battalion commanders had been wounded and evacuated, casualties had been heavy, and extraordinarily so among the officers.

The following day (Feb. 23) the attack was resumed, making limited gains. However, darkness found the weary troops digging in about where they had started out that morning. The day had not been without successes elsewhere, however. We had all been cheered to see "Old Glory" go up on the summit of Mt. Suribachi!

That night I was ordered to relieve the 1st Battalion at daylight and screen a tank attack as the corps' main effort. All available tanks were to be organized under a central command and hurled at the seemingly impregnable positions guarding Airfield No. 2. Our job was to keep the Jap infantry from swarming over our tanks and to consolidate gains made by them.

Historical accounts differ widely as to what happened that day. The truth is that the 100 to 150 tanks we were to screen never arrived. I had no other alternative but to order the attack without them, so that the advantage of the tremendous artillery barrage put down in front of us would not be wasted. Without time to redispose themselves from the screening formation, or to reequip with extra flamethrowers and bazookas, the men "jumped off," relying primarily on their bayonets and grenades.

With bloodcurdling screams they surged up and over the camouflaged bunkers, darting from one shell crater to the next. Pausing briefly to hurl a grenade into a fire port or through the back door, bayoneting those who dared to emerge, they smashed through the belt of defensive positions for a gain of about 700 yards.

In the first few minutes, Captain Clayton S. Rockmore, CO of I Company, was killed and Captain Rodney L. Heinz, CO of K Company, was wounded and had to be evacuated. Captain Daniel A. Marshall, a soft-spoken English professor back home, took over I Company and 1st Lieutenant Raoul Archambault, Jr., took over K Company and the attack continued unabated.

The fight for that hill has been described as one of the most dramatic series of events of the campaign. K Company, in hand-to-hand fighting, seized the hill, occupying the trenches from which they had driven the Japanese. Though I was constantly reporting my changing frontline positions, through some error they were not being correctly shown in the fire direction center. "Friendly" artillery fire came down on the beleaguered K Company and drove them off the hill, which was immediately reoccupied by the Japanese. Once again K Company attacked and seized the hill, and this time they were driven off by the Japanese. Once more the valiant and determined company smashed into the position and regained the hill.

The grim determination of those heroic men was beyond anything I had ever seen or anticipated. One sergeant was attacking a light machine-gun position aboveground, protecting the approach to a bunker. A burst of fire struck him in the leg, knocking him down. He struggled to his feet and hobbled forward. A hand grenade exploded just in front of him, knocking him down again. Once more he got up and stumbled forward, and I could see that his right foot was blown off, yet he continued on, his shattered shinbone sinking deep into the soft sand. Again the machine gun spat out a burst, striking him in the chest, ripping through his back. Somehow he made the two or three last steps and drove his bayonet up to the hilt into the machine gunner as he fell forward across the gun and died.

At a large bunker, a marine was methodically tossing grenades through a fire port. His buddy was standing by the back door, swinging a steel barbed-wire post he had pulled out of the ground, smashing the heads of the escaping Japs as they crawled out on their hands and knees. As he struck each one, he would drag the body behind him and stand poised, his post in the air, waiting for the next one. When no more emerged he and his buddy stripped several grenade carriers from the dead Japs and started on to the next bunker. Suddenly a fire port appeared in a hummock of sand where none had been visible before, then the muzzle of a Nambu jutted out and a staccato burst of fire cut them down. No quarter was asked and none was given, and scenes similar to those described were being repeated all up and down the line.

The midday administrative report by my staff staggered me. In the first hour and 45 minutes I had lost over 500 men, almost half my command. Other frontline battalions were in even worse shape and we still had a long way to go.

The battalion was in a most precarious situation. Our wedge-shaped salient deep into the enemy's position offered him an opportunity to envelop or enfilade both flanks, and we were in grave danger of being cut off and wiped out. Many bunkers that had been overrun or bypassed behind the front lines still contained numerous live and angry Japs waiting in darkness to attack from the rear.

K Company, across the airfield, was very low on ammunition, especially hand grenades. A trailer load of ammunition was hurriedly collected and the trailer hooked onto the rear of a tank. As darkness fell, a nameless hero volunteered to lead the tank through the minefield at the end of Airfield No. 2 and down the airstrip to the isolated company. Carrying a shielded flashlight, he walked slowly ahead of the tank through a hail of bullets and so guided it to the weary company, reaching it just in the nick of time, for the enemy had just launched the first of a series of counterattacks that were to continue throughout the night. Seventeen times, the determined Japs hurled themselves at that critical hill and each time were thrown back by K Company's stubborn defense. Archambault's reports grew fainter and fainter as his radio battery grew weaker. I sent two men with spare batteries, but they were cut down before they had gone a hundred yards. I sent two more and one of them finally got through and our only communication link was restored.

War has its grim humor. It was reported to me that when field rations were being issued the next morning in the growing light, four Japs had been discovered waiting in line with one of the platoons. They did not get breakfast that morning or ever again.

Daylight of the 28th found us once more crossing Airfield No. 2, on beyond Hill 199, the scene of K Company's valiant stand, passing through the 1st Battalion, 9th Marines. We attacked at 8:15 following a furious 30-minute artillery barrage. Our own artillery, the 12th Marines, were ashore now with plenty of ammunition and we jumped off, closely following a living curtain of steel, L and I Companies in the line, K Company in reserve.

In their usual slam-bang style, the line surged rapidly ahead, making excellent progress through the sandstone buttes and outcroppings, which became more numerous and larger in size as we moved north and east.

Watching the line from the top of a hill, I saw that it was gradually swinging from a northeasterly direction, the companies heading for Airfield No. 3, an unfinished field, which nevertheless offered excellent fields of fire. According, to the "book," I should have corrected the direction of attack immediately but a hunch prompted me to let them go. About noon an aerial observer reported a large number of Japs moving from the area around Motoyama village, our original objective in the direction of Airfield No. 3, and digging in with their backs to the airfield, obviously planning to stop us there. A few Jap tanks were speeding across the airfield and were taking up firing positions on the far side. Our misdirected attack had drawn them out of their prepared positions.

Stopping my companies where they were, I pulled L Company out of the line and sent it due east to seize Motoyama village, a village in name only since there wasn't a wall left standing. The foundations, however, provided excellent cover. The Japs were caught completely off balance, and L Company, commanded by Captain Edward V. Stephenson, swept into Motoyama on the run. Leaving K Company to guard the critical left flank, I swung I Company in after L Company and the route to the Japs was complete; they were running in all directions, but generally making for high ground to their right rear. Jubilantly I reported our advance of almost three quarters of a mile and requested the Division Reserve be rushed up to cover my flanks, for it looked as if we had split them wide open.

The exhilaration at our success was to be short-lived. An air strike of many of our planes was coming in to bomb that position, paralleling our front. Several of the planes overshot and bombed my front line. Frantically I tried to radio the flight coordinator but could not get on his frequency.

I ordered the line to lay out parking panels to indicate our front line, but all but one of the panel carriers had become casualties and the pilots apparently could not see that one panel for the smoke and dust in the air. I finally got through to corps on the field telephone as the last plane finished its run. I made our position clear and ordered the attack to continue. Once more the companies jumped off and were again moving ahead when a second strike peeled off and once again we caught the "overs." This was too much. Both companies dug in.

I planned to commit my reserve company and continue the attack but the guardian angel that had been watching over me for so long looked the other way for a moment. As I prepared to move my observation post forward we were spotted by the enemy and fired on by a large-caliber dual-purpose gun. The first round struck the retaining wall of the destroyed gun position we occupied, the force of the explosion slamming me against the gun mount behind me, knocking me out. My combat orderly and close friend, who had already saved my life many times, dragged me to the rear of the position and to safety before the next shell struck. I remember getting up and walking down the hill to my command post, where I found my foxhole, got into it, pulled my poncho over me, and passed out.

Success or failure is so often based on an infinite number of little "ifs":

If I had tried to talk to my executive officer;

If I had called for a doctor or a corpsman;

If my staff had not been so anxious to let me get some rest;

If my CO had tried to get me on the phone; or

If I had had some visible wound, my condition would have been discovered.

But none of these things happened. My staff assumed that I had halted the attack in order not to expose my flanks any further; I had been observed walking into the command post under my own power, and externally at least I was my usual irascible self. Indeed, I was out of my head in a state of shock and was not fit to command.

When I came to it was almost midnight. I could think clearly once more, and, except for deafness in one ear and persistent ringing in the other, I was "back to battery." In my stupor I had neglected to put blankets or equipment under me to protect me from the heat in the ground, for we were near the mineral springs area, and the ground was so hot you could heat a can of C-rations just by stomping it into the ground. My back and hips were blistered but all in all I was happy that I had been able to walk away from that one. The situation at the front was quite another thing. While I had lain for nine hours completely befuddled, the enemy had reoccupied their carefully prepared positions and our golden opportunity was lost.

I have refought that phase a thousand times, debating all the possibilities. Had I pressed on and seized the high ground, could we have held it throughout the night? I will never know the answers to these and other questions, but I will always keep asking them, for 900 marines were killed or wounded in the bloody week that followed, in desperate efforts to seize that little hillside that came to be known as "Cushman's Pocket," a hillside that had been offered to me on a silver platter the day before.

At daybreak I moved my observation post into Motoyama village at the northeastern end of Airfield No. 2, passed K Company through I Company, and ordered the attack to continue. My worst fears were realized. Both companies were stopped in their tracks with heavy losses. I moved along the line with Archambault trying to analyze what kind of resistance we were up against. Of 19 dead marines I carefully examined, 17 had been shot through the head and killed by a single bullet. This meant rifle fire by excellent marksmen. Pillboxes, bunkers, artillery, mortars, rockets, and tanks could not halt my veteran battalion, but skillfully employed defense by accurate rifle fire did stop us and stop us cold. I called down artillery barrage after barrage. The 81mm mortar platoon poured hundreds of rounds into the position. We pounded it with air strikes using napalm bombs, raked it with machine guns, and attacked again, and once more, were pinned down by that deadly rifle fire.

Days later we were to discover that the position consisted of a series of trenches, each trench a little higher up the hill than the one below, resulting in a tiered effect. From each trench a slanting tunnel led down as much as 75 feet to large underground shelters where the Japs would wait out our barrages in safety, leaving only a lookout in the trenches, which were covered by camouflage nets. When we attacked, the Japs manned their trenches and fired on us through the nets. So perfect was the camouflage, the trenches and troops were invisible to us. Crawling over the bare ridges, the marines made excellent targets for them. The unit defending the position was the crack 26th Imperial Tank Regiment fighting on foot. Its commanding officer was a graduate of our service schools and knew our tactics and equipment as well as we did.

The group was advancing along the edge of Airfield No. 2 in single file, well spread out, when I observed two Japs wheel a crude launcher out of a cave about 600 yards to my front. Lighting the fuse of the huge rocket in the V-shaped trough, they darted back into the cave. I marked the cave mouth for further attention and watched the bomb take off like a giant skyrocket. These missiles had been more of a nuisance than a threat, since they were so inaccurate, but not this one; it had our name written all over it. Like a perfectly thrown forward pass it came spiraling down, and all 100 pounds of it exploded in the middle of the command post group with disastrous effect. Lieutenant C. T. Jones, the communication officer, Staff Sergeant Mills, the construction boss, and six other men were killed and almost a score wounded, among them Major Minetree Folkes, headquarters commandant, whose leg was badly mangled. Just at that time a pair of machine guns opened up on the group from across the strip, hampering our efforts to aid the wounded. Doctor Weinstein, the battalion medical officer, a gynecologist in private practice, dragged Major Folkes into the shelter of the crater made by the blast and amputated the mangled leg, cursing the machine guns whose bullets were kicking dirt into the wound. When I last heard of Major Folkes he was a Virginia legislator, his life saved by our scrappy "Winny."

In the midst of this confusing melee a crippled B-29 came swooping in from a raid on Japan, approaching Airfield No. 2 over the enemy's positions. Frantically we tried to wave it off. The airstrip was littered with shot-up tanks and vehicles and was cratered with shell holes. On it came and crash-landed on the strip, slithering off one side. To our relief we saw the crew jump out and scamper to safety. To top that discouraging day we learned that a typhoon had flattened our tent camp back on Guam. It certainly looked as if our fabulous good luck had finally run out.

Airfield No. 1 was now in operation. Cargo planes were landing one after the other, unloading critical supplies at one end of the field, filling up with wounded marines at the other. The 4th Division to our right rear was making slow but steady progress in the "Meat Grinder." The 5th Division to our left rear had made substantial gains and was also moving steadily forward. In the 3rd Division's zone in the center a large gap existed between units due to the unfinished Airfield No. 3. It became evident that Hill 362 at the north end of the airfield was the controlling terrain feature and must be seized. Its seizure would outflank "Cushman's Pocket," which as of March 4 still remained impregnable. I was ordered to pull out of position at the "Pocket," take a circuitous route around the south end of Airfield No. 3, attack and seize Hill 362.

When I began a careful disengagement about 4:00 A.M., the Japs hit us with a counterattack that took time to repulse, which meant we would arrive at the jump-off late. The trail around the airfield was under heavy bombardment, which forced us to go farther south so that now we would arrive even later. But worst of all was the fog. It was so thick that visibility was reduced to a few feet, and I was leading the battalion across terrain I had never seen before into a very rough enemy stronghold. As we passed the area of the sulphur mines, its distinctive rotten egg smell blending with the battlefield stench caused many men to retch. The earth held many deposits of clay, which were vividly green or yellow or blue. Vapors and mists rose from many open fissures, merging with a thick smothering blanket of fog, laden with death. The hideous unreality of it gripped us all. Men were silent, their teeth clenched, the only sound the steady crunch, crunch of their footsteps and the rattle of the enemy's fire. I felt transported to a strange and unknown planet in space and not on this earth at all.

To quote from a description I once wrote of the attack:

> Shells come in increasing tempo now and there are more dust-covered bundles of dead and wounded. The line starts forming up, officers are moving back and forth, shouting to be heard above the din of our own thundering artillery. The line bunches and spreads out, men taking their places like

> football players after a huddle. Now they're fixing bayonets and giving their weapons a last-minute check. It's K-Hour. Our bombardment ceases so suddenly the silence hurts. "Let's go." The men lunge to their feet and dash forward, dodging, twisting, turning. Some fall. The others go on. The chonk, chonk of our mortar shells is steadily beating down ahead of them. Our machine guns are rapping out a rhythmic tattoo. The brittle crackling of rifle fire is heard now—the thin wavering line is closing with the unseen enemy hidden by the blanket of fog. The zinging pop of hand grenades tells they're very close. After a little while there is a lull. My radioman reports K Company is reorganizing. They need 30 stretchers right away. Soon after, the report from L Company. Captain Stevie Stephenson has been killed, and we are pinned down by heavy fire from antitank guns firing point-blank into our lines. I pick up my useless binoculars and head for L Company through the soupy fog. Stevie, a North Carolina druggist, had been leading his men in the attack. A capricious breeze had swept the fog away for a moment and Stevie found himself looking into the muzzle of a large caliber antitank gun only feet away. The gun roared, and Stevie, his gunnery sergeant, and his runner had been blasted into eternity. Only moments before his death, when he made his hourly report to me, he had concluded in his lighthearted whimsical way, "Better set the beans and sowbelly on the back of the stove, I'll be late getting in tonight. It's sure sticky up here. Anybody got any windshield wipers? Over and out."

We had done all we could do that day, and I ordered the companies to dig in. We were short of Hill 362 and had not reached our objective. I was called to the phone with a message that Diamond 6 (Major General Graves B. Erskine) wanted to speak to me. This could be very good news or very bad news. As usual he wasted no words: "Duplantis, I'm not satisfied with your advance. Your last report shows a gain of only 150 yards and you haven't taken Hill 362. What about it?" I thought here it comes—the ax.

Out loud I said: "That's right, General, but we knocked out seven fortified positions by last count and there's still one platoon to hear from."

"Tell your men I said well done. There'll be no attack tomorrow. Get some hot food and rest." He was tough but he knew his job and he was fair and just, and no man could ask for a better combination than that in the midst of combat.

For three more days we hammered away at "Cushman's Pocket." On the fourth day we held enough of the ridge to the rear to attempt an envelopment. Attacking toward our own lines, we came down on them from the rear and at long last they broke and flushed from their position like a startled covey. In an hour and a half it was all over: They were wiped out.

Boundaries between the 5th and 3rd Divisions were not readjusted, and the 3rd was ordered to attack across the front of the 5th and clean out Kitano Point, the northern tip of the island. The 1st and 2nd Battalions, 21st Marines jumped off in the attack going down steep series of terraces toward the sea. I was back with my parent organization now and watched the attack from a prominent hill in company with General Erskine and Colonel Hartnoll J. Withers, commanding the 21st Marines. When the battle-weary battalions finally were brought to a halt by sheer exhaustion, I was ordered to pass through the 1st Battalion and finish the job.

I positioned several tanks on higher terrace to fire in front of us with overhead fire, and down we went. With the 2nd Battalion joining in on the left we quickly eliminated . . . last three Japs retreating into the surf, firing their rifles while waist deep in water, grimly defiant to the bitter end.

This was the 16th of March and the official announcement went out: "All organized resistance has been eliminated."

Attack on Cape Gloucester

Island Hopping

Men of the 7th Division on Kwajalein Island

165th Infantry attacking Butaritari, Yellow Beach Two

Dick Bayman

My World War II Years

At various times throughout my life since the Cebu, Philippine Island, combat experience, I have attempted to talk to different people about certain events that occurred on the battlefield or about my friend Derrell Walton, who was killed in my foxhole only a few feet from where I was manning the machine gun, but I have always become very emotional and would have to apologize for not being able to talk any further on these subjects.

By television, I have watched veterans revisit places 50 years later where they saw action, try to recall horrible experiences, and invariably they would break up emotionally, so it is something we all who survived in combat must live with—those terrible and indelible memories that are a part of us every day of our lives. These are the mental scars of war, which are just as real as the physical ones.

Prior to my eighteenth birthday on June 30, 1944, I tried to enlist in the air force to become a tail gunner on a B-17 bomber, the same as my brother Bill, who had already been in the air force for two years and was stationed in England. George, the eldest brother, had been in the service of his country over two years, serving in the 45th Army Division, and was overseas in North Africa at the time. The air force had met their quota of recruits, with no available openings, and so I was put on hold, even though I was only 17 years of age at the time.

Many men in their late twenties and in their thirties, some with families and some without, who had more to fight for than 18-year-old boys, received military deferments, which I did not feel was fair. Either everybody who was physically able should have been inducted into the military—or nobody. One person who received such a deferment said, upon my return home two years later, that I was a sucker for serving in the armed forces of this country.

After being sworn into the army at Fort Hayes in Columbus, Ohio, on September 13, 1944, we were taken to Camp Atterbury, Indiana, to await assignment to an army base for basic training. While there, I told the assignment office of my efforts to enlist in the air force, so they held me over awaiting an opening, and day after day I was assigned to KP, which was a hard day's work lasting 14 hours from 4:00 A.M. until 8:00 P.M. After 11 days and still there, homesick and not able to get a pass to go home on, I went to the assignment division, where they told me they still had no openings in the air force. I made the mistake of saying I would even take the army to get out of there, as all the people I had been inducted with were long gone. Apparently they did not think I was kidding. The very next day they cut the orders and I was on my way to Camp Blanding, Florida, for basic training. There I would be assigned to a heavy weapons company featuring heavy .30-caliber water-cooled machine guns and mortars along with the basics of the bazooka, M-1 rifle, carbine, and the .45-caliber automatic handgun. The camp housed and trained approximately 60,000 troops at all times, and, though we had Nisei or American Japanese troops, no black trainees were seen on this base. They were being trained at other bases for support operations such as truck drivers and for work details, but not for combat.

In basic training there was always somebody trying to find a way to get discharged from the service. One such person said he would not be in the service for very long, so he pleaded he could not see. On the firing range he would always get "Maggie's Drawers." He never hit the target, and the marker would wave, which looked like somebody's underwear. What a shame for a coward! He was discharged a short time later. There also were bed wetters, and eventually their beds would be moved into the latrine, where others would not have to put up with them, but I never heard of anyone being discharged for it.

We were told we would receive 17 weeks of training, but that was cut short to only 15 weeks, which was totally insufficient in preparing teenaged boys for combat. It would put them at a great disadvantage and great risk when confronting a well-trained enemy that had been battle experienced from years of fighting. But when the generals call for troops, they get them regardless of how well prepared they may be, as they just want warm bodies to plug the holes created by casualties. If the battle is won and the general has met his timetable, this will be very favorable for his political agenda after the war is over. The generals receive all the credit for the sacrifices of the servicemen who fight and die and who come home in coffins or are scarred physically and mentally for life.

The forced marches in basic training, where you double time for miles carrying a mortar-base plate strapped to your back or the tripod of a heavy .30-caliber water-cooled machine gun cutting into your shoulders, were soul-testing times. Making these events even more torturous were the sandy terrain, swamps, and hills as you agonized trying to keep up and reaching your goal. The most dreaded training exercise to me was the infiltration course, where you crawled across a quagmire of mud and water, cradling your rifle with live overhead machine-gun fire and explosives going off all around you to simulate as closely as possible actual combat conditions. It was especially stressful as you finished the course to see machine-gun bullets peppering the sandbags just above your head as you crawled into the trenches and safety. Although the machine guns are locked into firing position at a certain height, an occasional round will spiral into the ground, and you do not want it to hit you. There had been serious casualties running this course, and we were told even some deaths occurred because some soldiers panicked under these conditions and got up and ran. Upon finishing, everyone would be loaded into trucks and returned to their respective barracks where we would take our mud-caked rifles into the showers with us to wash the dirt off both our bodies and the weapons. Once we were dried off and dressed, it was necessary to disassemble and lubricate each component part and the barrel to prevent corrosion. This weapon was now your best friend, so you took very good care of it as some day it may save your life.

One day while in basic training I had a wonderful experience as my brother Bill stopped at Camp Blanding to have lunch with me. Bill had been rotated back to stateside from England and a tour of flying bombing missions over Europe and Italy and was on his way to an air force base in Miami, Florida. They told Bill he could not have lunch with me, to which he replied, "The hell I can't; you cannot stop me," and so seeing my brother, for whom I had great admiration, and having lunch with him was a real treat and morale booster.

The WACs also used Camp Blanding as a training base to prepare the women for their part in the war effort, and, although there was a fence between the two areas, it was not enough to keep some soldiers from visiting some of their female counterparts. Somehow holes appeared in the fence.

Upon completion of our fifteenth week of training, we were mustered out in the company area, at which time about half the names of the soldiers in our company were read off and were told we were being assigned to the Pacific Theater of Operations. This was during the time of the Battle of the Bulge in Europe.

My assignment turned out to be Company D, 182nd Infantry Regiment of the Americal Division, a heavy-weapons company. The heavy machine-gun squads suffered extremely high casualties, in the range of 150-200 percent during the early days of the Cebu campaign, while the mortar squads' casualties were very light. As expected, my fate had been sealed, and I was now to become a member of a machine-gun squad, perhaps one of the most dangerous assignments one could receive. Your hopes of survival were pretty slim and were totally in God's hands.

After receiving our assignments to different rifle and machine-gun squads, we were taken up narrow trails to a hill adjacent to one where a battle raged between American and Japanese troops, and we watched it with field binoculars while being oriented on what was taking place and what we would be facing the next day when we would face our baptism by fire. Later that day some of us were used as stretcher-bearers to get the wounded to the hospital for surgery and treatment of wounds, as casualties were high from the battle that had just taken place. I was given the unsavory task of burying a man's foot, still in his combat boot, and part of his leg that had been blown away. It was said the soldier commented that he was very lucky because his combat days were over and that soon he would be returning stateside.

The next morning came all too soon and before we knew it we were making our way up the trails to Horseshoe Ridge to face death every second of every day that we would be in the trenches of the front lines on the field of combat. Strange things happened while we were in a holding mode on Horseshoe Ridge:

A Japanese sniper from another hillside was zeroed in on a bomb crater on Horseshoe Ridge. Every time a soldier passed by the crater he became another casualty. The Americans had a difficult time pinpointing his exact position until he came out of his hiding place to relieve himself, at which time he was killed by an Americal mortar barrage.

The thought of combat is so terrifying that some soldiers would do anything to avoid it, as evidenced by one who shot himself in the knee so he would not have to go on. This seemed very drastic even from such a desperate person.

Another soldier, whom I had trained with in Florida, was so terrified he froze in his foxhole and refused to come out as we moved out to engage the Japanese in further action. He was reassigned to a rear area job with the Eighth Army Headquarters where he would not be able to cost the lives of any of our combat teams. One of my other friends called him a coward, and their long-standing friendship came to an end that day, but I could not judge him, as combat is such a horrible experience. By the same token, I would not have wanted my life to depend upon him.

On the brighter side from Horseshoe Ridge, I remember watching heavy bombers drop tons of explosives on enemy positions up in front of us; then P-38s and navy fighter planes followed by strafing targets to further soften them up, which gave me a great feeling of security and satisfaction. This day the sky was a beautiful blue with a few tufted white soft clouds, so our view of the action was unimpaired as our planes continued to pound the Japanese encampments and other military targets. From the harbor the navy's destroyers and cruisers would also throw round after round of shells at enemy positions, which, too, was nice to see.

We were part of the big push to capture Coconut Hill and Ridge, D Company in support of C Company, starting before dawn and climbing steadily. We soon met with heavy enemy fire and intense resistance. Our advance came to a halt as we were pinned down pretty high up on the hill, at which time my assignment was to watch for any Japanese activity at the opening of a cave way down in the valley to my left side. At this time bullets were cracking overhead from sustained machine-gun fire, and, as I wondered if one had my number on it, I started piling what rocks I could reach up beside my body for protection. I lay there motionless on the hillside for some time watching the cave below at the adjacent hill until the target became someone else.

The fighting never seemed to end, and by nightfall I believe we were somewhere on Hill 20 and dug in to prepare for what would be a night of hell lasting for what seemed like an eternity. When you are not in the circle, have not been oriented on each day's objectives, have not seen any topography maps, and have never been told your location at the end of each day, you were at a loss to know exactly where you were. The important thing was just staying alive to fight another day.

During my days in combat, for whatever reasons, I never saw a black soldier on the front lines. They were all used in rear areas as truck drivers or on work details out of harm's way. Even at this time when we so desperately needed reinforcements, only white soldiers were brought up to help hold the perimeter against the Japanese counterattacks. Veterans of the Bougainville campaign stated that black soldiers were tried in a combat zone there and failed miserably, being extremely trigger happy, shooting at anyone and everything, especially at night, from which they derived the moniker "Night Fighters." It seems they fired first, before they knew what they were shooting at. Ill feelings were very prevalent between the white combat soldiers and the black servicemen on the island, with racial relations becoming so strained that combat soldiers wanted to do serious harm to them. Because we had our hands full fighting the Japs, a race war did not take place.

Nightfall came before there was time to explore the network of tunnels the Japs had spent years digging into the mountain, so we took refuge in anything we could that resembled a foxhole or reasonable cover to protect us from incoming mortar, rifle, and machine-gun fire. That night was a real live nightmare as the Japs tried everything they could to get us to reveal our positions. They continually clicked the bolts of their rifles, or you could hear them digging with shovels or pick axes in the rocks trying to unnerve you until one of our soldiers lost his cool, firing his weapon, which caused all hell to break loose when they saw the muzzle blast.

The next morning was a continuation of the nightmare, and, just as dawn was breaking and I was standing guard on the machine gun as the others were trying to get some sleep and rest, three Japs came running out of a tunnel we did not have time to explore the night before, throwing dynamite at our position, blowing my backpack to kingdom come. Then one Jap came running straight at me, and, when he came close enough, I hit him over the head as hard as I could with my carbine, breaking it into two pieces. As he lay on the ground another squad member made sure he was dead by firing three bullets into his head. He was trying to blow up our machine-gun emplacement and as many of our squad members as possible while creating a diversionary action as the other Japs took off in another direction trying to escape over the edge of the mountain to safety. As I held the stock of the carbine in one hand and the barrel of it in the other, I wondered how I would be able to survive. I always believed these Japs must have been high on drugs or sake to perform these acts, knowing their chances of survival were slim to none.

Each day of fighting was pure hell, and the nights were even worse, as the Japs were always digging in the rocks or doing something to get you to reveal your position, while at the same time preventing you from getting any rest. Fatigue was ever present, along with the dirt and filth. There was no water to wash with, and it was extremely dangerous to get out of your foxhole, especially at night, to take care of personal needs. David Bricker, a very close friend, got out of his foxhole one night to relieve himself and was killed by gunfire from his comrades who thought he was a Jap looking for Americans to kill.

April 12, 1945, we learned of the death of the President of the United States, Franklin Delano Roosevelt, which saddened us all, but this day was no different from any other as the assault on Coconut Hill continued with the going very slow. The Japanese put up a strong resistance as we were trying to drive them from the ridge, with both sides paying a heavy price in casualties.

The night of April 12th was one to remember as the Commander of the 182nd's Company G and his men moved quietly up the hill in the blackness of the night, crawling to within a few yards of the Japanese defenses and halted briefly, before suddenly charging forward the last few yards with a daring bayonet attack. This brutal assault completely caught the Japanese off guard, and the men drove to within 75 yards of the crest of the hill before halting to reorganize and hold on to their gains. This was the first time the Americans had ever tried this nighttime maneuver, something that only the Japanese had used before.

The actions from the night of April 12th had completely exhausted my best buddy, Derrell Walton, so he took refuge in my foxhole to try and get a little shut-eye and rest as another squad member and I manned the machine gun. Just a short while later, the Japanese counterattacked. Coconut Hill fast became a killing field: We were being peppered with incoming mortar, machine gun, and rifle fire, and we had our hands full just trying to stay alive. Casualties were occurring everywhere. Yet I was not so frightened: I felt an unexplainable presence about me.

The Japs must have thrown everything they had at us, and the scene was like a horrible nightmare; people were being hit all around as the Japanese pressed the assault with a vengeance. As the battle raged, I remember hearing two mortar shells explode and then nervously awaited the third one. That one was always on target and we were the target. Although I never heard it, I knew it had hit and hit very close by. I turned over to see my friend, Derrell Walton, with his stomach completely blown away, and I knew then that the mortar shell had hit right beside him, killing him instantly. This wonderful person's memory will forever be a treasure in my mind; he always tried to help and protect me in every way he could. With Walton dead I felt all alone and wanted to cry, but I hated those damned Japs too much for what they were doing to my friends, and all I wanted was to see every last one of them dead for destroying my world.

Walton's death impacted my life more than could ever be described in words; he was my best friend while in combat as we fought side by side. Being a battle-hardened veteran from the Bougainville campaign, he tried to help me all he could. We confided a lot in each other and he showed me pictures, which he said he had never shown to anyone else, of his wife and baby girl who was born after he left for overseas. I knew Derrell Walton for only a short while, but it was a rare privilege to serve with this man and all of the others whom I came into contact with during the Cebu campaign.

As I looked at what remained of Walton, my back felt very hot, so I reached back to feel why and brought back a handful of blood, which made me realize I had been hit by shrapnel, was in trouble, and needed help. So I got up and somehow made it back under my own power to where the medics were located.

When I reached the medics, they quickly administered morphine to kill the pain as they started cutting away my fatigues to get at the back wound. I remarked to them that I had also been hit in the hip, and the medics applied sulphur, a bacterial-killing drug used by corpsmen to reduce the possibility of infection to the wounds, and bandaged them as best they could for the long trek down the mountainside to where needed medical services would be administered. Later it was learned the shrapnel had missed the spinal cord by the narrowest of margins. The angels were surely present that day.

The chaplain said a special prayer for me, which was very comforting, and then some time later it was into one of the operating rooms. Learning of two more of my comrades succumbing to their wounds was really very frightening.

On April 17, 1945, approximately 30 of us litter cases were transported to the air strip on Cebu Island by ambulance and loaded onto a C-27 cargo plane as the Japanese continued to throw 20mm shells at the runway. My never having been on an airplane before made no difference; I looked forward to this flight to safety. Leyte had been secured earlier from the Japanese and now was being used by the Americans as a supply base with medical facilities to treat all types of wounds, amputees, and diseases common to the area.

My having been on the Pacific Ocean for more than a month aboard a troop ship, spending time in the hospital with pneumonia, through combat, wounded, back in the hospital once more, and spending time on two islands made it difficult for the mail to catch up; but then one day as I was lying on my bed the mail clerk delivered a bundle of 63 letters from home. The letters contained enough news about everyone back in Piqua, Ohio, and brothers Bill and George, both in the European Theater of Operations, to last for quite awhile, even though some of the information was weeks old. The good news of all the family was a much-needed morale booster that carried over for a long time.

Later on and a short time before Christmas that year, I remember seeing a mountain of boxes from all over the United States to be delivered to the Americans on the island. It must have been stacked 30 feet high and probably 50 feet or more around. The boxes received very rough treatment, as some were crushed and others were torn half open, but everyone looked forward to getting a package from home no matter what the package looked like. Regardless of the condition of the cookies or cakes, after several weeks in those packages tossed on open ground in intense heat, they were still well received as someone back home had remembered to send them.

While training for the invasion of the Japanese mainland and bivouacked in the foothills of the island, one of the truly sad stories of war emerged as the starving war-orphaned children would daily form a line near the trash cans and hold out their cans for us to put in whatever food we did not want so they could survive.

It was not until the war's end and after returning home that I learned of the heavy price in lost lives and bloodshed that we six Ohio friends, who trained and shipped overseas together, had suffered on the Island of Cebu—two were killed in action, two were wounded, one didn't see action, and one was reassigned.

People talk of closure when they lose a loved one, but I can tell you there will never be closure to World War II in my mind, my heart, or my soul as long as I live. The tears have flowed freely and frequently as I have tried to relive these events, which so dominated my life.

Edward W. Strickler

While stationed in Tacloban, Leyte, Philippines with the 393rd Aircraft Squadron, Fifth Air Force in late October 1944, we were doing repair on the airstrip. The rain was continual, as it rained nine months out of the year, so at night we got in our pup tents, wrung out our socks, and next morning put them back on soaking wet. This went on for weeks, as our barracks bags were lost after our transport ship was sunk the day after we landed. By the time we got dry clothes, one quarter of our squadron came down with the "jungle rot" in their feet and had to be shipped back to the States.

One other memorable occasion was when I was on sentry duty on top of a small mountain close to the airstrip. The Japanese "Betty Bombers" (we called them "Washing Machine Charlies" because of their loud noise) came over the mountain so low after their bombing run over the airstrip that their bomb-bay doors were still open, and I could see the aircrew inside. The "ack-ack" from the airstrip was hitting everything but the aircraft. I dove into a slit trench just to save myself.

George F. Norton

Okinawa

The first cruise of six months [on board the SS *Josiah Snelling*] was uneventful except for a hell of a typhoon in the South Pacific. Our first port was Noumea, New Caledonia. I remember only the boatswain stationed me on the aft mooring line, pointed out the fire ax on the bulkhead and said, "Sailor, when I give the order, chop that line." Well, here I am, just turned 18 earlier that year, practically by myself standing near the fantail with a fire ax in my hands waiting for the storm to hit. Talk about scared. The winds were at 80 or 90 miles per hour, I don't remember exactly. But I do remember thinking that Smith Center, Kansas, wouldn't be so bad right now. The rest of that cruise was relatively quiet, standing watches, cleaning guns, chipping, painting, and dreaming of getting back to the States. The "inport" period went fast, buddies leaving, and new personnel reporting aboard. Phelps and I had to get our beards cut off during the first liberty after getting our pictures taken, and, before anyone knew it, we were back again, not knowing where to, but at least the catwalks didn't seem so high this trip.

Each day underway, daily drills were held—pointing, training, sightseeing, loading, matériel casualty, and magazine loading. We were busy at all times when off watch, except sleeping periods.

Days later we departed for Guam. In Guam, we tied up at a pier just opposite a hospital ship. This hospital ship had just arrived from Okinawa. Litter after litter, the sounds, hour after hour, people being carried off that hospital ship. It was hard for me to take—especially since the word had gotten out that Okinawa was our destination.

Our ship was raid free until May 18, 1945. At 0801½, the plane struck us at the #1 hold. All guns, except #1 and #2 20mms, were ordered to stand by for further action. The plane came onto us at an angle between the #2 gun tub and the foremast, shearing off two cargo booms, one heavy steel-cable mast stay, one ventilator, demolished two heavy winches, went through the deck plates and exploded, bursting into flames on the cargo in the bottom of the #1 hold. This cargo, made up of sacks of cement and 12x12 timbers, absorbed the shock and saved the ship's hull from damage.

The explosion of the plane and the light bomb she carried threw flaming gasoline throughout the #1 hold and sent a column of fire up masthead high. The shock of the explosion blew the gun crews out of #1 and #2 20mm gun tubs, down the main deck, from which point they made their way aft to the midship house for treatment. First-aid and emergency squads turned to at the scene of damage. Forward ammunition magazine was flooded on orders to the second officer an account of fire in the #1 hold. At 0858 the ALL CLEAR signal was passed by the Naval Air-raid Warning Circuit, and we secured from battle stations.

A survey by the gunnery officer and the gunners mate showed both #1 and #2 20mms in operating condition. Sound power phone circuits to both gun tubs broken, and immediate repairs not possible. All other armed guard gear and equipment in good condition.

(Upon examination of the ship and NOI Hold, a 500-pound bomb was discovered, buried in the timbers and cement. A newspaper article stated that during May of 1945 the Japanese sent 600 kamikazes to attack the U.S. fleet off Okinawa.)

Donald Rapp

Service to Country

My unit was the 213th Combat Military Police Company, attached to the U.S. Eighth Army Headquarters Company. Our duties included security for General Eichelberger, his staff, the message center, and the Eighth Army facilities and staff.

At one point ten others and myself were assigned to enforce martial law in a village on Leyte, the Philippines. The village officials had been incarcerated for being pro-Japanese. After the Armistice was signed, we were shipped to Yokohama, Japan. Our unit was assigned to town duty there.

I was assigned as personal driver and security for Colonel Caldwell, Provost Marshal of the Eighth Army, and then reassigned as a sergeant and escort driver for the security and escort for General Eichelberger. During my duty as escort for the general, we made an inspection of Hiroshima, and I saw firsthand the devastation there. I couldn't believe the destruction. I really believe if everyone could have seen what I saw, there would never be any more A-bombs.

I met General Douglas MacArthur through General Eichelberger. Both treated us with dignity and understanding. General Eichelberger had a railroad train at his disposal. Two of the cars, the dining car and the observation car, had belonged to Prince Tojo. When we pulled into the depots, the Japanese attendants came to attention in respect for those cars.

I found the Japanese people to be very friendly and eager to please. I enjoyed my duties in Japan. I really felt good doing my part for my country and its people. Of course, we thought it was the "war to end all wars." If only that could have been true!

Irwin J. Kappes

After combat duty aboard the USS *Moale* (DD693) in the western Pacific, I was transferred to shore duty as a mural artist for the Fleet Recreation and Morale Unit in Oahu, Hawaii. This outfit operated recreation facilities throughout the island for officers and enlisted men. In June 1944, construction was completed on a large swimming pool near the Aiea Naval Receiving Station. It was the pride and joy of our officer-in-charge, Commander Hickey.

However, when it was learned shortly after that President Roosevelt was to pay an unexpected visit to confer with General MacArthur and Admiral Nimitz, the top brass panicked. They feared that Roosevelt might see the luxury as inappropriate when men were fighting and dying in the Pacific, so the multi-million dollar pool was hastily bulldozed and filled in.

As it turned out, Roosevelt's itinerary didn't even include Aiea, but he did come close. After a luncheon meeting at Makalapa, about two miles from Aiea, and after a few rounds of martinis, Roosevelt turned to Nimitz and said, "What you fellows need out here is a swimming pool."

Desert Sands: Africa

Sylvester "Pete" Zimny

After we were in the Mediterranean awhile, one of the higher army officers on the boat got a wild idea and had kerosene added to the drinking water available to the troops. He wanted to wean us from drinking water. I guess he thought he could make camels out of us in a day or two. No matter how thirsty you were, it was hard to get more than one swallow down at a time. We saved on drinking water the rest of the trip. We took saltwater showers, but it was hard to get lather from the soap. The showers were more or less a daily exercise.

In the sleeping quarters, the hammocks were six high with about 16 inches in between. Overnight the quarters became pretty ripe. It was enough to bring tears to the eyes. As soon as you got below deck, the temperature became very hot. We stayed on deck as much as possible because it was much cooler there. We did our exercises and would get quite hungry from the exercise and fresh air. When we went down the gangway to the mess room, we had the steam cooking smell and lost our appetites.

We knew we were going to French North Africa when they gave us a little book with a few French phrases with the English translations to study. I was first assigned to Boat Team 13. We didn't know if this was a bad omen or not. After awhile, I was taken out of Boat Team 13 and put in Boat Team 7. We were told this was done to average the firepower in each team. While we were unloading the ship, we heard about Boat Team 13 getting lost in the invasion and ending up trying to get picked up by a destroyer. Fort De Leau was firing on the ships. One of the sailors on the ship had a bullhorn and told Boat Team 13 to get the hell away from there before they got run over. They must have given them a direction, because they finally found the beach.

When daybreak came one of the boys, who was nicknamed "Mickey Mouse," was on deck looking around. A German plane came over and dropped a torpedo aimed at the ship. Mickey saw it coming and watched it skipping on the water toward the ship. Mickey always carried a rosary, and he sure worked it while keeping an eye on the torpedo. He said that the torpedo went in between the bow and the anchor chain. Mickey said he thought that was a miracle. I think that if I were there, I would go along with his way of thinking.

Sometimes the planes came over a couple times a night. They were Stuka dive-bombers and had a demoralizing effect. They would climb high, and just when you thought they were leaving, they would turn and start their dive. At the bottom of the dive, they would release their stick of three bombs. They would then come screaming down. Lying face down you would swear they would hit you in the middle of the back. The planes would climb back and go through the same procedure again and again. They would do this until they ran out of bombs. One night they came real close to us. When the bombs exploded, fragments flew in every direction. One twisted piece of bomb stuck in a cork tree a small distance away. One of the bombs sheared off a tree limb, which fell on my back. I thought, "My God, it's a bomb!" When it didn't go off, I turned and saw it was a tree limb. I got mad and threw it off, but when another plane started to dive, I reached out and pulled the limb on top of me again.

There was a lieutenant with a squad guarding an airport near the Mediterranean. The ground was low and wet. The water table was high. They had the runways covered with metal interlocking mats. This was used so the planes wouldn't sink in when they landed or took off. The guards had an old shack they stayed in. They said the lieutenant chose a spot by the doorway and gave orders that everyone would stay in the shack when the planes came over and the air raid siren sounded. He said that he would shoot anyone who ran out. The planes came over later in the evening, and the siren went off. The boys said the lieutenant took off running and that he looked funny trying to put on a pair of fatigue pants for a jacket! It took him quite a while to live down that one. He found out there was quite a difference between saying something and doing it.

One of the first things we did when we came to this location was to build a latrine. The site was by a small stream in back of the shed under a grove of eucalyptus trees. We dug a long narrow trench about three feet deep, as deep as we could dig with a long-handled shovel. At each end of the trench we set a post about even with the front of the trench and set about two feet above the ground. We got a long pole and secured it to the top of the two posts. Then we fastened a six-foot high strip of canvas to a row of posts and this became our screen. We were then open for business. A shovel was left for cover-up purposes. It was kind of tricky getting used to sitting on the pole. It was a matter of adjustment for the short as well as the tall soldier.

Some of the civilian cars burned alcohol. They had a coke-burning heater mounted on the rear bumper. There were coils of tubing that carried the alcohol through a heater. The heated alcohol was then ignited, making the motor run. This produced the power to make the car work.

Food became a problem; we didn't have any variety. They pushed corned beef on us. The cans read "Product of the Argentine 1917." I guess they thought the age made it better. We had corned beef three times a day with two pieces of bread. There was no limit on the corned beef. The cooks did not like it when we complained about the food. They said that no matter what they did to prepare it—whether it was roasted, baked, or fried—it was still corned beef. It was a tiresome diet. After several weeks of this, Captain Thompson said, "We have a company fund, and I think we should send a couple of people to see if we can buy some eggs, chickens, or other farm produce to change our diet." Private First Class Singer, a clerk in company headquarters, was one of the people appointed to try to buy some food.

At this time some of the antiaircraft gun crews had picked up venereal disease. Captain Thompson told one of the lieutenants to take some men and raid the cathouses. I was one of the soldiers picked. In the first house we raided, we found Private First Class Singer. The lieutenant said, "What the hell are you doing here?" Singer quickly said, "Trying to buy some eggs, sir." These houses had high concrete walls with broken glass imbedded in concrete at the top. You couldn't jump up and climb over. After we shagged Private First Class Singer out, the others must have found a hole somewhere. Some of them had hobnailed shoes, and it sounded like shod horses running down the street in the dark.

After this, no passes were issued for some time and a guard was put at the gate. This seemed to cut the traffic. One day, while on a pass, Private First Class McCoy (who claimed he was related to one of the feuding families from West Virginia) went downtown. He had a little too much wine to drink and became pretty aggressive. A colonel came by and McCoy didn't salute him. The colonel asked him if he didn't salute officers. McCoy said that he didn't think he owed the colonel a salute. He thought he probably had more time on KP than the colonel had in the army. The next day McCoy was walking around with his one stripe missing from his shirt and jacket.

The disease situation didn't improve among the American troops. Our company commander, to keep a close watch on the disease, initiated biweekly short-arm inspections. We were told to read the bulletin board every day. When we read there was a formation at 9:00 A.M. and the uniform was caps, raincoats, and shoes, we knew we were having another physical inspection coming up. It finally got to Private First Class Sam Sternlicht. He exclaimed, "They are looking at my penis! There is nothing wrong with it! I have a mouth full of bad teeth, but do they look in my mouth? No." He was trying to promote if it isn't broke, don't fix it, but if it is broke, fix it. Well, they never did anything for his teeth. He was 36 years old and all he had were a few snags in his mouth.

One day we hiked many miles carrying our barracks bags, and that evening we camped in the desert. The next morning we were told what to take out of our barracks bags and then to put the bags on a pile. A truck was to come and pick them up. We left them there, never to see them again. It seems that after we left the bags, German planes flew over, shot the bags up with their machine guns, and they burned.

During a lull in the firing one day, while we were all in our holes, the captain said he wasn't a religious man but he didn't believe the saying, "You won't get killed unless the bullet has your name on it." He said he knew if you kept your butt down, you would have less chance of getting a bullet in it. Then some guy piped up and said he wasn't worried about the bullets with his name on them. It was the ones they threw up with "To Whom It May Concern" on them that had him worried.

At that time, a private first class with overseas pay was getting about $75 a month. We were paying $6.60 per month for a $10,000 life insurance policy. I think they stopped deducting a laundry charge. There were a couple of times my folks almost collected my insurance.

During this time the officers said to forget about saluting. The snipers were picking off the ones that returned the salute. They also went to cloth rank. It wasn't reflective in the sunlight. We were told there were 17 people in the army backing up every soldier on the firing line. It was nice to know we had that much backing. We also thought we should be paid more than the people backing us up; they were paid the same wages we were.

Our mortar squad still consisted of two—the soldier from Chicago and myself. There are five in a full mortar squad. I don't know where the other three went. I never saw them again. We were told the average life expectancy of mortar- or machine-gun squad members was three minutes on the line. It was hazardous, low-paying duty.

The next morning was hazy with sand in the air. Captain Perry and a soldier carrying a flag came by. He said for me to come with them; they were going to put the flag on Hill 609. I took my rifle. I didn't know what to expect. We got to the top by the rock chimneys, and the Germans were gone. We tried to push the flagstaff into the ground. That didn't work because the ground was so rocky and dry. I went over to one of the chimneys and told the soldier with the flag to come over by me. I removed the rocks that had fallen in one corner of the chimney and had him hold the flag vertical in the corner against the stone wall. Then I piled the fallen rock against the flagstaff until the flag was standing free. It was something to see our flag blowing in the breeze where the day before a machine gun was shooting at us.

I went to company headquarters one time to see if any rations came in. There weren't any there yet. Some new replacements had arrived. One of the men was at least 40 years old. Captain Perry said he couldn't use him, and that made the old guy mad. He said he might be old but he came to fight and he didn't want to go back. The army could surely find a better place for a 40-year-old man. With inadequate food and no rest, even the young soldiers were having trouble.

We pulled guard duty every night because the Arabs could sneak up under the olive trees and after dark they would disappear like smoke. One night they stole some things from the captain's tent. When they were in the first sergeant's tent, they stole his dress shoes. They were pulling the blankets off him when he started yelling, and they disappeared under the olive trees. The Arabs had probably watched First Sergeant Johnson walking around in those brightly shined dress shoes.

One morning across the road from the hospital, hanging over the fence was a dead Arab with an army blanket. Although the American government would pay the French $100 if any American killed a horse or cow, if it was an Arab that was killed, the solder that killed the Arab was court-martialed and fined $1. After he paid the fine, he could not be tried again. On the way out after the court-martial, he would be handed a carton of cigarettes.

Some of the officers complained that we didn't keep our uniforms neat, especially when on duty, and we were representing the U.S.A. before the whole native population. Everything they tried didn't seem to work. One day a colonel came through and they asked him for advice. He told them on the next day's roster, add two people and during the inspections, give the two neatest MPs the day off. The change was miraculous. We got an old flat iron and ironing board set up in our room. I became quite adept at pressing pleats in my shirts and creases in my pants. I won the day off lots of times.

Once when we were pulling duty in Bizerte for a short time, the election for President was in progress. Private First Class Bonney was campaigning for President Roosevelt. For a podium, he was using a fourth-floor balcony. He had quite a crowd listening to his speech. There were some black French-African troops in the crowd along with some American and British soldiers with a sprinkle of natives. Bonney ended his speech with a flourish and the exclamation that, next to Jesus Christ, Roosevelt was the greatest man that ever walked the earth! Some of the American and French-African soldiers threw their caps in the air and gave Bonney a great ovation. As the time for election drew near, we were issued ballots and given instructions on how to fill them out. We had to vote and return the ballots by a certain date. They were mailed back, and later we were told that our ballots didn't make it in time.

While on detached service in a different area, I went to church one Sunday. It was in the fall of 1943. I saw a familiar face. After church was over, I went to talk with him. He was from Royalton, Minnesota, my hometown. We talked for some time, and he was about to leave. He asked me if I had received any mail lately. I said, "No, not in many months." "Maybe I shouldn't tell you this," he said, "but your father was killed in a farm accident." I didn't know what to think. The last time I had received any mail, it had been a partially burnt letter, but I couldn't remember when that was. My father had died on April 3, 1943. I wrote home and finally got a letter. The folks had been writing to me but didn't know I hadn't been receiving any of their letters. This also was a part of wartime army life.

(Excerpts from his book, *My WW II Memoir*)

Peter F. Gelcius

I remember quite a bit about my service time in World War II. There's no way to experience some of the things we went through without having it stay with you for life. There were some unique things that happened, but most things are probably very common to anyone who served during that time.

I was inducted into the army in February of 1942 at Fort Dix, New Jersey. I guess they needed truck drivers at the time, because my training lasted only about nine weeks, and I was on my way overseas. We went by boat from New Jersey to Nova Scotia, then were placed on a troop ship and sent off to Belfast, Northern Ireland. The Atlantic was rough, and I had what seemed like the world's longest boat ride going over there. My outfit was attached to a joint American-British force, which was headed for Africa. We fought with the British Eighth Army. I got to see many parts of Africa and a large part of Italy during those years.

Everything doesn't go smoothly in the army. Lots of "hurry up and wait." Lots of things that don't go the way they should. We even had problems making it to Africa. I was on an Indian ship that carried mostly troops. Our other ship carried most of our supplies and equipment. That ship never made it to Africa. It was attacked by a sub and sank.

I wasn't in a combat unit, but we certainly saw our share of the fighting there. My outfit was the 109th Ordnance, which supported the 92nd Infantry. Our job was to transport, supply, and repair the materials used by the fighting units. We were usually pretty close to the action. I spent a lot of hours in foxholes, being shelled by German guns or strafed by German planes.

I was very lucky, though. I never got wounded. One time I came back from seeing a movie and found that my tent had been blown to bits by German artillery. All in all, I guess God was looking out for me.

Others weren't so lucky. My wife, Valerie, lost her brother Joseph during that time. He was on a transport ship that got hit off the coast of Tunisia. He wound up in the ocean and died of exposure to the cold water. I saw a lot of other guys who got shot up or killed. We had an army hospital sitting right next to my unit during a period of my time in Africa. A lot of rough things happen in a war.

One specific memory I have occurred during a lull in the action. General Patton was in charge of the troops at that time and was passing through our area. Besides my getting to see him, he actually yelled at me for not wearing my helmet!

I also got to see FDR, Churchill, and Stalin. I think it was in April of 1943. We were in Teheran at the time, and I got to be part of the honor guard that marched where they were meeting. I never found out until much later that the meeting involved the D-Day invasion.

Most days were fairly routine. You knew what you were supposed to do, and you did it. When you were busy, you thought about your work, and when you weren't busy, you thought about home.

After the fighting in Africa, we moved into Italy. I remember it as a pretty country. I saw some interesting things while I was there. The fighting around Cassino was really something. It had rained very hard for several weeks, and the ground was soft and muddy. Our unit was camped out near some olive trees, and we were constantly being shelled. You always had to be on the lookout for a safe place to hide. Many of the shells that landed never went off. They just disappeared into the mud. Others exploded but from much farther down in the ground. If it weren't for the rain, we probably would have taken a much worse beating than we did. It's strange the way things work out.

I remember looking through the olive trees and seeing the German artillery set up on the next mountain. It was a strange feeling knowing that they could see everything we were doing. Of course, we saw everything that they were doing, too.

The Germans were hitting us pretty hard from their positions, and they had the whole area around Cassino bottled up. At some point, the brass decided to bomb the fortress. I remember seeing wave after wave of bombers flying overhead on the day they attacked. The sky was almost black with planes. When it was over, the area was covered with rubble and craters. It was quite a mess.

While I was stationed near Pompeii, I experienced an earthquake. I was in my tent when the ground and everything around me started shaking. At first I thought some of the guys were goofing around, but it turned out to be the real thing.

When we finally arrived in Rome, I had another unique experience. Several of us were picked to have a visit with Pope Pius XII. We were in the city when our lieutenant came over and asked which of us were Catholic. They marched us over right then and there. The whole visit lasted only a few minutes, but it was quite a thrill. I guess I was in the right place at the right time.

I also had a chance to visit my brother, who was stationed farther south. I can't say that I enjoyed the plane ride, though. The pilot was pretty green, and the trip was very bumpy. But the landing was the worst! We hit the ground so hard that we thought the plane was going to flip right over. Two of the officers I was traveling with actually kissed the ground when they got out of the plane. I don't think I'll ever fly in an airplane again. It doesn't pay to tempt fate too often.

Ultimately I accumulated enough points to be sent back to the United States and figured I was on my way home. I was stationed in Aberdeen, Maryland, but received orders to go back overseas. Before I left, though, fate stepped in. I was cutting the grass on the base when I ran into a colonel I had served under in Africa. He said it was good to see me, and he was glad that some of the guys he served with made it back. When I told him they had me slated to go back overseas, he got real angry. I told him I had to do what I was told, but he stormed off. It turns out he went to see the people in charge to get things straightened out. When he came back, my orders where changed, and a short time later I got to go home for good.

I think about the war now and then. I think about the guys I served with and the places I went and the things I saw. I even have some bad dreams once in a while. I wasn't a hero. I just did my job, just like everybody else.

Edward F. Mickens

April 20, 1944. This evening at General Quarters everything seems to be in order. A quiet and peaceful day; our seventeenth day at sea since we left

Norfolk, Virginia; our second day in the Mediterranean. At 2 o'clock in the afternoon a German reconnaissance plane flew directly overhead at a very high altitude and great speed. No firing took place; he was much too high to reach for our guns. Convoy was proceeding along fine and about 5:30 P.M. passed the large city of Algiers, where a few ships joined the convoy. At about 8:30 P.M., everything peaceful. Bill Milligan and I were leaning on the flag bag and talking about our past experiences, as we did every evening. All of a sudden on our port beam and straight ahead where I was looking, five or six flashes burst out. Then a loud boom, and flames leaped about 500 feet into the air. Beautiful yellow and red colors, but a sight that made all of us clench our fists. A tanker was hit directly by German bombers. It was dark now, and the very heavy smoke of the tanker poured into the sky and left a trail that could be seen for miles around. It sank in a matter of seconds in sight of the African coast. This was the S.S. *Paul Hamilton*. Another ship, the first ship of the first column, was also hit but was afloat and turned back to Algiers.

All of our guns opened fire, and so did everyone else's. Someone on the ship next to us seemed to be firing at another ship. Bernard Christopher and I were the first 20mm to open up on our ship. We fired over our port bow where a plane was coming out of a dive. He dropped two bombs near the ship in front of us and had a very near miss on the ship astern. It really was dark now and another plane was on our starboard side. All of our starboard 20s opened up; also the 3- and 4-inch guns. There were more lead and tracers flying around than on any 4th of July celebration. The action occurred within a few minutes, but every second seemed like an hour. We were at our guns waiting, but the Heinies did not come back, probably because it was pitch black. We waited until 11 P.M. and were up at 4 A.M.—all prepared to welcome him if he tried to come at dawn, but he didn't return as we expected. We don't know who will get the credit for the Jerry that was downed, but we hope it paid off for what damage he caused.

Sol Rubin

Leslie Howard

I saw Leslie Howard for the first time in the *Romeo and Juliet* movie, 1936. Despite some language limitations as a newcomer to the U.S.A., the Shakespeare lovers that end in violent death engrossed me. The second time I watched my favorite actor was many years later after WWII.

I was with a family watching a revival of *Gone with the Wind*. During the TV commercials there was a discussion about the private lives of the leading actors, Clark Gable and Vivian Leigh. I was preoccupied with a supporting actor, Leslie Howard. This soft-spoken, peaceful man, caught in a whirlwind of war and racial tension, brought back my memories of another conflict.

While with a U.S. combat outfit during the 1943 Tunisian campaign, Leslie Howard was in the news when he was killed in a plane crash. After we licked Marshal Rommel's forces, there was a brief period of army "normalcy" like getting passes to Tunis. I held one of the papers and was standing on a hot, dusty road, waving or "thumbing" anything that moved toward the capital. Images of Casbah scenes stayed with me from a movie with Charles Boyer and Hedy Lamar. The British tanks and artillery would not pick me up, since I did not wear their uniform. One of them remarked: "Bloody rules, you know!" The July heat increased and so did the stubborn hungry insects. A jeep rolled by, slowed down and backed up to where I stood. A smiling chap offered me a ride to Tunis. We got acquainted. He made reference to my "Non-Yank accent." I offered a bio-background and he remarked wistfully, "We are both Europeans." After my quotes from Shakespeare, he complained about the war ruining his career. That included sharing the stage with Leslie Howard. We rode in silence since the tragic news of the "gentle Leslie's death" was mentioned.

Finally, we reached the long-awaited Casbah and a problem—an OFF LIMITS sign to all troops with a blockage of military police, American, British, and the local French-colony forces. While these security teams were breaking up a fight between sailors and soldiers, I sneaked through the gate. The Casbah was the residence of the poor Arabs and Jews amidst the narrowest alleys I had ever seen. While wandering around in that new world, I had a reunion with the British chap who drove me there and was kind enough to take me back to my army post. He asked me suddenly if I could speak Yiddish and, after my affirmative response, related a surprising detail of Leslie Howard's life—the actor spoke fluent Yiddish to his father, an immigrant from Hungary. When the war was over and no security problems were involved, we learned that Leslie Howard served with the British Intelligence and was shot down by the Nazis.

Sabbath in Africa

We were standing around our commander and our walkie-talkie to learn about our next move. Cigarettes half discarded, no news, just hanging around at the tail end of the Tunisian campaign, 1943. During that lull, I heard chanting from the open door of a nearby building. The words were familiar, not the melody. Then, to my surprise, I realized that it was a Sabbath prayer emanating from a synagogue. I peeked in and noticed Arabic Jews dressed like all other natives in North Africa, with a sprinkling of a few berets since it was then a French colony. The captain readily gave me permission to attend the Sabbath service, adding a line: "If we need you, easily found," with a wry smile.

As I entered the house of prayer, everything stopped momentarily. All eyes were fixed on the unshaven, slightly disheveled soldier, dirty helmet, rifle, and belt filled with hand grenades. Some of the congregation came over to examine my presence with a mixture of shock and confusion. Not knowing the Arabic language that they exchanged in my direction, I offered a line in French: "*Je suis un Juif Americain.*" That is, I am an American Jew. This brief remark caused a cheerful uproar with all sorts of happy exclamations. Some of the people passed near me, kissed their two fingers and pointed them at me, a gesture of affection I guessed. Soon the rabbi guided me to the altar for a blessing. Then the services continued. At the end of the Sabbath prayers, someone who knew a few words of English, plus French, invited me to join them for a celebration, the birth of a son. I followed the congregation outside, stopped momentarily to get the commander's approval, then on to the home of the family.

I inquired as to who was the father of the child and was introduced to a man with an impressive white beard. Surely that must be the grandfather. I witnessed customs never seen in my part of the universe. The group sang strange-to-me melodies and clapped their hands as they walked the narrow paths. We entered the dwelling of the family. The singing and clapping now continued around a bed where a beautiful woman and infant were resting. One thing became clear to me—the so-called grandpa was really the papa of the newborn. It was difficult for me to visualize this young woman in bed to be married to this gray-bearded man, but I kept the tradition and complimented him according to our ancient customs.

The collation consisted of spicy African food, in contrast to the tasteless army rations, yet too tough for me to take a chance. I searched for a solution so as not to offend my hosts. Fortunately, one of my buddies showed up and yelled out, "Let's go, march order, on the double!" I offered a few fast "*Shaloms,*" peace to everyone, including the daddy-grandpa, the charming mama, and the little one.

When I returned to my outfit there were all the details of our campaign, Algeria. As our convoy rolled onto the hot dusty road, I noticed some poorly dressed, undernourished kids and recalled the newborn's peaceful, angelic face at the family party while being showered with blessings.

All Hell Broke Loose: Europe

U.S. Infantrymen with a captured Nazi flag

Hilltown ABLE

Excerpts from a unit memoir of Battery A-744th FA Battalion

The time at Camp Chaffee had had its compensating moments, but it hadn't been all beery bull sessions at PX 7, battery parties in the day room, and weekend passes to Ft. Smith and Fayetteville, North Carolina. There had been many hours of hard work under an intolerably hot sun or in rain and knee-deep mud, and there had been hundreds of foxholes and slit trenches dug only to inculcate the habit of digging. There had been close-order drill, stuffy parades, and hours of classroom monotony; and there had been heat rash and chigger bites and those damned MPs. So when final exams—corps and AGF tests—loomed on the horizon with the prospect of repeating training in the event of failure, the men bent an earnest effort to preparation and took the tests in the manner accredited to Grant at Richmond.

Camp Kilmer will probably be most remembered for its good meals, which included a bounteous Thanksgiving Day spread and retreat-to-reveille passes. Men living in the New York-Philadelphia area took advantage of these to spend a few final hours at home, while others accepted the opportunity for a last-minute look at the metropolis, bright lights, and a "fling."

But the New Brunswick, New Jersey, stay was a short one—just long enough for the fellows to decide the place was a bit of all right, and few were as anxious to leave as they had been at Chaffee. The "last mile" trek from the train to the ferry at Jersey City and from the ferry to the loading platform at the Staten Island pier taught us the wisdom of regulations limiting the luggage to be carried. The military band playing "Jersey Bounce" at the entrance to the pier was evidently intended to revive sinking spirits, but with most of us it was muscle and not spirit that needed a lift. The Red Cross ladies at the top of the incline to the boat deck pier twisted our arms and made us stop and sit down for a cup of coffee and a donut. Without that breather, we'd probably never have made it up the gangplank.

Once on the boat, a guide took us in hand, led us tripping over shipboard paraphernalia through a brief maze of batches and passages to a hole through which we looked down into a dimly lit dungeon. "That's it," he said, and disappeared in the blackness.

The next day we surveyed the steep stairway into the hold, wondered how we ever got down it with all that equipment without even a broken bone, and decided we wouldn't try it again without a rope and pulleys. The officer at the bottom said something like, "Climb-into-a-bunk-relax-and-stay-there." Bunk? So that's what those things were. We'd thought those pieces of canvas had just been washed and were put on those racks to dry. We climbed into one and wondered how long it would take us to learn to relax with a cartridge belt on, a packed musette bag on our back, a full duffel bag, carbine, and overcoat on top of us, and on top of that, the guy in the next bunk above, who was only partially supported by the sagging canvas.

The ocean trip was, for the most part, uneventful. No one ever got quite comfortable in the cramped quarters, and waiting in line for meals occupied a good portion of the day. But entertainment was organized and movies were shown. The most popular shipboard pastimes were reading, cards, and another game played clandestinely in secluded passageways with a pair of marked cubes. The South Atlantic weather was warm, but there were spells of bad weather and moderately rough seas and the usual number of men were introduced to the agonized indisposition of seasickness. After a few days, however, stomachs became adjusted to the roll of the sea, and most of those who had been victims were willing to admit they were glad they had not died.

While still a few days out of England, we watched the convoy's destroyer escort go into action off our starboard stern and could hear the detonations of depth charges. We were then within the patrol range of the British Catalina flying boats, and one of these could be seen circling the area over which the destroyers were racing under a full head of steam. There were reports later, none of which was corroborated, of several U-boats destroyed in the action.

The men found England interesting. The little differences in manner of speech and social and political custom (we found that they didn't even employ the simple implements of knife and fork the same way we do) aroused curiosity. And more than that—although of interest only to the single men, of course—the girls were friendly. The policy on passes was liberal, and there was ample opportunity to study the ways and byways of a country that was much older than ours and acted its age, a country that had been at war for over five years.

Some of the customs we didn't understand, like the daily cessation of all activity in order that undiluted effort might be given over to a ritual called "tea," and like the subservient reverence with which they looked on the sacred national traditions, some of which seemed to us pitifully outmoded and impractical. And there were things that amused us like the national institution known as "Time, please!" loudly heralded twice daily through the length and breadth of the land at the given hour of pub curfew, and the national addiction to the habit—amounting almost to a mania—of gum chewing, bringing upon the American visitors a hundred times a day the query, "Any gum, chum?"

There was sufficient evidence of wine, women, and song despite the long years of war. Although the "wine" consisted chiefly of two barely palatable (but much partaken of) potions called "mild and bitter," the women spoke the same language and song was entered into at the slightest provocation and often continued until the last baritone lost his voice. It was evident that England did not list her morale among her war casualties.

A few months earlier the Nazi armies, in frenzied flight before the Allied avalanche that had rolled out of the Cherbourg peninsula, had found the Seine a costly obstacle to their retreat. On the trip up the river from Le

Havre to Rouen we stood at the starboard rail and saw the wreckage strewn along mile after mile of the south bank of the winding stream—the modern and expensive equipment of an "invincible" army, destroyed and abandoned in the mad run for Nazi lives. The trip also afforded our first glimpse at what had been actual battleground in the war. Industrial sites that had spawned German matériel of war and therefore had to be eradicated by our air forces were twisted, crumpled ruins. Here and there a gaunt wall or two, rising tombstonelike out of acres of brick dust and ashes, marked what had been a town in which the retreating armies had elected to stop and wage a delaying action.

Evidences of France's war damage on the trip from Rouen to the front were largely repetitions of the scenes along the Seine. Some towns and villages were untouched or bore only minor shell and bullet marks. In others, especially the larger cities, areas totaling many acres had been reduced to rubble. France had caught some of the war's heaviest blows full in the face, and her scars would show for a long time.

At 1800 the convoy stopped near Ste. Chatteau for supper, and, although the only visible house was over a half-mile away, a dozen ragged children of from three to nine years of age almost immediately surrounded us. They didn't speak, but their anxious eyes and hungry faces pleaded for them. We studied their clothing, the most conglomerate collection of rags we'd ever seen beyond a remnants bargain counter and wondered what the younger of them, who had never experienced it, would think of a normal peacetime world. K-ration is meager for a hungry grown man, and that was all we had to eat on the trip, but when we left each of the children had a small box or two of K-ration odds and ends that we'd tossed his way.

At Marienborn, our next position, the situation was somewhat different and distinctly on the warmer side. After traveling 51 miles from Nerzweiler, we arrived at the position just west of Mainz at nightfall. One of the major air battles of the war had been fought over the area the day before, March 24th, and the enemy was evidently attempting to land a last-round punch in that battle as we came into the flat field where the guns were to be emplaced. To our south our "AA" was throwing up a cone of machine-gun fire, and the entire area was illuminated by hundreds of flares that evidently had been dropped from the planes. Thus illuminated, and with the air-ground battle to the south of us continuing, the battery went into position and made ready to fire. Meanwhile a lone unidentified but unfriendly sounding plane kept flying back and forth above our position, low under the heavy clouds, and we wondered what notes he might be taking on us to turn over to the enemy artillery.

The following morning our own planes patrolled the skies unopposed, but the situation still was not conducive to great comfort. Whereas in the previous positions we had had the advantage of concealment, and from our OPs could observe all the enemy's activity, here we now saw the situation was reversed. Our territory was a broad, level plain bounded on our left and left-front by the enemy-held hills, forming a huge amphitheatre in which we held the stage and the Germans occupied the box seats. Whether it was merely good fortune or the fact that the enemy was so preoccupied with the task of getting himself elsewhere in one piece that he didn't concentrate on returning fire, we'll probably never know, but the trouble we felt certain we were due for never materialized. On our third night in the position a fast and furious hail of 88s (48 of them landed in a little over a minute) came in close enough to rip things up and tear holes in the tent of an attached antiaircraft unit to our right rear. But no further damage was done, and the six-day stay in that position was marked by no other serious incident.

It was at Closewitz where the incident of the cook and his prisoner occurred. By this time, the speed of our armies' advances and the German retreat were too great for some groups of Nazi soldiers who were being left behind in little uncombed areas to face the prospects of giving themselves up or chancing starvation in their hiding places. Most of them did not hesitate long in making a decision, and, as a result, we were continuously encountering them, singly or in small groups, practically begging to be taken prisoner. Despite Nazi superman propaganda, these men were, as a lot, just a scared, hungry, dirty mob that were having more trouble finding someone who would accept them as prisoners than they were avoiding capture.

Nevertheless, our cook, whom nature and the years has made more fitted for cooking than prisoner taking, usually left such adventures to his younger comrades. He must have been feeling his oats (and being in the kitchen stood him in better opportunity to get enough oats to feel) that day when he talked another cook into accompanying him on a prisoner chase. It's unlikely that either of them went at it very seriously, and both probably were surprised when they did come across one who gave up after they had fired one shot at this retreating figure. Just as they were starting to search the prisoner for weapons, they heard the motors of the prime movers and realized that the battery was getting ready to pull out. Inasmuch as they were a half mile from the position, our cook's friend decided that he'd better go ahead and hold the battery, and amid loud protest from the cook he took off, leaving the latter alone with the German. The cook thus found himself not only alone with an enemy soldier but facing the possibility of being left even more alone if the battery pulled out without him, and it did not take him long to decide that this wasn't exactly a predicament he'd bargained for.

When the first sergeant approached the scene in a jeep a short while later, he found captor and captive involved in a mad race. The cook, having abandoned all thought of taking a prisoner, was well out in front but tiring fast in a headlong dash to elude the Kraut, and the latter, having evidently decided against accepting the prospect of being left behind, was rolling along easily 30 yards behind and gaining with every step.

In our movement into the next position near Riglasho on the following day the battery became involved in the most thoroughly and irremediably snafued situation we'd encountered yet—and we had encountered some. It all started when a guide and a road marker got their signals crossed and Able, which was leading the battalion, went past its release point on a rain-soaked single-lane road.

When we attempted to turn around, we found that there was no place to do so. One vehicle, a prime mover, went down a lane between two farmhouses and, after a great bit of difficulty, did get turned around and came back on the road again to come face to face with Baker battery's leading prime mover. From this writer's viewpoint, the only part of the tangle visible was those two prime movers, parked nose to nose in the one-way road with several individuals running around them futilely. We asked one of our noncoms what went on, and he summed it up, rather nicely, we thought, thus: "Our position's up there," pointing in the direction from which we'd come, "but we can't get there because B and C batteries are in the way. B and C batteries' positions are down the other way, but they can't get there 'cause we're in the way. And even if they do get past this first piece, they can't get by the next one because it's wedged in between two houses on opposite sides of the road and can't go backward or forward. And besides, even if we could get all our vehicles past all B's and C's vehicles, we'd still have to get by headquarters, and they have three trucks stuck in the middle of the road. Otherwise everything's all right."

A more or less tear-jerking experience occurred at a position near Landau, Germany, in April after we had crossed the Danube River where you must have read the sign at the approach to the bridge, JUST ANOTHER DAMNED RIVER. After passing through a German airfield to a new position, we saw a wire-enclosed hut area, and, upon cautiously approaching the same, we were shocked at what we saw. Emaciated, starving, haggard, pale, and weak-looking individuals started pouring toward us with outstretched hands, crying, kissing, laughing, and talking several different languages simultaneously and confusing us no end. When the excitement had abated, a Belgian professor stepped forward speaking perfect English. It was then discovered that we were the first Americans they had seen for nine or ten years, and, what was even more awe inspiring, we had liberated about 200 Nazi political prisoners who were lucky to be still alive. We later found freshly dug graves that bore out the story of Nazi brutality related to us by the Belgian professor. There were many mixed sentiments that afternoon among the "liberators," but one fact that was certain was that all had the feeling of hate for a nation capable of perpetrating such heinous crimes.

(Submitted by Elia Lorenzo, one of three brothers who
served in the war. Michael was in the air force;
William was in the 35th Infantry Division;
Elia started in the coast artillery and
then went into the field artillery.)

Sherl Hasler

A Country Bumpkin Boy Going to War

When war was declared December 8, 1941, I was working at a huge naval ammunition depot in south-central Indiana. I kept working until I was drafted into the service. On my first day in the army, we stood in line for shots, then it was on to the clothes-issue line. My feet were measured for shoes while standing in a sand pile holding a three-gallon bucket of sand in each hand. Then my tracks were measured. On down the line, I was handed a pair of size 12 shoes. I told the supply sergeant that they were too big, that I wore only size 7. He said, "Move on; they will fit." Moving on down the line, the shirt I was handed looked as if it would go around the neck of an elephant. When I told the PFC that the shirt was too big, he replied, "It's your size, soldier. Move on." By then, I decided to keep quiet about the pants. When I dressed in my uniform, the knot in my necktie hung down on my chest about where the top of my shirt pocket should be, and my pants wrapped around me like an Indian blanket.

After five days at the induction center getting all the necessary records and papers processed and one 18-hour day doing KP duty, washing 13,000 food trays three times that day, I was put on a train and handed a copy of General Orders and was told to memorize them by the time we arrived at our destination—which could have been 100 miles or 5,000 miles. About 24 hours later we arrived at the army air base in Richmond, Virginia. I was assigned to the 924th Engineers. Vigorous training soon commenced, and we were hit a double whammy, training for combat and also construction. Training became so intense that it was almost unbearable. I remember one morning at reveille we were told to be at a certain time in uniform with a full field pack. (I think the weight of a full field pack was nearly 60 pounds). When we started this hike, we were followed by empty 6 x6 covered army trucks and a kitchen mess truck. When we completed our hike that evening, we had gone 35 miles. We had stopped for three ten-minute breaks and a lunch break from the mess truck. If I remember correctly, nine from Company A were stiff on their feet when we arrived at the barracks, and the rest fell by the wayside and were picked up by the 6x6 trucks. I remember that we were unable to go to the mess hall that evening and doctors came to the barracks to doctor our feet, as blisters had worn through blisters into the red meat.

In February 1943 we were made into the 862nd Engineer Aviation Battalion, and in May we loaded on an ex-luxury ocean liner, the *Mariposa*. With other units on the ship, the total was nearly 15,000 people, plus ammunition and other supplies in the hole. We were escorted by airplane out as far as their fuel would permit, then we were picked up by airplane from England, when they could reach us. Unlike many of the ships, the *Mariposa* had too much speed to go in a convoy. The trip was uneventful except for one round with a submarine and one with bedbugs.

We docked at Liverpool and loaded on a train the next day. We disembarked and marched toward the airfield; while we were enroute to the airfield, the train was bombed and strafed. Later we were told that the train crew was killed. I was sure that the Germans knew we were on that train. They were either behind schedule, or we were ahead of schedule.

I was at Raydon Air Base for almost 11 months. It was designed and built to be a heavy-bomber base, though to my knowledge, heavy bombers were never assigned to the base. Fighter groups operated from there during my tour. However, I have seen many heavy bombers come in and out and in all kinds of conditions—holes in fuselage that a jeep could drive through, no landing gears and bellies in, complete nose gone from cannon fire, three motors dead from four-motor planes, wounded and dead on board, and many others too numerous to mention.

The archives say that the 862nd were loaded on LSTs and LCTs (types of landing ships) at South Hampton and arrived at Omaha Beach, Normandy, France, on August 6, 1944. I know that was not the case with some of us. I was in Normandy much earlier than that, and I sailed on a big ship and was lowered over the side of the ship by cranes in a motorboat and landed on Utah Beach. Fighting was very heavy a few miles inland at St. Lô. From this time on until the war ended, we were never far behind the front lines, and at times were up with the front. At that time, the 862nd was very busy in maintenance and repair of seven or eight airstrips in the Normandy area.

We never seemed to be able to work many hours without interruption. I remember in October when everything was a sea of mud, a B-26 crash landed on the runway with two injured crewmen. The airplane was demolished but none of the crew was injured in the crash. Three or four days later, a P-51 attempted to land and it crashed. The pilot was injured. Also in October, a P-51 out of gas landed and a B-26 landed with only one functioning engine. A B-17 with three dead engines and without landing gears bellied in successfully, two more B-17s made emergency landings, and later the same day, a P-38 made a crash landing on the runway. About midnight that same day a German FW-190 tried to land, but heavy equipment was operating on the runway. He landed alongside the runway but everything was a sea of mud, so his plane overturned after hitting the mud and the pilot was killed instantly. Just in the last six years I have learned why that German tried to land on the air base. Here's a paragraph from a letter that I received from an 862nd veteran, John Tapia, in 1995.

> An incident occurred which no one else knows about. When I was manning a similar weapon somewhere, one of the companies was working on a temporary landing strip day and night. My instructions were that in the event that I detected the sound of a German plane, I was to fire a red flare, at which time all the lights would be turned off and people would take some security. I had to leave the machine-

gun emplacement to take care of nature's call when I heard the unmistakable sound of a German plane. I ran to the emplacement, grabbed the pistol and fired, only to discover to my discomfort that the pistol contained not a red flare, but a green one, which indicated "all clear." It appears that the German pilot thought that the field was still in German hands and tried to land a high-speed fighter aircraft on a temporary landing strip—the pierced-plank type bordered by jerry cans—and splattered himself and plane all over the field.

In spite of all the adverse problems of bombings, strafing, wrecked airplanes, rain making everything a sea of mud, ice, and snow, the air base was completed on or about the middle of November, just two weeks after the expected date. When the runway was completed, a few of us were still at the site. We looked up and the sky was full of C-47 cargo planes going into their landing pattern. I can still see our company commander standing near the end and in the center of the runway, waving them off. A B-17 had crashed at the end of the runway, and he did not want them to land. The lead planes pulled back up and got back in formation, and they began to land in reverse procedure. In confusion, two planes loaded mostly with jerry cans of gasoline crashed in midair. All crew members were burned to death from the explosion and fire. The runways were built with steel pierced planks and secured to the ground with steel pins along the edges. After the 158 planes landed, the sides of the runway had pulled the pins and were at least 10 feet in the air, with mud, ice, and snow several inches deep in the center of the runway. If I had not been so wet and cold, I probably would have sat down, cried, and thrown up.

Work continued on the air base, general maintenance, bomb repairs, taxiways, hard stands, unloading aprons, etc. The weather became colder and colder each day. Our Company A was housed in an old glass factory on the bank of the Meuse River, near Namur, Belgium. All the glass was broken out of the windows, with no heat and with no way to get warm day or night. Temperatures dipped as low as -13°F. and water would freeze in our canteens. On December 15th, I was so miserable from the lack of rest due to overwork and cold weather, I slipped away (the first time ever I was away from my unit without permission) to the home of a person I met a few days before that had a heated home and would spare me a very small drink. When I started back to the unit about midnight, searchlights came on from miles around and could put any object in a cross many thousand feet high. The sky was lit up like Times Square, and I could see paratroopers coming down like falling leaves after a big frost in southern Indiana. Needless to say I was somewhat nervous but did make my way back to the unit. The Battle of the Bulge was on. Just as I entered into the shell of the building, the company commander, Captain Kingery, had just finished having a roll call. He said to me, "You were AWOL. When the time is convenient you will do two weeks extra duty." Sure enough after the Battle of the Bulge was stopped, each night after work I washed equipment with a bucket of water and a rag for two weeks in deep snow. This irritated me to no end and still does. I felt for two and a half years I had given all I had and this is the thanks I get.

During the next 10 or 12 days unmerciful cold, heavy fog, and cloudy and snowy weather kept most of our heavy bombers grounded. In Company A we were busy preparing demolition at the air base, preparing to blow up useful facilities, equipment, fuel, storage tanks, etc. Enemy planes strafed and bombed the field daily, and many dogfights occurred in the area as well. Flying buzz bombs seemed to be perpetual. On Christmas Day, a bomb from a very speedy aircraft dropped in the center of the battalion motor pool, killing six and injuring nine enlisted men and one officer. Much equipment and gasoline was also destroyed.

During this time period, the 833rd Aviation Engineer Battalion (the unit we relieved at Raydon, England) was taking a pounding in the Colmar Pocket, probably more so than we were. On or about 27 December, the fog and skies began to clear. Then the heavy aircraft (the first that I think I saw were from Britain Lancasters) began dropping supplies for the 101st Airborne, who were encircled at Bastogne. From our vantage point, I could see these airdrops plainly. With the aircraft back out in force, combined with the First and Third Armies under Omar Bradley and George Patton, the encircled 101st Airborne was liberated and the Battle of the Ardennes, also known as the Battle of the Bulge, was halted.

When the war ended in Japan (August 14), it was a happy day for me. The order of discharge was set up on a point system. My number, 96 points, based mostly on longevity, came up on or about mid-November. We were loaded onto a small liberty ship, the *Costa Rica*.

About the first of December, we sailed into the Potomac River and docked. Organizations like the Red Cross and Salvation Army came aboard passing out candies, goodies, and fresh milk. I drank two quarts of milk—the first I had in two and a half years. It was the best I ever tasted. I was soon shipped to Camp Atterbury, Indiana, and about midnight on December 5, 1945, I was discharged. Going home, when I topped a hill overlooking Bloomfield, Indiana, and saw the few hundred lights, I thought that I was riding into heaven at the age of 25.

Donald Ford

I was a staff sergeant in the 3rd Battalion of the 255th Infantry Regiment of the 63rd Division. We had been in Europe only a few weeks and were in position near the Rhine Canal in the town of Petite Rederching and had set up our aide station in the barn/workshop of a carpenter. At that time, we noted that we had about a quart of gas in each of two gas cans. To get them filled, they had to be empty. If we then emptied the one into the other, we could get just one can filled. So the MAC officer, Lieutenant Cohan, elected to give what little gas was left in each can to the carpenter whose shop we were using as an aide station to use in his motorbike. Thus, we now had two empty gas cans we could get filled.

To our surprise, an hour later the carpenter invited the officers to his house for a lovely goose Christmas dinner and the rest of us to come that evening for Christmas Eve celebration. So all 12 of us squeezed into the living room next to a live tree with real burning candles, drank wine, and sang carols in English and Alsatian French. About 11 P.M. there was a knock on the door. When it was opened, we saw a young girl all dressed in white with miniature wings fastened to her back. She came to check the children on their catechism. If they passed, each would get an orange (obtained from the battalion mess sergeant). All went well, the tree didn't catch fire, and the next day, bright and sunny, we watched as hundreds of bombers flew overhead into Germany to the cheers of all the townsfolk, who had no pleasant memories of the German troops who had occupied the town only a few weeks before. This was a Christmas Eve that none of us had expected—no casualties and an unusual Christmas celebration.

Ed Dennis

Chaplain's Log

At Normandy after the landing ramp went down, one GI said, "I ran and then buried my face in the sand and rocks and started to pray. 'Our Father who art in Heaven . . . ' The words came out haltingly but somehow they came out, and I thought that as long as I could keep saying those words, I was still alive. I then took another deep breath, looked around and remembered out loud, 'The Lord is my Shepherd, I shall not want . . .' I stopped for a moment, popped my head up, looked around again, then started to repeat 'The Lord's Prayer' again as I jumped up and ran like hell up the beach toward the unknown."

At Arawe, on the island of New Britain, I watched as the bodies were unloaded from a truck and laid out on the wharf where Father O'Brien said a prayer and gave each GI the Last Rites of the church regardless of his religion or what was on his dog tag. He said, "It didn't matter to God what the GI's religion was; he has just given his life for his country."

Forest Robert Bradley

We landed on Sicily right behind the infantry, and there was very little cleanup done by support troops. Actually, we were on our own. Nothing was very safe. We stayed clear of any beaches because of the land mines. However, any place on the island was fair game for hiding munitions. We were warned repeatedly not to mess around with any munitions cache if we were to come into contact. As in any service group, we were made up of several companies, such as headquarters, quartermaster, signal.

Our quartermaster company was made up of all black troops. I never knew why, but that's the way it was. A couple of these soldiers apparently had a problem with some civilian girls—a real big problem, big enough to try to kill them. Somehow they acquired some Italian hand grenades, concussion grenades as opposed to the shrapnel type, and decided to settle the score, whatever that was. Being in the quartermasters, they had access to a truck, a 6x6 with closed cab. Not being very well educated in the pros and cons of Italian hand grenades, they made a very serious mistake, maybe in the timing, maybe the grenade was unstable, hell, maybe they forgot to roll the window down. They drove up in front of this house, pulled the pin, and joined their ancestors with the utmost expediency. There were pictures taken of this and distributed with more warnings not to mess with munitions.

It was in 1944 in Rome, Italy, when this next little incident came about. My company had a detachment of men stationed out on the coast on the Mediterranean side, and we would take their mail to them two or three times every week. Well, I volunteered to do this because I was bored and I liked to drive the captain's new jeep. I was on the way back from Lido de Roma, a big resort town before the war. I was tooling down the road and passed a civilian car with man and woman occupants, lovers, it was obvious. I didn't think too much about it until a few days later the captain called me in and started a line of questions. Were you driving on the Lido road at such and such a time? Yes (he already knew that). How fast were you going? I told him flat out—maybe 60 in a jeep. The speed limit for military vehicles was 45 mph. He asked if I remembered passing a civilian car. Yep, it was a Fiat with a man and a woman in it. He gave me a commanding officer look and asked if I was sure about that. I said that I was pretty sure it was a Fiat. No, no, the occupants I was sure of—a man and a woman, and she was all over him. I was shown a letter from the group CO. He was angry about my speeding and recommended punishment (I was a corporal at the time and soon to be a private, I was sure of that). Captain asked me if I had told anyone else about what I had seen; I told him no, it wasn't worth talking about. Of course I didn't know it was one of my superiors, who was supposedly a big family man. Well, corporal, consider yourself severely reprimanded and confined. I said yessir, confined to quarters? He said no, not exactly, just Italy, I guess. However, you are not to talk about any of this to anyone, and you know exactly what I mean—now get out of here.

The chaplain's assistant was a pretty nice guy, a loner for the most part, and religious, obviously, so he didn't make friends with ordinary riffraff that made up the rest of the troops. I really didn't know him very well, as he was attached to headquarters and spent most of his time working for the chaplain. One afternoon a bunch of us caught the pass truck to go into Rome, and he went with us. He said that he wanted to visit some of the churches, however, and this had no place on our agenda. I'll have to say that if you were alone in Rome at night, you had better have a pistol in your pocket or be a linebacker for the Packers. Most of us always had a buddy or a gun. I acquired a Beretta and carried it anytime in a strange city. The pass truck left at midnight and, if you weren't at the meeting place, tough. Time to leave and no chaplain assistant. We knew he wasn't passed out in a bar or some other such place, so we had the driver of the pass truck hold everything, and we all split up into groups and went on a search and rescue mission to meet again at the truck in two hours. Well, a couple guys found him on a side street. He had been mugged and rolled and worked over pretty good. Young thugs roamed the streets at night and jumped anyone who was fair game. The chaplain's assistant recovered but was pretty careful after that about where he went.

While on a courier mail run to Lido (we had a detachment there), I saw some rather hectic activity at a place where I had driven by several times. Not being in a hurry, I decided to stop and check out the situation. What looked like the entrance to a cave turned out to be just that [Fosse Ardeatine outside Rome]. There was an Italian *carabinieri* on duty at the entrance, and he saluted me, much to my astonishment. I was carrying a sidearm and had a case under my arm full of mail for Lido. He must have mistaken me for an MP or officer, because they were the only ones who carried pistols. After talking to him for a couple of minutes, I learned the Nazis had executed 365 Italian civilians (one for every day in the year) in retribution for resistance. Most Italians hated the Nazis, and Italians are passionate people, very emotional. The *carabinieri* invited me to go on in. After walking in (there were lights, strung along for workers), I came to a large chamber. Along the walls stacked five or six high were the bodies of the people who were executed. They were covered in lime and, of course, the odor of death was pretty overpowering. I almost lost it, and it took me a few minutes of intense concentration to gain self-control. Daylight and fresh air seemed to be a very good idea, so I left that chamber of horrors. After getting into the jeep, I sat for a few minutes trying to block out that scene, but it lives in my mind to this day. It has been said that at some time in a man's life there is an incident or occasion when he grows up. It was that day when I suddenly changed from a boy into a man.

Our major was the group adjutant. Rumor had it that he had been an aide to a congressman in civilian life and got a commission when the war started. Good one, too. Had anything happened to the colonel, the major would have been in command. Fortunately for us, the colonel stayed healthy. The major would have a real problem commanding a Girl Scout Brownie troop, let alone an air service group. The major was about 5'6" tall and probably 190 pounds. Most of that was in his rear end—no doubt from sitting during his career as an aide to the congressman. Well the major decided he would like to go up to the front with his camera and his reluctant driver to show the folks back home what a hero he was. Not knowing where it was safe to go, the driver ventured a bit too far, and suddenly they were the objects of a German sniper's attention. They had left the jeep so the major could take pictures and were pinned down hugging the ground trying to disappear. I'd bet a month's wages that when that sniper saw the major's big can sticking up, he had a grin on his face when he squeezed the trigger. Well, the major had something to brag about—a wound in the most prominent part of his anatomy. His driver, the real hero, was able to load him in the jeep and get him to an aid station. The major got the Purple Heart. Whenever he wore it, the troops would sort of grin and try to keep a straight face. We called it the "Order of the Purple Butt."

Perhaps of all of the places in Europe where I served, Linz, Austria was the worst! At first it was difficult to understand, but all the soldiers that I mentioned my feelings to were in accord. No civilian could look an American soldier in the eye. We were hated desperately and passionately because of a dirty secret that was about to surface. Right outside the city there was a concentration camp that was really a way station for thousands of Jews on their way to execution. A blanket of guilt hung over this place and rightly so. These people knew what was going on and never offered an objection or any help. I don't think it was out of fear; I do think they supported the Nazis one hundred percent. Hitler was an Austrian, and all of his warped thinking and insane attitude was condoned and even encouraged by Austria. Linz is geographically located in north central Austria, not too many miles from Nüremberg, location of the war trials after the war. There is no question in my mind that a great many of these war criminals were never brought to justice, and I feel sure that they escaped to Austria to hide. The entire story will never be told, and the shame of Linz, Austria, and Germany is something that these people will have to live with.

After 20 months in Italy, transferring to Austria was a bummer. The weather was nasty, and so were the people. Hershing had been a base for the Luftwaffe, and it was probably the most unattractive place I have ever seen. It was downright ugly. When the Germans vacated, they destroyed most of the plumbing and electrical services but didn't have time to do a real number on the telephone system, just the main terminal. The commanding officer was plenty eager to get the inner office network going, so that was the first objective. After a few days of long hours and a lot of dumb luck, we were able to oblige him. He was happy for that. Now we set out to get the other buildings tied in. This took much longer, but eventually everything was up and running.

May 8, 1945—V-E Day. A sense of urgency to really get this group ready for the Pacific! Admittedly, no one was too eager for this, but that was the way the ball was bouncing. Damn! Were we going to spend another year or two in a foreign place? First things first, though. There was a large concentration camp within a couple of miles of the base. This had been a "holding cell" for thousands of Jews who were executed in the gas chambers. No wonder this place was so depressing. Now it was occupied by German prisoners of war and guarded by American and English infantry troops—no sympathy extended. Some of the Germans were just dumb kids, some old men, but quite a few SS troopers—easy-to-distinguish arrogant bastards. When it came to really nasty dirty-work details, guess who got them? One American guard I remember in particular was a Jewish kid whose parents emigrated to America. He could speak German fluently and always got more work out of any detail that he was guarding than anyone else. One day I asked him why he was so successful and he told me, matter of factly, "The first thing I do when I take out a detail is to promise each of them that if they don't do exactly as I say, I'll kill him." He meant it, and I knew it. The Germans did too.

William Lang Campbell

Point Man on My First Combat Patrol

In World War II, I was a combat infantryman in B Company of the 38th Armored Infantry Battalion of the 7th Armored Division. I was from Baltimore, as were my first sergeant, Lucas, and my company commander, Captain Meade. We all three survived the war, which is normal for first sergeants but not for junior officers. Although Captain Meade had a bullet or shrapnel nick in his combat jacket, I believe he was never wounded and that, too, is unusual for a junior officer who is so exposed. And Captain Meade was exposed. He was always in the thick of the action and a great leader. Most of the time we didn't have any lieutenants because they were quick casualties and in such short supply that they were not quickly replaced. My platoon sergeant, "Porky," was also the platoon leader because we didn't have a lieutenant.

I was "gung-ho" until my first combat patrol. The old-timers must have noticed my "gung-ho" attitude because they suckered me into volunteering to be point man on a combat patrol. We were at the Ruhr area at the Belgian/German border. It was winter and snow was knee-deep. Our patrol exited American lines at the edge of a wooded area leading to an open field about the size of a football field. In the middle of the field was a small stream so narrow you could jump over it in combat boots and loaded down. On the far side of the field was a high hill in heavy woods, and we could see some fortified foxholes, but we didn't know if there were any German soldiers there.

As the point man, I was the most vulnerable and most likely the first one to be shot so I was uneasy. I also feared stepping on a "*schu*" mine. The men that followed me walked in my tracks to reduce their chances of stepping on a mine. The rest of the patrol waited at the edge of the field in the woods until I had jumped the stream and safely arrived on the far side. I was terrified with each step waiting for a bullet to slam into me or to step on a mine.

We didn't find any German soldiers on the hill. They must have retreated early when they heard our armored vehicles from a distance. I was sure glad to get back into our lines in one piece and never volunteered for another combat patrol.

Steve A. Kallas

Dog Face

This is a story of my adventures while in the U. S. Army Infantry as Private Steve A. Kallas, serial number 35053700.

There have been many parts, events, and days not included. Actual dates for many events are impossible to retrieve, and the same is true as to the exact spot where events happened. We were not informed of much concerning our lives, that is why it is called infantry—infant. "Dog face" describes the infantryman.

My thoughts of why and how it happened still has me shaking my head today. I was extremely lucky. In 1943, the war was starting to need men at an accelerating rate, and the draft caught up with my number. I reported for induction on March 13, 1943. When it was time to board the train for Camp Perry, Ohio, I was not on the roster. How about that? I had already said my good-bye to my parents, and I could not go through that again. Since I was at the train station, they said you might as well get on board and come along.

I trained in several camps and was given the usual immunization shots. I was also given IQ tests and tests to see what skills I might possess to be most valuable as a soldier. Physically, I was in pretty good shape. The years of the 1930s were hard years economically for us as a family and as a nation. Walking was the primary mode of transportation in those days; consequently, marching in the army was not a hardship. I was sent to train with a Tank Destroyer Battalion at Fort Hood, Texas. From there, I was sent to Louisiana State University to study.

The ASTP, Army Specialized Training Program, was designed to help fill the colleges of the country with students. Regular enrollment in these schools was being drained by the military. The reason we were being sent to school, according to some of the professors, was because the country could not afford to lose all of the brains in the war. Our schooling was a rigorous accelerated five-year engineering study to be completed as soon as possible. All of the conventional subjects were given in addition to military training and physical exercise. My most difficult subject was English. I disliked it even more when the pompous Harvard-trained English professor would hold me up to ridicule in front of the class.

The school held dances for us on Saturday nights and many of the local young ladies were in attendance. One of the young ladies I danced with happened to ask how I liked the math professor. I told her he sort of limped around, talked out the side of his mouth, and was hard to understand. The following Monday I found out who her father was—the math professor, and he let me know it in no uncertain terms. We all studied very diligently and did not want to have any failing subjects. The regular army was the alternative should we fail. We did not have long to worry about what the army had in store for all of us; we were to be transferred to the infantry. The army needed soldiers for the invasion of Europe. Prior to leaving LSU, we were given one more test to determine our qualifications for medical school. Not many passed the test—hello the 99th Infantry Division, Camp Maxey, Texas.

I was in the 2nd Platoon of E Company 394th Regiment. Our training was intensified, and skills for survival were honed to include any and all weapons. A contest was held for the most accurate and highest score for shooting the BAR, Browning Automatic Rifle. It can fire 750 rounds per minute, but not accurately in automatic fire. The shooter must bump the trigger to get off a burst of three shots to achieve any accuracy. We fired the BAR in all positions—prone, sitting, kneeling, and standing. The prize was a three-day pass to Dallas, Texas. I won the prize, 236 out of 250 possible hits, and got a pass to Dallas, first time away from home, with little money and not much to do in Dallas without money. I forgot the other prize when I returned; it was to carry the BAR. Each platoon had three BAR men, and the company had four platoons, for a total of twelve BAR men in the company. The BAR weighs 21 pounds with bipod, each 20-round clip weighs one and a half pounds, and the ammo belt carries 12 clips. The total weight on your hips includes an entrenching tool, canteen, first aid kit, raincoat, and rations. Your ass is dragging and on top of that, there are times that the need to run was important for survival.

Our schedule for training accelerated, and after 18 weeks we were declared fit to go and fight the enemy. Later replacements received only 11 weeks of infantry training, far too little to be able to survive.

The trip overseas was on an English Merchant Marine ship. Our sleeping quarters were packed, and we slept in hammocks three high. The food was served at the lowest point of the ship, and the odors made many men sick. We were allowed on deck during the day and not allowed out at night. We were traveling in convoy to England. For me, the eleven-day Atlantic crossing was not too bad, but some of the guys were seasick the entire time. I enjoyed the rough weather and bouncing around of the ship. I made the acquaintance of one of the ship's Greek crew. After that, I ate with the crew and enjoyed better food than what was being served to the division.

In addition to our travels, we had free food and all the excitement we could handle. We were paid as privates—$21 per month. A private first class like myself received $65 per month for overseas and combat pay. We also were allowed to buy $10,000 worth of life insurance. The pay scale increased in relation to your rank.

The division spent a short time in England, and we did not get to enjoy the countryside. We embarked for France in LSTs to Le Havre and then to Aubel, Belgium. The ride was in open, uncovered 6x6 trucks. In early November 1944, the 99th was strung along a line of defense, approximately 21 miles. Facing us was the German Siegfried fortification line, a series of concrete reinforced bunkers and concrete tank traps. The line extended parallel to the French fortifications of the Maginot Line. The German troops in their concrete bunkers could take direct shell hits and not be fazed. Our positions were located in the Ardennes forest and opposite the Siegfried line bunkers. Our line consisted of foxholes, which we had dug, and they prepared us for what was thought to be a winter stalemate. We built some log cabins for drying our clothing, but they were mainly used as smoking and gambling centers. I did not want any part of it—too many men all in one spot and highly vulnerable to attack.

Our commanders did not think the Germans would launch an offensive through this area, this in spite of the fact that the Germans had launched an attack through the same area in 1941. Why would they want to do it again? The Germans had green troops facing them, and the American line was very thin with not much depth for resistance. Intelligence reports and briefings of serious movements and troop buildup in the German sector did not convince the American generals of trouble ahead. They all opted for vacations at this point; one wonders what was on their minds. Eisenhower, Bradley, and many other top-ranking generals did not believe the many ominous reports, and they, too, were on low alert.

The remaining days of November were spent improving foxholes and our fortifications. We had combat patrols to harass the Germans in their bunkers. Those were the order of the day. This was a diversion and training for the days to come. During one such combat patrol, led by the 2nd Platoon leader Lieutenant Buford Mabry, the patrol sustained one casualty. Mabry stepped on a land mine. It blew off his leg, sending it up a tree. He was evacuated to a hospital in England just before the Battle of the Bulge.

In early December, the weather was rain turning to snow. The German machine gunners in their bunkers started a continuous machine-gun fire aimed at us. This was to try and spook us, to keep our heads down, and to keep us from moving around. After a while, I started shooting back with my BAR. The shooting made some of our men jumpy enough to empty out the log cabin smokehouse. The combination of rain, snow, and firing of the BAR turned the BAR into a mass of rust. We did not have much protection from the weather. About that time, our chicken-shit colonel showed up to see what was going on when he saw my rusty BAR. He called Captain Patterson and read him the riot act and told him to break me from private first class to private. The captain was more realistic but had to reduce my high rank from private first class to private.

The evening of December 16th, Sergeant Al Paccino and I were on outpost duty. This was a post in front of the company in a small patch of woods. In front of our outpost were the German bunkers about three hundred yards straight ahead. On the 17th of December at approximately 5 A.M., the German artillery barrage started shooting with every piece of artillery they had. The sky was lit up like daylight and the crashing and explosions were deafening. The barrage lasted about two hours, and then the silence. Paccino and I decided to get back to the company and started running from our observation post. We were running across a wide-open area heading to the larger patch of woods. We were spotted running but could not turn back. Paccino was ahead of me running as fast as his legs would go. The German gunners unloaded a barrage of 88s at us, and Paccino dove into a slit trench. I landed on top of him. We finally worked our way back to the company area to find our area was flattened. Trees were chopped to kindling-wood size, but we had only one casualty, in spite of the heavy artillery barrage. The only Indian in the company, whom we called Chief, was killed. He was in the same foxhole with a guy who went bonkers and was evacuated in shock.

Orders came down around 11 A.M. for the company to retreat to the rear and take only our weapons and ammo. I was ordered to stay back with my BAR, give the company a half-hour start, then fall back to catch the company. During that time, I waited and patrolled the area. I searched one of the abandoned foxholes and found half a dozen D-bars. D-bars were enriched, hard as rock chocolate bars, used for quick energy. I was sustained physically the next couple days eating just D-bars. In one corner of my area, there were the remains of a fence. I rested the BAR on the fence waiting for the German assault. As I waited, I could hear the oncoming soldiers shouting, getting louder, nearer, and the Germans urging their barking dogs on. I was no hero or fool to wait any longer, one BAR to hold off five oncoming divisions of Germans. After the war, I confronted the captain as to why I was left behind, but that is another story. This had to be the poorest excuse of a defense—one BAR, but I did give the company its half-hour head start.

While I was moving back, I saw many trucks and material left behind in haste to be captured by the Germans. In one of the overturned trucks, I found a half-empty bottle of Canadian Club whiskey. I took my first taste of whiskey at this time, took a healthy swig of it, and tossed it away. As I continued my retreat, which by now was way back from the front, I caught up with Colonel Wortheimer, the chicken-shit colonel who had reduced me to private. He was in shock and did not know what to do—smoking a cigarette, walking around in circles, and wanting to surrender to the Germans. Captain McGee said the hell we would. He took over the command, and we kept going. The only reason I got as close to the colonel as I did was the fact I had cut my overcoat to a shorter length, which made me look like an officer. At this time, I picked up water in my steel helmet to drink. Some idiot said to me, "The water is not very clean." I laughed at this and said, "For the spot we are in, does it matter?" After the war, the tough colonel was reduced in rank to lieutenant.

Retreat is pure hell. The Germans utilized captured equipment and guns to shoot at us to increase the terror and uncertainty of our position. Who was shooting our guns, was it friendly fire, what direction do you go, and what was the destination? All day long a heavy ground fog, light rain, and snow contributed to the gloominess and feeling of death at any minute. The fog was so thick that visibility was almost zero. Daylight was fading fast, snow was falling at an increasing rate, and the temperature was dropping to zero. When the word to fall back was given, all nonessentials were to be left behind, and we were to take only our weapon and ammo.

Our officers and the remaining company took off. When I finally caught up with them, it was dark and there was no moonlight to see with. It was so dark we had to line up in single file and hold on to the soldier's coat in front. Someone at the head of this ragtag bunch of men was leading us somewhere. We were skirting just inside some woods, and the German artillery was trying to hit us. The American artillery was trying to hit the Germans on the other side of us. Many men were hit, and orders were not to carry the wounded. The medics would assist or treat them. The medics did what they could and left the wounded behind.

The terrain was sloping and hilly, wet with snow and muddy. Our leather-soled boots were wet, and we were slipping with each step. Earlier in the day I was lucky enough to find a blanket, same place I found the booze. I had it slung around my neck for later use. The trail we were following was heading down the slope and into open ground. Near the bottom of the hill was a shallow stream that had been filling up and becoming deeper and wider. Some of the men found some solid ground to cross the stream. I decided to jump the stream and not wait to find a safer crossing. All of my gear and ammo added at least 50 pounds to my tired body, and I underestimated the width of the water. The jump was short, and I landed in the middle of the water with all my equipment. I climbed out on the other side, wetter than hell, cussing at my poor judgment and cold as never before. On the other side of the bank, I took off all my clothes, boots and all. I wrung out all of my clothes, poured all the water out of the boots, and put them all back on. December 18th, not a good day, cold as hell, and I had to keep on going to reach safety and some unknown destination.

As I passed some guy lying on the ground, I couldn't see who it was. I heard this voice, which sounded to be deep within the earth, asking for my prized blanket. I gave it to him and kept on going. Movies and stories of helping the wounded are short of reality. Some guys stayed with other wounded to be either shot at or picked up by the German medical teams or captured. It turned out to be the latter—captured—and they were lost as valuable fighting assets. We finally made it to a huge barn and got inside out of the weather for the rest of the night and slept on the floor shivering and shaking—not much sleep! We had reached the safety of the 2nd Infantry Division. In the morning, we were able to gather up stragglers of E Company and what was left of the battalion. Out of the 394th, all that remained was less than a company of men, fewer than 200 men. We formed up what was left of Company E and any other stragglers that showed up. An order was given to occupy an area and to dig in for counterattacks. Anyone who felt he could not continue was asked to step forward and to fall out. Only one man fell out; he was another lieutenant.

The Elsenborn hills we were to occupy were a former German artillery range. Every inch of area zeroed in; that was our objective of the day. We were still very cold; the temperature was –20°F; no food or water since three days previous. It was snowing heavily. I satisfied my water need by drinking from streams and filling my canteen from any stream.

We were issued quarter-pound sticks of dynamite to be able to dig foxholes in the frozen ground. We were also given empty sandbags to fill for protection against small-arms fire while digging the foxholes. I used mine to put my feet in and afford some additional warmth to my feet. Our foxholes were spread out in a fashion to afford the interlocking defense pattern and fields of fire. Two men occupied each foxhole. Our days and nights were spent digging in the rock-hard ground reaching a depth of approximately six feet. We covered the hole as best we could with one of our raincoats and kept the opening as small as possible, just to be able to crawl out to fire our weapons and keep as much snow off as possible.

We finally received some K-rations and melted snow for water. Bodily functions were outside in the snow. Every night I had to go on patrol in and behind the German lines. Our GI issue of gloves was a joke—leather palm and fabric on the other side and not much comfort as to warmth. While on patrol, I would wear only one glove, right hand bare on the trigger, all the while sweating bullets. Getting back to the unit was another problem; we had to watch for the trigger-happy reception from our own troops. Find your snow-covered foxhole, jump in—saved for another day.

Every morning German artillery would try and blast us out of our holes with a barrage of 88s. We would sit in the hole listening to the high-pitched scream of the shells thudding into the frozen ground until the shelling would finally let up. We would take turns getting rations and getting water from any unfrozen source. We were given three rations—one for breakfast, one for lunch, and one for supper. After a while it was a struggle to eat any of the rations, had no appetite. This particular day it was Al Paccino's turn to get water. This in broad daylight: Sneak down to the creek, fill the canteens with water, and return. He had about six canteens rattling and the German artillery unloaded on him, wounding him seriously. He received a "slow healer" and never came back to the unit.

During the day, our time was spent in the foxhole trying to keep warm. The temperature was getting colder, -50°F! This was the coldest winter in 50 years. It was continuing to snow, and ice crystals were forming on the walls of the foxhole. I would think to myself, this foxhole is what a burial hole looks like from the inside. We were able to get gasoline to heat our K-ration cocoa or coffee. Included in the supper ration was toilet paper. You cannot imagine the feeling of distress having to answer a call of nature. Climb out of the hole, move away from the hole, disrobe in hip-deep snow, and hope that the enemy does not shoot you. Your position is so vulnerable, and you do not linger.

The result of burning the gasoline or the ration packaging to heat things in our foxhole was that my face was covered with soot. Except for my teeth and eyes, I looked black. I would brush my teeth as the only health sanitation. Shaving was out of the question. My clothing consisted of wool underwear with trap door in the rear, wool shirt, pants, sweater, and the M-43 fabric-lined outer jacket, wool socks, and leather boots. That was it! No fancy insulated jackets to keep you warm. Any fur-type insulation in our jackets was considered an infection if we were shot in the body area. Warm boots and snow packs came later, and after all the guys in the rear echelon got theirs. The leather boots were useless as to warmth, useless running in snow or ice. I did not take off the boots except to put on clean socks. Our feet would swell to the point of not being able to put on our shoes. Always kept a spare pair of socks under my sweater. With any clean clothing I received, I would put the clean clothes next to my body and the other on top. I would wear only one pair of pants over the wool underwear to be able to run. I looked huge due to the clothing. We would try to stay awake and sleep in turns of one hour on to one off, keeping watch while in the foxhole.

The Christmas truce allowed us to get a hot meal, one person at a time going to the rear for a mess kit of food. No bunching up of men at the chow wagon and no second helpings of food. Hurry back to your foxhole and eat the frozen dinner. Funny, I remember saying to myself, "Oh, Lord, I don't mind if I die, just don't let me die hungry." We were always hungry! The 24-hour truce was over and now back to business.

The snow was now hip deep, and about 20 other men and I were ordered to assault the German positions ahead of us. This combat patrol consisted of one BAR, ammo bearer for the BAR, light machine gun, light mortar squad, radioman for communications with headquarters, and artillery. We were dressed in olive drab and stuck out in the snow, visible to a blind man, and ideal targets. The formation was one scout out front about a hundred yards, BAR next, and the ammo bearer alongside the BAR man, me. The rest of the patrol was spread out, bringing up the rear. The scout was Lafayette Wadsworth, and, as we were approaching the jumping-off point, he found some candy in an abandoned foxhole. We were always hungry, and he shared these bits of candy with me. His demeanor and spirit were low, we were tired and hungry, and both of us felt resigned to our fate and impending doom. He and I talked about it and the uselessness of war and of getting back home. I had the feeling that Wadsworth felt his time was up. All he would say as to our fate was in four-letter words.

As we advanced closer to the woods, the snow seemed to be deeper and harder to maneuver. They had us zeroed in, and their machine guns began firing at us. Wadsworth got up, signaled with his arm to move forward when he was nailed, and down he went. I was on a small ridge facing the woods when the bullets were zinging at me and at my ammo bearer, Mark Goeblick. I rolled off the ridge down into the gully to avoid being hit, to position myself for a better shot, and to spot the German gunners. The Germans not only had camouflage suits but also smokeless powder; the U.S. Army used black powder. Their guns were impossible for me to spot. Mark froze on the ridge, not wanting to roll down with me. He got hit four times and was later picked up by our medics and was evacuated. My gun jammed and filled with snow. The machine gun Bob Hefiler was using jammed. I ran back to Lieutenant Holder to report our lack of progress. Just about this time, he was calling for a barrage of our artillery to hit near Wadsworth. The patrol fell back to another position when the German artillery started to shell us. Some started shooting at anything that moved, not being aware of what and who was a target. I walked over to one of our men to see how bad he was hit. He was lying face down; I found him dead. I took his helmet and his rifle, stabbed the rifle into the ground, and placed his helmet on the stock of the gun. This signified man killed. In the bat of an eye, someone started shooting at me. I remember the outline of a person in a prone position aiming and firing. I saw this fiery, white-hot object coming at me like a stinging bee. I moved my head to one side and it about took off my left ear. We regrouped and moved back to the safety of our foxholes. There were no winners today. I did not go out this night on patrol. I'd had it!

January and February 1945 were somewhat dull—a continuation of patrols, trying to stay warm, and not much to eat. Our positions were still defensive and in the same foxhole. We were always on the alert and had reports of Germans dressed in American uniforms.

Tensions were high, and the expected thaw of the weather only made living in the foxhole even more miserable. During one such break in activity, some of the men were sent to Malmédey for temporary rest, recuperation, and cleanup. Unfortunately, the area around Malmédey was not secure, and SS troops captured the town and summarily executed our men. This now became an "eye for an eye," take no prisoners, and kill the SS men we find. At the time, I felt put out that I didn't go to the rest area in Malmédey; after that I realized my luck was still with me. In late February, a group of us were sent to Eupen, Belgium, to shower and clean ourselves for the first time since September of the previous year. When I started to take off my clothes, some of my men could not believe their eyes. All the clothes I wore made me look huge, and now I was revealed as a skinny, underfed person.

The thaw of March became a muddy mess, and the trucks and tanks were having a hard time getting anywhere. We were given the task of chopping down trees, cleaning the trunks of branches, and cutting the trees in eight-foot lengths for corduroy roads. This was physical exercise for us after so much time sitting in our foxholes. The mud and water got even worse as the weather warmed. We did not get any breaks or R&R; we were the forgotten ones of war, expendables.

The Battle of the Bulge was over, and the rush was on to push the Germans back and to kill as many as possible. The Battle of the Bulge was the largest land battle of the war; it included 400,000 to 600,000 men at one time in a small area of the Ardennes forest. If the German thrust had been successful in reaching a much-needed gasoline dump in the area we were defending, they could have reached the port of Antwerp, Belgium. Casualties due to the weather—frozen feet and legs and the inability to move in snow accounted for many of the American dead and wounded. This battle was a classic maneuver and not as unplanned as some would lead many to believe. It was a maneuver of attrition. The Germans lost many men and materials of war, causing them to weaken even more.

In March, the weather was turning warmer and the trees were starting to bud. More important, our air force were flying in even greater numbers to clobber the Germans. We were on the move! Every town we approached with caution; every house had to be searched. An indication of super trouble was when the people were leaving town to avoid the fighting. Every day was different, and all I knew was that we were heading toward the unknown.

At this time, I had become a squad leader and was glad to get rid of the BAR. Promotion was due to luck and attrition of other men. Normally a full squad consisted of 12 men; we never had a full squad and operated with six or so men. E Company consisted of approximately 80 men instead of 180 men. Men would come in as replacements in the morning and be gone by afternoon, either wounded or killed. The odds were getting shorter for me, but I never doubted the outcome or that I would live. Life became a blur; thinking was left to the grand strategy of war. We were walking and digging foxholes all the way across Germany. It never failed to happen as we would attack our objective. We would be in the most vulnerable position in the open and with no cover. They would let us have it, starting with machine-gun fire to pin us down, mortar rounds, and then artillery to make sure we were not welcome. You cannot stay there on the ground, and you must choose to move or die. At times we were lucky to be in contact with our artillery and order a strike to flatten the opposition. The artillery corps developed, we learned later, a method to demolish the enemy. It was TOT, Time on Target, and it allowed the long heavy gun, shorter guns, and then even shorter guns to fire in time sequence, landing on target about the same time. For us it was an ass saver, but for the Germans much to be feared. The Germans experienced many duds in the artillery shells. Saved me many times while waiting for the worst.

Once in town, it became a house-to-house to find, kill, or capture the soldiers. At each house, the BAR man and others on the outside watched for snipers, and I would crash the door. One fast kick and the door would fly open, then I would race inside searching the house from top to bottom. The basement of the house was left to the last area of search. We would call out in German to surrender and no shooting. If we received no response, we would lob two to four hand grenades in the basement and out the door. This was the method used to clean out the town. As night would fall, we would pick a house to stay in and order out any civilians in the house. We would not allow any civilians to stay with us. We would post guard outside, and the company would settle down at the edge of town. We would eat any and all food in the house and drink anything in the way of refreshments left in the basement, usually hard cider. We did not receive any regular rations from the army, only ammo and grenades. The beds in the house we stayed in usually allowed rank its privileges. We shared our bed with our boots, keeping them on, lying on our rifle, and all sleeping under feather beds—almost like home. We did not dare take off our boots while sleeping for fear of an enemy attack.

We were not allowed to keep diaries or have any knowledge as to our whereabouts, as if that would make any difference. At this time we were west of the Rhine River and heading north to the German rocket-launching site of Peenemünde. At night we could see the rockets taking off for their destination—destruction in England. It wasn't the Fourth of July. About the same time, the bridge at Remagen was being assaulted by a group of the 9th Infantry Division. All reinforcements were to respond immediately. We were the lucky ones chosen. We were put on 6x6 trucks and packed like sardines, with the truck lights blazing in the black of night with no concern for our safety. Sitting at the outside end of the truck I was on was our only medic, Moore. He had his foot on the rear gate and under the gate bail. A German plane appeared from nowhere to strafe the truck convoy. The bunched-up men in the truck bolted out the back end of the truck like a shot. Moore was unable to remove his foot in time to avoid all our frantic bodies, knocking him over and leaving him dangling, head down and helpless at the end of the truck. We jumped from the truck to the side of the road and waited for other planes to attack the convoy; none came. The only casualty besides Moore was the division chaplain; he was sitting in one of the truck cabs, between the driver and another soldier. Goes to show you the unfairness of war.

We arrived in the town of Remagen about midnight, and the bridge was straight ahead. Shell bursts and heavy shooting from the other side of the Rhine lit the bridge as if it were daylight. The Germans had female artillery spotters in our area to direct the artillery barrage on the bridge. The artillery was trying to knock down the bridge and to prevent our troops from crossing. The female artillery spotters were found in one of the nearby buildings by our detection team. The detection team shot the spotters. That did not stop the shelling from the other side. Our orders were to get across the bridge as well as we could and to move out. We moved and started crossing in single file, in spite of artillery barrage trying to knock down the bridge. The machine-gun fire from the other side was hindering our advance. The bridge had taken quite a beating, and there were many open spots to avoid. In front of me was the squad scout, Samualson. His reflexes and reaction to a sudden shell burst were to drop to the girder we were on and to hold on for dear life. The company was behind me on the bridge, and Samualson hanging on the girder was delaying progress. The longer we stayed on the bridge the more precarious our situation. I could not run over him for fear of falling into the water. The water below was about 80 feet deep and there was no way around Sam. I gave him the choice either to get up or I was going to kick his ass off the bridge and into the water. He got up, and we kept on going. Our progress was slow, and daylight was coming on fast about the time we reached the other side. There were body parts all over the place and carnage you can only imagine. We made firm ground and off the bridge. There to greet me was a tank, one of ours. A head popped out of the tank; it turned out to be one of the men I trained with in the tank-destroyer group. He gave me a horselaugh, me walking, him riding. The division fanned out over the high ground adjacent to the bridge to protect and secure the area from counterattack. The bridge sustained many assaults from German artillery, frogmen, and air attacks to blow up the bridge. It lasted long enough for many men and matériel to cross. It finally collapsed under constant bombardment. Floating pontoon bridges were built to accommodate the continuing advancing American army and matériel. Our division continued to do what it was supposed to do, keep moving east toward Munich and beyond. Enemy resistance was weakening, and we were capturing at times what seemed to be entire divisions of men. In the city of Iserlohn, we received the surrender of 250,000 men and officers. It was the feeling of the German prisoners that they wanted to turn around and fight the Russians.

My thoughts now were to be extra careful, watch out for the unexpected. In every town and from house to house we would flush out soldiers not quite ready to surrender. As always when we would stop for the night, our actions were to dig in and to remain on the alert. My BAR man Ratterie and I usually shared a foxhole slit trench. We would use tree branches and any other material to line the trench, use one of our raincoats on top of the litter, and then sleep under the other's raincoat. Nights were not as cold, but sleep was not restful as each hole in the area used the one-hour sleep to one hour on guard for protection. This particular morning I was unusually quiet, and Ratterie spoke up to say that he dreamed I was shot and to be extra careful today. I said I dreamed the same thing, and that is how we started that day; nothing more was said.

The company was spread out and heading through some hilly, sparse woods. Ratterie and I were on the right side of the main group and approaching a deep ravine. At the bottom of this ravine was a surprised German soldier carrying a box and his automatic burp gun slung on his shoulder. I could see his sweat and fear; Ratterie wanted to shoot him on the spot. I thought it was useless to kill any more, and Ratterie and I argued about it. I prevailed and convinced the soldier to come on up and surrender. He was carrying PX rations for his troops. We took and ate the rations and used the prisoner to carry our loads of ammo and mortar shells. When we searched a prisoner, we relieved him of any weapons and his wristwatch. The reason for taking a watch is that it can be used as a compass. This soldier pleaded to keep his since his mother gave it to him. I let him keep his watch, but he didn't get far when our other men took it.

Later in the day it started to rain, and we put on our raincoats. On my raincoat, I had sewn an additional length to the bottom of the coat for added protection. We were about five miles from the next town, and it was raining harder; the question that was asked by the captain was do we stay in the woods all night or go into town? I said let's go to town and was directed to lead the group.

With my squad, we had an artillery observer and the only pair of field glasses. Along the way to town, we came to a branch road at the bottom of a hill. On this joining road we spotted a column of 80 or so German soldiers who had not seen us. We spread out; I took a man and climbed the hill above the road and to the left of the oncoming men. I directed Ratterie with his BAR at the junction of the road to fire straight up the road. The remaining men were to go to the opposite side on a hill above the road and to the right of the oncoming men. This was a guarantee for disaster, perfect ambush. As we commenced fire, Jarabeck and I started back down from the hill we were on and on to the main road. Jarabeck was ahead of me on the footpath when someone was shooting at us. He hit the ground, and I hit the ground directly behind him in the gully. My head was near his feet. I looked around to see where the bullets were coming from and to shoot back. All the while machine-gun bullets were thumping between his feet and my head and tracing alongside my body and head. I got up and yelled at Jarabeck to get up and get the hell out of there. He responded he couldn't move; he was shot. Instinctively, I finally realized it was coming from the other side of the hill, our men, friendly fire. I yelled and screamed and cursed until the shooting was stopped. Captain Patterson was about as mad as I was at the idiots who were shooting at us. The German soldiers we hit were left lying on the road. We carried Jarabeck to the town to which the German column and we were heading. Jarabeck was spitting pieces of lung; his body was filled with lead. We did not have any medics with us, and no transport to any aid station. All we could do was to wrap and bandage the lung wound. We made him as comfortable as possible and got him into a house, where he bled to death. The only excuse for this was that our raincoats looked like German field dress. That was one dream that did not come true for me, the day that I was to be shot.

For us the war was still on, and we did not know from one day to the next what to expect other than trouble. As the weather got warmer, we would lie down after lunch and nap for a while. We huddled in small groups, much like animals, to sleep and would be awakened to continue. One time nobody awoke us. It took us days to find the main body of our company after we woke up on our own.

In town we settled in a house for the night and posted guards outside. Around midnight, I received a message to see the platoon lieutenant. He asked me to gather a couple big strong men and take blankets and find and bring back the wounded men that were left behind. Oh yes, we will also give you a medal, he said while lying on his behind—thanks a lot! The men, like the lieutenant who knew where to go, did not want to go. I gathered two other men, some blankets, and off we went down the dark cobblestone road. Each step sounded like a drumbeat. We stopped in front of two houses. At the same time, I heard the sound of a cocking machine gun off to the right side of the road. Not good! We then squatted down on the road to lower our silhouette and held counsel as to our next move. We couldn't see a thing and decided to turn back and wait till morning for rescue. The next morning the mortar squad continued to shell the town and burn houses. We continued to advance to about where we were the previous night. We went in to find one of our men. The house was on fire, and the smell of burning flesh was overwhelming. The man was shot through the chest, his flesh was burned off his bones, and his skull smashed with his own pickmatic stuck in his head; there was a grin of death. We took his dog tags and left him and the house to continue to burn. Whoever dragged him into the house knew where he was, as did the lieutenant. I often think back, what could I have done better to save this person?

The war was winding down, but our daily routine still did not let up, town to town and house to house and many miles walking in between. Our next river crossing was the Danube River in Austria. Germans occupied the east side of the river. Our division was to cross in rubber boats and assault Salzburg. The three regiments of the division, 393rd, 394th, and 395th, were to cross simultaneously and as quickly as possible. The 393rd and the 394th crossed without too many casualties; the 395th was cut to pieces. They were sitting ducks in water.

I remember looking at the water and thinking the Blue Danube was really blue. We reached Salzburg with very little enemy opposition. There were, however, a number of tanks battling, shooting and tracking up and down the road; not safe to be outside. My squad and I ducked into the first house we could get into. Inside the house we found some very elderly women, and kicking them out was not considered. They were very frightened. The squad was making themselves at home and sitting on a very nice couch to clean their rifles. I was standing in an inside doorway, leaning against the frame. One of the new men thought his gun was clear of ammo when he pulled the trigger. The shot missed my head and hit the door frame. The old ladies about had heart failure, and the idiot almost killed me due to his lack of training. My luck was still holding up.

The war ended for us with a military service to all of our fallen men, taps, and a hurrah that we were still alive. The division and all other units were demobilizing, and men with the most service were being shipped home. Others were being prepared for transfer to the Pacific combat zones. Our company was transferred to the 26th Regiment of the 1st Division. Our duty consisted of guarding SS prisoners and directing the cleanup of Munich. The SS were treated well considering how they treated American soldiers. The prisoners were given two meals per day: coffee and bread for breakfast, soup and bread for supper. When they formed up in the morning for work, the formation was as if going to a parade. When they returned at night, it was parade formation marching into the camp and singing some parade song. What we did not know was that next to the compound was our army ration dump, and the SS had dug a tunnel to reach food.

The city of Munich was a pile of rubble; very few buildings were left standing. It became the job of the SS to break rock and clean the debris they helped make. Each noncom and three men were given 50 SS to guard as a work detail. One time an SS trooper slipped away to visit someone. When we found out one man was missing, we said we were going to shoot the remaining men. When the man returned, the SS disciplined him. Three of his own men grabbed him and beat him to a pulp with their shovels, then threw him on the truck.

It was hard getting used to the quiet and not hearing bullets and bombs going off, but the night dreams continued loud and clear, with all the screaming and yelling you can imagine. It took a long time, 10 to 15 years, for me to overcome the war and its horror. Sometimes, to this day, I jump with an unusual sound or motion.

In conclusion, I can say I did not chicken out under any of the many trying times, nor was I a hero of any importance. I know how it feels to be hungry, thirsty, cold, scared, and end up as an honorable man. The true heroes are somewhere dead, unsung, and not much appreciated for all they did.

Seymour Karpen

I lived on three boxes of K-rations along with bread and tea for the four days that it took to cross the Mediterranean Sea from Naples to Marseilles, France. K-rations were three wax-covered boxes labeled Breakfast, Lunch, and Dinner. Inside was chewing gum, a chocolate bar, a tin can of something with a small can opener, toilet paper, and a foil packet of Nescafe. I don't recall what else may have been included. I do recall that a company called Patton Foods made it. That's right—owned by none other than General George S. Patton! We arrived at Marseilles during the last week of January. I had just turned 18 on January 22, 1944.

We were loaded into boxcars called 40-and-8s (40 men or 8 horses). We were on this train for four days, crawling through the French countryside toward the Alsace Lorraine region. It was cold and miserable. I recall that on one of the many stops that the train made, we got out into a large train terminal and discovered a huge barrel car of wine. We emptied out our five-gallon cans of water, broke out the spigot, and filled the water cans with this "green wine." Needless to say, one of the days is missing from my life as carload after carload of soldiers was cockeyed drunk. We didn't feel too cold or miserable during that time. We finally arrived at our destination, unloaded from the boxcars, and were loaded into army trucks. I do not remember the time of day other than it was dark outside. We had full backpacks, gas masks, M-1 rifles, etc.—a total weight of about 60 pounds. My weight at this time was a whopping 135 pounds! We traveled for hours on the back of this truck, cold and uncomfortable. We arrived at around 2 A.M. at the headquarters of the 70th Infantry Division to be greeted by the general. We got out of the trucks and formed a circle. The general entered into the center of this circle to give a speech. He walked up to one soldier and said, "Do you know why you are here?" He answered, quite flustered, "To save the world for democracy!" He asked others the same question and got similar answers also based on the propaganda and patriotic fervor we had been filled with. The general then told us that we had given the wrong answers. We were there for one purpose only. We were there to kill Germans—men, women, and children. We were to make no distinctions. He then turned away and went back into his headquarters.

I was assigned to F Company of the 274th Infantry Regiment of the 70th Infantry Division. We brought the total in that company to around 170 men. When the captain asked me about my training, I mentioned that I was a radio operator with training in Morse code. He said he would use me as his new radio operator, and the sergeant handed me my radio. This was a 40-pound metal box, which was designed to be strung across the back and shoulders. Since I already had a 60-pound pack on my back, I was to carry the radio in my hand by its straps. When rifle, ammo, and gas mask were included, I was carrying very close to my total weight! The sergeant said to "move out" and to be quiet about it, as we were about two miles from the front lines and sound travels for long distances in the woods. We were going to relieve a company on the front line. We started to walk through the woods in a straight line. It was dark and cold and snow was on the ground. I had no idea where I was. After about ten minutes, I found that I was becoming exhausted from all the weight I was carrying. At one point I slipped and couldn't find the strength to get up. I recall lying on my chest with my face in the snow, thinking that I couldn't go on. One of the soldiers came to me and asked what was wrong. I told him of my exhaustion. He suggested that I throw away the gas mask and some other items and rest awhile. Then, catch up. Off he went along with the rest of the company, leaving me lying in the snow. As I saw them disappear through the woods and I realized that I was all alone in a strange place not knowing where they were all going (there were no signposts), I somehow got up, took what I could carry, and hurried to catch up.

The company had stopped at the edge of the woods. In order to get into this little town we had to run across about a quarter mile of open field. We were told to run one at a time since the open field was under enemy observation. The moon had come out, which made everything and everyone stand out quite clearly. My turn came to run. I picked up my load and tried to run across the field, frightened that I would be shot at. My attempt at running didn't last for more than 20 yards when I was lucky to keep walking. Fear gives one more strength than you can imagine. I made the village, collapsed, and threw everything down and off my back. I then noticed the rest of the guys carried only a small backpack, rifle, and ammo. They advised me of what we needed to carry. I gave the guys things they were missing that I had with me. The captain told me to stay near him, as I was radioman, along with one other radioman in the company. I was told to sleep, as I had to stand guard duty in a couple of hours. This was day one on the front lines in a village whose name I can't recall. I do remember that after we stood guard duty we were able to keep warm in a house and could sleep in a bedroll on the floor. Occasional shots rang out and a few mortars landed nearby. No one was injured, and we held our position this way for a few days. The other soldiers filled me in on the terrible battle they had fought for the town of Wingen, Germany, where they had lost almost two thirds of the company. It was why they needed replacements so badly. It seemed that intelligence reports came in and said there were only about 75 tired soldiers in this town, mostly from countries the Germans had occupied and forced into service. A wide-open field had to be traversed before getting into the town itself. They supplied the company with about five tanks to give the infantry protection as they crossed this open field. Halfway across the field all hell broke loose. These weren't tired soldiers the company ran into. They turned out to be crack SS troops armed with automatic weapons (fondly called "burp guns"), sniper rifles, and antitank artillery. Within minutes, using sniper rifles, they had killed about 25 soldiers with shots through the head. One tank was disabled, so the rest turned back and left the company completely exposed with only narrow farming furrows to fall into. They stayed like this for four days until help came in and the SS troops left. Some U.S. soldiers were caught exposed, tried to surrender, and were executed where they stood! Because of this, it was weeks before my company took German prisoners. When I came into the company, they were down to 75 soldiers from the full complement of 175 after the battle of Wingen. More replacements came in, and the company was again almost up to full strength. We were getting ready to attack, and I was ill prepared for what was about to unfold.

I strapped the 40-pound radio on my back, took my M-1 rifle, two cans of rations and followed the captain outside. I was told to stay near him, but not too close. The other soldiers were already out on this dirt road, spaced about 15 feet apart, on both sides of the road. When they saw me come out with the radio and the captain, I was told to keep far away from everyone. I asked why and was told that the first one the enemy shoots at is the radioman and his radio in order to knock out communications. I was the third radioman in this company. The others had been wounded or killed. I got on the road at the proper distance from the others, and we started to walk. It was just about daybreak, the woods were full of foggy mist, and the only sound was that of walking feet on the dirt road. It was eerie and very quiet. After about a half-hour's walk, the captain signaled to the troops to make a 90-degree left turn into the woods and to spread apart. I was to stay near him, which meant 20 feet away unless he called me closer. We walked into the mist around trees and shrubs with the only sound being boots on leaves. Quickly, bullets whizzed by, mortars exploded, and everyone hit the ground. When I hit the ground, the radio slid up my back and knocked my helmet off. Amidst cries of pain and "Medic!" the captain waved me toward him. I got my helmet back on and crawled up to him. The noise was deafening. I gave him the radio transmitter after contacting headquarters, and he related what was going on. All this while, bullets were whining around me and shrapnel was pinging off the metal casing of the radio. I was in battle for the first time and I was damn scared. Someone was trying to kill me! Time now became irrelevant.

I stayed with the captain wherever he went. We moved through the woods, running from tree to tree with bullets flying all around me. I saw soldiers get wounded and one, who was three feet away from me, got shot through his forehead and died instantly. Later the captain and I started to walk through the village together on this one dirt road that ran through the center with houses and barns on both sides. Suddenly, I looked to my left and two German soldiers emerged from one of the houses with cloth caps on their heads (not helmets) and their hands on top of their heads. They were surrendering. I pointed my rifle at them and yelled something. The captain hadn't seen them and was still fumbling to get his .45-caliber automatic out of his holster when I ran over and pointed my rifle into one of their stomachs. I had captured my first prisoners. They were a German captain and his sergeant. If they had wanted to shoot us, we would both have been shot. The captain was furious because our sergeant said all the houses were cleared of Germans. The battle was over. Some Germans surrendered and others ran away. We didn't trust the civilians so we rounded them all up and put them in one of the big barns. The door was locked and guarded. We weren't concerned whether they had food, water, or toilet facilities. We kept them like this for about three days until we moved on. The reason for this was that in a prior battle, when we came into town, one of the soldiers saw a young boy of about 10 or 11 years. He felt sorry for him and decided to give him one of the small bars of chocolate that came with our K-rations. As he put down his rifle to reach into his pocket for the chocolate, this sweet little boy pulled out a Luger pistol and shot him in the stomach. We then trusted no one and did not become good Samaritans again.

We set up positions on the outskirts of town and warded off a counterattack. Night fell, and we rested in one of the houses in town. We relaxed somewhat and ate some cold supper from our C-rations. C-rations were cans that held about 14 ounces of food. At that time there were about three choices: franks and beans, corned beef hash, and I can't recall the other. We had a small can opener that we carried with us. When you opened the can there was about a half-inch layer of fat on top. It did wonders for the intestinal tract. The idea was that you could cut a small hole in the top of the can and heat it over a fire and have a hot meal. Unfortunately, you ate from these cans when they were cold. Diarrhea was a fairly common ailment.

Guard duty started up for everyone—two hours on and four hours off. This was a daily chore dependent on the amount of men in the company. It could and did go down to two on and two off. I learned that sleep was something denied to infantrymen. One learned to doze off even when walking.

The chronology of events that followed has slipped my mind. I will write of what I remember whether it is in the right order or not.

After a couple of days in Spicheren, we got orders to march on to the next town. We got pinned down alongside the road that we were walking on. Suddenly a U.S. Army jeep came down this road with flags and general stars on the front. The general had decided to visit the front at this time! We screamed at him to get out of there, but he decided to get out and talk to us. He wanted to know why we weren't advancing and hiding behind rocks, etc. The answer came quickly when mortar shells started pouring in on the road and his jeep. He quickly left—and left us to suffer the rest of the bombardment. His visit caused several casualties and death.

At one point, I recall that some of the Germans had surrendered and come over to our lines. The captain called headquarters and asked them to send someone to take them back for interrogation. They refused, and we could not afford to send any soldiers to march them back about four miles each way. He called in one of our soldiers who had a submachine gun and gave him orders to march these prisoners back to headquarters and to return within 15 minutes. He came back in five minutes and reported that the prisoners were taken care of. (So much for the Geneva Rules of War.) It took all night to gather the replacements that ran off. After a few more days, we were relieved and sent back to rest for a couple of days. We had been on the front line for almost two weeks straight. We were tired, hungry, dirty, and needed to regroup.

We walked back a few miles to another small village. There we got a hot meal and took off all our clothes to take a shower. A shower was accomplished by putting water in a 55-gallon drum, which was heated by a gasoline-powered immersion heater. A pipe was erected with a bucket on top with holes in the bottom. You stood under the bucket and water was placed in the bucket and poured down over you. You stepped out and soaped yourself up while the next guy got wet. Then you got back under, and the water washed off the soap. You were shivering because there was not enough heat in the tent. You got dusted with DDT and were issued clean clothes to put on. The only things you got back were your original shoes. We rested for a day, got some hot meals and supplies, and reorganized for battle.

At this point in my writing, certain events are coming to mind that should be told in order to give the reader an understanding of what I felt like as a soldier and the frame of mind that I developed in order to cope with what I was witnessing and participating in. The stress was enormous. The fear of getting killed or maimed was with me almost all the time. The food from C- or K-rations was sustaining but gave me the runs. There was always the fear of getting caught with your pants down when an attack or shelling occurred. I drank water from mud holes using chlorine tablets when no other source was available. The mind has to regard dead and mutilated bodies as just another part of the landscape. There were times when we laughed or made dumb comments at the grotesque dead shapes we were stepping over and around. One soldier in my company was called "ringfinger" because he would take the rings off the dead bodies and save them. If he couldn't pull them off easily he would cut them off. We would laugh watching him do this. Another form of our "entertainment" was lining up wounded German prisoners and making them do exercises such as pushups and jumping jacks. Not easy when one has bandaged arms, legs, and torsos. I do not relate any of these things to make you laugh or because I am proud of them. I was not ashamed either. This is what sometimes happens in war situations in one form or another.

I recall standing guard duty one night outside the house where we were taking turns trying to sleep. It was pitch black and I heard footsteps. I asked for the password; the person didn't know it and spoke English. We knew that at times German patrols had soldiers that could speak English and tried to infiltrate. I was ready to shoot this person when the captain opened the door and stopped me. He had recognized the voice of a lieutenant from another company. I came very close to killing a fellow soldier.

Once, when we had pulled back from the front for regrouping, we got a replacement that had been in most landings from Africa to Europe. He was very quiet and withdrawn. He had been through a lot for years and never got a scratch. One of our new replacement lieutenants ordered him to dig a slit trench. (This was an infantry toilet about three feet deep, six feet long, and one shovel-width wide). He coldly looked at the officer and told him that he was a fighting soldier and didn't waste his strength on that kind of work. The officer started yelling at him, threatening court-martial, etc., for not following orders. I watched him take his shovel and start to dig in the earth. I offered to help him, but he refused my help saying it was something he had to do. I walked away and after about two hours, I heard the sergeant yelling like crazy at this soldier. He had dug a hole about 2'x2'x6'. The sergeant told him this wasn't a slit trench. The soldier calmly agreed and said that this was a burial plot for the officer. He was almost finished, and he would kill and bury the officer in it. I know he meant it by the look in his eyes. The sergeant calmly put him in a jeep and sent him to the hospital. I was sent to find the officer and tell him to disappear for a while. He then realized that you don't give orders to combat soldiers in the same manner that you do when in training. When the battle starts, no one knows where the bullets are coming from or who fires them. Officers did not wear any insignia or bars on the front line. They also kept away from radio operators like me.

It must have been about 2 A.M. We were sitting in this house with our backs against the wall, resting and warming up. We started to clean the dirt and mud off our weapons, talking to get the stress and fear out of our systems, when one of the soldiers who had not been on patrol came into the room. He started to make wisecracks but none of us was in the mood to smile or laugh. He then made a remark about us looking like some dirty Jews and some other anti-Semitic statements. All of us got silent, and I looked up and told him that I was Jewish and didn't take kindly to his words. At the same time I let the bolt forward on my rifle, which put a round in the chamber, and I pointed it at him. I think I was tired and angry enough to actually pull the trigger and try to kill him. He saw the look in my eyes and became profoundly apologetic. The other guys cooled me off, and I told him to keep away from me. Frontline soldiers have to be very careful about making ethnic, racial, or religious slurs. You learn that we are all in this mess together, and the bigotry of peacetime can be an extremely dangerous practice in war.

We stayed in this village for a few days, sending out patrols every night. One night a patrol came back and was sitting cleaning their weapons when one soldier's muddy hands slipped on the bolt and it fired accidentally. We all got frightened but were glad he had the sense to point the barrel up and not toward anyone. Unfortunately, one of our soldiers was upstairs in the room above us. He was bending over a bed where he had spread a blanket and was leaning over to lie down, when this bullet went through the floor and penetrated his chest and heart, killing him instantly. We didn't know this had happened until the captain came storming in screaming at us. I remember him saying that this soldier was a married man about 32 years old with two children. He was keeping him off patrols because of this. Accidents like this happened from time to time.

A major battle was shaping up. We were told that we were preparing to break through the Siegfried Line that consisted of concrete pillboxes with walls so thick that artillery shells just bounced off, taking little chips of concrete. Inside the boxes were small cannons, machine guns, and burp guns manned by a few soldiers. In front of the pillboxes, stretching for a distance of about 100 yards, were tank traps, barbed wire, and mine fields with the infamous "*schu*" mines. These were little boxes buried just below the earth with just enough explosives in them to blow off a leg or an arm. They were designed to maim, not necessarily kill a soldier, if you stepped on one. Sometimes they were hooked together, so if one went off it would set off dozens more. There was very little cover before these pillboxes. Frontal assaults were suicidal and useless. We called in the engineers, who crawled on the ground at night, clearing the minefields up to the pillboxes and marking the way in. This took a couple of days as they could work only at night without moonlight. Finally, some soldier made it to the pillbox and threw grenades into the slits in the concrete that were used to fire their weapons. This was how we crossed the line and took over the pillbox. There was fierce fighting and lots of casualties. Our soldiers occupied other German defense positions, and we had to fight off counterattacks. A machine gunner from E Company on our right flank either mistook us for Germans or went berserk. He began firing at us and killed and wounded several of my company. Our efforts to contact his company were fruitless. He had us pinned inside the pillbox. Anyone that went out was fired at. We dragged in one of the wounded soldiers who had been badly wounded in the stomach area. He was screaming from pain, and we couldn't get a medic with morphine because no one could get near us. We couldn't give him any water with this type of wound, and he kept screaming for water and from pain. We had to listen to this for hours; it was so terrible that at times some of us wished he would die and shut up.

We were waiting for it to get dark when we finally got in touch with E Company. They also couldn't get near the machine gunner, for he was shooting at his own company! Both companies sent out patrols and had to kill him. Finally we were also able to send the wounded soldier back for medical help. Our orders were to hold at all costs. We had started out to battle with almost a full company of 175 soldiers. We were now down to 40, and we all felt that our time was coming soon if we didn't get help and relief. Whatever the reason, the Germans stopped counterattacking and pulled back.

Replacements arrived around dusk and their sergeant began yelling for them to line up. We didn't believe our ears! He thought he was back in the States, not on the front lines. Sound travels for great distances in the woods, and we knew we would be in trouble if he didn't shut up. We told him to quiet down, but his arrogance and ignorance wouldn't allow him to listen to a couple of lowly privates. He had his replacements lined up and was beginning to divide them into platoons when shells started dropping all over the place. I recall running for some cover and jumping into a tank trap that was a man-made gully about six feet deep, ten feet wide, and went for a long distance. It was made to either trap tanks or to slow them down while they built bridges to cross the opening. The shelling lasted a few minutes; when I climbed out of the hole, the soldiers were scattered all over the place. The replacements ran in all directions, and it took hours to round them up. I was very frightened. When I met my buddy, I suggested that we take off since it was so chaotic and disorganized that nobody would know what happened to us. We discussed it for a short while and decided that we would look for the others since it would be desertion, and we didn't know where we were or where to go. Within an hour we found the others along with the sergeant who now knew enough to organize his men quietly. We walked around the woods and came to an opening in the trees. We were on top of a hill, and as we looked down we saw the town of Saarbrücken, which was our next objective. It didn't look like it would be fun. (As it turned out, my company helped take Saarbrücken without much fighting as the Germans had vacated the city.)

My buddy and I decided we would dig a foxhole for the night. We picked a huge tree, about three feet in diameter, and started digging next to the trunk. We got down about 18 inches and decided that it was enough as we were tired and the roots were giving us some trouble. It would also bring us down below the level of the ground. We made it wide enough for the two of us. Since we were behind the lines in a rest area, a jeep came up and brought us sleeping bags. Night was now upon us. We got into the foxhole, took off our boots (something you do not do on the front lines, but we felt we were in a safe area), and slid into the bags for the night. I put my boots next to me in the foxhole. My buddy put his boots on the ground nearby and put his eyeglasses into a boot for safekeeping. We fell fast asleep. I got up to take a leak just as dawn was breaking. Since it was cold, I hurried back and got into the sleeping bag. I am not sure, but I may have been spotted by German artillery because shortly after I got into the bag, a mortar shell landed about ten feet from our hole. I believe the tree saved us from serious injuries. The shell blew a chunk out of the tree and blew my buddy's boots and glasses to kingdom come.

The Germans had zeroed in on us and were waiting for us to get up and about. Since we were behind the lines, a kitchen jeep arrived to give us a hot breakfast. Since my buddy couldn't walk without boots or see too well without his glasses, I brought back food for us. After handing him his mess kit, I sat on the edge of the hole eating. It was February 27, 1945.

Suddenly, I heard the whirring sound of incoming 88mm artillery shells and saw one explode somewhere off to my left. I was leaning forward to fall into our hole when a shell exploded in the trees above us (this one I did not hear coming). A piece of shrapnel struck me in the back and literally threw me into the hole. The shelling continued for some time. My buddy knew I was hit and was talking to me. He could do nothing until the shelling stopped. He then yelled for the medic, as I had difficulty in yelling because it hurt to take in large gulps of air. There were many cries for medic at this time. When the medic came, I was able to stand up after he put some sulphur powder and a bandage over my wound, but I couldn't straighten up or walk too fast. We were behind the lines so jeeps and ambulances could come up to us. This was a bit of luck. The ride back to the medical field hospital (a tent) was awful. I felt every bump and turn. Luckily my wound was not bleeding, just painful. I think I was glad to be wounded and alive. I would be getting away from the fighting for a while. When I got to the field hospital, a doctor examined the wound, changed the bandage, and gave me a shot of morphine. He put a tag on my jacket stating what my wound was, plus other information. I felt pretty doped up by the time an ambulance came to take me back to the hospital that I believe was situated in the city of Nancy. It was the 5th General Hospital and I believe staffed by the Harvard Medical School. The ride to the hospital was fairly long but a blur due to the morphine. I recall there were four soldiers in stretchers on each side, one above the other, and three or four of us sitting wherever we could find space. We arrived at the hospital, and I recall the place was filled with wounded, stretchers all over the floor, and soldiers sitting on benches along the wall. I was placed on a bench near the wall. I was tired, groggy, and sleepy. I faded in and out of reality only half conscious of what was around me. I was glad there was no shelling. I was placed on a stretcher to wait my turn on the operating table. They took off my field jacket, and I remember telling them to give it back to me as this jacket had kept me warm. It was full of dirt and mud and had a hole from the wound, but it was a precious possession. I never did get it back, but I did get another shot of morphine, as there were so many wounded being operated on. This must have put me to sleep for hours. I recall waking up on the stretcher on the floor and looking up at an operating table about ten feet away. There were three or four people around this table and they were all covered with bloodstains. They looked more like butchers than surgeons. On the table was an anesthetized soldier who had a leg wound that started to bleed. I recall one of the people elevating the bleeding leg with one hand while eating a sandwich with the other. When the bleeding stopped, they moved him away and put me on the table. They put a needle in my arm and told me to start counting backwards from 100. I think I may have reached 95, but that is all I remember. They were giving me Pentothal.

I recall a funny incident of how one of the guys got wounded. He had been wounded across his buttocks, which is one of the slowest wounds to heal, and had to lie on his stomach for a long time. He had figured out that he did not want to be a front-line infantryman, so he volunteered to go out after the battles and pick up the dead bodies. He figured if the shooting was over his chance of survival was much better. One day, as he was bending over a dead body, a sniper decided he was a good target and shot him right across his ass. He kept complaining that this shouldn't have happened because he wasn't even carrying a gun. We told him to write a complaint to the German High Command. He couldn't understand why all the guys thought his story was funny.

One evening we heard the news that President Franklin D. Roosevelt had passed away. Although he was a great President, I did not feel any remorse. He was old and lived a full life. I knew too many young soldiers who had died before they had reached their twentieth birthday. My sadness was used up on them.

We were finally going back to our front-line units when the great news came that the war in Europe had ended. I can't describe the relief and elation we all felt. The general threw a party with food and liquor and music in celebration of our victory. There were five musicians in the group and my ears picked up at what sounded like klezmer (Jewish music) phrases. I walked over to the band during a break and spoke a few words of Yiddish to one of them. Three of the five turned out to be Jews, and I had them playing Yiddish music on and off all afternoon. It was great, and when my buddies asked what kind of music that was, I explained it away by saying it was European folk music.

We were a group of about 40 soldiers, and they didn't know what to do with us. There was no use sending us back to our outfits as the war was over and they would soon be dismantling the divisions. Since we all had combat experience, they decided to make us MPs (military policemen). They disregarded the fact that half of our group had severe mental problems, were unstable, and were not to be given any weapons. We were immediately issued .45-caliber pistols and other MP paraphernalia. We were shipped out on trucks and sent to Frankfurt, Germany. I remember traveling through Mannheim and being amazed at the utter destruction. There wasn't a building that didn't have part or all of its walls bombed away. We went through Ludwigshafen and saw the same except for the Ford Motor Company plant, which had only a few windows blown out. This was selective bombing at its worst because this plant had been making war materials for the Germans. I remember this with some bitterness because afterwards, when our government was asked why they didn't bomb the concentration camps or the railroad tracks leading into them, they answered that they couldn't waste the bombs. They could have used the ones they saved from bombing the Ford plant. Anyway, we arrived in Frankfurt and took over some housing to sleep in. We didn't have an officer in charge, only a sergeant. We had to spray ourselves and the whole house and beds with DDT as the place was "crawling." We were among the first occupation forces and were supposed to keep the soldiers from talking to or having anything to do with the German civilians. We walked around town and kept telling the other soldiers that they had to comply or be subject to court-martial. As I said before, we had quite a few in our group who had severe mental problems. They felt the rules didn't apply to them, as they kept bringing German women into our housing in spite of the rest of our objections. It didn't take too long for many to come down with gonorrhea. The drinking and drunkenness was rampant. A lieutenant was finally brought in to control our group. The trouble was he was fresh out of West Point and had no idea how to handle this group of combat veterans. One morning he decided to line us up and have a gun inspection like we had in basic training. None of us took kindly to this as we felt we had gone beyond this kind of training. Inspection required each soldier to have his .45-caliber pistol in one hand with the barrel pulled back for inspection and the clip of bullets in the other. When the lieutenant finished looking into the barrel for cleanliness, we were supposed to release the barrel, pull the trigger, and insert the clip of ammunition. What one soldier did was put the clip in, released the barrel (thereby loading a round into the chamber), and then pulled the trigger. Of course, the gun fired about 12 inches from the lieutenant's head, and all of us hit the ground as a reflex from combat conditions. The lieutenant was furious with the soldier, who apologized, saying he hadn't done inspection for so long he had forgotten how to do it. The lieutenant continued on with inspection and sure enough the same thing happened again. Only this time it went off closer to his head. He then dismissed the company, and the inspection was over. We never had another one or anything like it. I found out that it all was done on purpose. About two weeks later, we got another lieutenant who had been in combat and knew the score and how to deal with us. We became more organized and quieted down somewhat. Guard duty consisted of patrolling the streets and watching that soldiers didn't fraternize with the Germans. We stood guard at some of the displaced persons camps. This was where they put some of the survivors of the concentration camps after they were nursed back to health until they could figure out where they should be sent and to whom. It was decided that we should be sent to Berlin. This was about one month after the war in Europe had ended.

One of the first things we were ordered to do after arriving in Berlin was to clean out an area for the American troops to live in. It was a fairly large area of two-storied private houses. Berlin had been heavily bombed, but this residential area had been left pretty much alone. We were told that if any people were in the houses they had to leave immediately; no exceptions were to be made as they had been given three weeks to vacate their premises. If force was needed, we could use it. We went house to house in groups of three to four soldiers relishing the opportunity to push the Germans around. Some Germans tried to be "cute" by faking illness and lying in bed. If they didn't get up to walk on our commands, we would pick them up and throw them out, in some cases, literally down the stairs. After we did a few of these, the rest flew out of the houses. What had taken others three weeks, we accomplished in a few hours. The area was secured for the Americans to move in. It was fenced in, and one of our posts was to stand guard at the gates and throughout the compound. The area also included a section for the Women's Army Corps. We also would go into the streets and round up the German civilians, herd them into a nearby movie house, and force them to see the captured German films that had been taken at the concentration camps—the ones that showed the bulldozers push dead emaciated bodies into mass graves and the conditions and ovens in the camps that murdered six million Jews and six million others—truly, the most horrible films ever made considering that they were real. Most of the Germans would come out speechless. Some said they didn't believe them; it was American propaganda. There was no arguing. My dislike for the Germans intensified and stayed with me throughout the occupation.

The American occupation of Germany ended. The Americans, British, French, and Russians divided Berlin into four zones of occupation. When we arrived in Berlin all soldiers traveled freely from one zone to the next. We spent evenings drinking with the Russians, toasting each other with one word, "*Tovarish.*" We were the winners, and we were alive! Black-market activities were rampant. The Russians were buying everything they could get at any price. It seems that they had not been paid wages for years. (Why pay a soldier who might be killed?) They now got paid in occupation marks that they could not redeem back in Russia. They were buying things like Mickey Mouse watches, which the Americans bought for $2, while they paid $600! We would see Russians with six watches on each arm. Everything was for sale, and the greatest medium of exchange was cigarettes. Diamonds, ivory, art of all kinds, Leica cameras, gold, etc., were purchased with a few cartons of cigarettes. The Germans were starving and would trade everything for food. Soldiers and civilians would go over to Potsdamer Platz and do business together. I had heard that the first month's paycheck for Americans was about one million dollars, and they had sent home about four million dollars! I had arrived in Berlin too late to reap these benefits. We could send home only our paycheck, which was verified by our payroll card. Besides, I disliked the Germans so much that I preferred seeing them starve rather than sell them food or the means to buy it.

President Truman came to Berlin to raise the American flag over Luftwaffe headquarters. This was the symbolic end of World War II and our victory. We were given orders, being part of the forces that would protect the president, generals, and other bigwigs who would be there. Luftwaffe headquarters consisted of long buildings on three sides of a rectangular area with the flagpole in front of the center building. Our company was given the job of clearing out these buildings and making sure that no one entered. If we saw a head stick out a window, we were to shoot first and ask questions later. When the president's security tried to enter the building to check it out, they were immediately surrounded and almost shot. They left, secure in the knowledge that we were doing our job. My post was on the roof overlooking the flagpole and witness to the whole ceremony. It was very thrilling to be a part of this. Berlin was filled with generals and other big shots who came to witness this occasion. It then became our job to stand guard at the houses they occupied. Among these were General Eisenhower and General Lucius Clay. I recall standing guard at General Eisenhower's home on the midnight shift. He would come out to walk his dog and stop to chat with us at the gate. He told us we had to salute him only when he was with other important people! One night one of our company was standing guard at his house when he noticed a light on in the basement. When our man looked in, he saw a German woman there. He immediately started shooting at her, which aroused the whole house and a small army. It turned out she was doing laundry for the general. Our reputation was growing in leaps and bounds! One night General Eisenhower and Russian General Khruschev came home from some kind of celebration with more than a few drinks under their belts. As Khruschev was leaving, Eisenhower warned him to be careful because the guards at the gate might shoot his ass off. He stayed the night in Eisenhower's house.

One of our chores at Eisenhower's house was to raise the American flag before the beginning of the 6 A.M. shift. That chore was given to two of our company standing guard that night. I remember them as Big Chief and Little Chief. They were Native Americans who really loved their wine and were among the bunch that should not have been given a gun. That night they decided to spend their shift drinking wine, and they were really drunk. When daybreak started they remembered to raise the flag. The trouble was they raised it upside down and never bothered to look up. This was a signal of distress. They were replaced by the next shift that also didn't look at the flag. Tanks, armored cars, hundreds of troops all converged on the house. The two guys on guard duty didn't know what was happening, but they bore the brunt of the abuse that came pouring in on them. We all had a good laugh at this incident, but the rest of the army did not see the humor.

Rosh Hashanah was coming, and the army posted orders that any Jewish soldiers who wished to go to services would be excused from their regular duties for the day. I hadn't been to services for over two years, and, besides, I would get out of guard duty. When I told my sergeant that I was going to services he was furious. He was short-handed and the other Jewish soldier in the company wasn't going to go, so why was I? I told him that I was not going to stand guard that day but would be glad to stand guard on Christmas to make up for it. He didn't like it but couldn't do anything about it. A Reform rabbi chaplain conducted the service. There were about 30 to 40 soldiers there and, surprisingly, there were some German-Jewish civilians. After services, one of the women came to me and, speaking to me in Yiddish, asked if I came from New York City. I said yes and she asked if I would write home and ask my parents if they would try to contact her sister who lived in Brooklyn. She had not been in touch with her for several years and wanted her to know that she was alive. I wrote home as she asked and forgot all about it. When I got home after being discharged from the service, my mother told me what a good deed I had done. They had taken the Brooklyn telephone directory and called every one who had that last name until, unbelievably, they found the sister of this person! The tears of gratitude were tremendous, and these people made a special trip from Brooklyn to the Bronx to personally thank my parents for their efforts. I don't know if the sisters ever got together, but I hope they did.

Soldiers were being sent home according to a point system based on length of time in service, medals, etc. Musicians in the 298th AGF (Army Ground Forces) band were being sent home, and they needed musicians. Luckily, I had listed on my record that I played clarinet and saxophone. They asked if I would like to transfer to the army band. I was out of being an MP within 24 hours and, with a great sense of relief, went to where the band was housed and got a clarinet. I proceeded to practice for 16 hours a day since I hadn't played in two years and was very rusty. The guys thought I was nuts. We ended up playing every night at a place called Club 48. This was dance music for the enlisted men and women. I remember liquor was served for ten cents a drink. Each soldier was issued a case of beer per week and a fifth of whiskey every month if they wanted it. There was so much drinking at that time that I can't remember what went on between Christmas 1945 and New Year's of 1946. I do recall a huge New Year's party that we played at that was arranged by the allied powers. Our band was the entertainment for the United States. I recall drinking with the Irish Guard soldiers, which was Great Britain's entertainment. They all wore kilts and paraded with drums and bagpipes. I found out what they wore under their kilts—nothing! We ate caviar, lobster, all kinds of sausages from each country, beautiful cakes, and foods that I have no idea what they were. We drank the finest cognac, vodkas, and wines from each country. It was an unbelievable shindig with more important people than I could name.

O. B. Hill

My Normandy Invasion Experiences

Prior to the jump into Normandy, my battalion was placed temporarily at Folkingham airstrip in the Midlands of England. As I remember, we were there about five days preparing for the invasion. Prior to that time, we did not know when or where we would be involved with any combat action.

At Folkingham, we studied sand tables that had been prepared by our intelligence crew, known as S-2 people. They had constructed the sand table to show where we were supposed to land. Buildings, fencerows, hedgerows, rivers, etc., were on the table to give us a good view of the area. We spent our time studying that scene, packing equipment bundles, cleaning our rifles, playing cards, and shooting dice in the hangar building, attending movies, attending church services, and writing letters. The area was secured, and no one was permitted to leave for any purpose. We were fully ready to take off from the airstrip on June 4th, but the weather forced a delay of one day. With blackened faces, we loaded into the planes the evening of June 5th.

Every man in every plane was fully loaded with everything that he thought he might need. We were taking rations and ammunition enough for three days. There was ample ammunition, and many of us took several bandoliers over the allotted amount. This proved to be a worthwhile move, because most of us landed far from the scheduled drop zone, and we were behind the German lines for days before getting back to our unit. We also carried land mines, gammon grenades, hand grenades, maps, radios, smoke grenades, phosphorous grenades, and more.

At that time, I was the 1st Battalion Message Center Chief with the rank of buck sergeant. Normally, I would have jumped behind my company commander, Captain Gerard A. Ruddy. My platoon leader, First Lieutenant Charles J. McElligott, and the company commander were very good friends, and Mac wanted to jump behind Ruddy. As a result, I traded spots in the plane with him, and I was then the last man to leave our plane. This proved to be a lucky break for me because Captain Ruddy was killed very soon after landing. McElligott was shot through the stomach and captured, and most of the rest of those in the front of the plane were either killed or captured. McElligott is still around, and I thank him frequently for asking me to trade spots with him.

We left Folkingham, as I remember, at about 9:30 P.M. That is a pure guess because, to be honest, I was not wondering about the time as we loaded the plane and took off. We flew around for quite a long time getting all of the planes in formation for the flight across the channel. We could see planes in all directions around us during the formation period and, finally, we were on our way to Normandy.

Our formation crossed the Guernsey Islands and started to see flak around us. As we hit the Normandy coast, there was much more flak coming up from the antiaircraft batteries below. The formation then hit some heavy clouds. The combination of flak, clouds, and inexperienced pilots was the reason for our biggest problem. The planes started veering right and left in order to be certain that they were not going to run into the one on either side. We were standing up, all hooked up by this time, and, when the green light went on, we jumped without knowing that we were not over the scheduled drop zones.

On the way down, we were shot at with machine guns and rifles, and it looked very bad. We were not very high for the jump but it seemed like forever before we reached the ground. On the way down, I could see that there was lots of water below, and I assumed that it was the Merderet River. That was the river closest to where we were supposed to be. It proved later to be the Douve River, and I was to land about five miles from my scheduled drop zone. Also on the way down, some of the machine-gun fire hit a gas mask case that I had strapped to my side. I had left the gas mask in England and filled the rubber mask case with cigarettes. The bullets ripped the cases open, spun me around like a top and ruined my cigarettes. I then landed in water, and they were still shooting at me.

When I first realized that I was going to land in the water, I was sure that I would drown because I had far too much equipment on me at that time. Because of all the extra weight that I carried, I had to be helped into the plane. Many of us were loaded similarly. After hitting the water, I stood up, as it was just over waist deep. With the shooting still going on and bullets coming at me, I submerged again with just enough of me sticking out to allow me to breathe. The firing soon stopped, and I was then able to assemble all of my gear and start getting out of the water. It was still quite dark and there was action all around where I landed, so I kept as quiet as possible and started making my way in what I thought was the right direction. Our mission was to secure the area and prevent the Germans from reinforcing their beach troops. We also prevented many from retreating from the beaches. The 508th Parachute Infantry Regiment was to destroy the bridges crossing the Douve River at Etienville and Reuzeville la Bastille. As I was making my way in what I assumed to be the right direction, I heard men walking and did not know if they were enemy or some of our own. I stopped and lay flat on the ground, then realized that I was at the edge of a ditch that was about four or five feet deep. The men were walking in my direction in this ditch. I remained quiet and, as they passed me, I heard one of them speak and then knew they were the enemy. I could have reached out and touched their helmets as they passed. I was sure that they could hear my heart pounding, but they did not.

When they had passed, I jumped the ditch and continued until I heard someone say, "Flash." I did not even try to remember the correct response, which was, "Thunder." My reply was "Oh, shit!" I had completely forgotten the password for the moment. As it turned out, the person challenging me was one of my corporals. We compared notes and determined that we were going in the right direction and continued down the path that was there. Along the way we picked up more jumpers and soon discovered that we were not the only ones who were not in the proper place. We found men from the 505, some from the 507 and even some from the 101st Division. The 101st was scheduled to land around Carentan, which was several miles from our area. The 505 and 507 were also part of the 82nd Airborne Division, as we were. Just before daybreak we encountered a group of German soldiers at a cross road, and we engaged in a fierce firefight which lasted about 20 minutes. The time is a pure guess, but it seemed much longer. We drove them off and continued moving in the chosen direction. We were challenged two other times before we reached one of the main roads. At each of these points, we drove the enemy off. We were outnumbered each time and the only explanation for our coming out ahead is that we were more determined and perhaps better trained. We lost some of our men also. We had been trained for this and told what to expect, but seeing it first hand was not a good experience. At about 10:00 A.M. the first morning, we arrived at the village of Beuzeville. This was on the east side of the Douve River. We were at the bridge, which our unit was supposed to destroy, but we did not know that at the time. We were still under the impression that we had landed on the east side of the Merderet River. We had no idea where we were until later in the day.

There was a pocket of German soldiers at this crossroad and we discovered that there was more of our group across the road from us. Together we drove the Germans off, and we crossed the road to join the others. We then thought that there were still more of our men just up the road, and Mel Beets from my company volunteered to go get them and guide them to where we were. It turned out that the men up the road were the enemy, and Mel was captured. The two groups now assembled in fields behind a row of about seven houses along the road in Beuzeville. I located Staff Sergeant Ray Hummel from my company. We then realized that he and I were the ranking men in our group; we had no officers. We thought we should get up in one of the two-story houses and see what was around us.

We shot the lock off the back door of an occupied house, and the people in it were badly scared. They did not interfere; in fact, they smiled at us and gave us the run of the place. Ray and I went up the stairs just inside the back door, and Jim McMahon, who was then the corporal in the wire section of my company, followed. Ray and I went to a double window at the front of the house and were looking to see what was around us. We heard tanks approaching from the west and dropped down to keep from being seen. There were three French Renault tanks that the German Army was using in that area. The center one stopped immediately under the window where we were. The top hatch opened and one of the soldiers inside stood up to look around. While he was looking, I handed Ray a gammon grenade, and he dropped it into the tank. That tank was knocked out of action, and the other two were trying to figure what had hit it.

We left that building and once again joined the men in the fields behind the houses. If the two tanks had pursued us, we could not have stopped them because the heaviest weapons we had were our rifles. They did not tarry long and soon moved on their way going east from us. In the area behind the houses, we soon learned that we could not cross the river to our west, and we could not cross the floodwaters to the south. There were machine guns in both of these directions and nothing to cover us so that we could attempt to knock them out. Our only choice was to move in an easterly direction. We were plainly visible from the road as we jumped the hedgerows and crossed the fields, so we went two at a time while the rest tried to keep watch on the road. All went fairly well, and we made it to the next road, which we found was the approach to the causeway going to Chef du Pont. We could hear firing in all directions around us and could tell that some of the battles were quite fierce. It was easy to determine the sound of the German guns and our own.

When we got to the last field before the road, we were pinned down again by German fire. Ray and I had the men spread out up and down the hedgerows both in front of us and behind. There was a barn and a barn lot in front of us and a two-story house on the corner. The Germans occupied it, and we started firing at it in force. We could not proceed further with them in that house. In the middle of the firing, we heard an American voice shouting for us to stop or the Germans would kill them. Some of our men were being held prisoner in that house. This stopped the firing, but we were still being shot at from the road, and a sniper from behind us killed August Labate.

Along the way, we had taken the ammunition and other items from those who had been killed. This gave us some extra ammunition, but we knew that we could not hold out for any extended length of time. Ray and I discussed this, and we decided that we did not want to be taken as prisoners, so we would hold out to the end. This seemed to be the opinion of all in our group.

From the beginning of our ordeal on June 6th, we ended up with a total of about 52 men. We lost 13 and had some wounded along the way. We were pinned down in that final field for five days and frequently were challenged by the Germans. We proved to be a stubborn group, because we held our ground against every attempt to get us out. Both Ray Hummel and I agree that we did a pretty good job with what we had. Our men were from various organizations and we had little equipment, but we were certainly a thorn in the side of those opposing us. We slowed down the retreat of some coming from the beaches, and we kept some reinforcements from advancing beyond our corner. In S.L.A. Marshall's book, *Night Drop*, we were referred to as "a pack of strays." I guess that is a good description of our group. We did some good with little equipment and no guidance.

During those five days behind the German lines, many other things happened, of course. Pete Reynolds was shot in the head and did not realize this until he took off his helmet and the wool knit cap. We treated him also, though we had no medics in our group. George DeCarvalho had been hit in the ankle by a German rifle grenade. The grenade did not go off, but it did damage the ankle severely. Hummel buried Labate where he had been killed. A Frenchman who risked his life to bring us cheese, bread and wine had visited us in the dark of night. He also told us approximately how many Germans were around us. We were nearly out of ammunition and the situation was starting to look quite bad.

In the late afternoon of the fifth day, we heard firing from the direction of the causeway, which led to Chef du Pont. We recognized it as being from American weapons. The first friendly words that we heard were uttered by a master sergeant from the 90th Division who yelled, "Bring up that bazooka." All of us stood up and cheered. Remarkably, none of us were shot in the process. The 90th Division men then knew that we were there, and the Germans left that corner in a rush.

The sergeant told us he would send our wounded men back and would give us a guide to get through the mined roads and back with our units. We owe that sergeant and his men our lives, because we were down to our final clips of ammunition. We could not have held out for another day without supplies. Those of us who were in that field refer to it as "Hell's Half Acre." We all have memories of events that happened there. In comparing notes with each other, we find that even though we were in the same field, the difference in positions determined what each of us remembers.

We rejoined the 1st Battalion that day and learned that our battalion commander, company commander, first sergeant, and numerous others had been killed. I cannot explain the feelings that any of us had that day. We had lost some very good men and some very good friends.

Walter Lukasavage

As a young man, the thought of being a paratrooper sounded like a good way to serve my country. I volunteered on September 28, 1942, and spent the first day at Camp Custer, Michigan, doing KP duty. The second day, I was on my way to Toccoa, Georgia, for training with Company I, 506th Parachute Infantry, 101st Airborne Division. I always seemed to be doing much more than my share of KP and guard duty, but I never missed a long march, parachute jump, or other training. I remember having two days of sick leave to have my tonsils removed. The doctor gave me a shot of local anesthetic in my neck, which was supposed to deaden the pain, while he cut away in my throat. Hot tears were running down my face from the pain. When he was finished, the doctor said, "OK, son, back to your barracks." The training at Toccoa was very thorough and difficult both physically and mentally. Twice a week we ran a mountain called "Currahee" three miles up and three miles down. We didn't have tennis shoes in those days, just good old heavy army shoes. Each company tried to make the best time in running this mountain. Every day was spent pushing ourselves to the limit in 3-4 hours a day of physical training. There were many long marches of 24 miles and even one that was 136 miles. This type of training was being conducted in camps throughout the United States and overseas in England until June 6, 1944, the date of the invasion of France.

While in training, we made five practice parachute jumps, were considered paratroopers, and received our wings. This was only the beginning. We then jumped out of C-47 airplanes and made a couple of night jumps in full field equipment. At night you couldn't see the ground, and we hit very hard. It really made you wonder if you're still in one piece.

Ten days before the invasion of France, we were living in a special area—waiting—thinking—praying—knowing some of us would never come back. On June 4th Captain McKnight of Company I called for an inspection of OD uniforms. My OD pants were cut for shorts and worn under my jump suit for added warmth. The captain saw this and told me, "When I get back, I'll have you court-martialed." The captain never came back; he was held captive by the Germans for the duration of the war.

We made the jump on June 6, 1944, at 1 A.M. from about 500 feet, which meant our reserve parachutes couldn't have been used if needed. I spent 33 days in France. Harry Westerberg and I were in the first bayonet attack of World War II. Many men lost their lives in that attack. Harry was wounded, and I ended up in a large ditch with German machine guns firing over me.

Nearly all the planes flying over France in the invasion received some damage. It looked like a living hell below and we jumped right into the middle of it! I feel proud to have been able to serve my country so that people can live in freedom—but war is hell. I remember fighting in France and not being able to wash or put on clean socks. We were always hoping for some sleep time but never getting it. Each day was another war—moving—fighting on—digging foxholes and hedgerows. It was very thick. The seconds seemed like minutes, minutes like hours, hours like days. Your constant thought from day to day was just wanting to survive and that to do so, knowing you have to kill or be killed yourself. You can't read about combat and expect to understand it. You have to be there as a part of it.

After the invasion of France we returned to Ramsbury, England, to regroup. We lost many men to death, and many more were wounded and captured. In our squad of 12 men, I was the only one to return. My friends had many tears shed for them. There were many replacements in the 506th Parachute Infantry. Of the original 750 men, 615 were killed, and only 135 of us survived.

Charles "Chuck" Katlic

I was sent to the front battle line on November 9, 1944. The entire front of 70 miles was covered by four and a half infantry divisions. Under the conditions and terrain, one division should have covered 4 to 5 miles. The 99th Division was spread out on a line some 22 miles across villages, fields, forested hills, marshes, and stream banks in ice, rain, and snow. The line stretched all the way from Monchau in the north to Losheim in the south. The 99th sector was named "Buzz Bomb Alley" (in the path of V-1 rockets, or buzz bombs, headed for Antwerp and London). In the six weeks of occupying this sector, the men of F Company and all infantry companies constructed an unbroken line of resistance. During this time, the men improved their foxholes by lining them with pine branches and putting logs and dirt over their foxholes to give protection from tree bursts from German 88s and other artillery. We also built log huts for washing our feet and changed socks to lower the risk of trench foot and frostbite. We sent out patrols to bring back prisoners for interrogation.

On December 16, 1944, at 0500 in the morning, the great German artillery barrage began. All hell broke loose—you could feel the foxhole rocking! The magnitude of the attack stunned American soldiers of North Africa, Sicily, and Normandy. For those who lacked combat experience, it was unforgettable. It has been claimed to be the heaviest artillery barrage in the history of the world, and records support this contention. For example, 23 battalions of artillery supported the 47th Panzer Corps alone. Company F of the 2nd Battalion along with other units of the 99th were surrounded and cut off by the Germans for three days. The only way to fight those tanks was to blow the tanks with our bazookas. Once the tanks were stopped, we would hit them with Molotov cocktails, glass bottles filled with diesel fuel and gasoline with a rag for a fuse. When the bottle broke upon impact with the tank, the tank would heat up from the fire. The tanker would have to come out or fry. We managed to fight our way out and under cover of darkness. We got out of the clutches of the Germans and hooked with the other battalions of the 394th Regiment. We reformed on the Elsenborn Ridge and took up defensive positions and held off the Germans. The 99th was outnumbered 10 to 1. We were called "The Lost Battalion."

On January 30, 1945, in black, bitter cold and biting winds of night, we launched an attack across open fields of waist deep snow against the Germans, who were entrenched in the wooded area to our front. The German grip on this critical corner was finally broken, and the 99th "battle babies" surged cross-country over the snow-covered icy hills and gullies through the dense woods to completely clear the pocket. We then fought our way to the Rhine River.

On March 10, 1945, at 1900 hours, Company F, in one of the most important moves since D-Day, moved out on foot to cross the Rhine River into the heart of Germany. After a ten-hour march, we arrived in the vicinity of the Remagen Railway Bridge. At this point, we came under heavy enemy artillery fire, causing a number of casualties. It was very dark, and it was hard to walk without tripping over the dead and wounded bodies. We crossed the bridge at intervals of artillery shelling. Our company suffered 24 casualties in crossing the bridge.

James M. Burt

I was a tank company commander, 3rd Battalion, 66th Armored Regiment, 2nd Armored Division ("Benning to Berlin"). It was practically impossible to earn a medal in a tank. My tank company was attached to an infantry battalion with the mission to cut Aachen Gap, the supply route to Aachen. There was ground fighting for seven or eight days. In the first two days, infantry battalion lost all equipment and all its officers except two in rear echelon. Lost about 50 percent of its men. By emergency, I took over the infantry battalion and spent much of the time on the ground with them. They accepted me readily because they had seen me drag their wounded battalion commander to safety. I received the Congressional Medal of Honor. I was cross-trained artillery, infantry, and air support and used them all.

Leonard Dziabas

Company H, 351st Infantry

Saint and Sinner

MAGENTA, ALGERIA - DECEMBER 1943

It was a night problem and our machine gun was placed at outpost on the forward slope of a mountain. It was a bright moonlit night, with a relentless and frigid wind screaming across the Sahara and pounding against the slopes of the Atlas Mountains.

Eubanks and Zaverous were pulling the 0200 to 0400 gun watch. I was the first gunner, but this night was acting squad leader. It was during this watch that I decided to check on the gun. Approaching the emplacement, I found it unmanned, with nary a soul in sight. Cussing, I began looking for the two culprits. Above and to the leeward side of the mountain, I spied a posterior sticking out of some dwarf bushes. Taking deliberate aim and with great force, I shot my right foot into the center of the target. With a piercing yell, this soldier leaped to his feet. The silver bars shining in the moonlight were blinding and the crosses on the collar the largest I had ever seen. In a state of shock, I tried to explain to Chaplain Crowley of 1st Battalion, 349th that I was merely looking for my men. Regaining his poise, he asked, "Are you always so harsh on your men?" "No, Sir," I replied, "but, with these two, when an order is given, it always has to be ended with a great big exclamation mark."

The chaplain then explained to me how much more could be accomplished with human beings by using kindness in place of physical force. Upon finishing, he asked me to reach a box from his musette bag. This I thought was it—the name, rank, and serial number bit. Receiving the box, he opened it and asked me to have a piece of the best chocolate candy ever.

Still apologizing, I left to return to the gun pit. Lo and behold, there in the emplacement sat Eubanks and Zaverous, most alert and attentive, as good soldiers should be. Remembering the good chaplain's words and thinking he might still be in earshot, I merely turned, shaking my head, and returned to my squad position.

Eyes Right

HIGHWAY 6 - JUNE 1944

H Company, 351st moved as a complete unit in this attack; we were not parceled out among the rifle companies. H Company was lost, as we had become separated from the battalion. Where we were, where anybody was, we had no idea.

We entered a large farm complex. Lieutenant Buzick ordered our platoon, first platoon machine guns, to set up security around the buildings while Captain Church and the officers went into the farmhouse to orient themselves as to where we were and where the battalion might be.

The first section of machine guns moved out in front of the buildings. It was a moonlit night, but a fairly heavy growth of trees made the area semidark, with the exception of a wheat field to the right of the farm road. About a hundred yards down this road, we came to a highway. This highway was jammed with traffic, all moving north at great speed. Our section lined up along the roadside and watched this spectacle in silence for a while. Someone chimed in that these vehicles were not GI. After a short debate, we all came to the conclusion that they were definitely British. Somehow the officers back there in the farmhouse snafued and got us mixed up with His Majesty's Eighth Army.

James Besse ran to the farmhouse to inform the officers as to where we were. In a short time, we heard Lieutenant Buzick's short and heavy step trotting toward us on the gravel lane with Besse right behind. Puffing, the lieutenant came to a halt among us and taking a good hard look, he exclaimed in a surprised voice, "British, hell! That's the whole damn German Tenth Army passing in review!"

A Stinking Ambush

TUSCANY—JULY 1944

The 2nd Battalion was attacking. It moved in two advancing columns with about a hundred yards between. At midmorning, the air was still, hot, and humid. An unusual silence hung over the bright sunlit landscape. Topping a ridge, the battalion looked down into a small bowllike valley and proceeded down the slope. Cover was lacking, with the exception of a small vineyard at the bottom left of the valley.

As the machine-gun squad mounted the ridge, I detected an odor, a most obnoxious odor—the unmistakable smell of the German army. It came from our left flank. Within a second, John Simmons exclaimed, "I smell Jerry." Passing into the valley, we tried to see if there were any scouts on the ridge to our left. None could be seen. Our column was about one quarter of the way up to the right ridge. The two forward scouts were moving at port arms only a hundred fifty yards ahead of the battalion. The situation was all snafued. With the Jerry smell becoming stronger and the prickly feeling that we were being observed, I began moving my squad in the direction of the vineyard, hoping it would provide us with enough cover to bring our gun into action. Simmons and I kept our eyes on the lead scouts as they climbed the far ridge. The rest of the squad kept surveillance of the left ridge.

As the forward scout reached the military crest, he whirled to face us and raised his rifle over his head to signal "enemy in sight." Then he was dead. With heavy German machine-gun and mortar fire falling about us, we dashed the few remaining yards to the vineyard. Here, in the very first row, Dame Fortune smiled upon us. For there we found a lone narrow, shallow trench that would accommodate the entire squad. We all dove in head first, as if it were the old swimming hole. Reality came upon us with lightning force—the trench was a fresh and well-used Jerry latrine.

Me and My Machete

In June 1944, each machine gun squad was equipped with a machete, usually carried by the squad leader. The machete was more of a tool than a weapon. It was used to cut rails in the underbrush, clear fields of fire, clean mud off the boots, cut meat, and peel potatoes. It added glamour to the dress because it was so eye catching, but was a wearisome thing to carry in combat. Forever spanking, gouging, and nagging the bearer, the machete made it almost impossible to hit the dirt fast. As a weapon, it was only on rare occasions that one would find it useful. However, the enemy cowered in terror from it.

In all my combat days, the period just before or after Rome was the only time I wore the machete. What caused me to take it that time I do not know. One day, Sergeant Frank McCormick instructed me to emplace my gun ahead of the battalion in order to cover a crossroad. The terrain was flat, but to the left, a cornfield sloped gently away. I chose this field for my emplacement. Even in June, the corn was shoulder high, so I unsheathed the machete and began to cut a field of fire toward the road junction. I found a small gully, unseen from either the road or our position. As I raised the machete to cut the last stand of corn in front of the gully, I saw a German rifleman standing in it. He saw me at the same instant, dropped his rifle, and screamed "*Kamerad.*" My eyes followed the rifle to the ground, and I was even more startled to see a German machine gun and two gunners pressing themselves to the ground. I could not describe the frozen terror on their faces.

After taking the prisoners back to the riflemen, my squad and I went to inspect the enemy position. Looking down their field of fire toward the crossroads, I spotted two dead GIs spaced about 20 yards apart. They were apparently scouts from another outfit. I regretted my machete had not arrived there sooner.

Roma

JUNE 1944

It was a beautiful June day, the rare day that the poets spoke of. The columns stopped, and, while waiting, I pulled out my camel-skin wallet, which I had bartered for with a pack of cigarettes in Oran, Algeria. I took out a small notebook, which had been given to me by the Red Cross. On the inside cover was a 1944 calendar. On this calendar I would mark an "X" on each combat day that I had served at the front. I penciled in an "X" on the 4th of June 1944. Counting back the Xs I learned this would be my seventieth day facing the German armies.

As we moved down the hill, a scene opened up in front of us—a scene right out of the pages of my world history book. Roman buildings with tall columns in front of them, and mounted on top of the columns were statues of Romans. One even had a chariot pulled by horses on its top. The sun was near the horizon and caused the structures to appear in a bronze color. I pulled out my pocket watch. It was 6:00 P.M. sharp.

On the far edge of a park were two tanks. Their hatches were open and the crew was tossing candy and gum to about 20 or 30 Italians who had gathered around the tanks. As we came alongside, rifle fire broke out from the nearest apartment building. A sniper was taking pop shots at us. The riflemen made a mad rush for the building. The civilians were screaming their heads off and milling around like cattle. The tankers dashed down their turrets and slammed the lids shut. The tanks spun around and headed for the rear at great speed.

The Italians were now both screaming and sobbing and some were yelling, "*Medico.*" Doc Gulley, our platoon aid man, ran to assist them. He yelled back that two women had been wounded and that we would care for them.

The riflemen were still searching for the sniper. Feeling exposed in the open field, I led my men to a street that led from the park, which was the direction that the battalion had been heading before the distraction.

As we entered the street, nighttime enveloped us. It seems in Italy there is no twilight to speak of. As if with the click of a switch it turns from day to night. The street was wide and very still, as if we were in a cave. We moved down the middle of the street for about a block when a peasant dashed out of a house to my left. He tapped my arm and asked, "*Tedesco?*"

I said, "No, *Americano*." With that he shouted at the top of his voice, "*Americano*!"

Every door and window flew open on each side of the street. The light from the opening lit up the dark roadway, and from each opening the people were screaming loudly, "*Americano*." Like a tidal wave, the voices picked up in volume and speed until it seemed that the whole of Rome was yelling, "*Americano*."

The Italians stormed from their abodes and engulfed us tightly. We came to a halt; we were unable to move. Young *senorinas* surrounded us and began feeling our muscles. Two put their arms around my neck and began kissing me. Another one jumped up with her legs around my waist and started to kiss me on the mouth. Her jump caused me to lose my balance, and I was forced to steady myself by grabbing her buttocks. By quickly grabbing her, my hands had accidentally gotten under her dress. To my great surprise, her underwear was made of 100 percent pure silk. She also was wearing silk hose. This was unheard of back in the U.S.A.

Simmons was in a bit of a bind. Carrying the machine-gun receiver, he found he was unable to fend off the girls, so he handed the receiver to a middle-aged peasant who was saluting him nearby and began to devote his full attention to the young ladies. The rest of my squad were buried by humanity. I had no idea how they were handling themselves; however, I heard no cries for help.

In all my exuberance, I was interrupted by a nasty voice yelling, "Dzab, what the hell are you doing?" It was Sergeant McCormick. He had made his way up to find out what was holding up the line. He kept yelling, "We got to get the bridge before Jerry blows it up." This was the first that I heard of a bridge, and I had no idea where it was.

He then spotted Simmons covered with girls and the *paisano* standing by with the receiver on his shoulder. Mac went livid and had kittens right there in the middle of the street. He kept yelling and repeating his pet phrase, "I'm going to have you all court-martialed as soon as we get off the line."

Breaking away from the adorable girls, I fell in the column behind the rifle company that had cleared a narrow path through the crowd. The path that the Romans left us was narrow, with only enough room to pass through in single file. From each side they kept shoving bottles at us plus cookies, cakes, and breads. Also they pelted us with fruit and flowers. I even tasted some candy along the way. I would grab a bottle and take a big swig out of it and pass it on to Simmons, and John would take his gulp and pass it on to Tessoline, and so on down the line of the squad. Many of the sips I was able to recognize. There was a great deal of *vino*, Champagne, anisette, grappa, and even some peach brandy. We should have been totally intoxicated and passed out from the amount of liquor we had drunk, but outside of sweating like overworked horses we were perfectly sane and steady on our feet.

After a long delay the battalion moved alongside the curvature of the

Coliseum until it reached its northern end. We then turned into a wide avenue on our left and crossed a very distinctive bridge with a column of men on each side. There was no sign of Jerry or of any attempts to blow the bridge. Jerry must have been in a big rush to get out of the city.

Entering a narrow street, it was apparent that only a jeep would be able to move into its narrowness. As the columns neared the top, it placed my squad about halfway up the hill. Two Jerry machine guns opened up at the top of the hill, firing with rapid and deadly fire down the line of each column.

My squad hit the ground, pressing against a garden wall built of stone. The fire was so close we were being pelted with a rain of pavement and stone fragments. I spotted an iron gateway in the garden wall and yelled to my men to follow me. We hit the gate with great force and it flew open. As we dashed to the other side of the wall, another machine gun opened fire on us from within the garden. The fire was even angrier than on the roadway, so we retreated back through the gateway. I then realized that the only way to save my squad was to get on top of the thick wall. We all scaled the wall with haste, and it proved to be a good move, for all the fire was below us. However, the top of the wall had broken bottles cemented into it. Lying on top of these broken glass fragments proved not only to be painful, but they also tore holes in our ODs [olive drab uniforms] and made us a bloody mess. Before we could get any of our weapons into action, the shooting stopped and all that could be heard were the cries for medics.

Somebody Loved Us

LAIATICO - JULY 1944

The attack on Laiatico was an oil painting come to life. The moon was very bright, the night warm, the curtain of artillery and mortar phosphorous shells moved at a walking pace with the soldiers following a few yards behind. Each man was spaced properly and was very erect, and the shadow from the moon made each appear ten feet tall.

The faces of the men were hard, as if cast from an iron mold, cold perspiration running slowly to the point of their chins. Shell fragments and phosphorous were falling among them, but none caused them to flinch or change their course. The only way the attack could have been more perfect was if they had used small-arms fire with their movement.

A farm was on the outskirts of Laiatico. My squad, moving across the farmyard, had to traverse the bases of some hayricks, which had two or three feet of new-mown hay in them. John Simons and I, carrying the machine gun, had already passed the ricks when our ammo bearers, following behind, let out several howls. I heard one shout, "There're Jerrys under this hay, and they're grabbing our feet." I yelled back, "Shoot them!" As John and I moved on, I heard Rocco Dechester say they couldn't do that, but some riflemen walking along the side of the rick settled the problem. I heard their squad leader say, "Save your ammo, we'll take care of them with our bayonets."

By this time, John and I had turned down the farmyard road and were well away from the melee. We paused on the left side of the dirt track and while waiting for the bearers to catch up we did what was second nature to our squad. I plopped the tripod on the ground, John set the receiver on it, and we seated ourselves ready for action. The machine gun faced across the road, which was very dark under the shadow of large trees and shrubs. A dirt track met the road about 15 or 20 yards from us. At the intersection lay the body of a dead lieutenant, his bars sparkling in the moonlight. He should have been instructed to remove them before going into combat.

Sergeant McCormack, coming down the right side of the dirt rack, spotted us and called, "What are you doing there, Dzab?" As I started to answer, he became alert and asked, "You hear something?" We answered no, and then Mac said there was a cave with someone in it. Our empty gun was pointing into the cave, so John and I crouched and steadied the weapon as if it were loaded and ready for business. We all yelled, "*Rouse*!" Receiving no answer, Mac fired a round from his carbine into the cave. The quiet of the moment was broken by a multitude of voices, all screaming, "*Kamerad*." Over 50 Jerries, hands on heads, walked out in single file—all petrified by the machine gun they were facing. With the last one apparently out, Mac tossed a grenade into the cave and marched the prisoners to the rear. The rest of the squad caught up, and I moved our prisoners into the cave. We set the machine gun at the entrance, facing the road intersection. Exploring the interior of the cave with lighted matches, we found a virtual arsenal of German arms and munitions.

The moon went down later, and all became quiet and dark. John and I were on watch behind the gun when we heard rapidly moving footsteps on the gravel road. We were able to see the outline of a man, who seemed to be a GI, coming at the emplaced gun. Taking out my .45 pistol, I stepped in front of the gun and reached with my left hand to stop him. It was then I saw he was a German. I grasped him by the throat and buried the .45 into his stomach all the way up to the safety catch. There was not an iota of fight left in him. He dropped the papers he was carrying and went limp as I relieved him of his P-38 pistol. We saw then he was an officer, of what rank we didn't know. As the ammo bearers led him away, he kept pleading, "*Potograps, potograps*."

Thus a whole Jerry company was scratched off by one empty machine gun.

Karma

Arno River - August 1944

The battalion was perched on the last foothills before the Arno River. Our machine gun was dug in on outpost while the battalion awaited the order to move to the river's edge. Slightly to the right rear, an artillery observer set up his OP. Here, one was able to peek through the scope and see an anthill of German activity on the road running parallel with the river.

At twilight, we moved toward the river. Our platoon's mission was to secure the left flank. After crossing the road without opposition, we came to a large farm complex. A large building on the northern edge of the courtyard functioned as a barn with the family living quarters on the second floor. The platoon came to a halt at the edge of the compound. Sergeant Frank McCormack told Jim Besse and me to investigate the large building. Finding a large double door in the center of the building, we assured ourselves it was empty. We proceeded to the southwest corner where there was a smaller door. We heard a stirring within. Being armed only with .45s and not knowing what firepower we might have to face, we decided to announce our presence with a grenade. The door was ajar an inch or so. I readied myself to one side to kick it open, while Besse pulled the pin and positioned himself for throwing.

I opened the door with a violent kick, and Besse let fly with the grenade. Instantly it flew right back out, landed between us, and we heard the click, which spelled our doom. Instinctively we hit Mother Earth. The blast shattered the still night; a huge white bulk thundered over us. A cow came shrieking and howling out of the house and streaked across the courtyard. The beast must have been standing at the doorway and, as the door opened, it started out as the grenade hit and bounced back out.

James E. Gatten

Eyewitness to History

APRIL 5, 1944

Under cover of darkness, the 83rd Division was moved from the staging area to New York harbor and onto troop ships. State Rooms? No! The hold of the ship was reminiscent of the proverbial sardine can. The bunks were a piece of canvas stretched on a pipe frame, stacked four and five high. I was young and accustomed to adverse conditions, so I slept well. On the passageway to breakfast, I realized the ship was moving. While I slept we had slipped out of the harbor and were on the open Atlantic. We were sternly warned to wear a life vest at all times and never to remove our wool uniform. It was midmorning before we were permitted to go up to the open deck. There was a sight that took my breath away. Wherever I looked, in every direction, there were ships, many more ships than I could count. If ever there had been a doubt in my mind concerning us winning this war, that doubt was gone. I was certain we would win. I learned later I was on the flagship *George Washington* with twelve thousand troops on board, so we were in the center of the convoy. A few hundred yards off our starboard side was the mighty and majestic battleship *Texas*. Every hour of every day for 14 days, the *Texas* was in that same exact position. I assume the life of a sailor can also be boring. All around the outside perimeter of the convoy, only specks on the distant horizon, steamed our destroyer escorts. As I was a farm boy, they reminded me of faithful dogs herding a flock of sheep.

The 83rd Division launches its first full-scale offensive in the hedgerows of Normandy. It was one of the most miserable places American troops have ever been committed. Daily progress was measured in yards, and casualties were counted for every yard gained.

July 19, 1944

The worst day yet for the reconnaissance troop. The entire troop was committed, on foot, to assist (backup) an attack by our infantry in the hedgerows. We were stopped by intense fire. The battle reached a stalemate, which lasted several hours. Finally, the Germans pushed a large tank into our flank. The tank was supported by ground troops. We were unable to stop the tank with our weapons. The only alternative was a hasty retreat.

Operation Cobra

July 25, 1944

A day that remains so very vivid in my memory. There was a radio message to halt and return to a designated location, a small apple orchard. There were literally hundreds of little orchards in Normandy. All were enclosed by a high hedgerow. We parked the vehicles and relaxed in the bright summer sun. Very soon we heard a sound unlike any we had ever heard before. It was a sound no one will ever hear again—the sound of massed propeller-driven heavy bombers. We had no previous information of what we were about to witness. The powers that be made the decision for this great gamble. Some three thousand of our heavy bombers would fly from England to concentrate on a spot of the German front line—an area two miles wide, one mile deep. The theory was to make a hole in German defenses that would provide the opportunity for our infantry and General Patton's tanks. If we could get a strong force through that hole blasted in the enemy line, we might be able to get out of the miserable hedgerow country.

I would estimate I was about three miles from the target area. The bombers came in from behind us, passing directly overhead. As the first wave reached the target, I was amazed to learn the Germans had so much firepower. It looked as though our planes were flying through a hailstorm. As I watched, one of our planes exploded in a ball of orange flame and black smoke. At that distance, it seemed as though I were watching a movie. It seemed difficult for my mind to adjust to the reality of the horror I saw. Those pieces of black debris in the backdrop of the blue sky included the bodies of ten American boys as they dropped on the soil of France. As the bombs exploded three miles away, the earth vibrated. The concussion came in waves, ruffling my clothing like a 40-mile-per-hour wind. After dropping their bombs, all the planes followed the same course, banking like graceful eagles as they turned to return to England. After the first few waves of our bombers, the German guns became silent. Our planes kept coming, wave after wave, for about two-and-half hours.

There was also tragedy unexpected. Some of the bombs were short of the target, killing and wounding several Americans. One of the unintended victims was Lieutenant General Leslie McNair. He had gone forward to observe the operation. I have a snapshot of Lieutenant General McNair's grave, taken when I visited the American Cemetery at St. Laurent in 1986. The three-star general has the same size marker and grave space as the nearby privates. Is this a symbol of democracy or the fact that death itself is a common denominator?

July 26–27, 1944

In spite of the tragic errors, Operation Cobra was successful. A few hours after the aerial bombing, the reconnaissance troop drove through that black hole. (The grass and foliage was black.) The road was blocked by a terrific jam of military vehicles. Lieutenant B jumped down from his armored car, and I followed. Very impatiently he took one of our jeeps and began driving through the fields, bypassing the road traffic. He stopped when we reached a road intersection. Here again was a sight never to be forgotten. Stretched down a road, heading east, almost bumper to bumper as far as I could see was a line of Sherman tanks. Patton's tanks were through the hole—these steel monsters, assembled in American factories, shipped across three thousand miles of ocean, hundreds of tanks in France ready to roll into Germany, the unbelievable production of American industry.

For many people in the small towns and villages of France, we were the first Americans they had seen. It is difficult to find the words to describe their reaction. The tricolor flags of France had been carefully hidden for four years. Now they were waving everywhere. There were times when those French civilians actually overwhelmed us, crowding into the street, crawling onto our vehicles. They were impeding our progress. It was truly an emotional experience that will never be forgotten. I am sorry that more of our troops could not enjoy that first flush of liberation excitement.

Our platoon stopped briefly in a little town in Luxembourg. There was a deserted old school building opposite our car. Lieutenant B jumped down to the street, Tommy gun slung over a shoulder. He went inside the building alone. After a few minutes he came out with a piece of yellow chalk. On the outside of the building he printed these words:

IF THERE IS ANY GOOD THING I CAN DO, LET ME DO IT NOW, FOR I SHALL NOT PASS THIS WAY AGAIN.

He offered no verbal comment, and none of his men said a word. He climbed back into the car, and the column proceeded down the street.

APRIL 1945

This month will always be remembered as the most tiring and stressful of my life. At the same time, April will be remembered as one of the most exhilarating periods of my life. Organized enemy resistance was broken. Once again the cavalry was used as the planners had intended. The highly mobile cavalry swept out in front of the infantry in an effort to maintain contact with the enemy. In France we had come as liberators. In Germany we came as conquerors. Once again we entered villages and small towns to be the first Americans the citizens had seen. But we didn't see them, not even a child. It was as quiet as though uninhabited. No colored flags were waving, but a piece of white cloth hung from every home and building. It was an eerie feeling to see the universal symbol of surrender—a proud and arrogant nation thoroughly defeated. In the excitement of the moment, I don't recall remembering the fact that there is some German blood in my veins.

Robert Toledo

Operation Cobra—Thunderbolt Across Europe

First Machine Gun Squad of M Company, 331st Regiment, 83rd Infantry Division was assigned to perform a suicide mission against the Nazis. Only the first squad was to simulate a counterattack east and west of the St. Lô Perrier Road and south of the city of St. Lô in the swampland in Normandy, France. Orders came from command post by a lieutenant and a first sergeant and made an observation post in a foxhole next to my .30-caliber machine-gun emplacement. Their objective was to take all details of enemy-fire activity and a plan of the area width and depth. My duties were to fire at the enemy from the hip along the 100-yard length of hedgerow. This left dead Nazis and cows in the swampland. Some of our boys were also wounded. We drew so much fire from Tiger tanks with 88mm guns and machine guns that I was told to stop firing. Mission had been accomplished. The lieutenant said the object of this was for an air raid. The date was midday July 24, 1944. The evening was quiet through the night.

July 25, 1944, also midday, so much rumbling in the sky. We were thinking that Jerry and his planes were going to bomb and strafe us as usual. What a surprise as we were looking up into the sky. What a beautiful sight—thousands and thousands of planes of all types P-47s, P-38s, P-51s, B-17s, B-24 pursuit planes and bombers. This was the largest carpet bombardment that I had ever seen. This achievement annihilated the 17th S.S. Division, 6th Parachute Nazi Regiment, and many Tiger tanks. There were burnt bodies all over their mechanized equipment. This was the breakout of Normandy, the bottleneck of the swamps where thousands upon thousands of American heroes died. The odor was stagnating and breathing impossible. First Squad also volunteered to pick up our dead warriors and to load them on trucks with their dog tags—one for the mouth and one for the driver. This was sad, and most were decomposed due to heat and rain.

Martin Milco, Sr.

T/5, Headquarters Battery, 405th AAA Battalion

Inching Along!

During those early days of the Normandy invasion, when our infantrymen were painfully slogging it out from hedgerow to hedgerow and from town to town, I recall a day on the road to St. Lô. I was assigned as the battery commander's driver in Headquarters Battery 405th AAA Battalion. The infantry was engaged in heavy combat in the town of St. Lô, and we could not move forward until they took the town. Nothing was moving, and I was thinking about the butcher's bill they must be paying up ahead. I was just a small cog in this great crusade, just trying to get my CO to where he had to go. He had a commanding officer, and that guy had a CO and so on up the line. Just a very few of our best generals had put this whole show together. But those guys were too far above me for me to give them much more than a passing thought. I was just a GI trying to inch his way forward, trying to get to Germany, end this thing, and get home to my wife and the son who was born 55 minutes after I shipped out from New York back in October of '43. Yeah! I was just trying to inch forward.

Out of the corner of my eye, I glimpsed a fender of a military vehicle slowly inching along to my left. It was some other guy trying to inch forward, trying to get to Germany ahead of me, maybe trying to get home before me. I was piling up eligibility points to get home as soon as possible. I wondered how many points this guy had. Where the hell did he think he was going! The foot sloggers hadn't taken St. Lô yet, and nobody was going anywhere till they did. Well, he started inching up a bit more and I could see it was a staff car—one of those heavy-duty, open jobs. The rear door of that vehicle was exactly abreast of where I was sitting. It was a GI all right, just inching his way across France toward Germany. I looked at him, and our eyes locked onto each other. His seemed to be saying, "I'm doing my best, son, to get us moving." For an instant I felt like it was me and "Brad" and all these other guys—all of us pushing, inch by inch, against the Germans, trying to push them back to the Fatherland. Two GIs on the road to St. Lô. For about 20 minutes on that summer day in Normandy I was side by side with the guy they called the "GI General," Omar Bradley. What a privilege—a memory to last a lifetime. Years later, when General Bradley peacefully passed away, a cartoon appeared in the newspaper. It showed the familiar crosses and stars, row upon row of an American military cemetery in France. The caption simply read: "Hey, look guys, it's Brad!" and I remembered the day that Brad looked at me—the day two GIs were just inching along.

Marvin R. Spencer

HQ Company 3rd BN-317 Infantry, Reg. 80th Div.

We camped on King George the 8th RAACE Track and had advanced battle training. General Eisenhower was "roughin'" it too, in the King's Palace with his lady friend. Finally, they decided we were ready for combat. I was one more than ready (had been for a year just tired of "doggin'" around.) So finally we crossed the English Channel to Omaha Beach, France. This is where friendship ceased and hell began.

I don't recall all the small towns, which were many and rough, too. I lost many of my good buddies along this route. It seemed like there was always another river or hill where the Krauts were looking down our throats.

Argentan was worst of all for me. This was the only hand-to-hand battle of the war for me. When I went over the hedgerow, there was the biggest German I ever saw waiting for me. He was on his knees when I hit the ground; he raked me with his bayonet. But he didn't do his job well, just cut the skin for about six inches. No intestines came out—just luck. So I did him in.

The battle began at two minutes till five; the first I noticed my watch it was 10:30, the battle was over, and it didn't seem like many men were left. You couldn't take three steps in any direction without stepping over a dead or wounded man. I seemed kind of in a daze, you know, kind of like the world had come to an end or something. I had not had time to think of myself yet, but when things simmered down a bit, Corporal Bowman from 305 Medics came to me. He put a few stitches in my belly and said everything's going to be all right. He cleaned me up for the next battle.

I feel we were fighting for a just cause. I gave it all I had until the medics took my gun away and hauled me out near Mt. St. Jean. Lots of my friends gave more.

Carter B. Strong

Scott Field and Reception Center

Scott Field looked strange and bleak to us the morning of March 15, 1943, as we gazed inside from the gatehouse. As soon as we could, we dashed into the building to where we were directed from the gate. It was the Identification and Receiving Building where we were to turn in our orders and papers, and where we were to be given our first issue of toilet articles and be assigned to barracks. Then I saw my first glimpse of the army's policy of deliberately splitting up friends. Dave and Norm were assigned to one barracks and Bud and I to another.

Our first GI haircut was a lulu! They left little for the imagination. As Bud put it, "Twenty years to grow it; two minutes to lose it." The charge was only 35 cents, but that was little consolation for what we thought was a terrific loss of dignity. From there we went over to the PX. It was a new experience to me seeing all that stuff available exclusively for the men and at greatly reduced prices. Candy, gum, cokes, etc.—there were many things that were becoming so scarce outside.

Our barracks sergeant was a big fellow who had been in over a year already and was way down in the throes of the usual filthy language and habits that the army can breed. Of course, he tried to scare us half to death and, being new, we naturally fell for a lot of it. Also, as we were college men, he took special delight in poking cracks at us. It was the general opinion that his IQ was no doubt somewhere in the seventies.

We were impressed with the big mess hall, and the food was very good. We who were still in civilian clothes had preference in the chow line, which saved us standing out in the mud. We didn't mind that at all. After the first couple of days, though, that honor went to other groups arriving after us.

The thought of the dreaded KP hung over our heads, because as soon as one was through processing, he was eligible for it, and once he was assigned to it, it meant a four-day siege from 4 A.M. until 11 P.M. But on the fifth day, when the KP list was read for our group, my name was not on it. I later learned why. I was to be shipped out with a contingent that night, March 19th.

Camp Robinson and Basic Training

Our first week in camp was more or less an orientation week supervised by the company officers and noncoms. I took several more examinations—clerical, college—and was in on anything good that came along. Some of the exams were in anticipation of the new Army Specialized Training Program whereby we would be sent to a college in uniform and would study such things as engineering and foreign languages for the army. Other activities included learning all about our individual equipment that we had been issued. One evening we had to clean up our brand new rifles. Ours was just about the first training group to get the new Garands [M-1 rifles], and I was especially glad to see them because I was familiar with them from ROTC.

Our first few days were filled with physical training, gas mask drill, lectures, movies, and assembly and disassembly of our rifles. Our inside work was done in large cement-floored buildings on the edge of the huge training areas. Several hundred men could squat on a floor and follow through various operations under the direction of a few officers. The outside work included running the obstacle courses, a series of fences, walls, and ditches about a hundred yards long. Bayonet drill was the most unpopular and the most strenuous, but it took up a lot of hours on our schedule. Gas-mask drill included a session in the gas chamber where our masks proved their worth. While inside, we had to take off our masks and run out the door. That was all done to give us confidence, and the gas solution was not up to full strength anyway. Hand-grenade drills were fun, but I was always a headache to the instructors because I was left-handed and had to do everything exactly contrary to their orders.

Camp Maxey and the 99th Infantry Division

I was one of about 30 assigned to Company G, 395th Regiment, 99th Division. We were shown into the dayroom and told to make ourselves comfortable until breakfast. Looking around the room as it grew lighter, I noticed only one man from my company at the ASTP program at Louisiana State University—Glenny Blanchard, whom I had known only slightly at school. I must have been the only one he recognized right away, too, because we got together and buddied up. This was the beginning of a friendship that was to continue to be very close for the rest of the war.

A short time later we were marched over to the big recreation hall, where the officers of the regiment spoke to us. We were told that in spite of our not having had any sleep the past night, we would begin a full-day schedule of getting settled. We were told in so many words that we were in the infantry now, and if anyone had any different ideas for himself that he had better dismiss them. The attitude was, of course, that they were proud of this outfit and that they were going to make us live in it and like it. We were also told that it would take an Act of Congress to get a man out of the 99th Division, and by gosh, if they weren't just about right. I don't know of a single man who managed to get himself transferred to another camp.

Our group from LSU was divided equally into the 393rd, 394th, and 395th Infantry Regiments of the 99th Division. Ours was only the first of several groups to arrive from various ASTP colleges during that week, and by the end of ten days there were several thousand college men in our division, all assigned as trainees.

During a routine interview I talked to the special service officer, Lieutenant Ernest Zinger. He had noticed by my records that I was also a musician and that I was interested in playing in a dance band he was organizing within the regiment. There were four men interested in playing trumpet but since there was room for only three, one had to go. Since I could fake it a little, I squeezed out one other man. Other sections had no competition within them, and it worked out that we were able to have a good 12-piece band. The weekend of July 16th saw me released from all company duties because of work with the dance band. We played for parties at the service club Saturday night and Sunday afternoon, for which I was $6 richer by Monday morning.

My first promotion to PFC came on July 18th, and I was probably rather hard on my men when I drew prisoner guard duty the next day. Though it was only one stripe, representing $4 a month, it at least meant that I was off the bottom of the pile at last.

Camp Miles Standish and Port of Embarkation

Tumbling off the train at the docks, we lined up in formation and waited for the next move. A few minutes later a WAC band began to play for us, and Red Cross women came through our ranks with hot coffee and donuts.

The women were mostly the motherly types, so it was real nice. We must have made a sight there, all clean-shaven and fairly rugged looking, loaded down with a pack that would have made a mule shudder, and invariably leaning on our rifles. The weight of those steel helmets alone made our necks ache after an hour or so until we became used to them.

Soon a Transportation Corps man began to call off our names, and we slowly moved toward the gangplank. "This is it," we said and staggered up. Just as I was halfway up, someone behind me hollered out in a loud voice, "Is this trip necessary?" With our duffel bags on our shoulders and our packs on our backs, we filed up ladders, down ladders, through hatchways, down more ladders, and past a maze of strange looking objects, always following the man in front of us until one by one we were assigned bunks. I was separated from the rest of my squad, but it was to work to my advantage when duties would be coming up. Yes, it was going to be fine to be away when the squad leader was looking for men for details.

It wasn't until late in the evening of September 29th that we pulled out of Boston Harbor. It was a cold evening, but I stayed on deck a long time. It was a peculiar sort of thrill seeing the lights of the harbor grow dimmer, feeling the cold spray that flew up over the decks, and realizing that that might be our last glimpse of the good old U.S.A. for quite awhile. A lot of thoughts ran through our heads as we stood there, our life jackets tied around our shivering bodies, but there was relatively little talking. Exactly where we were going, how long we would be gone, what would happen to us in the months ahead—all were questions we knew only time would answer. Finally the harbor lights disappeared in the mist and we went down to climb into our bunks and go to sleep.

Germany

On the evening of December 10th, I received my first Christmas box from home. Mother had mailed it in October in accordance with overseas regulations, and it was one of the first to arrive at our company. It was a box full of little original things all wrapped in Christmas paper, and I had a wonderful time opening it. Some of the most appreciated items were some clean handkerchiefs and underwear.

We didn't know it at the time, but in December we were beginning to be a part of what the newspapers were describing as "First Army opens new attack below Hürtgen." However, we were not too much interested in general concepts when our feet were freezing and we were generally miserable otherwise. I was told to stay with headquarters platoon until something more definite developed, so I proceeded to dig a foxhole with Gene Eldredge near the CP.

We weren't very battle wise yet and didn't know the best ways to combat the extreme cold. This night was a good example. We dug a medium-sized foxhole and then pitched our tent nearby. With so much snow on the ground and the wind so penetrating, our tent furnished us very little warmth. On the other hand, if we had known better, we would have dug our foxhole big enough for two men to lie down in it, covered it, and used it for our bed. Being down below ground level, we would have been protected against shellfire and also sheltered from the cold much more comfortably than with the tent. But we didn't know, so we did the best we could.

Eldredge and I crawled into our tent early and tried to get some sleep; then it was our time for guard shift. It was a painful process to put on our boots and coats in that cold temperature and go out into the cold night for two hours. It was really a beautiful night and under any other circumstances, we could have enjoyed it. But we both agreed that it was the most miserable night either of us had ever spent up to that time. Several others agreed with us. We walked around on the snowy paths in the woods to keep our feet moving. Nearby was a kitchen tent where we could hear voices inside of the officers who had gone in there to spend the night. We knew it was the only place in the whole woods that wasn't below freezing, and how we despised them all for that comfort. We knew the reception any of us would have gotten if we had stuck our nose through the tent flap after two hours of guard duty. Periods like that made the morale droop badly.

Because of the cold, our pack straps did not work very well, and to make them fasten at all it was necessary to take off our gloves. Then, before we were all set, our hands were all raw and numb.

Our objective was behind the Siegfried Line. That meant plenty of fireworks before we would ever get through that line of fortifications, and it was quite certain that many of us never would get through. With the bitter winter weather against us too, it wasn't a pretty picture.

Many thoughts were running through our minds as we moved at a snail's pace through the woods. Coming to a clearing, we saw several large guns, artillery that was backing up our attack and beyond. We came to another, better road where trucks were moving forward. We joined the movement, taking up the paths along the edges of the woods that had been made by the advancing battalions ahead of us.

In midafternoon we stopped and dug in for the night. We had to dig until well after dark, so it was then that we decided to make the hole wide enough at the head and shoulders and simply slip down in it. When it was large enough, we undid our packs and spread out what little we had. However, since we were so closely packed in the hole, our blankets wrapped around us with no trouble, and we made out very well. It was fine being down out of the wind, and, even with no covering on the hole, we slept twice as well as we had the night before.

Getting away to a good start, we crossed the road and moved down the path on the other side. It had snowed some more during the night, making it very advisable to stay on the path. A half mile along we began to see the results of what was up ahead. Medics were bringing walking casualties back down our path to the rear. Some of the men had bandages around their heads, others had arms in slings, and nearly all were dirty and bloody. We looked at them and said nothing. Every man knew that they were shrapnel wounds, shrapnel from the dreaded German 88s that we could hear only too plainly in the distance.

As the day of December 14th wore on, we could tell we were getting closer to action. By afternoon our battalion was in the lead. Climbing down one hill and up another, we were suddenly told to drop our packs except for our raincoats, bayonets, and rations. Then we moved on again. A half mile further we were shelled by the enemy as 88s began falling near us. I saw the medics pick up a man on a stretcher and carry him along the path to the rear. It was no use; he was dead.

Stumbling down the forward slope of a high wooded hill, we were again shelled. Some landed within 50 yards of me, and I noticed medics struggling with casualties, trying to get them up that slippery hill. A few moments later we went down the rest of the hill to the open valley floor. Then, one man at a time, we dashed across the open space, slogging through the icy stream in the middle, and moved up the wooded area on the far side. There was a pillbox that could see this area from up the valley. No one wasted any time in getting across to the woods. This was the northern edge of the Ardennes, some of the roughest terrain in Europe, and we were learning just exactly how rough it was.

Going through narrow places along the sides of the roads made it very difficult to keep contact with the men in front, and several times we had to run as hard as we could to catch up. We got very discouraged with so much rough walking and welcomed those stops that came all too seldom. We would lie down right in the snow to catch our breath during those periods. The reason we were allowed no regular rests was that no one knew exactly where the Germans were, and it was thought best to get out of the whole area as quickly as possible.

We did stop once while the officers suddenly had a conference. Word had been received that our marching orders were false and that we never should have left our positions that afternoon. Our battalion commander had fallen for a trick German radio transmission on our frequency, not having bothered to check the message for authentication. When his mistake was learned, he was relieved of his command by the regimental commander on the spot. The battalion executive officer, Captain Boyden, was immediately put in charge of the battalion and made his decision. We were going back into our positions.

None of the men knew what had happened, and most of us didn't realize that we had gone back until we reached our old area where we had been that day. On the way back, we passed along the edge of the woods opposite the town of Krinkelt and observed a terrific battle going on within the town. Tanks were burning, shells were bursting, tracer bullets streamed through the sky, and a good share of the town was in flames. Another regiment of our division was battling near the town, too, up ahead of us and to our right.

When we did learn the situation, we discovered that our pulling out permanently would have left this other regiment exposed on its flank. So Captain Boyden's decision to get us back into position was the right move.

The next night the weather was the same, only a little colder. We slogged down the same roads and over the same streams and fields. We reached the town of Elsenborn, only eight miles from where we had started, but it took us at least six hours to travel these eight miles—giving some indication of what kind of terrain it was that we traveled over.

Big guns were booming from positions all along the road, and we decided that this town was going to be defended. This was the northern hinge, or "hot corner" of what was later on to be called "The Bulge." The blasts of the guns were deafening, and since our nerves were on edge at this time, we were all cursing them in spite of the fact that we were ever so grateful for their presence. A buddy sounded off at one gun crew along the side of the road, "Turn that damned thing off, or I'll come over there and personally hang every one of you from the highest limb of that tree!" Then in a lower voice to us near him he said, "How in the hell do they expect us to get any sleep tonight with their big mouths blabbing off every five minutes?" We all gave out with a big roar of laughter that eased much of the tension that had been accumulating for the past week.

The morning of December 21st was cold, and we were grateful for being able to stay inside most of the time. Our supply sergeant over at G Company had now moved some things into the school house, so Marvin Wilson and I went over there to see what he had. To our pleasant surprise we found that he had a complete stock of new clothing for us, from underwear to overcoats. Did we have a swell time going through all of it and taking what we wanted! I picked a new pair of shoes, a new shirt, a pair of new pants, another set of wool underwear, some socks, and a mackinaw. Going back to battalion and our room, I then took a piecemeal bath and shaved. What a feeling—it was as though I were a new man completely.

Shortly after daylight the chow jeeps arrived, and we enjoyed our first kitchen-cooked full meal in two weeks. It more than made up for our miserable night and loss of sleep. After breakfast, I got out my entrenching tool and started digging a hole for Wilson and me. We worked all day and kept warm from the exercise. We chopped ourselves some trees to make into logs for the top of the hole, and by late afternoon we had a good roof.

We received some more mail that day, and I was lucky in getting two more boxes from home. I went over to G Company and found Glenny Blanchard and Harold Veney, and we all ate up the contents of the boxes. Since we couldn't carry any more on our backs, it was the best policy to consume all that we could while we were still in one spot.

Christmas Day. A fine Merry Christmas, starting out by being strafed. We could think of much nicer ways of spending the holidays, but at the same time we wasted no tears in brooding over it, since we knew it wouldn't do any good.

Anyone moving down the road these days was easily spotted from the enemy lines because of the snow outlining our darkly clothed bodies. Once I was fired at by small arms (rifles) and had to hit the ground, but at such a great distance a man was difficult to hit. Another time several of us were walking down the road together when the enemy sent over some mortar shells.

A real highlight during my stay in Elsenborn was the trip to Eupen for a shower. The engineers had set up an extensive shower- and change-of-clothing service in Eupen for the army units all around that area. It was a bitter-cold day on January 20th when I went. But I was extremely lucky in being at the right place at the right time and was able to ride in the cab of our truck. Arriving in Eupen, we immediately went in and took our showers. It was such a treat that the men had to be shoved along out of the shower rooms in order to let other groups in. For me, it was my first real bath in three months.

The company then spread out in a sparsely wooded area north of Elsenborn that could be located only by following paths and being careful about direction. Due to the positions being so far from the main roads, it was nearly always impossible to get vehicles in, so that meant no hot meals. K-rations were brought in by horse and sled and later by the new Weasel, a caterpillar-tracked truck that could move over the snow and ice without bogging down. The runners had to go with Weasel nearly every trip because of the changing of drivers and the fact that they couldn't remember all the routes into the various companies.

We were to move on up through the woods and relieve elements of the 1st Division, which had broken through the Siegfried Line near Hollerath. The roads were icy, so marching up and down the hilly roads of the Ardennes was no easy job that night. We had only one stop for a rest during the three or four hours of marching, so twice my arms went dead on me under the weight of my pack. The blood having partly left them, I couldn't even raise them, and several times I almost dropped my carbine from my shoulder. It is a most helpless feeling not to have control of your arms, but that often happened during marches while carrying full packs.

About 10 P.M. we reached the "Dragon's Teeth" fortifications and marched on through. But a half mile beyond we turned around and came back to the woods just outside the line. Some of us were so exhausted that we just sat on a log and hung our heads to rest before settling down. It had been a fast and tiring march. Wilson and I fixed ourselves a spot beside a jeep trailer, and after a shift of guard duty, we turned in. We didn't do any digging but just laid our stuff out on the ground and crawled in for the rest of the night. That was a miserable night with much confusion evident, and we were glad to see morning come. Taz [Nelson] and [Frank] Ryan had slept in a booby-trapped foxhole that night without realizing it and lived to tell about it only because it had failed to go off. Another boy did trip on a wire, and it cost him his foot, which all showed that the Germans hadn't left without dropping a few souvenirs in the area.

While at Hollerath, some rumors began to circulate to the effect that we were going to be taken back to the rear for a rest area. That was hard news to believe after having had nothing but dirt, misery, and work for over three months. On the other hand, we had been on line for 94 days, which was a record surpassed only by two other outfits on our front at the time. So after thinking it over, we figured we did deserve a rest if anyone did.

As all good things seem to come to an end, so did our rest period. The news came suddenly that we would move on the afternoon of February 27th; our fun was over. We passed through Aachen, going east. That city amazed me. I had no idea it was so large, the population being about 300,000 before the battle began. But it had been practically shelled into uselessness now with only a small portion of the place capable of being used by our army. Mass destruction was the scene all the way from the Siegfried forts on the west side of town through the east side.

Ruhr Pocket

The morning of April 13th in Meggen was a sad day for us when we first learned of President Roosevelt's passing the day before. It was a surprise to all of us and hard to believe, but nobody thought that much would be changed because of it, so we thought about it as little as possible and went right on with the war.

As we moved out along the river we looked like a strange outfit, having accumulated so many German vehicles here and there and keeping them. There were regulations against their use by Americans in such cases, but their finders always kept them until authorities made them give them up.

The whole Ruhr pocket was now only a couple of days away from being completely wiped out, and everyone seemed to sense the climax. What encouraged us so much was the mass surrender, the likes of which hadn't been seen since the big traps back in France the year before. The original estimate of a hundred thousand Germans in the pocket was proving to be only a third the actual amount.

Prisoners were coming back in numbers again, but on foot in this area, and were being herded into fields on the rear side of town. In this group were several young women, husky as their men and putting up a much bigger fuss. They were babies in a situation like that, but the men didn't seem to pay any attention to them. G Company alone captured three generals and their entire staffs. We came across E Company, and what a sight to behold—150 were trying to look after a couple thousand prisoners.

We later learned that the situation was so confused that Germans were capturing Americans, and then later were coming to our lines as prisoners of their captives. Collins, G Company jeep driver, had the experience of being captured in his jeep alone during the night. He spent the night in a cellar as a prisoner while his captors decided what they were going to do. They finally decided and told Collins to take them to the Americans as his prisoners.

Orders had come down a couple days before April 22nd forbidding troops to use German houses for shelter anymore since they were not supposed to be healthful or something. Did that burn us up! We griped and cussed and fumed constantly. I guess the whole Third Army, which we were now a part of, echoed our gripes, because as I understand it, General Eisenhower sent down an order overriding Patton's, and we were once again allowed to use the houses.

The next few days brought the collapse of the whole European War while we sat in Altfrauenhofen resting, taking pictures, getting cleaned up, and enjoying a movie and band concert. It was a wonderful feeling to relax again after the previous two weeks of relentless attacking. Eldredge and I moved down with the other runners as soon as the G Company lines were laid, and we had a lot of fun absorbing the sun and taking it easy when the weather warmed up again.

Gradually we were now able to get our clothes and ourselves washed up a bit. Back at Altfrauenhofen we made a deal with a German woman to wash our combat jackets for some chocolate. Mine hadn't been washed since February and was thoroughly filthy. Little by little I managed a bath and a shave and to wash out some of my underwear. My hair was dirty as usual, but I didn't want to wash it until I got another closer haircut. We seldom washed our hair during combat. It took too much water, too much soap, and it would flop in our eyes.

May 20th was a big day for those of us who like to write letters, because on that day we received a new set of censorship regulations, which practically lifted censorship altogether. We were now free to tell where we were and any of our experiences that didn't involve describing our equipment in detail or our combat tactics. The Jap war was still on, and though the U.S. didn't care about a lot of information getting to them—figuring it would only serve to scare them a bit—there were certain things that were thought best not to talk about.

Formal surrender ceremonies took place aboard the battleship USS *Missouri* in Tokyo Bay on September 2nd, so all thoughts were now on how soon could we get home. I was no exception. Under final recomputation of points, I now had 56. This projected to a departure date from Europe of approximately February 1946. Men in my category were beginning to be transferred to the 79th Division for shipment to the U.S. Band members were specifically excluded. I didn't mind, at least for the moment. We were enjoying our life. It amazed us from the time the war was over we never had any kind of trouble from the civilian population. Everyone was very cooperative. In fact, we could never find anyone who would admit to having been a Nazi. Ha! They were a pretty desperate people economically and constantly courted our favors for anything we might give them.

(Excerpts from his military memoirs titled *To Hellenbach*)

Donald Wallace

Camp Maxey and the Infantry

Infantry training consisted of marching, maneuvers, hand-to-hand combat training, and something called an infiltration course. This latter consisted of crawling under barbed wire and through smoke while a machine gun fired over our heads. There was a night exercise with smoke, as well as a daylight exercise.

I didn't do well on the rifle range with an M-1. I flinched every time I pulled the trigger, and the shot would go astray. They would wave "Maggie's drawers" many times for me over the target. One good buddy "penciled me in" so that I would pass and stay in the company with my buddies. I later qualified with a carbine and was made a runner.

Overseas with the 99th

On September 29, 1944, we boarded ships in Boston for the long trip across the Atlantic. It was one of the largest ocean convoys of the war. We could see ships as far as the horizon in all directions. The ships had to zig and zag to hide from German submarines as they crossed the ocean. We arrived in Scotland and, after debarking, made our way to the south of England and lived for a spell in tents. It was always raining there, and it was mudsville—sloppy, mushy mudsville. We got one 48-hour pass into London and for the first time witnessed a city in blackout. On November 6th we boarded barges to cross the channel to France, got into open trucks, and crossed into Belgium. As we passed through villages, French and Belgian citizens threw apples to us and ran alongside the slow-moving trucks pouring wine and passing it up to us. It was very heartwarming for our cold bodies in those open trucks.

Battle of the Bulge

On December 11th we moved to a clearing in Buchholz, Belgium, where we were in division reserve. Sometime during the peaceful days before the battle, I used a can of gasoline from a jeep nearby to restart a fire from embers of a fire of the night before. (Stupid thing to do!) A flame crept up, spilling the fuel; my hand and arm caught fire. I rolled over in the snow to snuff out the flames but had a badly burned left hand. Blisters eventually formed all over my left hand. (I was a southpaw.)

The shooting war began soon after the artillery barrage east of our position. From the farmhouse yard we could hear popping sounds coming from near the station. German troops had come out of the woods, and L Company had taken them on. I couldn't shoot from my position, because I really couldn't tell who was who. I crept along the yard in the front of the farmhouse to a small berm and the hedges there. It was a little misty, and vision wasn't too good. I watched some of the firefight near the station until I drew fire from somewhere northeast of my position. Twigs were snapping on the shrubs above my head.

Sometime after the initial battle when the German advance broke down there was an artillery barrage laid on L Company and the 3rd Battalion headquarters. We had dug slit trenches in the yard but instead (and without thinking) scampered into a boxcar that was low to the ground without its wheels. The barrage lasted awhile, and the noise was shattering and ceaseless. No shell ever hit the boxcar directly, but it was very scary when I realized during the barrage that I should be in my foxhole. In examining the boxcar afterward, we noted that shrapnel had torn through it leaving gaping holes all along its side down to less than two feet above ground level. The yard was full of holes from artillery explosions. Again I felt lucky.

During the day on the 16th, I carried messages from the farmhouse down the road to Buchholz Station. Once in awhile, a single artillery round would be lobbed in. These were not part of any barrage, but played psychological havoc with their suddenness. There was absolutely no warning. On one of my trips to the station, I was within about 20 feet of the railroad overpass, when one of those shells exploded on top of the overpass. The concussion tore off my helmet and knocked me to the ground. When I realized that I was OK, I thought about how lucky I was!

During the night, 3rd Battalion headquarters pulled north into the woods. Word came down that German paratroopers with GI uniforms were in the area and moving about. We had to inform everyone of this, and I delivered the message to L Company that they should remain perfectly still during the night. Anything that moved was to be treated as hostile and shot. Later I was startled to learn that I was to deliver a change of password to L Company. It was the belief that the old password might be known to the Krauts. I said, "But the guys will shoot anything that moves!" The message had to be delivered, however, so I went. The forest was dark and so very quiet. Every step I took during my search for the company I thought to myself, "Gawd, I hope I don't step on a twig." I was scared and in the darkness I didn't want to make a sound. Suddenly I heard, "HALT!" To this day I remember my immediate response, "Don't shoot! It's me, Wallace!" The guy knew me. I recognized his voice, and he recognized mine. I felt lucky again.

Sometime after I got back to the battalion area in the woods, a group of us were led off in the darkness. We avoided towns and made our way north across rolling open fields that seemed to be farmland. I tore the seat of my pants going through a barbed-wire fence. We hit the ground as burp guns spat behind us and bullets kissed the air around us. When I looked back once to my left rear, I saw a village not more than a quarter of a mile away glowing in the night as it was blasted by artillery.

Later we hoofed it out to Elsenborn Ridge to join the remnants of the 3rd Battalion and L Company. We dug in behind the high spot of the ridge. The Germans were in the woods beyond us. I was given a bazooka and a

BAR (besides my carbine) to help defend our positions there. On Christmas Day after dark we were brought cold turkey sandwiches. (Turkey was a tradition that would not be ignored.)

At least one day was cloudy. There were low clouds with a small break here and there. A German reconnaissance plane, probably looking for ground activity, passed above one of these breaks for an instant. I could see the pilot, he was that low! When the clouds cleared overhead, we watched dogfights and saw planes go down leaving smoke trails. We watched pilots bail out of their aircraft and parachute toward the ground. It was just like the movies, but this was real.

At the ridge, one buddy was out relieving himself in the early morning. A single artillery round exploded nearby and killed him. I was sent on a detail to carry his body to the rear, but I was beginning to feel the weakening effects of a hand infection. (In order to be able to fire my carbine, I had bitten open the blisters after that flame incident. One area on my hand became infected.) I tried but didn't have enough strength to lift him, so I had to pass off that duty to another guy.

On January 4th I was very weak and was sent back to a hospital in Liege with blood poisoning. I remember telling the nurses that I didn't feel right about being so muddy and dirty and put in bed with clean sheets. (I know that sounds stupid, but these things stand out.) They found my lack of dexterity later and would not send me back to my outfit. I missed the guys so very much.

Life in Gay Paree

Before I reached my twentieth birthday, I had been fighting out of foxholes and sharing the camaraderie of close buddies. They were back there still fighting while I was being cared for in three different hospitals. First there was a MASH unit, followed by a hospital in Liege and one in England. In Liege buzz bombs flew over, sounding like big trucks passing overhead. We'd cringe when the rocket motor cut off. After a minute, there would be an explosion as it hit. It was scary. I was eventually evacuated to a hospital in the south of England. Then I was sent to Paris.

I was trained in a medical attachment in suburban Paris in the art of giving shots. I gave shots of penicillin to GIs who hadn't used preventive methods. Once when a colonel came in for a tetanus shot (or some such thing) and I didn't know how much to draw into the syringe, I gave him a shot that turned out to be double what he was supposed to get. He got very sick.

I visited the art museums, historic places, and palaces in Paris, but I was too young to appreciate these finer things. Much of the time our fun activity was not classy. I look back on times like this as being foolish. We spent many evenings at the Concert Mayol, a show that featured a topless chorus line and comedy acts. We actually sat in alcoves on the side of the stage. The girls would wave to us when they danced by, as our frequent visits made us well known to them.

When the attachment was discontinued, I was transferred to a general hospital outside Paris and still later to a unit that administered prophylactic care to guys who fooled around with wicked women and needed care to prevent diseases. We were stationed in major hotels, had our offices there, and lived like kings.

Of course, there was temptation. It was difficult to avoid. Pigalle was an area that was loaded with girlie shows, but there were hookers all over Paris. When we needed a little extra cash we would sell some cigarettes, candy, and clothing. (I worked in clothing supply at the general hospital.)

Eventually I was shipped home and discharged nine months after the war had ended. By that time the brass band celebration had ended, and I came home without fanfare. My folks were really glad to see me, and I was glad to be home.

Raymond A. Trayes

We arrived in France on November 2, 1944; Belgium, November 6, 1944; and Germany, November 9, 1944. We were committed to line at Kalterherberg, Germany, in a defensive position that lasted five weeks. Our usual procedure was to dig a large pit to put the mortar in so that we had some protection from artillery shrapnel. In this case, we dug the pit extra large, about 8'x8', and covered most of the opening with logs and put dirt on top. This made room for several men to sleep in the hole with the gun. During this type of defensive position, only one half of the squad would be out in the woods with the gun. The other half would be having its turn staying in a house in the village for a few days and then alternating.

All during combat we were under orders not to eat any food that we found in the houses because of the possibility of its being poisoned. However, several of us "country boys" had a different view on this occasionally. One day when we returned to the house from the gun position we discovered the carcass of a small slaughtered pig hanging in the attic, and everybody was frying fresh pork of various cuts and descriptions.

Ed Higgins, who became my best friend all during combat, joined us while we were at this position. On December 11, 1944, we started an attack in the vicinity of the Manchau Forest on the left flank of the 2nd Division. We met heavy opposition from pillboxes between the towns of Krinkelt and Billingen. Our company had its first casualty and fatality.

On the night of December 16, 1944, I had to dig my foxhole on a pine-tree-covered hillside in ground loaded with shale. I dug a hole that I could sit in with my knees up in front of me and put the mortar-base plate across the hole above my head. At that time we had not yet received our winter jackets or boots. During the night when my feet became cold, I kicked them against the end of the hole. By morning I could not feel anything when I kicked. Early in the morning I was included in a detail of men to carry food and ammunition to the machine gunners up on the front. I really stumbled along for a while until I got some circulation in my feet. I think this forced hike saved my feet. Later that morning our lieutenant told us that we were surrounded and that the decision to fight our way out or to surrender had not yet been made. We were told to discard anything German in case we were taken prisoner. I was wearing a pair of high knitted woolen socks, but since they were the only ones I had, I did not discard them.

While we were moving around that afternoon trying to determine what we were going to do, I heard an artillery shell coming in that I knew "had my name on it." I flopped to the ground near a clump of small trees, and the shell landed about 20 feet on the other side of the trees but did not explode. Thanks to some "slave laborer" who "fixed" that shell, my life was spared. This was the first day of the German Ardennes breakthrough, better known as the Belgian Bulge.

On the night of December 19, 1944, after the enemy intercepted our code, they ordered us to withdraw. We traveled all night with the fighting on our right and ended up in the morning back at our original positions. We were extremely lucky!

During the early days of the Bulge there was a lot of confusion. English-speaking Germans dressed as Americans infiltrated the area and changed road signs. We were in the area of the northern hinge of the Bulge. We finally made a withdrawal through the 2nd Division to Elsenborn, Belgium, on December 20, 1944.

We went into the 9th Division's reserve and set up a defense outside Elsenborn. Christmas Day was spent in a foxhole at this position. Most of the men received packages here but, since I had been a replacement, my mail was still very slow in arriving. I do not remember when my packages arrived. Christmas was a sunny day, and, therefore, there was plenty of enemy aircraft activity. New Year's Day was spent in the same position with no celebrating and a lot of enemy aircraft activity.

On January 5, 1945, we relieved the 38th Infantry of the 9th Division and were still outside Elsenborn. We did a lot of firing here and received a lot in return. As the result of some blizzards, we had snow three to four feet deep. There was a schoolhouse in Elsenborn where we could go occasionally to clean up and enjoy a cooked meal. It was on my first visit to the schoolhouse that I trimmed my beard into a mustache.

We moved into the woods outside Hollerath, Germany, on February 4th and the next day walked through the German dragon's teeth defenses to Hollerath and saw the first signs of the mass death of the German soldiers caused by our artillery. We relieved the 1st Division units in a defensive position. On February 12th, units of the 69th Division who were on line for the first time relieved us. We spent a wet night in the woods.

We were pulled back from the line on February 14th and went to Folander, Belgium, a temporary rest area. Our rest was interrupted by being assigned to help the engineers load stone and brick rubble from destroyed houses and yard walls on trucks to be spread on the muddy dirt roads. Occasionally we would find a personal article of some sort in the rubble. One fellow found two cloth bags about the size of a five-pound bag of sugar. He tore one bag open and discarded the bags because the contents were moldy. Another "country-boy" and I each grabbed one, and I discovered that I had a homecured smoked picnic shoulder. We had great eating that night when I fried it.

As we crossed Germany, it was interesting to see how the civilians tried to protect their belongings. We found a console-size radio hidden in the hay in a haymow. Once, when the snow had been mostly melted away, we saw spots of clay in the garden. I probed several of the smaller spots and found crocks filled with *Schnapps* and food items. One large site had a galvanized tank stuffed with clothes. We did, however, occasionally find some smoked meat hanging in the smokehouses, which we eventually discovered were built into the house chimneys in the attics.

At one point, we dug a pit about six feet in diameter and about three feet deep to put the mortar in so that we could fire over a house. We did have to cut down a small apple tree to get the necessary clearance, however, and a neighbor man took sharp exception to that. One little old lady occupied the house we were in. The first day we were there she returned from the bomb shelter while we were gathered in her kitchen having coffee. She was a nice, cooperative lady, and we tried to be considerate of her. In fact, we became the guardians of the rabbit she had in a hutch in the backyard by stopping other GIs from taking it. When we wanted a rabbit to eat, we went elsewhere for one. We did, however, slip and discovered that somebody had taken the rabbit. We set out to replace it but could not find one as large as the one she had had. When we left her house, she had two small rabbits in her hutch!

On the night of March 9th we walked several miles back to a crossroads and bunked down in the same tavern we had slept in on our way up to the Rhine. About midnight we were awakened and loaded on trucks to be hauled to a bridge that had been captured. The roads were loaded with tanks and trucks, and we finally walked about the last six miles. This bridge was the double-tracked Ludendorf Railway Bridge to Remagen. As we approached the bridge, I saw that both sets of rails had been covered with large sheets of three-quarter-inch steel plate. I marveled at how the army engineers had located the steel plate and installed it in such a short time. It was not until I was reading an account of the fiftieth anniversary of the capture of the bridge that I realized the Germans put the steel on the tracks so they could use it to evacuate their remaining troops on the western side of the river. Those troops never were evacuated.

While staying in a house in a little village on a mountain, Ed Higgins and I caught some chickens and cleaned and fried them and, together with some fried potatoes, had a nice meal on the table. When an American tank on the very narrow roadway scraped the side of the building and shook the supporting beam, a lot of plaster fell from the ceiling onto the table, and we were unable to eat the chicken and potatoes!

On March 14th we attacked Butenbuch. During this attack Sergeant Currie was killed and Sergeant Bryan suffered severe shell shock while they were looking for blankets in a knocked-out German tank. Sergeant Bryan was in the tank and Sergeant Currie was standing on top of the tank when a German artillery shell hit it. Sergeant Bryan returned to the front a few days later, but the shock was so great that his effectiveness as a fighter was gone.

When we entered a village we started a house-to-house search to make sure all the soldiers and villagers had left. I went down the basement steps of one house with a flashlight and saw that the basement was jammed with old men, women, and children. I just waved to them and retreated up the stairs, figuring that was a good safe place for them to spend the rest of the night. We then chose another house to stay in while we were in that village. We chose the house of the village doctor, but the vestibule and stairway were completely knocked out by American artillery hits. After we found a ladder to get to the second floor, I found some dry clothes to replace my wet ones.

We were now riding in trucks a lot and mopping up behind the 9th Armored Division as needed. The 6x6 two-and-a-half-ton army trucks that we were using fascinated the German civilians. These trucks would speed down the Autobahn at 55 miles an hour and, when interrupted by a bombed-out bridge, would go cross-country and grind and growl through a woods, wade a stream, groan up a steep embankment to the Autobahn, whine through a series of gear shifting, and once again speed off. I agreed with the people who said that these trucks played a big part in our victory in this highly mobile war.

For the first time we freed Allied prisoners at Loar on March 23rd. A British captain asked to see my .45-caliber automatic pistol while we were having a "coffee-break" and complimented me on my gun-safety habits when I unloaded it before I handed it to him. He did not realize it, but I would never give my loaded pistol to anybody over there!

On April 10th we started clearing the Ruhr pocket that was created when two armored forces that had bypassed this industrial area joined forces again on the other side of the area. Thousands of German troops were surrounded, and their officers marched them in formation to surrender. We were called upon to help the MP units handle the prisoners. We lined them up in fields several yards apart and then examined their belongings on a one-on-one basis. They apparently did not expect us to feed them because they all had a loaf or two of hard crusted dark bread and a jar of white animal fat of some kind that they used as a spread. We let them keep the bread and fat but, of course, had to take away the knives.

The original diary from which this was prepared was completed on May 27, 1945, when our primary duty consisted of doing guard duty at a former German army-camp complex. Included in this complex were a bakery and a warehouse that had some beet sugar and grain in them. We were informed by a member of the 6th Squad, who was a former Tennessee hillbilly, that these were all the ingredients necessary to make some "mountain moonshine." Four or five of us, including the hillbilly, decided to make some. We used a woodburning laundry tub as a cooker and fashioned a still, using the copper gas line from an old German truck as the condensing coil. The stuff tasted pretty good but was extremely strong.

During this period everybody was counting and recounting their "points." It was sometime during this period after the moonshine affair that some of us realized that, since we had somehow arrived safely at this point, there was now a pretty good chance that we would be returning home after all. This was something we did not count on during combat. This change of attitude also included a change in our habits and actions.

Since I had had more active duty time in the U.S. before going overseas, I had more points than the rest of the men. And since the total accumulated points each man had determined his discharge date, I was transferred to the 83rd Division for occupation duty and eventually my return to the U.S.

Richard A. Boe

Battle of the Bulge

On March 5, 1943, I was sent a letter of Greetings from our President, Franklin D. Roosevelt, stating I was to report for induction in the U.S. Army at San Francisco, California. As I was a Canadian citizen I was not able to volunteer, therefore, I was drafted. From San Francisco we went to the Presidio of Monterey for classification, then, because of my extremely brilliant mind I was sent to the infantry. However, they wanted volunteers for parachutists at Toccoa, Georgia. Upon arriving we immediately went into intensive training. The medical doctor said I had flat feet. Boy, was I surprised! He also said I was color-blind. I was wondering why they accepted me in the first place. I was sent to Camp Blanding, Florida, for basic training. After ten weeks of training we were the regular soldiers of the 66th Infantry Division. We were transferred as a division to Camp Robinson, Little Rock, Arkansas. At the U.S. District Court I received my citizenship papers. I went through some rigorous training, was sent to a special school, and there I received my Ranger shoulder patch. I was one of the best they had, as I was the best expert rifleman. I tied with the best in the nation at 700 yards rifle range. From there we went to Camp Rucker, Alabama, for more training. There the call went out for volunteers for the parachutist; again I was accepted. At that time I was an 18-year-old staff sergeant, a very young age to have this responsibility. I left the 66th Infantry Division, went to Camp Miles Standish, and was on the first available ship to England, the S.S. *Wakefield*.

We arrived at Liverpool, England, and proceeded to Nottingham, England's Sherwood Forest where Robin Hood spent many years. This area was beautiful with its many trees. Although we were in squad tents, I finally found out this was the famous 82nd Airborne Division Company E for the 505th Parachute regiment. What a stroke of luck! Our general was General James Gavin, the youngest brigadier general in the U.S. Army, and he loved his men. This was the reason we would do anything for him. We received our jump training nearby in an airfield that had C-4 planes that were used for parachute training. The first and second jump went well; the third almost cost me my life. I remember my friend Zudeck, who jumped in front of me and went all the way to the ground. His chute didn't open and he was killed instantly. On my third jump, at about 900 feet, we all stood up for equipment check. Everything was all right, the green light went on, and we were moving toward the door. This time I was scared about the jump. I left the plane shouting "Geronimo" and, as I was falling through the sky, nothing happened. My parachute didn't deploy. I was falling faster and faster. I didn't know what to do. No time to pray, but God is merciful. I landed on top of another man's chute, right in the center. It felt like a cloud as I tried to get up, but my legs started to collapse his chute and I realized I must get off it. So without regard to my own life, I lay down and swam off his chute. There I was free falling all the way to the ground. My face was turned upward. My whole body blacked out, for how long I did not know. Then I heard voices saying, "Is he dead? He hit awfully hard and he's not moving." I tried to breathe but couldn't. All the air was knocked out of me. I know now the holy angels were encamped around me, and I was given a breath of life again. I got up, to the amazement of the other troopers. I was OK, but my canteen was flattened. There wasn't anything wrong with me. No broken bones, and I walked off the jump field a new man. Praise the Lord. He loved me!

On my fourth and almost fatal jump again, I stood up as the red light went on and was given an equipment check. A-OK. The green light went on, and I was scared again. Then out the door I went. I saw my chute go over my head and blossom into fullness, but again the same thing happened to me. I was too close to the trooper in front of me. I acted as a clock pendulum and swung through his raiser (lines) up into the apex of his parachute. I couldn't believe it. Again, I was in trouble. As I came back down off his chute, I took four of his lines with me. Because this is unreal it caused his chute to spill excess amounts of air and he was tilted, but all my lines were captured by his four lines, as I was heavier than he was. As I was falling faster, my chute collapsed again, and, about the last 50 feet, I fell and again the ground came up very fast. I hit like a ton of bricks, but again no broken bones or bruises. Boy, you'd think I would have given up by now! But being young I wanted to serve my country. The fifth jump everything went well and I received my parachute wings. Now I was a real trooper. This is what I wanted.

Here I learned to love the British way of life. I was introduced to fish and chips wrapped in the local newspaper. I went to one of their dances where they were doing the Lambeth Walk, and I was intrigued by their English accent. They didn't love us but tolerated us Yanks, as they called us, and we were glad we came to help them in their finest hour, as Sir Winston Churchill said.

As the war went on, our training became more rigorous. Sometimes, however, we were given weekend passes. I always went to London, which was about two hours by bus and train. When we arrived at Queen Victoria Station, I was impressed by the size. It was huge! The amount of trains that were there! I really enjoyed sightseeing and went everyplace the underground train would take me. I remember one night during the blackout I went to see a stage show at the Palace theater where they had vaudeville. A German buzz bomb roared overhead, and everybody in the theater froze. No sounds. The noise stopped, and the buzz bomb plummeted to earth several blocks away. There was a huge explosion that rocked our theater. Fire engines raced past us, then everyone went back to performing as if nothing had happened. They were so used to the bombings that life went on. I went to the outskirts of London high up on a hill to overlook the city around 11 P.M. As I looked up at the darkened sky, I saw a weird sight. An arcing of fire was dull red, and, as I watched, it reached the apex and started to fall on London. I didn't realize at the time, but it was a V-2 rocket. It hit London with a brilliant flash that lit up the sky, followed by a loud bang. I had just witnessed a V-2 and realized that the people that were there were surely dead. This was my first taste of what war was all about— people killing people.

Late in December I heard a loud noise and went outside my barracks and looked up. What I saw was a Flying Fortress B-17 drop two red flares and one blue flare. I didn't know at the time that it was the signal for all planes to group into formation. I saw one group from the right, one from the left joining in the middle with fighter escorts overhead flying protective cover for the B-17s, and they all headed for Germany in close formation. It took more than 20 minutes for them to fly over my head. I realized that it was a maximum effort and that there were over 1,000 bombers headed for Europe. This massive destruction force would unleash its fury on the people and soldiers. This thought scared me, and I was glad it wasn't us on the receiving end of these destructive bombs.

The next morning, January 1, 1945, we started to advance into German-occupied positions. They booby-trapped a horse with a saddle, and one of our troopers jumped on for a joy ride and lost his leg when the bomb exploded. Soon after this happened a German Panzer tank came at me. He was about a block away and opened fire. An 88mm shell exploded over my head. The white-hot metal rained all around my body. The ground was smoking like a ring of fire. Again, the tank fired his 88. Again, a ring of fire. I know the angels deflected the sharpness and saved my life.

As we were advancing across no-man's land, I ran across a civilian U.S. Salvation Army man handing out Hershey Almond Chocolate Bars right between the Germans and us. I couldn't believe my eyes. The Red Cross wouldn't do this. They even charged us a nickel for donuts and coffee. This is why I think a lot of the Salvation Army. They were there when we needed them.

Meanwhile, overhead, two B-25 Marauders were strafing a German column just over the hill. They caused a lot of damage to the men and vehicles. However, they were able to knock out one of our attacking aircraft. There were two men that were able to bail out of their aircraft. Both parachutes opened. One fell right in front of me, the other drifted toward the German column. We rushed across the snow to rescue him. Boy, was he glad to see us! The Germans left everything behind and fled north. The column was badly mauled. Tanks, trucks, guns were everywhere for our taking. Because of the cold weather (10°F.), my feet finally got frostbite. I realized I must take off my combat boots and thaw out my toes. I couldn't put my shoes on. It hurt me, so I carried them and used my rain boots filled with straw as I was carrying ammunition. I saw a lady rush out and welcome us and was shouting she was free again. She had wine and bread. I took the bread and gave her my combat boots. As my feet hurt, I kept falling farther and farther behind my outfit. Limping along, it took me all day to find them again. We crossed into Germany and through the Siegfried line. There was still snow on the ground. Later that day I was out in the field by myself and here comes a fighter plane P-47 Thunderbolt, and he flew right over my head and dropped a bomb on me. I guess he thought I was a German. As it hit the ground, it didn't explode; it was a gas tank. There was enough gas for my stove.

I was walking down a snow-covered road and saw the biggest tank that I've ever seen. A monster called King Tiger, 65 tons, that was stalled in the middle of the road. A fearsome sight. There I captured my first German soldier. He looked miserable, but he didn't care. He yelled, "Comrade!" and then he surrendered. I took him back to be interrogated by our G-2 intelligence team. We moved to a hillside observation point into this dugout at night, as the dragon teeth and German pillbox were within a block of our position. I was looking out and here was a pair of new parachute boots standing right in my eyesight. I grabbed the boots and pulled in an officer, a second lieutenant, who was spit and polished. No combat clothes. I could not believe it. He was giving away our position. The next thing we knew the Germans were shelling us. I told him the next time I would kill him. I found out he had been recruiting in New York, and they flew him into the front lines within three days. I told him he was lucky to be alive walking along the hill like it was a Sunday picnic.

I remember our sergeant went down to the water's edge. There was a German tank and nobody around. He went to investigate, and, as we walked around, a German machine gun opened up across the river and he was shot with five bullets into his midsection. His last words were, "Tell my mother I love her," and fell over dead. That's the way the war goes. You never know.

Several days later we were relieved by regular army groups, and we went back to France for rest and training. There I saw Marlena Dietrich's stage show. I want to mention the jeep shows where Mickey Rooney came to entertain the troops. He was very, very good. We really enjoyed him, a real professional. Thanks to the USO. They brought home to us in France.

On the way to Berlin, Field Marshal Von Rundstedt was defeated at the Battle of the Bulge although he knew he couldn't win. Hitler had ordered an all-out attack in Belgium and Luxembourg toward Antwerp, thus cutting the Allies in half. However, this failed and the German soldiers' losses were over 100,00 casualties. The American casualties were 81,000. Approximately 800 battle tanks on both sides were lost in battle.

We were in Epinal, France, when General Jim Gavin called us together as a group and informed us to pack our gear; we were going to Berlin, Germany, to keep the peace. We were given a section, as were the Russians, French, and British in postwar Germany July 1945.

We finally arrived at the railroad station in Berlin, heavily damaged by air raids and artillery. We all loaded into army trucks and proceeded toward Potsdam. We came across many knocked out tanks and vehicles, and the city was in ruins. We marched into the barracks, former SS soldiers' quarters. My first duty was to guard a German prisoner-of- war camp just outside our barracks.

A few Germans escaped from the compound, and we had work forces outside the camp to gather wood for stoves. When not on guard duty we went to downtown Berlin on local trains. We could cover the whole area down at the Brandenburg Gate, the victory arch, with the heart of Berlin almost totally destroyed.

While there I tried to locate Hitler's bunker nearby, but there was too much rubble. There were Russian soldiers and women everywhere trying to barter for American cigarettes and watches. I even heard that a Russian had bought an American Sherman tank. Of course, he didn't get to keep it.

I noticed a large hole in the street, and, as I looked down, there were underground trains four tiers below. They had stopped before they fell in the hole. A delayed-action bomb dropped by our planes caused this hole. Later I smelled a horrible stench coming from underground. I was told that the SS had blasted a hole in the river channel, thus causing the water to flood the underground tunnels, causing the death of thousands of innocent civilians who were using them as underground shelters. The SS diverted the river to keep out the Soviet soldiers who were using it to enter Berlin.

I went to Femina Palast, a very high-class nightclub for entertainment and dancing. One of the ladies, who was part Jewish, told me her dad was picked up by the SS and sent to a concentration camp. She never saw her mother or dad again. So in retaliation, she gained the confidence of the German SS, then told the Russian MPs, who took them to prison.

The following week, General Gavin told our company commanders that we would be honor guards to parade at Templehoff Airfield before three

Russian field marshals Koniev, Zhukov, and Rokosovsky, Field Marshal Montgomery, and General of the Army Eisenhower. What a time in history. All this brass. Yes, the 82nd was making history. What an honor that I was part of this parade. There was a parachute jump as part of this display, but there was a casualty to one of our troopers as he jumped out of the C-47 jump plane. As he was falling, he landed right on top of a high portable radio antenna. It broke in two and killed him. After that an officer landed right in front of me and hit the cement hard and landed on his knees. Nothing broken. He was OK. Then all the marshals and Eisenhower came to inspect the 82nd Honor Parade. What an exciting moment to see all the high-ranking officers.

Next day I went to the train station, and all these women were holding photographs of their sons and fathers that were captured in the Battle of Stalingrad. That is where Field Marshal Von Paulus surrendered a whole army of over 107,000 Germans who were marched into Siberia to die in the frozen north. These women were hoping their loved ones would be on the train. But only about 5,000 came back alive.

General Marshall informed General Gavin that the 82nd Airborne Division was selected to go to New York City and march down Fifth Avenue. This was to be the WWII Victory Parade to honor all those soldiers who had fallen in WWII. We were proud to do this parade.

No, I was not a perfect soldier, as I went AWOL and they sent the MPs looking for me. They were ordered to pick me up as soon as possible because the adjutant general wanted to talk to me. Well, when I got back to the SS barracks, I was put under house arrest. My punishment was to dig a 6'x6'x6'-deep hole and fill it back up. Then as further company punishment, I was put in charge of the battalion's beer hall. I gave the GIs one glass of beer for you and one beer for me! Boy! I liked this punishment—hic!

There was great interest in giving U.S. soldiers in Berlin an opportunity to learn a trade while there. My CO asked if there was anyone who would like to learn automotive repair, so I volunteered and enjoyed my school lessons. We received Field Marshal Göring's touring car, and our group tuned it up and sent it to the motor pool.

At the school was a large manufacturing building that housed our field mess hall, which served three meals a day. While eating my lunch, I looked out the window and saw a large line of women and children standing next to two large garbage cans. These lines were several hundred feet long. Later, I went outside and gave them some of my leftover meat. The mothers were not asking anything for themselves but for their children. After that I always made sure that I saved apples, oranges, or food to give to them; I didn't want them to beg. However, some of our soldiers did throw their food into the garbage cans. For them, I apologize. Children are innocent of the crimes of their government.

U.S. soldiers in food line

Mountain Men

U.S. Infantrymen during winter operations

U.S. Infantrymen guarding German prisoners

Alan Blackwell

Italy and Southern France

It was decided that 2nd Regiment of the First Special Service Force would assault Mount La Difensa in Italy. Patrols had been going out looking for the best assault route, and finally one was chosen. It would take The Force over to the right of the hill, but required the scaling of a steep escarpment. Though it presented our troops with several obstacles, this line of attack was chosen for its shock value; it was unlikely, our leaders speculated, that the Germans defending La Difensa would expect opposition from this direction.

We had been training hard for several days when the order came to assault the mountain. Everyone was ready, and on December 1, 1943, 2nd Regiment moved up with full gear to within a half-dozen miles of La Difensa's base. After getting off the trucks, we marched in darkness for six hours, slogging through mud and pouring rain to a spot that offered protection from German fire on the mountaintop. While we dried clothing and checked weapons, Colonel Frederick gave us a truly grim picture of what lay ahead. First Regiment, we learned, was assigned as reserves. Third Regiment, meanwhile, was given double duty—its members were to serve either as litter-bearers for 2nd Regiment (a task that fell to 1st Battalion) or as reserves to be used when and where needed (2nd Battalion). Second Regiment would lead the assault.

I was in 3rd Company, 2nd Regiment, commanded by Lieutenant Colonel Tom McWilliam. After what seemed like an eternity, The Force got the order to begin its final assault. We started the grueling climb of La Difensa itself and quickly came to appreciate all the training we'd received in mountain climbing. The night was cold and rainy; we cursed and puffed our way up the hill, wondering when the fighting would begin. Dawn found us all in position, still concealed from the enemy. It stopped raining, and we were ordered to fix bayonets.

The sight before us was unreal; I can honestly say it was like walking into hell. Allied artillery had started softening up the German positions at sunset the night before and were still pounding away at the mountaintop as we readied for our final assault. We learned later that 22,000 rounds were dropped on La Difensa during the night and, believe me, it showed.

We were told to hold our fire until 6 A.M., but some men slipped while moving into position and sent gravel rolling down on the Germans. Flares went up, and all hell broke loose. The battle for La Difensa was on.

The fighting was ferocious. Both officers and enlisted men were involved in hand-to-hand combat atop La Difensa—a real rarity in the Second World War. Fortunately, as a machinegunner, I wasn't involved in the close-quarters stuff; however, I was pinned down by German machine guns for nearly an hour and able to move my position only after some of our troops dislodged the enemy.

Because two previous assaults on La Difensa by other units had failed, Fifth Army staff anticipated it would take three or four days to secure the mountain. We did it in less than four hours. Our success, I think, can be attributed to the element of surprise and superior firepower; our sudden appearance on the mountain caught the Germans flat-footed, while our Tommy guns and submachine guns produced a hail of bullets.

Though we succeeded in accomplishing what others had failed to do, the victory on La Difensa was bittersweet and was achieved only with much sadness and loss of friends. Heavy mortar and artillery fire took its toll—Lieutenant Colonel McWilliam was killed and Major Ed Thomas was wounded with a bayonet. Dozens of others lay dead or wounded.

The battle etched images in my memory that can never be erased. One in particular stands out, and it can be described only as both horrible and unfortunate. In an effort to gain an insight into future enemy troop movements, we were told to take as many prisoners as possible during the assault. With this in mind, when a group of our men took a machine-gun nest near my position, they called for the enemy's surrender. A group of German soldiers emerged waving white flags, yet when one of our officers went to take the men prisoners, he was shot and killed. The results were as predictable as they were bloody. The German soldiers, even those who'd taken no part in the treachery, were instantly mowed down by machine-gun fire from our troops. Needless to say, the incident ended our campaign to take prisoners.

I can't forget how, in this instance, one thoughtless action by a German officer resulted in the loss of many German lives and that of at least one good FSSF officer. It wasn't the last time this would happen, either; during my five years in the army, I witnessed several incidents in which one self-centered individual sacrificed the lives of many good men simply for the sake of prestige or self-esteem.

The 142nd Infantry finally relieved us, and we came down the God-forsaken mountain never wanting to look back. We'd all seen enough blood, both the enemy's and ours. We now had time to rest and consider the events of the past few days. It seemed no matter how hard I tried, I couldn't forget the boys who'd been killed or wounded—or the scene atop La Difensa after our first battle. Dead Germans had lain everywhere and, among them, the bodies of our own fallen comrades. Punctuating this grisly sight was the menacing flicker of Allied artillery from the valley below; not to be outdone, the Germans responded with "Screaming Meemies," those six-barreled rocket launchers that, while none too effective, made a hell of a noise and demoralized almost everyone.

The Force received several assignments in the mountains that winter, and our casualties were high. It was cold, and the land was blanketed with heavy snow. Many of our men suffered from frostbite, while others contracted trench foot (a nasty ailment that landed me in the hospital for five days).

Shortly thereafter, we headed for Anzio. Closer to Rome and behind

German lines, this new landing site pitted us against four German divisions commanded by Field Marshal Albert Kesselring. The Force moved into position along the Mussolini Canal. Ordered to hold the ground at all costs, we dug in and covered our shelters with logs, tin, and anything else we could find. In the end, our preparations undoubtedly saved many lives, because it wasn't long before the Germans started dropping "basket bombs" on us. When these container-like parcels hit the ground, they'd break open and scatter phosphorus bombs the size of eggs everywhere, severely burning anything with which they came in contact.

Of course, we didn't just sit in our holes and take whatever the enemy hurled at us. Every night, we'd blacken our faces with camouflage paint and send patrols into the German lines. On these sorties, we'd harass the Germans unmercifully, then leave our own unique calling cards—stickers that bore the spearhead insignia of The Force and the German phrase, *Das dicke Ende kommt noch* ("The worst is yet to come")—on their positions and dead. Our calling cards and blackened faces apparently wreaked psychological havoc among the German troops, because they began referring to us simply as "The Black Devils." At the very least, we got them thinking, as the diary of one German attests. "These Black Devils are all around us," one Wehrmacht soldier wrote prior to capture. "We don't know where they will strike next."

It was on one of these night patrols that I had perhaps my worst scare of the war. It involved a German mine nicknamed "Bouncing Betty" by Allied troops because when triggered, it jumped about four feet in the air before exploding and throwing shrapnel everywhere. My patrol was working its way out through a minefield at night when I stepped on a "Betty." Feeling that horrifying click as its trigger depressed, I thought: "This is it." Much to my relief, though, the mine turned out to be a dud. Troop mate Ray Elizonda was behind me at the time, and we couldn't believe our luck. (Years later, at a Force reunion, Ray turned to my wife and said: "Did this guy ever tell you how lucky he can be?" Of course, she didn't know what he was talking about, because I never shared any war experiences with my family.)

Our tour at Anzio was grueling. The Force was defending a large area with about two thousand men; though vastly outnumbered and subjected to horrific artillery barrages from the enemy, we held our ground. In later years, our somewhat unorthodox tactics and nearly unmatched military record inspired the popular book and movie, *The Devil's Brigade*. At Anzio, though, our nightly raids served a more useful purpose; indeed, it has been suggested that they led the enemy to overestimate our numbers and probably discouraged them from mounting a deliberate attack.

Thinking over battles fought and comrades lost, I often wonder how some of us survived almost unscathed. I lost two buddies at Anzio; we'd trained together from day one. Bert was one of them. One night, he came to me and said, "Blackie, I'm picked for patrol tonight. I can't refuse, but I have a bad feeling that I won't be coming back." His words proved prophetic;

when the patrol returned, he wasn't with it. I never learned what happened to him, and he is still listed as "missing in action." A few days after Bert disappeared, our platoon was moving up a nearly barren valley when we came under mortar fire. My other buddy, Art Knapp, was only a few feet from me. When the shells started falling, we all dived for cover, which unfortunately was scarce. Screams and yells filled the air, competing with the sounds of exploding shells. Many men were wounded and several were killed, including Art. Though at least one mortar shell had landed squarely between Art and me, he was the one to die. I didn't receive so much as a scratch.

Gordon Stanley Hall

(as told to his son, Doug Hall)

After spending about three months with the Royal Canadian Regiment in Italy, Father volunteered for service with an elite infantry unit named the First Special Service Force. This combined Canadian-American group is presently better known as The Devil's Brigade. The FSSF was disbanded in December 1944, and as a result, Father was sent back to the RCR in Europe, with which he remained until the end of the war in May 1945.

Before going overseas, Father was stationed in New Brunswick. He recalled that he once went AWOL and that after he had been AWOL for some time, he was returning to camp and met three members of another unit, the Governor General's Horse Guard. Just in conversation, he told them that he had been AWOL, and he was on his way back to camp to face the music. Despite the fact that he was returning to camp in any case, the three members of the Governor General's Horse Guard tried to put Father under arrest. Father had a rather smug look on his face when he said that these men did not manage to arrest him, and he subsequently returned to camp under his own steam. About four o'clock in the morning, however, he was awakened and charged with being AWOL and resisting arrest. He was not let out of prison until it was time to board the boat for overseas.

This boat was in a convoy, whose commander was Lord Mountbatten. So far as I know, the trip was uneventful. Many years later, however, he did say that he had a girlfriend while in England, and, since she worked for the British government, she knew how many ships had been lost to German submarines in the transatlantic crossing. He said that he might not have been in such a hurry to join the army if he had known this in advance.

The initials A.A., as in the 100th A.A. Battalion and the 2nd Heavy A.A. Battalion, are pronounced "Ack-Ack" and stand for AntiAircraft. Father recalled that he slept for some two years with his boots on because, when the air raid sirens started to blow, he had to be up and running immediately. They used radar to shoot at the German aircraft, and Father recalled shooting one down—a Heinkel 111. Apparently, it had five men on board and a full load of bombs when it went down. Father went to see the crash site afterwards and said that there was a large crater and that he had never seen so much blood in his life. There were houses nearby, and the gore was hanging off the houses.

During the very early period of Father's stay in England, it was required that all armed forces personnel be prepared to wear a gas mask at any time; so it was necessary to carry a gas mask even when off the base. After some time, however, an announcement was made over the radio that this would no longer be required, and, accordingly, Father went without his mask to a bar just outside the army base on which he was stationed. On exiting this bar, a senior officer took father to task for not carrying his mask. Father tried to explain that it was on the radio all over England that this was no longer required, but the senior officer would not be deterred, saying that it had not been officially announced yet on Father's army base. Quite some time passed after this with no repercussions, and Father felt that his transgression had been forgotten. The day came, however, when he was marched in to see the commanding officer. His explanations were to no avail, and he was fined 40 dollars.

His army pay was 40 dollars per month, but half of this amount had to be sent home every month; so, in effect, his fine was two months' pay. Father was outraged by this and said, "Well, I just made up my mind that if I could live two months without being paid, I could survive without being paid at all." At that time, the legion in Erin sent Father a carton of cigarettes a month, and his relatives sent him another carton. Also, he managed to buy an iron (a scarce commodity in those days) and apparently had quite a roaring business in pressing clothes for other soldiers, especially the officers. Thus, he was able to support himself through the black market in cigarettes and through his ironing business.

In Italy with the RCR, Father recalled the muddy season in the Po River valley. Apparently, at a certain time of the year, everything there turns to mud, and this gave rise to what he called the worst night of his life. They started to advance through the mud at night but very slowly as they would move only about six feet at a time and then there was an interminable wait before the man in front of him advanced and he could move again. As this was going on, he was standing in deep mud carrying a heavy pack and a rifle, which he was unable to put down because of the mud.

One night when they were encamped in Italy, someone heard noises in some nearby bushes, and Father said half the camp came out and started firing into the bushes. The next morning some of the men decided to go into the bushes and see what caused the noise they had heard. They found an old Italian woman shot to death.

Just after D-Day in June 1994, Father volunteered for the First Special Service Force. Better known as The Devil's Brigade after the movie, it was an elite force of about three thousand men, about one-third Canadian and two-thirds American. To join this outfit, he said you not only had to volunteer, but, after you volunteered, you had to be selected. Also, he had to sign a piece of paper stating that he was willing to jump by parachute, but, in fact, they never did jump into battle while he was a member of the unit.

He did, however, become a member of the 1st Airborne Task Force, a ten-thousand-man group composed of the First Special Service Force and two American commando units. They were charged with securing the flank of the invasion forces at Normandy by fighting from Normandy through the area of the French Riviera to the Italian border. It is said that the Germans fought back tenaciously since they thought that the purpose of the task force was to push them into the Allied forces still fighting their way up the Italian peninsula.

"One time, while on a ship on the Mediterranean, right on the border between France and Italy at a place called Menton, the navy came in and bombarded a mountain, setting the whole mountain on fire. The next morning, they sent me and 19 other men out on a small boat to capture the mountain. The mountain was captured with no resistance because of the bombardment, and that was all right until the following morning when the Germans counterattacked. The first I knew they were being counterattacked, I was replacing another man on the machine gun, and they shot him through the heart. All I can remember about that day is that, in the excitement, I forgot my canteen on the machine gun and can never remember being so thirsty in my entire life. The Germans managed to chase us off that mountain all right, but by the time we got down to the bottom, there were only ten of us left alive. There were hundreds and hundreds of men going up on top of the mountain to counterattack the Germans again.

"The ten of us who were left alive were put in reserve at the bottom of the mountain. Well, that was all right until the following morning when the Germans counterattacked again, but, instead of coming across the top of the mountain, they came around behind. When I woke up that morning, we were being shelled by 88s. It's a good job I had a safe place to sleep that night, or I wouldn't be here. And when the 88s stopped coming in, we could hear the small arms fire break out; so we knew that we were being counterattacked, and we started running like crazy to get into the line. My lieutenant was running about ten feet in front of me, and I watched as a bullet went into his neck on one side, and a big puff of blood came out the other side. Well, the lieutenant fell over dead. But for me, I could see where that bullet came from. And where it came from, there was a pile of rocks, and I went and looked inside the rocks, and I could see a German officer. Well, I couldn't quite get my rifle in through those rocks to shoot him; so there was a man on a machine gun nearby, and I knew that man had a pistol; so I ran and got the pistol, returned to the rocks, put my arm in and shot him. I always hated killing that man. We took some pictures off him afterwards, and he had a really attractive wife and two young children. But after he killed the lieutenant, he just had to die. And besides that he was already up through our lines behind the machine gun. At the end of that day, there were only four of us left alive. And of the four of us that were left, two men had to be sent home immediately because of nervous breakdowns. Of the 16 men that were killed, three of them, including my lieutenant, were standing right near me when they were killed. There was only me and the sergeant left. We took their medals and Luger pistols; the French Resistance took their rifles and grenades; and then the civilians took everything else."

Later on, Father was in the city of Nice, and he spoke of going uptown and hearing a shot. He went to investigate and found a man lying dead in the street, and there was a large lineup of French partisans, all with pistols, filing past this dead man. As each one passed, he fired a shot into the corpse. Then, Father also saw a truck, and in the back of the truck there were six men. As he watched, an old woman got into the back of this truck, took off her shoe, and went to each of the six men and beat him violently with the shoe. When she was finished beating these men, she was so tired that she fell off the truck into the arms of the men below. Father inquired as to what was happening in this place, and he was informed that the man lying dead in the street was a collaborator who had tried to escape, and that the other men, in the back of the truck, were also collaborators who were at that very moment being taken to a place on the outskirts of town to be shot.

Once, when they were encamped in Germany or perhaps Holland, two Germans on bicycles came up to their camp just at dusk. The guard on duty said, "*Halt*!" whereupon the two Germans threw down their bicycles and fled across a field. Father chuckled as he recalled, "The whole camp came out to shoot at them. Even the commanding officer was there shooting at them with a pistol." The Germans got away. They were too far out of range for anyone to hit them.

Also in this area, he recalled approaching a farmhouse, and a nearby tank put a shell into the house, thinking that the Germans might be hiding there. After the shell exploded, a woman holding a baby in her arms came running out of the house to a nearby woodpile. Not seeing her, the tank then proceeded to put a shell into the woodpile, whereupon the woman, still with the baby in her arms, ran back into the house. Still not seeing this, the tank put several more shells into the house. No one would go into the house and check on them afterwards, and as they left the area, all they could hear was the crying of the baby.

Another event that occurred about this time, either in Germany or Holland, involved the shooting of a German soldier in the foot. "We were in a small village, and I was crouched down beside a building when I saw two German soldiers come around the corner of the building carrying an Allied soldier in a stretcher. I kept watching for the Allied soldier who must be guarding them and, as I was watching, a bullet went right by my head, and I saw it plow into the foot of one of the German soldiers. He immediately dropped the stretcher and began to hop around on one foot screaming in pain. At this time, the Allied soldier guarding them came around the corner, and upon seeing the antics of the German soldier screamed, 'What's the matter with you?' The German soldier pointed to the blood oozing from his foot, whereupon the Allied soldier leveled his gun at the hapless German and screamed again, 'There's nothing wrong with you! Pick up that stretcher and get moving!' The German soldier quickly complied."

There were more serious memories such as this one: "An armor-piercing shell went right through the company headquarters, and it took the commanding officer's head right off. And then after that, our remaining officers were all in one building sleeping, and a shell landed right on that building killing many of them outright, and those that were not dead were so badly wounded that they had to be sent home immediately. When we were approaching Appeldorn, many of the men were heard to remark that they could remember coming out of battle a few times with no officers, but they could never remember going into battle with no officers.

"I was wounded in Holland at Appeldorn. We were walking behind the tanks in single file, walking in the tank treads to avoid land mines. Suddenly, they started shooting at us with mortars, and the mortars came down on us like rain for half an hour, exploding all around us. We jumped for the ditch and, when the mortars stopped coming in, we got up out of the ditch, and, believe it or not, not one man was wounded or killed. But just after we got up out of the ditch, they opened up on us with 88s. I jumped for the ditch again, but it was too late." Father was wounded by shrapnel in the left chest and the right knee. It was April 13, 1945, just three and one half weeks before the end of the war.

Father's trip to the hospital became an ordeal. They were loaded into an ambulance—four of them and a wounded German soldier who was well enough to hold a bag of blood up for a wounded Allied soldier. No one was guarding the German soldier, for apparently at that late stage of the war, it was not necessary. In any case, as they approached a railroad track, there was a train coming toward them and the ambulance accordingly stopped. The train, however, also stopped. Several times afterwards, the ambulance started to go, and when they did so, the train also started to proceed. Eventually they came to a stop with the train up against the ambulance, and the ambulance up on two wheels. They had to call another ambulance to take Father and the other men to the hospital.

"Medic!"

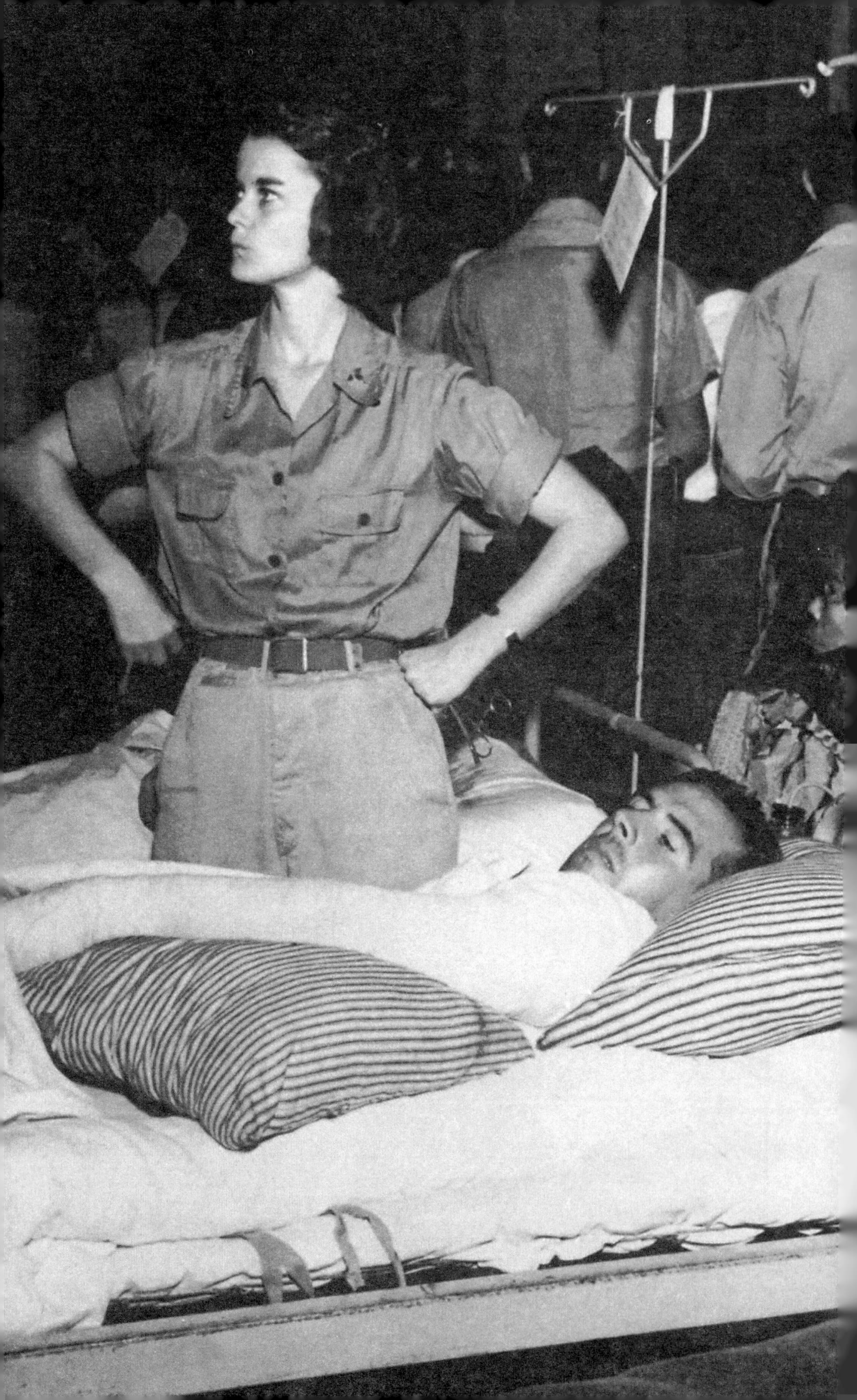

Angelo Vicari

Co. K 395th Inf. 3rd Platoon, 3rd Battalion

After attending the full Medical Basic Training at Camp Barkley, Texas (Dec. '42), I was assigned to the 233rd Station Hospital at Camp Maxey, Texas. They were in training to become a mobile field hospital overseas. I was assigned to the Orderly Room taking care of service records and other clerical duties. One day an officer came into the company office and asked to see the personnel files. He then made out a list and told our CO that the men chosen were going to the A.S.T.P. [Army Specialized Training Program] We had never heard of it, but found ourselves enroute the next day to the University of Arkansas. Three terms of Basic Engineering went by, and instead of going home on leave, we were shipped to the 99th Division at Camp Maxey. There we went through 13 weeks of intensive infantry training, day and night, along with the original members of the division. Hearing that the medical detachment was under strength and was putting former truck drivers in as medics, I let them know I had Medical Basic and was promptly transferred to Medical Detachment, 395th Infantry.

At first we felt that the original 99th men resented us A.S.T.P.ers, but by the time we were sent overseas we were assimilated and one group complemented the other; we became a good team, each respecting the other, and we became like brothers.

I was sent overseas with K Company of the 395th. After spending a month in Dorchester, England, the division was shipped to France. I remember on the English pier some GIs found an open door on a freight car and pulled out OD turtleneck sweaters knitted by a Connecticut Red Cross unit and earmarked for British troops. The officer in charge at the pier looked the other way as the sweaters were passed around and shoved into our duffel bags. They were superior to the GI issue V-necks. This I wore up to the front line. My gloves had been stolen in an English pub before leaving. No replacements were available at that time.

The battalion commander gave us a "pep" talk the last night of bivouac in Belgium before moving by truck into Germany. It certainly boosted morale when he told us that one out of five would be killed and two or more would be wounded.

Eventually we moved up into the forested hills, fog and mist in the air, to the village near Hofen, hating to walk the last part up to a row of farmhouses atop a ridge. No trucks or vehicles were permitted on the line. Little did we know that the enemy was on the ridge opposite us. I recall how our platoon leader, Lieutenant Peterson, helped dig a latrine alongside the house that was to be the CP [Command Post]. I suggested using a homemade ladder found in the rear barn as a latrine seat, what with irregularly spaced rungs affording a seat for every size man! As the platoon medic, I tried to make myself useful, as we had to make this shelled house as comfortable and secure as possible. We put logs in the wet basement, piling straw over them, to make a cushion for our sleeping bags. Men from the foxholes took turns sleeping in relative warmth and shelter. Sand-filled crates were secured in the basement windows to deter grenade attacks at night by German patrols. We hung blankets inside the "front door" for blackout and closed the "L" series of foxholes running out on the ridge behind the houses facing the enemy. A draw with a hedgerow ran along the line.

The food supply hadn't caught up with us yet so for a few days we ate C-rations of meat and vegetable stew left by the armored outfit we replaced. Field kitchens were finally set up in a cottage factory behind one of the houses. (There were textile machines in this one.) On Thanksgiving Day they sent up one half of a roast turkey for our platoon plus a mortar squad, which was using our CP as an observation post. Some of us saved our half slice of white bread and ate it for dessert!

Once a cow was butchered back at battalion and we were given some. Smelled delicious, but it was so tough we couldn't chew it. I received some packages from home that contained various goodies, which I shared. They had been mailed months before.

On some nights, German patrols would pass by the house along the road outside the room used for the CP. On one such occasion Lieutenant Peterson fired a grenade launcher out the upstairs window, getting return fire from a "burp" gun. Next morning the lieutenant called me to go outside and see the dead German soldier lying along the road. He asked me to take him back to the company aid station approximately three-quarters of a mile back. I mentioned to him that it was the first time I had ever seen a dead human being, not even at a funeral. We then picked up the German and put him into an old wheelbarrow taken from the barn. I paraded down the road with the wheelbarrow in bright sunshine, at the same time seeing a hole through the dead man's head. He was wearing one of their reversible field jackets, the other side being white to wear in snow. At the medics I dumped him out and returned "home." Sometimes at night in the darkness, someone would open fire at an old tree stump, swearing the next day that they saw something move out there. We were lucky if any of us got more than two hours' sleep any one of the 40 plus nights we were there.

One day a fellow was brought to me complaining of difficulty breathing. With the lieutenant's permission I walked him back to the medical aid station in late afternoon. Upon arriving there, they sat him in an old chair. At the same time, he stopped breathing altogether. I gave him artificial respiration for quite a while till he came around. (Mouth-to-mouth procedure was not heard of then.) He received a sedative to induce sleep, and he did—for three days. By the time I was finished attending to the artificial respiration, it was beginning to get dark. They wanted me to spend the night there, but I felt I was expected back at platoon CP where I belonged. Walking up the road I was aware of men from other platoons pointing their M-1 rifles in my direction from partially opened doors in houses. I thought sure that they would open fire if I started to run toward my platoon, so I started whistling "Yankee Doodle" and walked boldly up the road, shaking in my boots until I reached the CP. It was now totally dark. I knocked on the door, and told them who I was, whereupon the door was opened and I was yanked inside, surrounded by my comrades with sidearms drawn. They didn't expect me to return that night and were taking no chances.

One night Lieutenant Peterson had a call on the telephone line, which connected other units with ours. The voice kept calling "Peter, Peter" (Lieutenant Peterson's call name) evidently trying to lure him outside in the dark. The next day we saw where the communications line had been cut and spliced on the outside of the house by a German patrol. They often prodded cows to meander down the Monschau-Eupen road to set off possible mines. A few had gaping holes in their sides but continued to graze along the road. This road came in to Hofen, and probably was used later by tanks.

Early in the morning of December 16th, the 88 artillery shells were coming in at us from the Germans, to "soften us up," I suppose. As I was heating my C-ration breakfast on a coal stove in the CP, I was called to go outside to aid a man who was hit. I grabbed my medical bags, and, wearing my helmet (now with Red Cross markings we ourselves belatedly painted on the line) and my turtleneck sweater, I ran out to find our men placed along the hedgerow in the draw; rifles aimed down the side of the hill. Snow had fallen during the night, an inch or so, enough to blanket the ground white. I asked where the wounded man was, and they said, "It's Duncan down there." Lieutenant Peterson was partway down the hill, crouched behind the old tree stump, and Duncan was lying face down a few feet away. I climbed over the fence and walked down to them. There was absolutely no cover except for the tree stump. I hit the ground when I realized that the enemy was at the bottom of the hill, scattered behind the trees Indian style. The lieutenant asked me to hand him Duncan's rifle, which I did. At that moment, a German opened fire with his machine pistol, sweeping the ground near me. They had held their fire while I walked down the hill. I could see the snow being kicked up by the bullets, coming closer and closer to me. Evidently, I was the target! Within a matter of seconds I was hit. The force of the bullet entered my right side and rolled me over to the left, my arms flying into the air. Now as I lay on my belly, the lieutenant asked me if I could crawl up the hill to the hedgerow. I said I would try. Getting up on all fours like an animal, I started to crawl up the hill. The enemy again held their fire, and three-quarters of the way up I glanced back and saw a path of red blood behind me in the snow, realizing at once that it was *my* blood. All I felt before this was a stinging and burning sensation through the middle of my body, and then afterward an aching back. Upon reaching the hedgerow, my buddies held my back down in order for me to slide under a trip wire attached to an instant grenade. Letting myself roll down the slight embankment to the draw, ending up with my face down, I realized I could no longer move my legs. The platoon sergeant started to run toward me, at the same time pulling off his belt to use as a tourniquet. He suddenly stopped, ran the other way, yelling for everyone to run away. He had tripped a wire strung across the draw, which was attached to one of those gray-box antipersonnel mines mounted in the hedgerow less than four feet from where I was lying. They yelled at me to run, but of course I couldn't. I pushed my helmet back on my head, threw my arms around my head, and waited. Nothing happened! The mine never exploded! When they thought it was safe, several men ran back to help me. The sergeant put his belt around my left thigh to stop the bleeding. Unfortunately for me, the wound was in the left butt further up. A short time later, medics came up in a jeep, breaking the rule about motor vehicles up on the line. Placed on a litter, I was strapped to the hood of the jeep. I asked, "Where's Duncan?" They said they had him. Someone else was on the hood alongside me facing the other direction. I don't remember who it was. Perhaps it was Duncan.

Back at the battalion aid station, they gave me blood plasma and eventually evacuated me to regiment medics. At this point (I believe it was regiment), I was to go into the operating room that had been improvised in the basement of a building. I remember two chaplains deciding "who I belonged to"—the Catholic chaplain winning out. While I lay on my litter on the floor, he heard my confession and gave me what I thought were the Last Rites of the church. After an injection of sodium Pentothal, I went to sleep and they debrided the wound. I remember receiving transfusions of whole blood afterward. When one bottle was empty, I pinched the tube and called for a nurse, and it was replaced with a full one. I heard someone say that I was bleeding from the bone! This was in a "Recovery" tent with army nurses in fatigues. I still didn't know the extent of my injuries, although I had one hell of a backache! I remember that night waking up in a room with other wounded men lying on cots. By this time it must have been two days since I had eaten anything except for coffee sucked through a rubber tube a couple of times. The distinctive aroma of Campbell's soup filled the room. The medic said that was his, but he brought me coffee and a couple of crackers. By this time the young fellow in the bed next to me was stirring. He would sit up and start to unwrap the bandages on his left hand, the size of a catcher's mitt. The medic told me a grenade went off in his hand. He was delirious and was trying to get out of bed, at the same time falling over me. By now my sense of self-preservation was taking over, and, yelling at him, I called the medic. For someone to even lean on my cot at this point caused me pain and anguish. Finally he received a sedative and relaxed. The medic told me everyone else had left, leaving him in charge of us, waiting for more ambulances to evacuate us to a safer area. In my ambulance there were two others besides a dead German and me. The German was on the litter beneath me. I looked down and saw his yellow face. Looking forward through the windshield, I could see columns of tanks going on the road in the opposite direction. We were bumping along, crossing an onion field with deep furrows; I was now lying on my belly to lessen the pain. The driver's assistant was holding a blacked-out flashlight out the window to see where we were going—no headlights were permitted. (After the war I found out that my father's helper in the store was in one of those tanks going up to the front. He inquired about me and was told that I was being evacuated.)

At last we arrived at a hospital in Verviers, Belgium, where I was accepted. That night the city was bombed and all ambulatory patients were told to go down to the shelter. A few of us could not, of course, so we remained in bed with the window shades pulled down. Bomb bursts were heard outside, and after a while it stopped. Next morning we heard that another wing of the hospital had been hit although the target was the railroad yard nearby. Fortunately, the medical train that was to transport us to Paris was not hit, and we were put on board. British Red Cross women came aboard to cheer us up and handed out Milky Way chocolate bars.

After being evacuated to a small building near Le Bourget Airport (what was left of it), about 20 of us were left on our litters on the floor for one week including Christmas Day. French girls brought us small cups of onion soup, and our meals were brought in. No medical attention was given to us during this week. We had to go outside to the latrines. Somehow a package from home was brought to me. How they located us I don't know, but I sure wasn't complaining about that. In it were items I had requested a month or so earlier: candles, food, and things that were needed on the front line. A box of cookies was the best part, and they were passed around for all of us to enjoy. A Red Cross worker came in, nailed a pine branch over my head on the wall with a few strands of silver tinsel, and gave us a few cigarettes to make our Christmas Day. I was wondering what hell my buddies were going through during the battle up on the front and if they were even still alive.

Walter J. Shuster

C/77 Armored Medical Battalion. 7th Armored Division

Miracle in Metz Woods

It was my first trip driving an ambulance to the front. In the Metz Woods we found the captured German bunker, dark and filled with our wounded. Outside, a courageous Asian-American officer, Dr. Robert Kinoshita, was atop the bunker ordering men to stop running and protect the wounded. Inside, I reported to a medic, who tersely ordered me to turn around and be ready for a load.

The road was very narrow with a thick hedgerow on the left. On the right was a line of trees. Between them were dug-up mines and a ditch. I would need help to zigzag back and forth to turn around, but my assistant disappeared, which angered me. No time to look for him—firefight up ahead getting close—have to turn ambulance around alone and quickly.

I ran my ambulance into hedgerow on left—back up a little right—get out—see if back wheels are aimed between tree and a mine. Screaming 88 shells coming. I duck between back wheels—explosion—deafness—rain of dirt—ambulance window frame is welded to doorframe by a ragged shrapnel hole where my head would have been. Outside would have been the assistant directing me, and we would have both died. But a miracle saved us by separating us beforehand. I forgot to be angry at him—just grateful that he was responsible for saving us both by his disappearing at the crucial time. The shell exploded about six feet from where he and I would have been discussing how to turn around the ambulance.

After kicking open the driver's door, two dazed medics headed for safety with a full load of wounded. (One, a tanker, besides having a most grievous belly wound, was burned over most of his body when blown out of his tank.)

An Ambulance Driver's Day to Remember

On a hill across the Moselle River, the infantry officer gave me a requisition to bring back 25 blankets and 25 replacements (men) next trip.

Back at the pasture, the light bulbs in our surgery trucks were being shattered by concussion of a nearby artillery outfit that moved too close. Leo Moscardini, a hometown friend, came across the stone wall that separated his gunnery panel from where I had set up my shelter-half. Surprised and happy greetings had to be short. I had the urgent task to take off with my assistant driver to pick up the first five replacements and return to the front quickly. Frightened to begin with, they watched in apprehension as I navigated between exposed mines on narrow roads, climbed a dangerous steep, loose gravel incline and across an aboveground canal bridge, and slid into narrow tracks of a pontoon bridge over the Moselle River under a smoke screen. More foreboding was driving uphill through a minefield marked with white tape, while on the left was a barnyard full of dead, decaying cattle stinking horribly of death.

Up ahead, eerie sounds came from between clouds as Jerry and GI artillery shells flew overhead where we were headed. Looking at the men in back, I saw eyes bugged out in terror. There was a quiet period when I dropped off the replacements at the infantry CP for the coming night at the frontline—what the bravest soldiers dread most. Night fell just as I finished digging my slit trench for the night when I was called to take back three casualties for surgery. Two were replacements I'd just brought up.

Very dark now; impossible to see anything, even your shoes. I was reminded of such a black night, as a CCC boy in an eastern Connecticut valley. The road there had swamps on each side, no railings, and I had to get on my knees to feel where the roadside ended with my hands—slowly, one step at a time.

Back in France now, it was my turn to be frightened, and three wounded men and my assistant driver depended on me to get us out of there in one piece. Here there was no road. The only landmark was the CIP tent I was next to. Everywhere else was one big blackness all around—one big blank. I walk into the dark, carefully feeling the ground with my feet for 30 or 40 feet, I hope in a straight line from the ambulance—turn around—blackout lights get me back to the ambulance. With assistant driving, I lead him the 30 or 40 feet I had checked out. This routine is repeated over and over. We get stopped by artillery barrage when I didn't return to ambulance once to lead him. He left the ambulance to find me dazed in an abandoned muddy slit trench I fell into. The light of a nearby shell explosion showed him where I was. A left turn was what I was looking for. It would be marked with the white tapes. To the right would be German ground. The slow clanking sound of tank tracks comes from front and right of us! German? I call out the password. The clanking stops. No answer. I call the password again. No doubt someone must be seeing our blackout lights. If German, they could blast us!

Finally, a voice in English asks for name and where we are going. I don't give my German name. Instead I ask, where in hell do I get the ambulance with three moaning patients down the hill! The voice gives me a dirty sarcastic GI remark and the clank of tracks moves on, unseen, in the direction we came from. Great relief it wasn't German, or was it?

Having spent most of the night creeping around in the dark looking for the path we came upon left me exhausted and at the end of my rope. I stop to cool off and I pray. As if by magic, a breeze springs up with the sickening odor of those cows we had passed on the way up. A miracle! Follow the smell downhill from that nightmare. Things start to look better.

On the level, I drive now by dead reckoning again looking for the bridge from a broad plain of deep mud. A guard with a blacked-out flashlight stops me at the river's edge, guides me to where the pontoon bridge is, then aims my wheels to slide down the muddy riverbank onto the narrow tracks of the floating bridge, getting us across the Moselle River, homeward bound to the west.

At early light we pass a half-track that slipped off the side of a gravel incline, went down and turned over during the night—12 men killed or wounded. At home base, I'm told my friend Moscardini was wounded by an incoming 88 while I was away bringing three more casualties. The list that day that I knew of was 16.

Happy and grateful to be back safely, I was too sleepy and tired to think of anything but hitting the sack after one tough day. Only later did I get to thinking how incredible it was when a miracle was badly needed, it came precisely at the right place and exact time when I couldn't do any more myself. Coincidence? Granted the army made possible blackout lights, scouts for tanks, dead cattle, assistant drivers, casualties, etc.—but who made the breeze and my nose to follow it?

Another medic was ambulance driver Harold Cooper from New York State who became a "General" by his courage and common sense. As his assistant was driving, Cooper was trying to keep a patient's exposed brain alive. An officer with a nonlife-threatening wound was threatening Cooper with court-martial for ignoring the officer's "direct order" to give him extra morphine. At a hearing later, the colonel told the officer, "When you're in Cooper's ambulance, you are a private. Cooper is a general."

For me, driving an ambulance or leading a litter squad to the front were part-time experiences I'll never forget. As a full-time corporal, picking men for small details around camp (as corporals do) earned us a bad name among privates. But after VE Day, one private gave me a great compliment. He said, "Shuster, you're going to be famous for making latrines, from the beaches to the Baltic." They dug those latrines for 2,000 miles!

P.S. Discharge time in the U.S., two disgusting homefront "warriors" called us "pill rollers" and flicked cigarette butts our way because we were medics.

Dorothy Ahlswede Baker

I was an army nurse in World War II. It was indeed a pleasure to serve our country for two and a half years. I served on a hospital ship, the *Wisteria*, for a year. We took German POWs to Europe and brought back our patients. Many of these soldiers had been fighting for two or more years. As we came to New York harbor and they saw the Statue of Liberty, they broke down and cried.

Later, I was stationed at Camp Kilmer, New Jersey. From here I took war brides via train to the West Coast and made sure they got off at the right stop. Sometimes their husband and family met them. If they did not, I would make arrangements with the Red Cross to take care of them. I met so many interesting people.

After a few months of duty at Fort Lewis, Washington, I asked for Pacific duty and was placed on the troopship, *Fred C. Ainsworth*. We carried dependents to the Orient and brought back our troops. We made three trips to Shanghai, Japan, Korea, and the Philippines. This is where I met my husband, Captain Horace M. Baker. He was one of the surgeons on the ship. We had our first date in Japan and were later married in Seattle.

John Favicchio

The Seed Was Planted Early

I shall be forever grateful to the army for giving me the opportunity to see other parts of the country and Europe, to meet people from different backgrounds, and, most of all, to acquire firsthand knowledge of the workings of the mind. When I was drafted at the age of 23, I knew very little about the wonderment and intricacies of the mind. In the 18 months overseas, I got an education that was priceless. It would help me cope with three devastating experiences in civilian life.

My outfit, the 226th General Hospital, was crossing the English Channel in October of 1944 on our way to Le Havre where medical facilities were badly needed. It was on my maiden voyage to France that I was exposed to the healing power of words, a technique that is widely used and accepted by the medical profession—mental imagery and visualization.

I was leaning against the wall reading a paperback when I noticed this soldier sitting alone across the room crying. Everybody was preoccupied and ignored him. "What's the matter, soldier?" I asked, as though I couldn't see the fear written over his youthful face. "There're German subs out there. We'll never make it." The captain of the ship had announced on the public-address system that we were crossing dangerous waters. "Many ships got through," I said. "The English know how to avoid 'em. Back in Banbury, I got letters from GIs who are now in France. And we'll make it, too." "How'd ya' know?" In the morning at chow time I saw this kid on line smiling. We nodded. We didn't cross paths again. I hope he came out of the war well and a wiser human being.

Over five decades ago, when I gave that kid what I thought was good sound advice, I knew of the potential danger of the German subs—a direct hit and we'd all be goners. But for some reason I didn't dwell on it. Maybe because I had always been an upbeat, positive guy and carried that attitude into the army.

When we set up our hospital in the tiny bucolic village of Maumalon, France, I was a T/5 in charge of a ward and the stretcher bearers. A rumpus erupted on the ambulance compound where the wounded from the Battle of the Bulge were being transported. This one GI was screaming and waving his arms at the German POWs who were carrying him.

"What's the matter?"

"I don't want these Krauts carryin' me. Chase 'em away."

I ordered the POWs away and had our own men carry the patient inside.

Later, this same GI was causing another commotion on the ward. I left the nurses' station and went to him. "What's the matter, Jim?"

"Please give me more morphine," he pleaded. "The pain's killin' me."

"I can't give ya' another shot too soon after the last one, Jim." "Tell the doctor how painful it is."

I went back to the station and told the head nurse. "Fix him a saline solution," she said. (That's sterile water and salt.) I returned to the agonized patient and gave him the pseudo-shot. Almost instantly he stopped shouting and banging the bed. He closed his eyes and became as quiet as a kitten.

At that time I knew very little about the placebo effect, but the nurse explained that we had just tricked the brain into thinking it was getting the real stuff. "But the wound is still there, Lieutenant," I replied, not satisfied with the answer. "The pain . . . . ?"

"The body gets its orders from the brain. If it says it's okay, it won't be overruled."

If that wasn't proof enough, I witnessed another GI who was suffering from mental fatigue and demanded tranquilizers constantly. The nurse told me to give him sugar-coated pills. They had the identical placebo effect.

Paul W. Kulp

I landed on Omaha Beach as a casualty replacement assigned to Company C, 1st Battalion, 320th Regiment, 35th Infantry Division as a rifleman and scout. After breaking out of the Normandy hedgerows and heading for St. Lô, we were transferred to General George Patton's Third Army. After the St. Lô battle, Company C helped rescue the "Lost Battalion" and capture Hill 317. After repeated attacks, I was wounded by shrapnel and evacuated.

THE UNITED STATES OF AMERICA
TO ALL WHO SHALL SEE THESE PRESENTS, GREETING:
THIS IS TO CERTIFY THAT
THE PRESIDENT OF THE UNITED STATES OF AMERICA
HAS AWARDED THE
PURPLE HEART
ESTABLISHED BY GENERAL GEORGE WASHINGTON
AT NEWBURGH, NEW YORK, AUGUST 7, 1782
TO
PRIVATE FIRST CLASS PAUL W. KULP, UNITED STATES ARMY
FOR WOUNDS RECEIVED
IN ACTION
FRANCE 11 AUGUST 1944

Irwin Pontell

87th Infantry Division, Co. 1, 346 Regt.

How I Got My Purple Heart

On January 6, 1945, we were fairly safe in a monastery near the town of Tillet, Belgium, waiting for our next move. We thought this would be a quiet day, but in midafternoon we got orders to attack the town of Tillet together with another infantry company from our battalion.

Jump-off time came but the other company never arrived, so off we went downhill through open farmland. The fire was murderous but we kept going till we were pinned down on a dirt road. I carried a walkie-talkie for the captain, but somewhere on the trip to the roadway my aerial had been clipped off by a bullet or shrapnel, and it was useless. Soon after, we captured a German whom I was covering with my rifle. Suddenly my rifle broke apart. A piece of shrapnel broke the stock in half.

As I was the captain's radioman without a radio, the captain told me to go back to see if I could find the other company or get some help from anyone. Crawling and running, I started back up the hill, when suddenly I was hit. It felt like it was the bottom of my foot, but later it turned out to be my thigh. I lay in the snow for a while and then decided to crawl; but every time

I moved, someone fired at me. Fortunately, he was not very accurate. Dark came early and two of my buddies—walking wounded—helped me limp to the aid station. They told me I wasn't wounded, because there was no visible blood. However, my thigh started to swell from internal bleeding, and X-rays showed a bullet that had entered my thigh and traveled into my abdomen. I spent three months in a hospital in Hereford, England, where I actually received the Purple Heart. An officer showed up at the hospital one day with an armful of medals and dropped one off at each bed. Another month in a convalescent center in Coventry and back to duty.

Of the approximately 100 men who jumped off that afternoon, by the time Tillet was taken three days later, only 30 odd were not dead or wounded. Of our six officers, only one lieutenant walked out.

Desmond T. Doss

Infantry Medic, 77th Statue of Liberty Division, 307th Infantry, Company B

Medal of Honor Day

It was time to go up on the escarpment again. Although in the heat of battle it isn't always possible to remember which day is which, it is believed from reading other sources that this was on Desmond's Sabbath, May 5th, 1945.

Desmond was reading his Bible when Captain Vernon approached him and said, "Doss, would you mind going up on the escarpment today? You know, you are the only medic we have left, and we really need you."

Desmond bowed his head in prayer. He figured he was ready to join the group in about ten minutes. Some told him it was half an hour. But none of them were anxious to go up and fight, so they were glad for the delay.

The soldiers actually thought the hardest battle was already fought and that this day was just a mop-up job. Desmond did mention prayer to Captain Vernon, but he said, "Sorry, Doss, we've already started to push off." So nothing more was said.

The 155 men left in Company B went up the escarpment. Right away they faced the hell of war. Everything seemed to go wrong. One Japanese position the group could not seem to rout. The Americans heaved satchel charges (bags of TNT) and other high explosives into the Japanese position, but they pulled the fuses out before they exploded. Finally, several of the men grabbed five-gallon cans of gasoline and heaved them over into the Japs' foxhole. Then Lieutenant Phillips threw a white phosphorus grenade.

The resulting explosion was more than they anticipated. There was a terrific explosion in the foxhole itself, but even more further down in the hill. Evidently all of the high explosives the men had thrown into the foxhole went off but also an ammunition dump down below.

Then what happened was unexpected. Japanese came from all directions from other foxholes and trenches—probably figured it was now or never. There were so many Japanese, and they fought so hard; it would have been suicide to stay up on top. The soldiers were told to retreat. It was supposed to be an orderly retreat, but it ended in panic.

Desmond was up on top with his men—until they all left. But what about the wounded men who were scattered around on the top of the escarpment? He couldn't go off and leave them. He knew many of them had families at home. He started for the nearest soldier—he was badly hurt. Desmond dragged him over to the edge of the escarpment and looked around to see what he had to use. There was a litter and the one rope they had used for hauling up supplies. He rolled the wounded soldier onto the litter and tied him on as well as he could. Then he dropped him over the edge as he hung onto the rope. Partway down he thought he was going to lose the man, but the rope held and the litter landed safely 35 feet below at the bottom of the cargo net.

Some of the fellows had dropped to the ground at the bottom of the cargo net to rest for a minute before proceeding on down the cliff. "What on earth is going on?" they wondered as they noticed the litter coming down.

"Take him to the aid station pronto," yelled Desmond from up on top. "He's hurt bad."

As a couple of fellows started on down the cliff with the wounded man, Desmond pulled the rope back up. It took a long time to lower that man. Then he believes God brought to his mind that bowline knot he had tied back at Elkins, West Virginia. He tied the bowline knot with the two loops, brought another man over to the edge and slid the two loops onto his legs, doubled the rope again and tied it around the man's chest. Then he let him gently over the edge. The Lord even provided a tree stump on top of the hill. Desmond wound the rope around the stump and let up on the rope gradually. That took the load off him as he let the man down.

Desmond kept praying, "Lord, help me get one more." Why the Japanese didn't come over to the part of the escarpment where they were and finish them all off, Desmond didn't know. His only explanation was that God took care of him and his men, and later he had time to thank God. It took him about five hours, but he rescued all of the wounded soldiers. It was a tired, thankful, blood-soaked soldier who came down the Maeda Escarpment that day. And, unbelievably, he was not wounded.

The members of Company B who had witnessed this conscientious-objector-soldier medic doing what he did were astonished, and it wasn't long before the rest of the company heard about it, too. Then others.

When he arrived back at the bivouac area, he heard welcome words. "Doss, those fatigues are blood-soaked. Besides you are covered with flies, and we don't have any fly spray. We're going to have to find you some different fatigues." It wasn't long before he was dressed in a clean uniform. He decided to go off in a quiet place somewhere and read his Bible. He certainly had something special to thank his God for this time.

While he was gone, General A. D. Bruce from the 77th Division headquarters arrived at the camp. He had heard of Desmond's feat and wanted to shake his hand. He also suggested that he should receive the Congressional Medal of Honor and asked those who could start the process to get it going. Desmond was told this later because he was not there to shake the general's hand. He wished he had been.

How many men had Desmond let down from the escarpment? The top brass said, "Let's see. We had 155 men go up and only 55 men got down the hill on their own. So you must have saved 100 men."

"Couldn't be," said Desmond, modestly. "It couldn't have been more than 50. I wouldn't have had time to save 100 men." So they compromised at 75, and that is the number on Desmond's Congressional Medal of Honor Citation.

(Excerpts from *Desmond Doss in God's Care*
by his wife, Frances M. Doss)

U.S. Army Air Forces Liberator bomber flying over U.S. P-40 fighter planes

The Battle Above

SB2C in landing circle on USS Yorktown

TBF (Avengers) flying in formation

Ann Wood-Kelly

Pioneering Aviator

Wood-Kelly learned to fly in the same class as her brother at Bowdoin College in Maine. President Franklin Roosevelt, foreseeing the need for war pilots, had instituted the Civilian Pilot Training Program to train classes of 12 at a time for free. Because it was a federal program, one of the 12 could be a woman. Bowdoin, an all-male college at the time, refused to let Wood-Kelly into the class. Short one student, the college advertised in the paper asking for a male who wanted to learn to fly for free. No one came. Rather than lose the program, Bowdoin's president decided Wood-Kelly could get her wings. It was a summer class, he reasoned, and no one would know she was there.

After she got her license, she taught Bowdoin students to fly. But Pearl Harbor left her with only a handful of students as the young men left to fight in the war. Wood-Kelly herself wanted to join the war effort and had written to everyone she thought could help. But every avenue seemed a dead-end. Meanwhile, America's foremost woman pilot, Jacqueline Cochran, had approached the country's top generals. Even the general responsible for hiring women to be in the Air Corps refused to let women fly.

But over in Great Britain, pilots were being stretched too thin. Seven civilian British men who wanted to serve but were too old or had some impediment decided if they couldn't fight, they could ferry aircraft. One of the men, a World War I veteran, had only one eye, one leg, and one arm. "But he was a good peacetime pilot," Wood-Kelly said. The seven men formed the British Air Transport Auxiliary (BATA) and flew planes from factories to bases. Eventually, the civilian BATA would grow to 700. Some 173 BATA men and women lost their lives in the war.

Cochran saw the BATA as her opportunity to serve. And Pearl Harbor galvanized her to send out her famous telegram to 300 women registered with the Civil Aeronautics Administration in Oklahoma City. The telegram began, "On behalf of British Air Transport Auxiliary, I am wiring all the women pilots whose addresses are available to ask if you would be willing to volunteer for service with a nucleus to constitute initial contingent of newly formed American women's section of ATA for service in British Isles."

Wood-Kelly leaped to seize the opportunity. She had the minimum of 350 required flight hours. Some women had as many as 3,000. But of those, some were older and had families. Cochran didn't want them to desert their children," said Wood-Kelly. So Cochran chose young, single Wood-Kelly to join the BATA.

After initial training, the BATA sent Wood-Kelly to a pool of pilots based at Leicester. The BATA had taken over a man's home and airport. The man, a member of Parliament, and his wife essentially ran a boarding house for the BATA. Every day, Wood-Kelly walked 10 minutes to Ratcliffe Airfield for a day of flying. One day she moved eight aircraft.

From 1942 to 1945, Wood-Kelly's logbook recorded hundreds of flights in 75 different types of military aircraft—every Allied fighter type and various bombers and transports. Of the 75, she was probably not checked out in more than a half dozen. "They trained you in a basic aircraft and felt that once you had conquered that aircraft, you could then do at least 10 other aircraft that would be similar in weight and speed and such," she explained. "It was absolutely true." Some aircraft, such as the Spitfire and the Hurricane, made check rides impossible anyway, because they were single-seater fighter aircraft. There was no room for an instructor to ride along to test the pilot.

All her flights were solo. And since this was before the day of the computer, she navigated by maps and time and distance—effective under ideal conditions but not when there was a strong wind or wind change. Because she flew by visual reference, she flew only during the day and in good weather.

She felt fully accepted by her male colleagues—civilian and military. "You do different things when there is a need. And all the normal obstacles get obliterated."

Wood-Kelly refrained from flying under bridges—all but twice. The first time, she followed two friends in an airborne version of follow-the-leader. The second and last time, she was on her own and did not realize it was high tide until it was too late to turn away. After barely squeezing between the bridge and the water below, she gave up that trick.

Fear was not an issue for Wood-Kelly. Still, she said, there were petrifying moments. While she was in Europe, her engine stopped on only one occasion, which she confesses was partly her fault. She was doing a loop in a Miles Magister. Unlike some planes, the aircraft did not have an upside-down carburetor, so the engine cut out at the top of the loop. Wood-Kelly landed safely—or so she thought—in a farmer's field. "The farmer thought I was German and came after me with a pitchfork," she recalled. But after realizing she was not the enemy, he gave her some tea and let her call the nearest base.

(Excerpts from Gloucester *Daily Times*, February 18, 1999)
[Ann Wood-Kelly later became the first female vice president of Pan American World Airways.]

David M. Wilkins

In the late 1930s and early 1940s, I was working at Lockheed Aircraft Corporation in Burbank, California, building P-38 fighters. In 1942 I decided that I ought to join one of the military services to better help fight the war. In November 1942 I enlisted in the Army Air Corps Cadet Program and was called to duty on February 4, 1943. I went through the testing programs and qualified first as a navigator and second as a pilot.

My crew and I were eventually assigned to the 494th Bomb Group and sent to the island of Angaur in the Palau Islands. We arrived in early March 1945 and were assigned to the 866th Bomb Squadron. While on Angaur, we flew five missions; the first two were in the Philippines and the last three in the Palaus. During the month of June, the 494th Bomb Group was stationed at Yontan Air Base on Okinawa. From there, we flew five more missions. The first one on July 18th was a strike against a major Shanghai air base, Wusung. The next mission, on July 29th, was intended to be a strike on Japanese capital ships anchored at Kure Naval Base. The day before, 79 B-24s had attacked the base and two B-24s were shot down and 14 others damaged. The crew and I flew the same mission the following day and expected the worst, but a layer of clouds completely obscured the target, so the squadron bombed the secondary target, Nobeoka, a city on Kyushu. We flew two more missions from Okinawa—Marti Shima and surveillance of the China coast before Japan surrendered.

Chester J. Kanach

46th Troop Carrier Squadron, 317th Group—known as the "Jungle Skippers"

GI Haircuts

The fastest GI haircut I ever experienced was by a one-eyed barber operating a shop in the PX at our base. I had hardly settled in the chair when he was done. Next time around he wondered who gave me the lousy haircut.

The slowest cut was by a Filipino who was provided a tent and was permitted to do business in our tent area in Cat Clark Field in the Philippines. He was so slow he could restart the first side after finishing the second.

While being sent to the southwest Pacific, there was a lengthy layover in Honolulu where I got my hair cut by a female barber. That was an unknown in the U.S. in those days.

Cowboy Pilots

While on one flight the pilot observed a Filipino plowing with a walk-behind plow pulled by a water buffalo. He decided to frighten the farmer, and he did, by flying so low the man released the plow and ran to avoid the plane. How low were we? We had to climb to clear a fencerow.

On another occasion during a two-plane flight, the other plane decided to get his wing tip under ours and raise it. He did.

Cargo Hauled

The best cargo our crew ever hauled was the cast of the Broadway show *Oklahoma*.

Yes, they were pretty!

The worst cargo was a second-hand outhouse. No, not on the preceding flight.

Virgil W. Preston

We were to fly to Oran, Algeria, with a load of aircraft mechanics and their tools for the First Fighter Group, flying single-seat Lockheed P-38 Lightnings. We were to fly single ship without lights in purely dreadful weather, throttled back to only 125 miles per hour to conserve fuel. When we got to the Rock of Gibraltar where there was an RAF airport, we were to ask whether to continue on land. When we reached the Rock the next morning, we were told to land. It seems the Vichy French were still contesting our invasion. We did get to Oran without incident—only to learn that we were to sleep on the ground or in our tilted-floor airplane and whatever sleeping bag we had. There were no tents. We would live like nomads during that period trading anything the local Arabs fancied for tangerines, eggs, and potatoes. Furthermore, we had to refuel our 1020-gallon tanks from five-gallon cans dumped in a big pile from trucks from the Port of Oran.

On verbal orders, we flew anywhere with anything that our airport people told us was needed—begging food enroute. This was the Tunisian Campaign of 1942–43. Most of us spent our time flying men and supplies to frontline airports in Tunisia and flying the wounded back to field hospitals.

In June 1943 we moved to Sidi Bou Goubrine, Tunisia. The Germans and Italians had surrendered in April, and the Americans and British had occupied the whole country. We didn't know it at the time, but we were headed for the initial airborne invasion of Sicily. We would carry in gliders and parachutists of Field Marshal Bernard Montgomery's First Royal Airborne Brigade. On July 9th we were called to the operations tent and briefed. For our first mission that night, we were to tow the British in American CG-4As to Syracuse, Sicily. One hundred nine C-47s and C-53s towed the same number of 15-place gliders, taking off from Tunisia an hour before sunset headed initially for the island of Malta. The temperature was 95°F. and the air was terribly turbulent, with wind from the northwest gusting to 25 miles an hour. The intercom lines to many of the gliders broke loose and cut off communication with the glider pilots. We turned north around Malta in the dark and headed toward Sicily's southeast coast. Soon we saw antiaircraft tracers ahead of us. Then all hell broke loose as ships directly under our flight path began firing on us and shooting up star shells on little parachutes, the better to see us. We were flying at only 200 feet above the water and the hostile "friendly" ships soon broke up our formation.

We had navigators only in the lead ships of our four-plane, four-glider elements, and the rest of us became badly lost. We had to wander up and down the east coast looking for landmarks in the quarter-moonlight until we found where we were and then head for the coast to release our gliders. We were to release three thousand yards offshore at 1100 feet, but most of us released considerably higher because the wind was blowing offshore and seemed considerably higher than had been forecast. To make a long story short, 73 of the gliders fell into the sea and many of their men were drowned. Only a handful were within a mile of where they were to have landed. This small number of men, nevertheless, was able to accomplish their objectives before amphibious troops landed the next morning. We lost no tow planes, somehow.

On 13 July, we ran head on into trouble. That night, 10 C-47s and C-53s of the 60th, 62nd and 64th Groups flew 1,700 British "Red Devils" of the 1st Parachute Brigade to drop around the seven-span Primasole Bridge over the Simeto River just south of Catania, Sicily, ahead of Field Marshal Montgomery's British Eighth Army. We flew a little higher that night—600 feet. Again ships opened fire on us and broke up our formations. We nevertheless did a lot better that night. We got 41 planeloads of paratroops within a mile of the bridge and another 22 planeloads within five miles. However, we had six planes shot down at sea and four more over land and another 34 planes were severely damaged by both "friendly" and enemy antiaircraft fire.

Louis Loevsky

On March 22, 1944, the Eighth Air Force 466th BG flew their first mission to Berlin. Our B-24, the "Terry and the Pirates," was hit by flak over Berlin and we lost the #1 propeller. A midair collision ensued, causing "Terry" to lose props #2 and #3. Len Smith, a bombardier, was trapped in the "Terry" nose turret. The electrical and manual systems were rendered inoperable by the crash. The turret would not turn so that its doors could open to let Len out. He sustained substantial injury. For me to extricate Len from his predicament was most difficult since he was in shock and kept removing his gloves (at 35°F. or below) and oxygen mask (at 23,500 feet). I repeatedly tried putting his mask and gloves back on while trying to spring the nose-turret door open. I put an arm around his chest and pulled him out. That was quite an achievement. Eventually I got him out and released the bombs in train. Thirteen of 20 crew members were KIA, five "Terry" and eight "Brand." After assisting Len to bail out, our pilot, Bill Terry, yelled, "Hey, Lou, wait for me!" I waited until he left the control column, then bailed out through the bomb bay. Distrusting the Germans, I free fell and saw one parachute open above me, which had to be Terry's. While free-falling, I realized that with the "H" (which meant Jewish) on my dog tags, I risked being shot as a spy if I ripped them off and threw them away or as a Jew if I left them on and fell into the hands of the Gestapo or SS. I left them on. While free-falling, I thought of the gross of condoms scattered in every pocket of every uniform. My parents will think they raised a sex fiend!

When I finally opened my parachute, I found I was being shot at from the ground. Slipping and spilling air, I became an instant expert in maneuvering the chute despite admonitions to keep our "cotton-picking hands" off the shroud lines. I got away from a small camp where they were shooting at me toward another small camp where they were not. Selecting a small tree in Berlin, I crossed my legs for posterity, crashed branches off one side of the tree, chute caught on top, feet whipped over head, back injured, blacked out briefly, came to with toes touching ground. A shaking Home Guard (*Volksturm*) had a gun in my ribs, repeating: "*Pistole*? *Pistole*?" Two Wehrmacht troops appeared and took over my custody. While still getting out of the parachute harness, three SS arrived, apparently from the small camp where they had been shooting at me. The SS argued with the Wehrmacht. They wanted to take custody of me, and, since my parents sometimes talked Yiddish, I could understand. Fortunately, the two Wehrmacht troops retained my custody. As they marched me through the streets of Berlin to their headquarters, the angry civilian mob was yelling in perfect American English: "String him up," "Hang him," "Lynch him." As they were closing in, the Wehrmacht troops had to draw their sidearms to keep the ugly lynching mob at bay. I believe Bill Terry was shot from the ground as he floated down in his parachute.

I was now a POW at Stalag Luft III in Sagan, Germany, until the Russians got close in January 1945. After that, we were evacuated at 2 A.M. in a freezing blizzard. From there we reached Stalag VII A in Moosburg by marching in subzero weather and being crammed into 40-and-8 boxcars. [These were World War I railway cars designed to carry 40 men or eight horses.] We were improperly clothed and fed; our conditions were unsanitary and inhumane. Imagine hundreds of American officers and enlisted men lined up evacuating their bowels in full view of German women and children when the train stopped at a station. We were treated like swine! We were liberated by General Patton's troops on April 29, 1945.

Epilogue

When the B-24, "Terry and the Pirates," was fatally damaged by flak on March 22, 1944, Harry Schuster was a 16 year old in an antiaircraft battery in Berlin. Harry allegedly "shot Lou's B-24 down." After 50 years he decided to try to locate any living survivors of that B-24. Harry's story was that when "Terry" came down it was so close to the flak battery they all had to duck! Although it was *verboten* for him to leave his post, like any teenager he ran to view the nearby wreckage. He and a friend with a camera took two photos of the pile of mangled aluminum that had been the plane and made a note of the serial number.

When Lou questioned the version of the story that Harry had "shot Lou's B-24 down," Harry replied: "In Germany they say that in a lumber mill where very large circular saws are used (with hundreds of teeth per blade) if a person cuts or loses a finger, who is to say which tooth did it." Needless to say there were hundreds of flak batteries in and around Berlin.

After their meeting, Harry wrote to Lou. "We were very excited to finally see you in person and have the chance to sit down, talk to you, and get to know you. Despite all the terrible experiences we both encountered during the war, I was especially pleased that we could put the past behind us and enjoy the present as friends."

Harry died unexpectedly a short time later. His passing left a saddened Lou pondering the mysterious twists of fate that, after a half century, would bring him together in true friendship with one of his country's wartime foes, then sever the bond with death only days later.

Donald Tate

One of the 50 missions I completed began with the operations officer informing us that we were scheduled to fly the next day. He would waken us at 2:00 o'clock in the morning and tell us breakfast would be ready in 30 minutes. We would take our mess kit and cup to what is called the mess tent. Our breakfast would usually consist of poached eggs, burned bacon, burned toast, and coffee or milk. After breakfast we would return to our tent, put on our flight clothes and go to the briefing tent, where we would learn our mission for the day.

One of the most heavily defended targets in Europe was the Ploesti oil fields. By the word defended, I am talking about antiaircraft guns and German fighter planes. The group commander would not tell us the target, and about all he would say is that the name of the target is Ploesti. He did tell us what time we would take off, and it would probably be around 6:00 o'clock in the morning. Before we left the briefing tent, our chaplain, Captain Eastwood, would say a prayer and offer communion to anyone who wanted it. We would get into a 6x6 truck and be delivered to our airplane. Each man had a particular job to do before takeoff. The pilot and co-pilot checked the plane for any visible problems. The engineer and assistant engineer checked any and all mechanical things. Armament people checked guns, ammunition, bombs, and bomb racks. My job was to make sure that all the bombs had safety wires in them. We would wait for a flair-gun signal, then board our plane and start the engines. In the 464th Group, a mission would consist of four groups of seven planes, each making a total of 28 planes with ten men in each plane. The first of seven planes would take off and fly a straight line for seven minutes. He would then make a left turn and fly in a circular pattern. Then the second plane would take off one minute later and fly in a straight line for six minutes, and so on until the seventh plane took off and flew in a straight line for one minute, then that pilot would make the left turn and you could see from this that all seven planes were up and in formation. The second, third, and fourth groups would be doing the same thing and all 28 planes would end up in formation. The seven-plane formation consisted of a lead plane and right- and left-wing planes; the fourth plane was in the center with his wing planes (one on each side of him), and the seventh plane was in the center at the end.

Sometimes our plane was the lead plane, or we could be in any part of the formation. Once in the air and the group had formed, we headed for Ploesti. After we left Italy in formation, we headed across the Adriatic Sea, and each man had a job to perform while the plane was in the air. Fighters would never hit on us over water. The pilot and copilot checked all gauges to make sure the airplane was in good condition; the navigator gave us directions; the bombardier turned on the bombsight to check it. The radio operator checked the radio; the engineer checked all gauges and mechanical parts; the nose gunner checked the oxygen supply and the nose turret; the waist gunner positioned his guns (one on each side of the center of the plane) and checked ammunition; the tail gunner checked out his turret and the ammunition (at the tail of the gun); and I was the ball turret gunner (the turret on the underneath part of the plane), which I lowered so it was on the outside of the airplane and checked my ammunition. Before entering the turret it was also my job to arm all of the bombs, which consisted of pulling the safety pins or safety wires on each of the bombs. Then I would enter the turret, plug in my heated suit, put on my intercom, and adjust my oxygen mask. The rest of the crew were turning on their intercoms and adjusting their oxygen masks. While over the Adriatic Sea and on command from the pilot, each position test fired their guns. By that time we were usually over Yugoslavia on our way to Ploesti, Romania. All of this time we had been climbing in altitude.

Most of our missions were at 23,000 feet, which is between four and five miles high in the air. Every one of the ten men in the plane was on constant watch for German fighter planes. Most of the German fighter planes were ME-109s, and the one in that part of Europe had a yellow nose. It has been said that these planes and pilots were the elite of the German Air Force, commanded by Herman Göring, one of the most feared German commanders. On our way to Ploesti, we would avoid going over any towns because of antiaircraft fire. Those antiaircraft guns on the ground were 88mm. When we were 200 to 300 miles away from Ploesti, we were usually hit by German fighters. We didn't know where they were coming from, but the first strike would usually come out of the sun, and they could come from any direction. But each crewmember on our plane would call out the position of a fighter attack, and, at this point, the gunners had control of the radio and we were not to be interrupted by any other crewmember.

When we were within 150 to 200 miles of Ploesti, the Germans would shoot what they called marker flak, a brown smoke to find out our altitude. On some of my six missions to Ploesti, the Germans had reconstructed a B-24 with tail markings the same as ours, and would fly out of range of our guns, and then radio our altitude to their antiaircraft batteries on the ground. This brown could be seen for 50 to 75 miles before we arrived at the target. As we approached the target, the fighters would break off, and then we would be hit by antiaircraft fire. Being in antiaircraft fire for just ten minutes seemed like a lifetime. We would then hit what we called an IP (initial point) for the bomb run, at which time the bombardier took over the guidance of the plane. He had complete control of direction and, through his Norden gun sight, he could tell where the target was and prepare to drop the bombs. He opened the bomb bay doors and had a toggle switch to drop the bombs. The lead plane was the master plane and, when its bombs were dropped, all of the other planes in the group would drop their bombs. I, being in the ball turret (on the bottom of the plane), was to stay in the turret and observe where the bombs hit, reporting any fires or destruction that I saw. The entire time we were over the target, the antiaircraft guns on the ground were firing at us. We would get out of the range of the antiaircraft fire as soon as possible. If we were fortunate enough not to have mechanical problems and could stay in formation, we considered ourselves lucky. German fighters would come in again and prey on planes that had to drop out of formation for some reason or another and were vulnerable to attack.

I remember only two times that we dropped out of formation and were attacked by German fighter planes. One was when our tail guns were not working and a German fighter came in. He was too high for me to get a shot at and too low for the top turret gunner to get a shot at. The good Lord made the German fighter run out of ammunition before he could hit us and shoot us down. After turning away from the target and heading back to our base, we had to drop out of formation because one engine had caught fire and had to be shut down. The fire was extinguished. As we headed back to our base, another engine lost power and was "windmilling." By that I mean it was carrying its own weight but was not producing any power. We cleared the mountains on the coast of Yugoslavia, which were 10,000 feet in altitude, and headed out across the Adriatic Sea. Over the water we threw out everything that was loose to reduce the weight in the airplane—guns, ammunition, flak vests—anything but the rubber boat.

Arriving at our base, we were the last to land. The first plane to land was any plane with wounded aboard, and they would indicate this by shooting a red flare. The next to land were all the planes that were not damaged. The last to land were the planes that had been hit and were damaged. This mission consisted of eight hours in the air, four hours of preparing, and from one to two hours of debriefing. Our entire crew and all the other crews, separately, went to the debriefing, where we described what had taken place on that particular mission.

Rolf Slen

Angaur to Clark Field, Philippines—January 2, 1945

At the same time that the Japs bombed Pearl Harbor in Hawaii at the start of the war, they also bombed our airbase at Clark Field in the Philippines—destroying most of our B-17 bombers on the ground. Soon Japanese ground forces invaded the Philippines and captured Clark Field. They converted it into their main airfield in the Philippine Islands.

General Douglas McArthur planned to invade the main northern island of Luzon where Manila and Clark Field were located. It was the duty of the 494th Bomb Group located on Angaur to destroy the Japanese installations at Clark Field before the invasion.

We were rousted out of our cots at 2:05 A.M. I doubt that I was sleeping at the time. I never slept much, if at all, the night before a mission. My head was always filled with thoughts of distances, directions, times, check points, turning points, and bomb runs.

Fear was always present, too. What if we had to ditch? What if we had to bail out? What if . . . The greatest fear was flak. On this mission we were told we could expect lots of it.

Japanese fighter plane attacks were also possible.

During the bomb run, I was hunched down by the bomb bay manually holding a lever to make sure that the bomb bay doors did not accidentally close as we headed toward the target. The flak was heavy and accurate. Dirty black puffs of exploding shells were very close. The smell of burning powder drifted into the plane through the open bomb bay doors.

Suddenly there was another explosion. I looked out and saw a huge orange ball of fire explode beneath us. The separated wing of a B-24 drifted under us. A parachute drifted into the ball of fire and burned up. The crewman attached to that parachute plummeted like a stone to the jungle below. The smells, sounds, and sights of this scene combined with fear almost caused me to throw up. What stuck in my mind so clearly for many years afterwards were the colors—the green jungle, the black puffs of flak, the orange fire, the silver wing of the B-24, and the white parachute.

The B-24 that went down was leading our three-plane element at the time. It had sustained a direct hit between the #3 and #4 engines causing its right wing to break off. We were flying directly to the right and slightly behind it at the time. None of that crew survived. I knew the pilot and navigator quite well. We had flown on a number of previous missions with that crew.

The flying time for that mission was 14 hours and 20 minutes—one of our longest missions of the war. It covered 2,300 miles.

Angaur to Corregidor, January and February 1945

We pounded Corregidor day after day with hundreds of tons of bombs. Each of my six missions was a 12- to 13-hour flight. A typical mission to Corregidor involved arising at 2 A.M., taking off at 4 A.M., bombing at noon or 1 P.M., refueling at Tacloban on Leyte Island in the Philippines at 4 P.M., and then returning to Angaur before going to bed at 10 P.M. One time, we did this three days in a row.

On that third day we took off again, as usual, at 4 A.M. with a full load of gas and bombs.

Emil Turek, our pilot, turned west northwest on the usual heading, got up to our usual cruising altitude, and set the automatic pilot. The next thing I remember Lee Colvin, flight engineer, was tapping me on the shoulder. I jumped because I knew I had been sleeping. I looked out my window and saw the familiar outline of an island in the Philippines. I had slept for 700 miles; everyone else on the crew did, too. The plane flew itself and we were right on course. After dropping our bombs and starting home again, I took a "no doze" pill. It not only kept me awake the balance of the flight but for the entire night after we returned. I never took one of those pills again.

Imagine a B-24 bomber loaded with gas and bombs flying by itself for 700 miles with ten men aboard, all sleeping while they were on their way to bomb a Japanese target. They used to shoot sentries who fell asleep during wartime, didn't they?

"Taloa" and "Lonesome Lady"—The Aftermath

It was many years after the war before I could reconstruct what happened to the men in our squadron who bailed out of their stricken planes during our mission against the battleship *Haruna.* A lot of investigative work was done by others after the war with respect to what happened to them. Based on what I have been able to find out from various sources, the facts are here briefly stated.

Of the twenty original men in "Taloa" and "Lonesome Lady," thirteen survived being shot down and captured. Most of them were taken to a military prison in Hiroshima and killed when the atom bomb was dropped on that city. Only two men out of the twenty survived the war. One was Lieutenant Cartwright, the pilot of the "Lonesome Lady," who had been taken to Tokyo for further questioning and thus escaped the blast at Hiroshima. The other was Cartright's tail gunner, William Abel, who hid in a hollow tree on a mountain and escaped a search party of Japanese farmers. He came out of the tree at night and escaped detection for nine days. Then, desperate for food, he actually boarded a passenger train and gave himself up to a Japanese military man on that train. He was imprisoned and taken to Yokohama and released when the Japanese surrendered.

I did not personally know the men in the crew flying the "Lonesome Lady." They were a replacement crew flying only their second mission of the war. But I was well acquainted with the men on "Taloa." They were an original crew that left with us from Lincoln, Nebraska, and were good friends of ours for many months before their tragic deaths. Our own atom bomb apparently killed all of them who survived being shot down at Kure Harbor.

(Excerpts from his *Memoir of World War II*)

Doug Ackman

My "Funniest" Experience as a Kelly's Kobra

Early in January 1945 my buddies and I joined the 866th on Palau as replacement crews. We had come by ship, the *APA Grimes*, from Seattle, by way of Hickham Field, Kauai, Johnson Island, Saipan, Guam, etc. The usual route. With the exception of myself, a corporal (because I taught in the radio school at Scott Field, Illinois), all the other enlisted men were privates or privates first class. As we all knew, according to the TO [Table of Organization], the radio operator and engineer were supposed to be tech sergeants and the balance were to be staff sergeants. Well, our pilot, Lieutenant Bill O'Brien, along with all other pilots, put in for our increases in rank each month. Nothing happened. After a few months I got tired of all the bitchin'.

There was an officer on each post who was supposed to hear all serious complaints without any repercussions to the complainant, so I, having more gall than brains, decided to do something about it. I dressed up in my best short pants and got permission from our first sergeant to go see him. Everyone, including the first sergeant, said, "Don't do it. You'll get in trouble." I ignored them all and went to the 494th HQ and asked to see this person, who turned out to be a bird colonel. I was ushered into his office, came smartly to attention, saluted properly, and asked if I could state my (our) problem. He advised me to go ahead, which I did. When I finished, he seemed "shocked" and said he couldn't believe this oversight, but it would be remedied immediately. He then asked for my name, rank, and serial number, to which I replied "Corporal Jacob D. Ackman, 15339057, 866 Squad." The minute I gave this information, I thought I might be in trouble and I was. The first of the following month every one of the new crew's "enlisted men" but ol' Doug got their proper rating (rank). On payday they would call out the master sergeants by name, tech sergeants, staff sergeants, and buck sergeants and pay each of them. Then they would say, "Now for the corporals. Where are you 'Acky'?" I was the only corporal on a flight crew in the 866th and perhaps in the entire 494th group or Seventh Air Force, for all I know.

I never did get my proper rating and was discharged in September 1945 as a corporal, but managed to survive because we all had to allot all of our pay but $10 per month home . . . so what's the problem?

We flew on the Kure Naval Base run, the first 1,000-plane raid on Japan, and, as I remember, we were the only crew of the ten planes from the 866th to make it back—not even a scratch.

I wouldn't want to go through the war again, but wouldn't take a million for the experiences. I had enlisted, volunteered for overseas duty, and was refused same because of my poor hearing. But when I pinned a former world-champion wrestler, Everet Marshal, at a bond drive in Colorado, everything changed and the examining physician declared me "fit" without a physical. I would have felt terrible had I not been able to serve my country in combat.

Robert H. Bentley

I enlisted in the U.S. Marine Corps in March 1942, completed U.S. Navy flight training, and was designated a naval aviator and second lieutenant, USMCR, in July 1943. From then until the end of World War II, I served in several USMC fighter squadrons. The experience described here took place while I was serving in Marine Fighter Squadron (VMF)422 during the last stages of the Okinawa campaign.

VMF-422 was based on Ie Shima, a small island off the west side of Okinawa. It was one of four fighter squadrons and a torpedo squadron that comprised Marine Air Group (MAG)22, which was one of four that made up the 2nd Marine Air Wing. VMF-422 and the other fighter squadrons were equipped with the F4U-lD Corsair. VMF-422's primary mission was flying combat air patrols over U.S. Navy ships and U.S. Army and U.S. Marine shorebased installations and airfields to protect them from Japanese kamikaze aircraft, fighters, and bombers. The secondary mission was conducting fighter/bomber strikes against airfields on Kyushu and down the island chain south toward Formosa (now Taiwan).

As time passed, Japanese air activity slacked off and life became quite routine. Then, on August 6, 1945, we received some rumored reports that the Army Air Corps had dropped an extremely large bomb somewhere in Japan. We had no source of news media, so what we heard was word-of-mouth stories from someone who was supposed to have heard about it from someone who knew. Needless to say, we learned very little and did not give it much thought. Then, on the evening of August 8, 1945, I was one of 12 pilots from VMF-422 who attended a briefing at MAG-22 headquarters. Also present were pilots from the other fighter squadrons in MAG-22. To the best of my recollection, I would say there must have been 36 or more pilots in attendance. We were not given much information about the mission that we were to fly the following morning, except that we were to take off before dawn and rendezvous with a PBM flying patrol boat and a radio frequency on which to contact the PBM. We were further instructed that once we had rendezvoused with, and were in radio contact with, the PBM, we were to follow its instruction and to protect it from any form of enemy attack at all cost. This meant not leaving it to go chasing after Jap fighters, unless they were attacking the PBM.

Needless to say, the rendezvous of about 40 fighters with the PBM the next morning in the dark was pretty "hairy" but somehow we managed to assemble without a midair collision. The PBM instructed us to divide up so that there would be groups of fighters over him at intervals up to over 20,000 feet. The PBM then headed north, and the fighters took up their assigned positions above him. As we flew north dawn broke, and as we approached Kyushu, the PBM veered in order to follow the west coast of Kyushu and to stay 10 or 15 miles offshore. We flew in a northwesterly direction following the coastline and staying well clear of land for about 150 miles, at which time the PBM started to orbit a position offshore.

Looking to the east, we could see a city that was totally on fire. We were not then familiar with the characteristic mushroom cloud associated with nuclear explosion, but of course that was what we were seeing. We were witnessing the aftermath of the atomic bomb that an Army Air Corps B-29 had dropped on Nagasaki shortly before our arrival. We continued to orbit offshore, during which time four or five Jap fighter planes came nearby but made no hostile moves toward the PBM. So we left them alone, as we were ordered to do. A short time later, the PBM notified us that he was returning to Okinawa and that we should remain over him until we got there. It was a very long and tiring mission (six and a half hours), and one for which we did not then understand the purpose or value.

Only much later did we learn the purpose of that mission and that we had been witness to the immediate aftermath of the atomic bomb, which largely destroyed Nagasaki on August 9, 1945. The PBM had been dispatched to the area offshore of Nagasaki to provide air/sea rescue (ASR) for members of the B-29's crew that dropped the bomb in the event that the B-29 had been shot down by the Japs and had been forced to "ditch" or bail out over the ocean. We in the Corsairs were there to protect the PBM from attack. As we now know, the B-29 was not attacked and after delivering "The Bomb" on Nagasaki, it returned safely to its base on Tinian in the Marianas. Thus, the PBM was not needed for ASR, and when it determined the B-29 was clear of the area and headed safely home the PBM returned to its base on Okinawa with its fighter escort.

Thus ended a historic event in which the army, navy, and marines were all participants. This mission and the one flown three days earlier resulting in the destruction of Hiroshima were devastating to all involved, especially the residents of Hiroshima and Nagasaki. Those two bombs resulted in the death of over 106,000 and injury to more than 91,000 Japanese.

Grover Donald Hughes

Lightning Ace

1942 - EARLY NOVEMBER. Operation Torch. Entered Oran. People cheered us as we went through town, offered us fruit. Marched two miles to the (La Cenena) airport where a terrible fight for the airport had taken place by ground forces the previous day. Several U.S. tanks put out of commission, most hangars destroyed; 10 to 20 good airplanes burned up.

EARLY DECEMBER. Captain Fulmer shot down but phoned from the desert and said he was on his way home by camel. Our P-38s flew over Tripoli. Nine of our pilots missing: Lieutenant Cole, Williams, Skinner, Butler, Guskie, and Captain Lewis.

Lieutenant Guskie came in from being shot down. He said he saw Williams hit the ground and Cole down in flames. He got one Me109 and damaged another before two got on his tail and shot one of the engines out.

LATE DECEMBER. Tebessa was again bombed. Gerry above the overcast at 8,000 feet for about five minutes. Lieutenant Smith from UCLA and I were in a trench together, had a long talk about skiing in California while the bombing was going on.

DECEMBER 24. What a Christmas Eve! Went down to Captain Wallace's tent where the rest of the 48's pilots were, drinking and talking about last year. Score so far was 29 aircraft for 48th, 25 for the 49th. If we had had a few more airplanes to replace our losses, we could have doubled the score. We received word from the RAF that one of their priests buried Lieutenant Williams, one of the nine missing pilots. He was the only confirmation.

Bad time for the 14th and the Germans. The 49th lost their commanding officer, Lieutenant Morris, the second CO they have lost. (Captain Lewis the other). He went down in flames near Sousse. The 48th lost three planes. Lieutenant Virgil Smith, six victories, was down in flames after three Me109s got on his tail. Lieutenant Curley Smith (UCLA) and Lieutenant Carroll missing; they were swell fellows and were not made to be fighter pilots. (That's the Smith I was talking with about skiing.)

1943 - EARLY JANUARY. Received word that Captain Lewis was burned after his guns jammed and four Me109s got on his tail. Ju88 over field this morning, shot down. Plane exploded. Shipman found a few pieces of legs, arms, etc.

More bombs dropped at Tebessa. Captain Bing shot down but was safe. Captain Wallace chased home by four Me109s.

The 23rd was a dark day for the 48th. They came out of a fog right over Medessa Airport. Ninety-two German planes on the field. They were outnumbered to start with and were in enemy territory. Six men missing. They got only two Me109s. Tripoli fell, and they reported the road from Tripoli to Gabes jammed with fleeing Germans in orderly retreat, tanks, trucks, etc., on the road and on both sides.

At this stage we had lost 24 pilots out of our original 55. This was a heavy loss even though we had 70 victories. Fifty percent of our old gang dead or captured, and it was telling on the pilots, who were becoming nervous and high-strung. Shipman's story follows, amazing as it seems.

> He was shot down about 30 miles behind German lines by three Me109s. He got out of plane and each of three 109s made three passes at his plane and shot it up, but they did not shoot at him, 100 feet away, but tipped their wings at him. He burned plane up and started walking. A gang of Arabs came up and took his pistol, shoes, socks, helmet, shirt, and escape kit, and then fled. Mark tore off legs of pants and wrapped them around his feet in place of shoes; also took off undershirt, as it was white, and put in pants.
>
> He continued and suddenly found himself in an Italian camp, but he walked through practically unnoticed. Five Italians about 200 yards away looked at him, but that was all. After getting out of camp, four more Arabs caught him, took away his wristwatch, and he chased them off when they tried to take his wedding ring and Catholic necklace. At sundown,

another Arab on a camel offered to lead him through the lines for 1,000 francs, and Mark said OK. Also offered to let him ride on the camel for his gold ring, but Mark said no. Mark ditched the Arab in the dark and, after 36 hours, was picked up by American outpost.

The old pilots were to be sent home. Terrific celebration. All our planes turned over to 82nd. It was sure hard to see the boys we knew go home. They were a great bunch. Had the best record of any group in Africa—over 75 victories and 20 probables.

Heard that Captain Virgil Lusk was killed over San Diego when his plane and Captain Mark Mourna's ran into each other. It was hard to believe that old Lusk, tall, good looking, very polite, should go through the English and North Africa fight and then be killed in a training accident in California. Mark Mourna parachuted to safety, but Lusk's chute failed to open. Lusk had Air Medal with three oak leaf clusters and D.F.C. Lusk, a New Mexico boy, was buried in New Mexico. His ashes in the Capitol. The governor and all state departments took day off. Lusk was New Mexico's first air ace. He shot down five planes, six probables.

LATE MAY. Another raid by B-17s on airdromes in South Sicily escorted by 36 of our planes. Big dogfight. One pilot saw 20 FW-190s around him. Three men from 49th were reported missing (one was Lieutenant Little), but all except Little turned up. Lieutenant Snyder was missing, his first mission. His plane was seen in the water about 10 miles west of Sicily. His chute was seen to open, so probably he was picked up by the Germans.

Five-fighter sweep of Sardinia with 36 planes in all. Each plane carried a 500-pound bomb. #1 mission Captain Ross hit 400-foot ship and sank it, also small boats and wharf and strafed workers on docks. #2 Major Owen and three hit big railroad bridge and tug and car on road. #3 hit entrance to railroad tunnel and town. #4 hit seaplane base, destroyed three planes on ground. #5 hit central Sardinia bomb on zinc works, barracks, and warehouses and shot down three German light bombers. No enemy opposition except for light flak.

Twenty-four planes (1000-pound bombs) bombed two dams in central Sardinia. Both power stations blown up. A hole was seen in one dam with water rushing out. Another raid of 12 planes in northeast Sardinia, one hit on huge three-decker two-stacker troopship. Three of six oil tankers on fire. Two V-boats strafed; two lighthouses strafed. A man on a house was backed off as planes buzzed him. A lieutenant from 49th had to bail out over target due to engine on fire. One Italian seaplane shot down by 49th.

EARLY JUNE. 49th and 48th with 12 ships each, dive-bombed gun emplacements at Pantelleria. 37th led by Major Bright to bomb Calagri but missed Sardinia due to compass error; he had eight Japs and two Germans. 10,000 Italian prisoners taken at Pantelleria.

LATE JUNE. More raids on west Sicily airports. Many convoys seen on road going east, ports full of ships, excess planes and pilots, great tension in the air—expected an invasion.

MIDDLE JULY. On July 10 at 3 A.M. the invasion of Sicily began. Four hundred C-47s took paratroopers across; troops poured in all along the southeast: Americans on left, Canadians in center, British on right. Eight missions, strafing and dive-bombing behind the lines, tried to slow up Axis troops, tanks, etc. Three trains destroyed, many trucks and cars, etc. The boys reported the roads full of Axis equipment going up. On the fifth mission, the 49th shot down five Me109s and lost one P-38 (Lieutenant Booth). On last mission two from 49th shot down by flak with loss of three men. Changed from dive bombing and strafing to escorting B-26s over Messina. Messina itself had about 200 bombers over it and seemed to be on fire from end to end.

Lieutenant Stidham, missing since mid-July, returned with an amazing story:

> He was shot down and taken prisoner by Germans, taken to Div HQ where there were some generals and other high officials all running around in a dither looking at maps and very excited. They took no attention of him but finally an intelligence officer questioned him. He told Stidham that, due to American bombings, he thought he had the right to use any means to get information from him. The threat did not work, and Stidham refused to tell him anything more than his name, rank, and serial number. They put him in a prison camp with an RAF pilot. This camp consisted of a tent with a poor barbed wire fence around it. The two waited until dark and then slipped out after the one guard had gone by. They walked for four nights and hid during the day. They were then in the Mt. Aetna region and were making their way toward Catania. They ran across lots of ammo stored on the hills.
>
> They were challenged several times each night by German guards, but by keeping quiet the guards took no further notice. At Catania they were captured again in the front lines and taken to the rear by some guards when a shell hit in their midst, killing the Germans but hardly scratching the two prisoners—so they took off again southward in the midst of a heavy British barrage and rifle fire from Germans who could see them escaping. After about one hour dodging from

hole to hole they finally reached the British lines and came home.

Once after Stid was first captured, he was in a German truck convoy going to the rear and saw some P-38s about to strafe. He motioned to the Germans, and they stopped and got into a ditch. The 38s shot up all the trucks, burned four. None of the Germans or Stid was hit. Stidham says there were many signs of German hatred by Italians. The Germans told him that the Americans could thank the Italians for the North African victory. Also, once when a small Italian tank passed on the road, the Germans pointed to it and said "Italian Panzer," and then they all laughed.

LATE DECEMBER. Christmas Eve, December 24. Officers' Club up just in time for Xmas Eve. What a difference from the previous year. We could at least eat and keep warm.

1944 - MIDDLE JANUARY. Raid by B-17s on Me109 factory in southern Austria. Lieutenant Smith of 37th collided with Me109. Wing on 109 fell off. Tail boom cut in two, also one motor failed. He was reported lost but came in on one engine. A great feat. One other of our planes went down. The pilot chuted out and was followed down from 25,000 to 8,000 where he entered a cloud. His chute had not opened. We claimed one 109 destroyed.

(Excerpts from reminiscences of Colonel Grover Donald Hughes.
Compiled for the *P-38 Lightning Aces of the ETO/MTO, Osprey Aircraft of the Aces*, Vol. 19.
Submitted by Suzanne C. Wochos, wife of Colonel Hughes)

LTC Archie F. Maltbie

Flames at My Feet

Well not yet, but with gasoline bubbling onto the cockpit floor and flames coming out of the engine cowling, it was a matter of precious moments before my Thunderbolt would be engulfed in flames. But maybe we should start at the beginning of this fateful day. It was August 19, 1944, and I was a fighter-bomber pilot with the 388th Fighter Squadron of the famed 365th Fighter Group, known in the 9th Tactical Air Command as the "Hell Hawks." We flew the P-47 Thunderbolt and were a part of the Ninth Air Force, and our mission was to provide close support of our ground forces in Europe with our dive bombing and strafing of troops, tanks, motor transport, trains, bridges, bunkers, ammo dumps, airfields, flak towers, marshaling yards, no-ball targets, factories, heavily fortified areas, or any other damned thing that was impeding the advance of our GIs. We also used napalm bombs and five-inch aerial rockets to achieve some of our destruction. There wasn't anything that could be asked of us that we wouldn't attempt on behalf of our beloved GIs. We knew the conditions under which they were slugging it out with the Nazis, and many of us had brothers down there. We considered our job to be anything we could do to make it easier for them and to save lives.

On this particular morning, I was assigned to the mission scheduled for takeoff at 0748 hours. At Q700, I and the other 11 pilots were in the briefing room being given the details of the mission plan by the operations officer, weather officer, communications officer, armament officer, and the intelligence officer. The orders had come down as usual from Ninth Tac—we were to patrol an area from the mouth of the Seine to Elbe to prevent enemy forces, which had escaped the Falaise Pocket, from making an escape over the Seine. The squadron leader was Captain James E. Hill leading the 12-plane squadron consisting of red flight, blue flight, and white flight—a flight being four planes, each led by a flight leader, and number-three position in each flight designated an element leader. At the conclusion of briefing, having received detailed information on enemy-flak defenses in the area, armament information as to type, fusing, and size of the bombs we were carrying, and information as to the ammo our eight 50s would be spitting regarding frequency of tracers, armor piercing, etc., and a map of the target area, routing to and from the assigned area along with ground controllers, and any special radio frequencies for the day, we had the usual banter and boasts and wished each other good luck and good hunting and headed for the weapons carriers or jeeps outside the briefing, which took us to our planes.

On arriving at my revetment, my ever-faithful crew chief was there to greet me. He would assist me in the preflight check of my plane and help me climb into the cockpit of this monster fighter known as the P-47 Thunderbolt and affectionately called "The Jug" by those of us who flew her. This was nervous time as I settled into the cockpit, and that ever-present fear was there in the pit of my stomach as I buckled up. It was no worse and no better than all the other missions I had flown and had to deal with. It helped knowing it was normal and natural to have survival instincts, that this was what I was trained to do, the job had to be done, and the better it was done, the sooner this war would be over and we could all go home. Start engines was 0748, and all twelve of those Pratt & Whitney R-2800s roared to life with their 2,400 horsepower eager to get the day's mission started. The sound of this powerful engine dispelled the fear and started the aggressive juices flowing.

Captain Hill, the squadron leader, and his wingman taxied toward the end of the runway followed by red-flight element leader and his wingman. I was flying as blue-flight element leader, so I was leading the fourth set of two planes to the takeoff point. In combat operations, takeoffs and landings must all be accomplished in the least time and most efficient manner possible, because that is the time we are most vulnerable to surprise enemy attack. As each two-plane element arrived at the end of the runway we ran up the engine for a power check and tested the control surfaces for free operations, then applied throttle for takeoff power, and, at 15-second intervals, two fighters roared down the runway and rose into the air. The squadron leader would make a lazy climbing, and his element leader would soon be tucked into formation; then blue flight and white flight would come into squadron-combat formation, and we would climb out on the heading for today's route to the prescribed altitude.

In about 22 minutes we arrived over Louviers, just south of the Seine, and dive-bombed a bridge, with poor results. It was damaged, but we failed to knock it down. Captain Hill then led an armed reconnaissance of the area and strafed and destroyed a truck near the bridge. We then spotted some MT south of the river, and Captain Hill ordered me and my wingman, Lieutenant Shoup, to dive down to treetop level and check them out. As we discovered they were ambulances, we did not attack but received plenty of ground fire for our trouble, and, about that time, our top cover, white flight, was bounced by 13 Me109s. We immediately climbed to rejoin the squadron, and, at about 8,000 feet, I saw three planes in the haze above and to my left, and, as I closed, I saw they were Me109s. As I prepared to attack the number-three plane, I checked for my wingman, and he was not there. It was then I noted two more 109s slightly below and to my right. I could see they would be on my tail if I continued my original attack, so I turned to my right into the number-two man, got him in my gun sight and fired. I had closed so quickly that he blew up right in front of me, and I flew through the debris. Something heavy, perhaps the engine, hit my plane with a big shudder, and in seconds I had flames coming out of my engine cowling and gasoline on the floor of the cockpit. I knew I had precious seconds to get out before she was a fireball or blew. I cut the throttle, jettisoned the canopy, set the trim tab for a gentle climb, unplugged my oxygen tube and earphone plug, and as soon she started to stall, I stood on the seat and dove as hard as I could, as though to drive my head through the wing. Of course, I missed the wing and just avoided the horizontal stabilizer by inches.

I had never jumped before, but I remembered everything the instructor had said when he described how to get out of a P-47, and I was grateful to be safely out; but I made the mistake of pulling my ripcord too soon, instead of free-falling to lose some altitude quickly. I was surprised by the jolt when my chute snapped open at about 6,000 feet and by the silence and tranquility as I floated toward the earth below. It all seemed so still and peaceful, but the spell was quickly broken when I saw a ball of flame off in the distance as my plane exploded and a couple of 109s made a turn around me and flew off into the haze. At about 2,000 feet, I drew some 20mm cannon tracers and other small-arms fire from the ground. Several rounds went through the canopy of my chute. Minutes later the forest below was coming up pretty fast, and I saw I had a chance to make a small clearing if I could just slip the chute a bit and miss getting tangled up in one of those big trees. I just made it, and, as I passed the treetops, I got a sense of how fast I was falling. As I hit the ground, my knees buckled and came up and hit me in the chest. It knocked the wind out of me, kind of dazed me. But, I thought so far so good, I'm safely on terra firma.

Quickly I was on my feet and unbuckled and gathered up my chute and hid it under some leaves in the undergrowth. I knew the Germans had seen me come down and would be searching for me, so I crashed through the ferns, as tall as a man's head, that covered the floor of the forest. Shortly, I came upon a well-worn path, and I took off down it as fast as I could run until I was near exhaustion. I then left the path, taking care not to break any flora or fauna or leave any trail. About 50 yards off the path, I found a group of large rocks which provided cover and from which I had a view of the path. This looked like a good place to rest and get a bearing as to where I was and to plan how to proceed with my escape. In about an hour, a party of six Wehrmacht troops and two dogs came along the path, apparently in search of me. They stopped near the point where I had left the path, and my heart was in my mouth, but, after a few moments, they continued on their way. At that moment my hand instinctively went for my .45, and, just as quickly, I made the decision this would be foolish against six with automatic weapons. If they discovered me, I would just surrender and my war would be over. An hour or so later, they returned, going in the direction from which they had originally come. I decided to remain in hiding the rest of the day to let things cool down and to start moving at dusk in a west-southwest direction toward Allied lines. During this quiet time, thinking over the events of the day, I realized why Lieutenant Shoup, who was always very reliable, had not remained on my wing. I was flying a later model plane, fitted with a paddle prop, which had a much higher rate of climb. I had simply climbed away from him in the haze. I felt better knowing this. The fault for being alone was simply mine.

In the evening I started down the path. After a short time, I was startled by a large wild boar and several smaller ones as they crashed out of the brush to cross the path directly in front of me. The compass from my escape kit now took me in a direction from the path and into the forest. In about 30 minutes, with darkness approaching, I heard a commotion ahead. I paused and heard voices speaking in German. It appeared to be an antiaircraft-gun emplacement, so I gave the area a wide berth and continued quietly on my way. Sometime later it had become so dark and difficult to travel that I decided it was best to bed down and travel again at first light. I broke some ferns and gathered up some leaves to put on top of them and tried to get some sleep. But before long, I was disturbed by an approaching herd of wild pigs. They were feeding on something and fighting among themselves, making a fearsome noise. As they drew ever nearer, the fighting sounded even fiercer, so I climbed a nearby tree for my safety. They stayed around that tree the rest of the night making a nuisance of themselves. I learned later that they had been imported there from Russia for a British royal hunting preserve established in the Forst LaLonde. During my night in the tree, there were several spectacular fireworks displays as nearby antiaircraft batteries opened up on Allied bomber formations passing overhead. In the early morning hours, a fine rain started falling and, before long, I was thoroughly soaked, cold, and miserable. About dawn, the pigs left and I climbed down, eager to be on my way again.

It was much easier with the light to make my way through the forest, and in about two hours I came to a clearing. I could see in the distance a small village, which was LaLonde. Between the village and myself was a small thatched-roofed cottage. I followed a hedgerow down to a vantage point where I could observe the house. The sun was now well up, and I was enjoying the warmth. After some time of observing, a young woman came out of the house and sat on a stool near the hedgerow peeling a pan of potatoes. It all looked OK, and I decided to try for some help. I approached the girl, and, using my French phrases from my escape trip, I tried to tell her who I was. Fortunately, she spoke a little English and told me to stay hidden while she spoke to "Mamma." After what seemed an interminable time, she returned and told me to hurry into the cottage. She introduced me to "Mamma" (Madame Barbey) and to herself, Rollande. Madame Barbey immediately produced some of her late husband's clothes and had Rollande explain to me that if they were to help me escape the "*Boche*," I would have to give them my .45 automatic, my flight suit and A-2 jacket, my escape kit and dog tags, and anything to identify me as American military. I would also have to give them my word that if I were caught in the company of French friends, I would never admit to being American military. Madame Barbey's husband had been taken by the Nazis and died in slave labor, and Rollande's fiancé, André Rieff, who lived in the nearby village of Bourgthereulde (I never could pronounce it), was a member of the Maquis. That was good enough for me, and, besides, it was the only offer I had, and I was happy to have it from two such brave women. They could, and most probably would, have lost their lives if caught helping me. Madame Barbey then fixed me a breakfast of eggs, salt pork, toast, and a glass of hard cider. When I had finished breakfast, Rollande insisted I get some sleep, and she showed me to an old-fashioned down feather bed and promised to contact André after he came from work. I sank down and floated off to a wonderful, much-needed rest.

When I awoke, André was there, and I was impressed. He was much older than Rollande, a tall, muscular, big-framed guy and good looking in a rugged way. He was very self-assured and just the type you could see relishing the Maquis underground action resisting the Nazis. Through Rollande he told me he would take the passport photographs from my escape kit and get me false French identity papers so I could travel. It would take several days; in the meantime, I must keep a very low profile and remain indoors. This was August 20, 1944. General Patton's 3rd Armored was on a wild dash across France, and the Germans were in general retreat through this area. The next morning, Madame Barbey, Rollande, and I were having breakfast, the kitchen door open and chickens wandering in and out. Suddenly, a German jeep came rattling up the lane and stopped right outside the door. Two soldiers jumped out, one with pistol drawn stood at the door, as the other walked right in. I was sure they were there for me, but I continued to eat as nonchalantly as possible. The German took the butter and saltshaker from the table and the remainder of a loaf of bread from the sideboard, turned, smiled, muttered something, and walked out. As they drove out of the yard, I was nearly choking. Rollande and Madame had a good laugh. They were very pleased with how I handled the situation and with their assessment that the *Boche* must be in very bad shape for such an incident to happen.

That evening, André came back, and, after some soup for supper, he told me the Maquis were working on the documents I would need if I were stopped by enemy troops. As he was telling me about German emplacements and gun batteries around the village, all hell broke loose when mortar and artillery shells started falling nearby. This continued for the next day or two and was my first experience of being under attack on the ground. I must say it was very frightening. In the ensuing two or three days, I was witness to some great attacks on German tanks on a road about a mile from my perch in some trees. I never realized the power, the terrific noise, and the concussion of 500-pound bombs exploding as the P-47s dive-bombed the tanks. Then, after they had bombed, they swooped back in, firing those eight .50-caliber machine guns with armor-piercing shells. I was awestruck with the firepower and fully realized now, for the first time, why the Krauts so feared the "Jabos." [German *Jäger Bomber* or "hunter bomber"] I also saw several dogfights overhead with P-47s and P-51s against FW-190s. In most cases, the 190s were shot down or sent flying for home. It was almost as exciting as being a part of it.

Finally, on the fifth day, André came with my forged documents. My *Carte d'Identite* with my escape-kit photograph showed the name Francois LeGuehenec and that I was born October 16, 1919, in the Department of *Finistere* in the Brittany region of France. André told me this was chosen to explain my inability to speak French, because in Brittany, Basque was spoken, and, though many Germans spoke French, few would speak Basque. André also gave me a payroll slip showing I worked for a Jean Blard of Rouen as a woodcutter, a bicycle, and a combined ownership certificate and license, as well as three different-colored ration stamps. I never did know what the stamps were for. To this day, I still have these documents in my VMI souvenirs.

Now that I had my "papers," André could hardly wait for the evening meal to be over to take me for a walk around the village to show me the gun batteries and location of armor. As we were walking down the road, we were met by a column of Wehrmacht troops retreating single file on each side of us. The Jerries paid little attention to us except for a few curses and spits in our direction and an occasional smile. I was more than a little uneasy even though they were a really beat-up looking group. As we approached an antiaircraft battery, we were stopped by a sentry and asked for *papiers*. As André had previously told me to do in such a situation, I showed my identity card to the sentry and grunted "Breton." He took a quick look, passed it back, and gestured us on. By the time we had made a circuit of the town, I was much relieved to be back at the relative safety of the cottage. André said that the fighting was getting closer, that arrangements were being made for the safe houses I was to use on my way back to Allied lines. He would give me instructions as soon as he had them. The next couple of days André and I took evening strolls, and I saw some gruesome sights. On one little road a short distance from the cottage in about a one-mile stretch, there were over 100 dead horses with the ammunition carts they had been pulling strewn about their bloated bodies. There were several burned-out tanks and hundreds of dead German soldiers in the chaotic mess. Then it dawned on me that this was the result of the P-47 attacks I saw a couple of days ago from my perch in the trees.

Finally, on the evening of the seventh day, André had my instructions. I was to set out the next morning for the home of a doctor in the village of Lieurey. I was given the address and a map on an edible wafer I was to eat if apprehended. The doctor would have the instructions for my next leg. Madame Barbey and Rollande gave me a good breakfast and tearfully said their good-byes. I thanked them most sincerely and told them I would be back for a visit once they were free. I mounted my bike and set off toward Lieurey.

Immediately upon reaching the main road, I started meeting German troops and equipment in full retreat. I was grateful they were more interested at the moment in running than in fighting, as I would be passing through no-man's-land and the possible crossfire. About midmorning I encountered a French-Canadian light-armored column in hot pursuit. I jumped off my bike and approached a halftrack. I told them who I was, but, as I had no identification other than my forged papers, they treated me, as they should, as a displaced person. They dispatched a jeep and two soldiers to take me back to their battalion headquarters.

The next 24 hours I was taken by truck back through the British Army units all the while picking up other displaced persons until late in the afternoon on my ninth day we arrived at the British Detainment Center for displaced persons on the outskirts of Caen. The camp was in the charge of an old British colonel of the Home Guard type. When it was my turn to be interrogated, I told him of my situation, that our MIA reports went out ten days after the person was missing, and that I had been missing nine days. I requested to be returned to my unit immediately, so my parents would not receive such a notice. I also explained that my unit was based at Balleroy, only about 30 miles from Caen. The colonel then informed me that regulations required I be sent to an interrogation unit at Manston, on the south coast of England, for debriefing, and then, if my story checked out, I would be returned to the American authorities. I said OK, if that is the way it has to be done, will you please call my unit and inform them I'm here and all right. He refused to do even that, again citing regulations. I was not happy.

On the way back with the Canadians, I had met another escaping P-47 pilot by the name of Stephens. He was from another group in 9th Tac. He also was not happy with the results of his interview, so we decided to plan our early "checkout" from this detainment center. As soon as it was good and dark, we timed a sentry and climbed an apple tree we had spotted earlier and dropped to the ground on the other side of the barbed wire enclosure. We made our way into Caen, which was in total blackout. At this time, Caen was British Army Headquarters on the continent. Our good fortune was to come upon a jeep with American markings parked at the curb by some buildings. We stood in a doorway and staked it out. Finally, a couple of guys came out of one of the buildings and got into the jeep. We approached them and told them our story. As it turned out, they were CIC (Counter Intelligence Corps) guys and they got a kick out of our "escape" from the British, so they agreed to drive us to Balleroy. Once at our base, my intelligence officer identified me for them, and I promised I would have Stephens checked out before releasing him. Stephens and I spent the night at my base. Early the next morning, I took our battle-damaged P-47, which had a second seat installed behind the pilot, and flew Stephens down to Ninth Air Force headquarters where we were debriefed and had our MIA reports killed, just prior to their being sent out later that day. I then flew Stephens to his field and, after he was ID'd for me, said my good-byes and wished him well.

I then flew back to Balleroy, not knowing exactly what to expect. I knew that generally, when one had been down behind enemy lines, that person was not allowed to go back on operations in that theater of war again. It had something to do with the Geneva Convention and the rules of war and being treated as a spy rather than a POW if later captured. Well, I wanted to stay with my unit, and, after two weeks of pleas, applications, physicals, and psychiatric exams, I was finally ordered back to operational status with the 388th Fighter Squadron. During my ensuing duty, I found several occasions when I could fly a little L-5 observation plane we had down to LaLonde. I would land in the pasture next to the cottage to visit Madame Barbey and Rollande. Each time I would take them chocolate, whatever food I could, and cigarettes for André. It was always a very warm welcome and such a pleasure to see them enjoying their new freedom. My wife and I went to visit them once after the war. We were given a grand welcome, and it was our pleasure to present Rollande with an appliance for her home, one she had long desired. It was good to be able to express my thanks once again. Rollande Rieff is still living, in a rest home in Bedarieux, France, and we are still in touch, but Madame and André are long since deceased. It was a long and exciting road, and I continued on to the end of the war and a total of 98 missions with the 388th. Never a dull moment. I had taken off on my 99th mission, leading the squadron, on May 6, 1945 (the day after the war was supposed to be over) to Prague, to check out a report German jets were operating down there, only to have a runaway propeller that required me to abort and turn the squadron over to blue flight leader.

I guess this story will really never end as long as any of us "Hell Hawks" are still alive. The squadron operations board on May 5, 1945, showed Major Hill, Captain Mast, Captain Luckman, and myself as the only pilots on operational duty who had been with the unit previous to D-Day when we flew cross-channel missions from England against the continent. Some were reassigned, some became unfit to fly, some were serving on TDY [temporary duty] as ground observers with armored outfits, and some had finished tours and gone home, while others were lost in England and across France, Belgium, and Germany. We still get together every two years. We are growing older now, our ranks are rapidly being thinned by time and age, and many stories will go untold, as this one would had it not been for the urging of my brother Ken. I do not have the words to express the bonds we pilots formed with one another and the absolute love we shared for the P-47 Thunderbolt, to which many of us know we owed our very lives. Nor will we ever forget our crew chiefs, armorers, and radiomen who kept them operating at top efficiency for us. I would be remiss if I finished this tale without dedicating it to the memory of comrades who paid the ultimate price for our liberty and also to the two brave women of LaLonde, Madame Barbey and her daughter, Rollande Rieff, who were so instrumental in making it possible for this story to be told.

(Submitted by his brother, Ken Maltbie)

John T. "Red" Cochran

Excerpts from the Trip Log

MARCH 2, 1945

We got to Gander [Newfoundland] during a nice warm spell. The snow was still piled up from one to ten feet. We were now overseas as far as the army was concerned. We ran afoul of censorship, foreign money, and food that was a bit new. We had a big blizzard one night that kept us there longer than expected and, when we did leave, it was a bitter-cold night, so cold in fact the tires of the plane would freeze to the runway if allowed to stay in one spot over a minute.

MARCH 6, 1945 GANDER TO AZORES

This was our first flight over water and after 9 hours and 15 minutes of night flying we finally caught sight of the island.

MARCH 7, 1945 AZORES TO MARRAKECH

Up bright and early and started out for Africa. This was the beginning of what we later learned to call the "Rocket Run," meaning land at a place one afternoon, sleep, get up early, and head for the next place.

MARCH 8, 1945 MARRAKECH TO TUNIS

Africa from the air looks pretty good so far but as yet we haven't reached the desert. Tunis is a beautiful seaport town from the air, but the harbor still has remains of the war, and the airport has wrecked planes (Allied, German, and Italian) all over, as well as plenty of planes all over the countryside.

MARCH 9, 1945 TUNIS TO BENGHAZI

Not a building without bullet holes, and lots of buildings are condemned. Ships and subs sunk in the harbor. The rubble is just moved out of the street in town, and no moves to build the place back to prewar standards. The town changed hands about seven times in the war and now there is nothing but Jews and Arabs in it; no Italians allowed.

MARCH 10, 1945 BENGHAZI TO CAIRO

And we're off again. This was an interesting trip because we were flying right over all the big spots of the African campaign. Tobruk, Mersa Matruh, El Alamein—and there is plenty of evidence a war was fought out there. Wrecked tanks and planes still dot the desert; tank tracks everywhere. Fighter strips are so common there you wonder where they got the planes for them. As we were told in briefing, though, don't try to land on one unless it is an absolute emergency, and, if you come to a stop in one piece, don't wander around because the whole desert is still solidly mined. As we got to Cairo, we really saw a sight. The Nile Valley is beautiful from the air, green about 20 or 30 miles, and right in between miles and miles of desert sand. We circled the pyramids and took some air-to-ground pictures.

MARCH 11, 1945 CAIRO

We saw several pyramids of all sizes. We came back early and rested up for the rest of the trip, which by now had narrowed to a race between three of the eleven crews who started out from Mitchell Field together. We were leading up to here and wanted to hold on. The trip up to now had taken 38 hours and 40 minutes.

MARCH 12, 1945 CAIRO TO ABADAN

Off again early for a trip over Jerusalem, Bethlehem, and Nazareth to Abadan in Old Persia. Landed at Abadan and found out why it is one of the hottest places on earth. Temperature was over 100°F., and the boys there were dreading summer and hot weather to set in. We are still ahead in the race.

MARCH 13, 1945 ABADAN TO KARACHI

We were told right off that this wasn't the end so we were issued more clothes, slept, and took off once again at 5 A.M. See what I mean now by Rocket Run?

MARCH 14, 1945 KARACHI TO ONDAL

Still traveling, and I guess this will end it. Total time: 58 hours 40 minutes from New York to India. Ondal. We are here; no one knows why, or where we will go, when we go, or anything else. We have been assigned to the Fourteenth Air Force but cannot get to China from here.

APRIL—JUNE CHINA

Numerous hump flights and bombing missions.

JULY 25, 1945

We flew our first mission off Okinawa and it was easy. Primarily it was a weather reconnaissance, but we had six 1000-pound bombs to drop on shipping if we found any or on an airfield if no shipping was found. 'Twas on the island of Kyushu, and we were up there flying all over Japan by ourselves in broad open daylight. No flak or fighters, so it was a milk run.

AUGUST 15, 1945

Took off from Leyte for Morotai. Landed a little after noon and found out from the Red Cross girl who met the plane with iced drinks and cookies that the war was officially over. Our first news of it, and what a wonderful feeling it gave us.

MID-OCTOBER—NOVEMBER?

Plans for an eventual departure for home! This included a touch-and-go situation with flyable airplanes and seniority among the crews.

THIRD LEG KWAJALEIN TO HONOLULU

Uneventful leg. One notable part of the entire trip so far was that, as we were ready to take off each day from those island airports, a B-29 was landing and taxiing in after overnight flights into the same airports we were using on our return home. This plane was the *Enola Gay*, which was the plane that dropped the first atomic bomb.

Robert Tuthill

Air Force Mission #178 Remembered

The date was January 20, 1945, and one I shall never forget. My outfit was the 759th Bomb Squadron, 459th Bomb Group, 304th Bomb Wing, Fifteenth Air Force stationed in Cerignola on the Adriatic Sea in southern Italy. I was a corporal rated as a radio operator-waist gunner. I was about to go on my fourth combat mission. The crew named our B-24, "So Round, So Firm, So Fully Stacked."

The bomb load for this mission was forty 100-pound bombs totaling 4,000 pounds, or two tons of destruction. The target was a marshalling or railroad yard in Salzburg, Austria. We hoped that it wasn't going to be like our first two missions when we had to make emergency landings on the tiny island of Vis just off the west coast of Yugoslavia, southwest of Split, Herzegovina.

Our ten-man crew consisted of Pilot Kasmir Ulaky; Copilot Ted Bidwell; Navigator Forrest Haynes; Bombardier Ernest Biglow; Flight Engineer-Gunner Wally Comegys; Radio Operator-Waist Gunner, yours truly, Robert Tuthill; Left Waist Gunner Bill Wells; Ball Turret Gunner Bob Estep; Nose Turret Gunner Jake Egel; and Tail Gunner John Hancock. Our flight to the target was normal except bad weather required us to climb to 27,500 feet, where we had to wear oxygen masks as we did on every mission in excess of 10,000 feet. The outside temperature was –60°F.

As luck would have it, shortly before the bomb run we developed an oil leak in #3 engine, and I could see frozen chunks of oil flying away from the plane. This caused some concern, but we reached the impact point and dropped our bombs on the target. We did experience some moderate but accurate flak. About then, the pilot attempted to feather #3 prop, but there was not enough oil pressure left to turn the blades into a feathering position. This resulted in a "runaway" prop, which wasn't desirable. After turning and heading home, we soon found that we could not maintain sufficient air speed to stay with the group. Soon we were coming back over the Swiss Alps alone. It is not recommended to leave the group, but we had no choice, and to complicate matters we were losing altitude. At 14,000 feet, we were hit by accurate antiaircraft fire and raked from nose to tail. Our location then was over Udine in the Po Valley in northern Italy, a German fighter airfield. This was not exactly where we wanted to be and especially since we could count six Me109s on the ground. Happily for us, because of the bombing over the last year of the oil refineries and storage tanks, they couldn't get off the ground. I suspect it was during the aforesaid antiaircraft fire that Left Waist Gunner Bill Wells's parachute chest pack ripped. We both had them on when the flak hit the plane. He must not have noticed it when it happened.

It was about then that our #2 engine failed, and Pilot Ulaky nursed our crippled aircraft toward Yugoslavia. We were getting ready to bail out. He asked Navigator Haynes for a new heading and changed our course to a more easterly direction. We were now about 10–15 miles east of Fiume, a city at the north end of the Adriatic on the west coast of Yugoslavia. It is now called Rijecka, Slovenia. The pilot, captain of our ship, gave the order to bail out at 11,000 feet over the Juliske or Istrian Alps of northern Yugoslavia. I was the last one out, wearing my soft-soled flight boots, and as I jumped, I lost my flight helmet, which left me bareheaded. I also lost my GI shoes, which had been tied to my parachute harness. Bill Wells's parachute failed to open when he bailed out and we lost him. After the war, Graves Registration Teams failed to find any remains of Bill Wells.

I landed in approximately 18 inches of snow and sprained my right ankle. Luckily, I carried an army trench knife strapped to my leg in keeping with my motto "always be prepared." With my knife, I was able to cut strips from my parachute to strap my sprained ankle and also a kerchief to keep my ears from freezing and to protect my head from the bitter winter weather. I may not have looked like a fashion-plate, but I did keep my head warm. We found out later that the Germans, who saw us bail out, sent out a ski patrol from Fiume to take us as prisoners. Fortunately, our pilot, copilot, and I were picked up almost immediately by one of Marshall Tito's Partisan Freedom Fighters who was hunting game in the area.

He didn't speak or understand English, but we were able to advise him in Italian and German that our gas supply was gone and we, "American airmen," had had to hit the silk. It had started to snow again as he motioned for those of us who had found each other to follow him. We then walked in deep snow from about 3 P.M. to midnight until we reached a partisan command post in Merzla Vodice. Fortunately, the new snow covered our tracks, and the German patrol didn't find us.

On January 21, 1945, we left Merzla Vodice and walked to either Delnice or Skrad, where the tail gunner and I were able to sleep in a bed for the night as guests of Captain Vranes, a Yugoslav partisan officer, his wife, and young daughter. That same day, our bombardier Biglow joined our group, and that made six of the ten-man crew. The next day in the town of Skrad, we met British Captain Harrison of the Royal Engineers. He had parachuted into northern Yugoslavia to assist Allied escapees and evadees. We were evadees. He had radio contact with Fifteenth Air Force Headquarters in Italy and advised them of our status, so we were still MIAs and not prisoners of war, as we very nearly might have been. Captain Harrison provided us with some canned food and tea to supplement the meager Yugo diet of *parlenta*, a blanket, English sweaters, wool hats, and high-topped shoes. The shoes, although not of exact size, were a most necessary item and a blessing, because we were going to walk 200-250 miles before returning to an Allied-controlled area. Because of his aid and assistance to us and the fact that he did not seem to have a watch, I gave him my GI watch issued to me as a radio operator. He was most grateful and certainly needed it in his work.

The winter of 1944-45 in Europe, and certainly in Yugoslavia, was much colder than normal with more than the usual amount of snow and ice. This made it more difficult for the evadees but also hindered the enemy. On January 23rd, 1945, Flight Engineer Wally Comegys was finally able to join our group after playing games of "hide and seek" with the Krauts for three days in the snow, but this led to his having severe stomach problems during the remainder of our evasion trip back. Because the partisans were themselves divided between Tito and General Mikhailovich and the politics were so murky, when we were asked our opinion of the current political situation, we all agreed to reply in Yugoslavian, "I do not understand."

After walking east or inland for about two and half to three weeks, we made a forced march south to cross the German front lines at night. This was between Karlovac and Zagreb located about halfway between Fiume on the coast and the western border of Hungary. That's when we found out that the Benzedrine sulphate tablets in our escape kits came in very handy to keep us alert and awake during that stressful trip. I must mention that along the way we had picked up a lot of others also seeking to cross the lines. It was a motley crew of about 500, and indeed a sight to see. There were evadees, POW escapees, labor camp escapees, and wounded partisans on sleds drawn by oxen. It took almost 31 hours without sleep to get all across the German lines without getting caught. Looking back on it all and the number of people involved, it was a miracle we got away with it. After it was over and the Benzedrine wore off, you could fall asleep standing up.

After that, for the first time in about three weeks, we encountered some mechanized vehicles. The partisans had acquired some British Dodge trucks to transport us to the Adriatic port city of Zara, now known as Zadar, which had been vacated by the Germans only one day earlier. The only problem was to get all our men and a few others into the truck assigned to us. It was so crowded that there was no room to sit down, so we all stood for the day-and-a-half ride to the coast. Upon arriving, we were invited aboard an American oil tanker that was in port. The captain, seeing how hungry we were, had his cook make a very big breakfast of bacon and powdered scrambled eggs, toast, and coffee. It was our first real food in quite some time.

Victor C. Rose

I flew 51 combat missions over Europe in 1944–45 in a B-26 Martin Marauder Medium Bomber while assigned to the 344th Bomb Group, 495th Squadron.

I had a man in my barracks who had grown up in a small town near my home. I had never known him in civilian life; we met when we were flying missions in France. It was a sad day when his crew did not return from the mission. Most of the time when planes were lost, the crews never made it; we did not know at the time if anyone survived. After the war I discovered he had gotten out of his plane and was captured by the Germans and held in a prisoner of war camp. He had injuries from his experience and was released from the prisoner of war camp when the land troops came to the prison and set them free.

Would you believe that those in the army ground forces opened the prison doors to set their GI buddies free? Picture the excitement—to have been injured and held prisoner, then the doors suddenly open, and friendly American faces are there to free you. The prisoners rushed to greet those who had come to set them free. This big GI in the lead swung open the gates, and as he entered he was given a bear hug in the arms of my friend, who still had bandages over his face. This was no surprise to these troops;

this wasn't the first prison camp they had liberated. But this encounter was different. There was a strange feeling when the one with the bandaged face called him by name. What a shock! How would a prisoner being saved from a prison camp in Germany know who he was? Again his name was called. He was being released by a good friend who had grown up within a few miles of his home. The reunion made a story I will never forget. It has been an encounter that touches me every time I give it a thought.

Johnny Bloemendal

One Sad Day

This is a reminder that war can come to anyone, at any age, and sometimes the most innocent are the victims of the insane cruelty that is war.

It was August 23, 1944. At the little village of Freckleton, in rural Lancashire, a young teacher in the Holy Trinity Church School had just told the five-year-old tots of her nursery class to put their heads down while she read them a story from the Bible in an effort to quiet their fears. Outside, torrents of rain were beating on the roof and windows of the school, and violent winds were ripping roofs off houses and blowing over huge trees that had stood for decades.

Close by was an American air depot, where ten thousand soldiers worked day and night repairing and modifying bombers and fighters for use by the American Eighth Air Force. Every bomber and fighter had to be flight-tested after work was done on each. Although it was the second largest American airbase in England, only a handful of top-level military people and the local villagers knew the place existed. It was officially Base Air Depot #2. To those serving there, it was "BAD 2."

First Lieutenant Johnny Bloemendal, test pilot, was waiting at the edge of the main runway in a B-24 Liberator bomber for the control tower's order to take off. His copilot was Tech Sergeant Jimmy Parr. Flight Engineer was Sergeant Gordon Kinney. (There weren't enough test pilots on the base to enjoy the luxury of an officer copilot, so an enlisted man always rode in the right-hand seat on test flights.)

Behind Bloemendal's plane, Lieutenant Pete Manassero waited in another B-24 with Sergeant Dick Pew in the copilot's seat and Sergeant Lawrence "Frog" Smith, fight engineer, watching over their shoulders.

It hadn't started to rain yet, though it looked like a normal Lancashire day, cloudy, with probable showers soon. It was wartime, and no one could wait for ideal flying weather. Combat units sorely needed the planes 200 miles south in East Anglia.

The tower gave the "go"' signal to Johnny. The big Liberator started thundering down the runway, and Pete Manassero eased his plane around to follow Bloemendal. Moments later both planes were airborne, and each crew started flight-test routines.

As they gained some altitude, the pilots heard a radio call from the tower. General Ott, area commanding officer, had ordered all aircraft to be recalled to the base. A bad storm was approaching from the southeast.

Pete and John acknowledged the call and began landing procedure. They headed out over the Irish Sea, made a 180-degree turn, and started down toward the long runway. The two flight engineers lowered landing gear and went back to check that the gear was down and locked. Then, suddenly, the storm hit them. Pete could no longer see Johnny's B-24 ahead of him and neither crew could see the ground! Johnny keyed his microphone and announced, "My instruments are going crazy. I can't tell if I'm right side up or inverted!" Pete called him on the command set and said, "Let's get out of here and head north toward Scotland." Johnny replied, "OK."

In the second aircraft, Pete swung out to one side to make sure he would not hit Bloemendal's plane and shouted for Sergeant Smith to get the gear up to cut down the drag. He called to Sergeant Parr, "Give me war emergency power!" Jimmy rammed the throttles past the safety wire and grabbed the control column in front of him. Both men hauled back with all their strength in an effort to make the big Liberator climb. It just roared ahead, right on the treetops. The storm was trying to push the plane down, and it wouldn't climb at all. They continued on like that for nearly ten miles till the bomber broke out of the storm into sunshine!

Pete reached for his cigarettes, but his hand was shaking so hard he couldn't light one. He called Johnny on his radio but got no answer. Later, as the storm blew out of the area, Pete radioed the tower for landing instructions and was told to come in. As he circled the area he could see smoke coming up from the village of Freckleton.

Witnesses on the ground saw lightning strike the doomed bomber that Lieutenant Bloemendal was flying. Pieces of it came down as the B-24 crashed into the school below. Parts of the plane tore loose and crashed into a cafe across Lytham Road. The 2,700 gallons of high-octane aviation gas ignited and set fire to the school, adjoining houses, and the snack bar across the road.

Older children in the other classrooms climbed out of windows and ran out into the storm. Neighbors took many of them into their homes to give them shelter. But 38 little five-year-old tots perished in the fire with two young teachers. Americans and villagers rushed to the scene. Soldiers hauled five little ones out of the burning school, wrapped them in overcoats, and sent them to the air base hospital in the ambulance that had arrived.

Two of the tots died in the hospital. Two little boys and a girl survived but were to spend the next two years in hospitals for treatment of their terrible burns. When little George Carey was rescued, all of his clothing except his shoes had been burned off him. The other boy, David Madden, had been brought to Lancashire by his parents from their home near London to get him away from the German bombs that rained down in the London area every night. When Ruby May Whittle woke up in a hospital bed, she was covered with bandages from head to foot with just her fingertips and part of her face exposed.

Thirty-six children and the two teachers were buried together in the Holy Trinity Church yard cemetery. Two other families wanted their children buried elsewhere. At the funeral, two American soldiers carried the little caskets. Other soldiers stood shoulder to shoulder from the church to the grave as a Guard of Honor.

As Sergeant Tom Miller from Baton Rouge, Louisiana, set down the casket he had helped to carry, he saw the nameplate on it. It read "Sonya Dagger." Tom decided if ever he was married and had a little girl he would name her Sonya. After the war, Tom did get married, and he and his wife, Bernadine, named their daughter Sonya. When Sonya Miller was grown up and also married, she accompanied her parents on a reunion trip to the old air base. They visited Freckleton, and Sonya met the Dagger family.

On the way to the village she said, "All my life I've thought about doing this, but I never dreamed it would happen." The Daggers "adopted" Sonya into their family when they learned the story of how she had been named.

Epilogue

Neither David Madden nor George Carey was able to participate in sports as a child, due to the damage the fire had done to their legs. David eventually became a civil engineer. George, who had missed so much schooling, never learned to read or write. As an adult, he learned a trade doing plastering work. Ruby May has a spot on the top of her head where hair won't grow as the result of scar tissue. She married Brian Currell, and they went to live on the Isle of Wight. She learned to put her fears and memories of that terrible day behind her and became a cheerful, happy young lady.

Every year on the 23rd of August a group of villagers and members of the BAD 2 Association (Americans and British) hold a short ceremony at the gravesite. Little markers surround the grave with the names of the children buried there. A large stone monument stands at the head of the grave with all of the names engraved on it.

No one in the village ever criticized the Americans for the disaster. They realized that the only one to be blamed was the madman in Germany who had brought on the war.

Americans who return to the area on visits always head for the cemetery in the churchyard to offer a prayer for the little ones they will never forget. In America on the Sunday nearest the 23rd of August, altar flowers are offered as memorials in many churches. The BAD 2 Association has held five reunions over there. They have been welcomed back by the villagers, many of whom were children attending the school in 1944. Some of the villagers, including George Carey and Ruby May (now Currell) have attended BAD 2 reunions in America, as have other villagers. Out of the ashes of tragedy have risen bonds of friendship between the villagers and the Americans.

In recent years, when Holy Trinity Church (over 150 years old) needed some repairs, members of the BAD 2 Association contributed $7,000 to restore the old building. A new school and a memorial hall were built in the little village, partially with money contributed by soldiers on the air base in 1944.

Veterans who return on visits from all across America refer to their journey as "going over 'ome."

(Submitted by Ralph G. Scott, Secretary, BAD 2 Association)

Robert J. Ziesche

After one year of training as an airborne radio operator and mechanic in Pennsylvania, North Carolina, Florida, Illinois, Wisconsin, and Georgia, I went overseas on the French liner *Louis Pasteur* with a British crew. Food was not edible, so most of us lived on cookies and candy bars bought from the ship stores that opened once a day with a three-hour lineup.

We went overseas unescorted (no convoy) zigzagging for a week. It was winter in the north Atlantic and the ocean was very rough and nearly everybody was seasick.

We disembarked at Southampton, and I was sent to a Repple Depple [replacement depot] outside London for more training as an infantry replacement, but I was assigned to the 21st Weather Squadron as a radio operator and sent to Ascot. This was the headquarters for Supreme Allied Command. We were bombed every night, as Germans were trying to hit General Eisenhower's headquarters. We were warned if we were wounded inside a tent we would be court-martialed, so we had to "hit" the foxholes every bombing. I also took schooling in radio operator code transmissions.

I was then sent to Greenham Common Airbase near Reading, finally my permanent outfit and a tremendous, outstanding group—the 438th Troop Carrier Group. I was assigned to the 89th Squadron as a radio operator on a C-47 plane. Our CO acquired a very high-frequency directional finding mobile radio station. As I was rated radio mechanic, I was assigned to the station. Our call sign was "Natty," and we were in a network with two other airfields with directional finding antennas. We were the master control. When a pilot was not sure of his location, he would call us for a heading back to our base. We operated 24 hours a day, seven days a week, and I am proud to say several pilots came to the station to thank us for help.

On D-Day, General Eisenhower came to our base at Greenham Common and gave his historic preinvasion speech to the 438th Group and the 101st Division paratroops, as we were picked to lead off the D-Day invasion dropping 1430 paratroops of the 502nd Parachute Regiment from 81 C-47s near the town of Ste.-Mère-Église. The 438th was awarded a unit citation.

We returned towing 50 gliders with the 80th Antiaircraft Battery and field guns. The 438th went to Italy and dropped paratroops and gliders for the invasion of Southern France and helped supply Patton's Third Army units for their push across France. We also flew two much-appreciated supply missions to the 101st Division that had been cut off during the Battle of the Bulge.

I served in several other campaigns in France, Italy, and Holland. We were one happy bunch when Japan surrendered after the A-bombs. Most of us had been overseas almost two years.

Upon returning to the United States and seeing the Statue of Liberty in reverse, I arrived back at Camp Kilmer, New Jersey, from where I shipped out, only to find out I was a "Dear John" letter victim, losing wife and daughter because of being overseas two years.

Letters Home

William Wilson's wife, Jane, and daughter Johanna

A selection of holiday V-mails from Leonard M. Owczarzak

Joseph Phillips

[This letter was written to his nephew, Phil Blocher. Phil's father, Colonel Sam Blocher, was Joey's brother-in-law and was also stationed in Africa.]

January 1, 1943, from Africa

Dear Phil,

I'm almost completely out of envelopes, which is why I'm using V-mail. I don't like them, never have, and never expect to, but at a time like this, I can't very well afford to be choosy about such things.

Your December 6 V-letter got here yesterday, and I'm answering it promptly in refutation of your charge that I don't write to you. If I recall correctly, I've written to you three times in the past three weeks, which I think is doing pretty well, and I want no more remarks concerning the mooching I do. I just sent your Dad half a box of cigars. When anybody can mooch that many cigars from me at a time, that is mooching of a very high order indeed! My photography is coming along very well, but I am running out of developers. Think you can pick some up for me?

Your knife came in handy last night. My tent was blown out from over me during the rain and I used it to cut twigs to make temporary stakes. I might say that I got very wet indeed during the process. My blankets still contain an excess amount of moisture.

Last night I was awakened by what sounded like a small-scale battle—machine guns, Tommy guns, rifles, pistols, carbines, flares, and about every other kind of weapon you could think of. It took me a few minutes to realize that it was just a New Year celebration in the army's own quaint and inimitable fashion.

Love, Joey

Leonard Owczarzak

Dear Mom and Dad,

You haven't heard from me for quite some time because I have been making quite a few moves since arriving overseas, the latter part of September. Had a little submarine scare on our way over but the destroyer leading our convoy took care of it!

We are now setting up in our new location to protect the airstrips here from enemy attack. Those Japanese are sure stubborn. They sent planes to welcome us when we were making our landing and visit us almost every night. You might almost get the feeling that they didn't like us! Now their buddies on land have also taken to shooting at us.

We put up a couple of tents for shelter. It means a lot when it rains every day. Our kitchen crew came in and is doing a good job preparing chow for us. What they have to work with leaves something to be desired. Have a fast running stream to wash in, so we are living in luxury compared to the guys in the infantry. Air raid siren started sounding so will cut this short for now.

Love,
Your Son Leonard

The following letter shows how some soldiers got around the rules of censorship:

Mail call brought me a letter
Oh! - straight from Heaven above,
Memories of happy days bringing
When it comes from the one I love.

Every sweet thought that it carries
Arouses my love once again,
Rose-tinted paper—a perfume divine,
Enchanting me—Ah, my Lorraine!

Inside that sweet packet is my life –
Now opened with fingers afire –
Feeling her love so close to me,
Inspiring my soul with desire!

"John, I know you'll understand –
I met him at a dance. The band
Was playing a romantic tune and all –
He is handsome, dark, and tall.

"I love him and he loves me.
This is our destiny.
We were married yesterday,
Yours," with S.W.A.K.

Mail call brought me a letter,
I thought it was from Heaven above,
But it doesn't really matter –
It's just from the one I love.

Written by a disappointed soldier in 1941
(The first letter of each word in the first 14 lines reads MOM WE ARE IN FIJI.)

Harold A. Childs

4th Combat Camera Unit

The following letter was sent to Childs's future father-in-law on September 5, 1944:

Dear Mr. Graves,

For several months now, I have been intending to answer the swell letters you sent me shortly before the invasion.

It came at one of those times that confusion and uncertainty are running rampant. There are times when an experienced person's outlook has a quieting effect. I'm kind of stumbling around trying to express myself. Thanks a lot for the letter, Mr. Graves.

Janey does wonderfully in her letters, but as you know, nothing can equal her presence. She has a wholesomeness and humor that no one could help but love. I could go on for hours on what a wonderful daughter you and Mrs. Graves turned out. You have the envious pleasure of seeing her every day. Please excuse the babblings of some guy who hasn't seen her in ten months.

Our war is going pretty well. You would be as proud as I of America, if you could have been in Normandy. The way those fellows drove themselves in, in spite of one of the best and heavily fortified armies in the world, convinced me that America can hold her head up in any company. I guess you've read all this in the papers. I just want so badly to have people realize what they went through by sheer guts.

I'm glad that Jane could go to Michigan and see my folks and meet Randy. I imagine that she must have low moods at times. I'm sure that wars are harder to handle on the women than the men who go away. In my lower moments, I wish she hadn't met me and been forced to go through all this. A couple of times, when the current price on lives was pretty low, my greatest worry was about her.

I don't intend to carry on in this morbid subject, but I guess you know how much her happiness means to me, and I am fully aware of how much it means to you.

Jane writes that Fran has joined the WACs. I hope it will help her to find what she wants. Being an idealist in this sort of a world is a hard row to hoe.

I enjoyed so much seeing the Graves family live and the tactful way the younger element was handled. Coming from a family with just my sister and I contributing to the problems, it was a wonderful experience and made me realize what the words "A Good Home" really meant.

The Yanks crowded the Browns out of 1st place today much to the indignation of the GIs over here. The average American is about mentally 50% at home when he is engaged in a war.

I'm going to have to stop soon. In the event you can't translate this Mr. Graves, Jane might be able to help. At least she seems to reply to some remarks I make in my letters. Being under a strain at this time, it's hard to concentrate on any letter.

I'll say goodbye now. I hope you are all well and very happy and that this thing will be over soon. I know that your work kept you very busy. We all deserve a rest.

Give my love to the family and especially Jane.

Your friend, Hal

Austin Cox

Love Letters to My Bride

My dearest Jeanne,

I am in my little home, which is about three feet underground, sometimes called a foxhole. I've always wondered why they call it that, now I know; it's not the nicest place in the world, but at times you sure wouldn't trade it for anything else in the world.

I have your picture right over my heart, and every night I can lay here and look at you until it gets too dark to see you. I know your ears must burn an awful lot for every night I have a nice long talk with you. I guess you will think I'm nuts, but it sure makes me feel a lot closer to you.

We can never be beat now for every mile we go is bringing us that much nearer to home and to the ones we love.

All my love to the sweetest girl in the world, Austin

My dearest Jeanne,

Well darling, today is the 4th of July, the day they shoot all the fireworks at home. I can't say that I'm missing any of the bangs this year. I got a new issue of clothing today. I was beginning to feel pretty badly with the ones I had on. How I wish I could take you in my arms now. It seems I miss you more than anything about this time every evening, for I just lay here and do nothing but think of you.

All my love, Austin

August 8, 1944

My dearest Jeanne,

I have the most trouble writing now than I ever had. I guess it's because we are on the move so much here of late and I can't get myself settled down. It's just my nerves, that's the only thing I can blame it on. There was another beautiful sight in the sky today, thousands of heavy bombers. It's enough to make anyone cry with joy because they make everything easier. Every time they come over you can always see the prisoners list get bigger for they just come right over and give themselves up by the hundreds.

All my love, Austin

May 1945

My dearest Jeanne,

I could write a book about all that has happened since I was last with you, but I would rather wait until I get there with you and then we can talk to our heart's content.

I dream about that every night when I lay down, how we shall lay close together at nights and talk about all the many different things we have done and dreamed about since the day we parted. There are some things that I want to forget, for there were some pretty nasty experiences, and that can only be forgotten when I am once more with you.

The lights are about to go out now, my darling, but some day soon I hope to be able to keep them on all night if we want.

Forever and Always, Austin

Michael J. Chmieloski

Being a support group assigned to the 300th Bomb Group with the functions of communications, control-tower operations, weather station, range finder, homing range, etc., we had all functions necessary for the B-24s to get into the air and on their way with favorable conditions for a successful bombing mission. Having had easy access to the radio shack, I would scan for broadcasts from all over the world. The broadcasts that really intrigued me were the ones from Tokyo Rose in Tokyo and Helen and Betty from Radio Jakarta. They were the enemy demoralizing propaganda DJs who supervised the Sunday one-hour broadcasts permitting the prisoners of war to broadcast messages over the air to their loved ones. I began to wonder whether these POW messages were in any way being intercepted and whether somehow they were being conveyed to their families. I decided to miss Mass on Sundays and go down to the radio shack and tune in two receivers to ensure that I would get the complete message in the event of a receiver fading out. It is here that I believe that speed writing was invented, as I had to use shortcut words and abbreviations in order for me to put down on paper everything that was broadcast in each message, such as name, rank, serial number, home address, names of loved ones, and other incidentals. Being in the bush country, stationery was lacking, but the Red Cross was kind enough to supply me with boxes of envelopes and writing paper, which I used to compose and type a letter from all the info I had written down.

I intercepted about a thousand POW messages but was able to type up only about 500. At the beginning, the censor at the APO tried to stop these letters from going out, but an officer interceded on my behalf, as there was nothing in the rules and regulations to prevent these letters from being mailed. I received about 65 replies thanking me from the bottom of their hearts as in most cases my letter was the only positive news in two years, after they had received a missing-in-action letter or telegram, that their loved one was alive. I received letters from Australia, Canada, Burma, India, England, and the United States. These letters were indescribable classics, as their appreciative elation was put in writing that came from the heart, and it made me feel good that I had contributed a little extra to the war effort.

One day I was scanning on the receiver and I picked up a broadcast from San Francisco, where it stated that a high school had undertaken a project to intercept these POW messages. I felt a sigh of relief and prayed to God that they had become involved early enough to intercept some of the 500 messages I did not type and forward.

Gerald Cagle

My Brothers

I will never forget the day when, as a child, my mother took me into a back room of our home to "show me something"—those military unit pictures on the wall that I had seen so many times but did not know their significance. I was no more than five or six years of age at the time, maybe younger. She began to tell me about two brothers that I had whom I had never heard about. It was confusing for me, but exciting in an odd way. There on those pictures were faces of people I did not know, but who were brothers to me. I had two brothers still alive at that time, so I knew what it was like to have brothers, but these felt different. What my mother told me that day became a lifelong quest of trying to get to know two brothers whom I could never know in the true sense of the word.

I have forgotten much of what my mother told me that day, but I have never forgotten what my brothers did in their service to our country. I have always thought that if I could honor them in my heart, it would not matter very much if no one else honored them. But as time passed, I have realized that what they did was important. They were no more, no less, than so many who went "over there." But these were my brothers. What they did in the war mattered. Private First Class Clyde F. Cagle and Private First Class George M. (Melton) Cagle paid the ultimate price for the United States to remain free.

Being born after my brothers were killed, I could not in my youth and still cannot imagine what my family had experienced just a few years before. They never recovered from their loss. How could a parent recover from this kind of loss? At one point in World War II, my mother had three sons and five brothers in service at the same time. How she must have worried. As far as I know, all of them saw action or were in battlefield theater of operations. One of my brothers who was in service in World War II survived. Another brother missed the draft.

My brother T/5 William R. (Richard) Cagle was in Battery B, 325th AAA Searchlight Battalion. He was responsible for the requisitioning, receiving, and distributing all publications for the central Pacific area. Richard was my best friend. He was my big brother, my hero. He had some hard years after the war. He could never talk to me about the other "boys." He had some days of deep, dark depression that would, at times, almost overwhelm him.

Clyde was in Co. L, 121st Regiment, 8th Division. They went into Normandy on July 4, 1944. I know very little about the battles that were fought, but the fighting must have been very intense. On July 12, 1944, Clyde was killed in action somewhere outside St. Lô. He was killed instantly by an 88 and is buried in the Normandy-Colleville Cemetery.

Melton served in Co. D of the 786th Tank Battalion. He was killed accidentally as he was cleaning the machine gun on his tank on March 3, 1945. I have never understood how this happened, but I have been told that it was a fairly common accident. My parents never did find out any more than this about Melton's death. I don't think that they really wanted to know.

Melton's death was a terrible blow to my parents, who had already lost one son. I have heard that, upon the arrival of those who informed my parents of Melton's death, my mother said with much despair, "Not again." I have tried to picture that scene. The fear of seeing that military car pull into the yard must have been unbearable. I think that all parents have a horrible fear of losing one of their children. Think of losing two sons to a war that was being fought in such a distant land. Two sons, who left in tears, promising to come back home soon, but were never to be seen again. Melton is buried in the Henri-Chapelle Cemetery in Belgium.

Melton's death was such a shock that my parents didn't even fill out and return the form for his life insurance. In all the turmoil in their lives, they must have just forgotten. It may be that they just could not bring themselves to receive any money for the death of another son. They had been convinced to do so at Clyde's death, but my daddy always thought that receiving this money was the same as receiving "blood money." He just didn't think it was right to accept payment for the death of his son.

All this was forgotten over the years but was discovered in the late seventies. It created quite a stir in the Veterans Administration when they found out that parents of a deceased veteran who died in a foreign country in time of war were not receiving his life insurance benefits, even though he was not killed in action. An investigation revealed that the form had not been returned, so there was nothing that could be done. It was discovered at this time, though, that my parents should have been receiving much more money over the years. I am not sure of the reason for the underpayment, but the VA [Veterans' Administration] did correct this problem at this time. How much easier it could have been in years past for my parents if they could have been drawing this larger amount. I remember how badly my family needed this small amount every month. It wasn't much (maybe $40 or so), but it did put some food on the table. It seems to this day a very small amount for all that they lost. What price could be put on the lives of two sons? How much would really be enough?

The following letter was written to my uncle John ("Jake") from overseas. Uncle John was medically discharged just before Clyde's unit went overseas. Uncle John and Clyde had been together from the time they entered service.

April 29, 1944
Dear Jake,

How is everything going by now? Fine I hope. As for me I am doing fine. I received your letter last night, which I was glad to get. They wrote me about Melton being at home on furlough. I am glad he got it. I was surprised to hear about Roy getting another furlough. I believe that makes him two. It is good that he can get to come home now while he is in the States. I hope him and Melton don't have to come across. Maybe they won't. I'll be glad when all of us can come back across. It is good that Wade is close enough that he can come home pretty often. I will close for now. Keep everything going.

Love,
Clyde

Mr. Cagle:

I guess you will wonder who I am, but I am Ed Ray. I was your son Clyde's platoon sergeant. And I got wounded in France. I want to tell you that Clyde was a very dear friend of mine. I was with him when he got killed. We were about ten miles from St. Lô. Some time about the 9th of July we got cut off by the Germans. Our company lost about 25 men in that same battle. Clyde was with me. There were only a few of us left. I got up and started around a fence. Clyde called me and asked me did I want him to come. And I told him yes. And about that time I heard some shells coming and I hit the ground, and after they hit I ran back. And there lay Clyde with his face down on his machine gun. He never did speak after he was hit. He had been with me ever since he came to Fort Leonard Wood, Missouri. He was just like a brother to me. And one of the best soldiers. Nobody felt his death more than me. I can say it and tell the truth he was one of the cleanest living boys I have ever met. I have heard him talk about his home and I wonder it is an awful price to pay in war. But I am lucky to be here. I will stop this time.

Yours truly,
Ed Ray

War Department
The Adjutant General's Office
Washington, D.C.
August 1, 1944
In reply refer to AG 201 Cagle, Clyde F. PCN ET0139
Dear Mrs. Cagle:

It is with regret that I am writing to confirm the recent telegram informing you of the death of your son, Private First Class Clyde F. Cagle,

34,473,221, Infantry, who was killed in action on 12 July in France. I fully understand your desire to learn as much as possible regarding the circumstances leading to his death and I wish that there were more information available to give you. Unfortunately, reports of this nature contain only the briefest details as they are prepared under battle conditions and the means of transmission are limited. I know the sorrow this message has brought you and it is my hope that in time the knowledge of his heroic service to his country, even unto death, may be of sustaining comfort to you. I extend to you my deepest sympathy.

Sincerely yours,
J.A. Ulio
Major General
The Adjutant General

Bulletin of Information
Headquarters 121st Infantry
APO 8, New York, NY
19 December 1944
Dear Mrs. Cagle:

The Regimental Commander, the Officers and men of the 121st Infantry Regiment wish to express their deepest sympathy to you and your family in the loss of your son, PFC Clyde F. Cagle, 34,473,221, Co. L, 121st Infantry who was killed in action in France on 12 July 1944. Your son was performing his duty in a most courageous and excellent manner and was held in high esteem by all those who knew him. We want you to know that you are not alone in your loss, for it was ours also. Our prayer is that God may be close to you in your sorrow and that through His grace you may find comfort.

Yours sincerely,
James F. McCrary, Chaplain

The following letter was sent to my uncle John, who was medically discharged just before he was to be shipped overseas.

Tuesday night December 5, 1944
Hello John,

I received your letter while I was on a furlough. About Clyde—we went in France July 4th and fought from there on. Most of the boys either got wounded or killed. Perry, Lt. Huffham, CC Knight, Johnes, Hunt, all got killed the first day. Me, Hoare, McCuistion, Adkins got wounded. Oh yes, Sgt. Thompson got killed. Bradley too.

John, an 88 shell got me, and that is what got Clyde. We were pinned down, and the captain sent me to bring them up closer. I got up and started. And Clyde followed me. And he forgot his gun. And he went back to get it. And just as he picked it up, a shell hit him. It went through him. And I ran to him but he never did speak one word. I got the gun out from under him and laid him on his back. And that is about all there was to it. I can say Clyde was a good boy, one of the best. And I felt it as if it had been a brother of mine. Well, John, when you find time write. So long.

Yours truly,
Ed

Following is the letter that informed my parents of Melton's death. How hard this letter must have been to read. I can't imagine.

War Department
The Adjutant General's Office
Washington 25, D. C.
In reply refer to AG 201 Cagle, George M.
PCN ETO 073
23 March 1945
Dear Mrs. Cagle:

It is with deep regret that I confirm the telegram of recent date informing you of the death of your son, Private First Class George M. Cagle, 34,636,747, Infantry.

The official casualty report states that your son was killed on 3 March 1945 in Neurath, Germany. The report further states that he was killed accidentally by a machine gun of tank while cleaning the weapon.

I fully understand your desire to receive as much information as possible concerning his death. Recently provisions were made whereby there will be sent directly to the emergency addressee or the next of kin a letter containing further information about each person who dies overseas in the service of our country, and if this letter has not already been received, it may be expected soon.

I sincerely regret that this message must carry so much sorrow into your home and I hope that in time you may find sustaining comfort in knowing that he served his country honorably.

My deepest sympathy is extended to you in your bereavement,

Sincerely yours,
J. A. Ulio
Major General
The Adjutant General

There are many other things that I would like to know about my brothers, but my knowledge will never be complete in this life. I am thankful to know as much as I do about their lives and their sacrifices for their country. What they did ultimately bought my freedom. I thank God for them, and I thank them for being willing to do what they could.

I can say that the world will little note, nor long remember what I have said here, but it can never forget what they did. We must never forget. Our freedom depends on it.

Arthur P. Renkosiak

The following press release was sent to the parents of Arthur P. Renkosiak in 1945:

The following story concerning your son was released today to Chicago newspapers. I thought it would be of interest to you.

William K. Holt
1st Lt. U.S. Marine Corps, Public Relations Officer

A Marine Corps Correspondent Dispatch—1945
By Sergeant John W. Chapman of Webster City, Iowa,
a Marine Corps Combat Correspondent

Somewhere in the Pacific—(delayed)—A 48-hour sea-bound prelude to Iwo Jima packed more action than Marine Private First Class Arthur P. Renkosiak of Chicago experienced in any like period of time during his 26 days under fire on the island itself.

Within those few hours, the LST 477 carrying Renkosiak, as well as other members of the Third Marine Division, suffered all of the following misadventures:

The death of a naval officer and the wounding of a sailor in an accidental explosion.

Eleven more deaths and 20 additional casualties when a Jap bomb tore a gaping hole in the starboard bow, blew another hole in the main deck forward, damaged two Marine Sherman tanks, created a stubborn fire, and fouled the bridge-controlled steering apparatus.

Twice rammed a beached LST on its way to the harbor.

"We were prepared for Iwo after that," Renkosiak stated philosophically.

The LST 477's adversity began on the morning of February 21, when an emergency charge the officer was explaining to the sailor suddenly detonated. Burial of the officer at sea with full military honors took place in the early afternoon and had a quieting effect on the entire ship until evening chow, the Chicagoan said.

Renkosiak had finished his meal on the fantail and was listening to a radio version of the battle for Iwo with a group of about 100 Marines on the port side of the lower tank deck when the ship shuddered violently. "Someone said a magazine must have exploded," Renkosiak recalled, "and we dashed up the ladders with general quarters screaming in our ears."

He found that a Jap bomb had torn through the main deck and exploded, its concussion blowing the amidships freight hatch covering into the air and inflicting casualties among the men who were using it as a dining table. Most of the dead were up forward in the area where the plane crashed, he said.

Renkosiak busied himself loading 20mm guns on the bridge while other members of the battalion battled the flames on deck.

"The next day," he continued, "We buried the dead and repaired the damaged tanks and steering gear. We got the idea that our bad luck had run out, but the following morning as we sailed into the harbor at Iwo we crashed into the side of a beached LST. We reversed the engines and moved away, but when we moved ahead again, a sudden sweep of wind carried us smack into the side of the same LST a second time."

A member of the battalion ordnance crew, Renkosiak admitted that he had had his share of danger during the Iwo Jima campaign—especially during the three days he spent in the front lines launching rockets at Japs—but credited his experience aboard the ill-fated LST as "something I'll never forget."

(Submitted by his daughter, Sharon Renkosiak Smogor)

William Wilson

November 8, 1944—Camp Pendleton, CA—Preparation to leave the States, Letter #59

My darling:

It is real nice here today. The sun is out in full and there is a slight breeze coming off the ocean. I am setting her on my "sack" writing now, after packing my sea bag. We have done very little here in the way of training. About a half hour of drilling each day and that is all the actual work. We have turned in to the quartermaster our green overcoat, blouse, and one pair of pants, keeping only one pair of green pants.

We had a physical examination yesterday—complete and teeth checked. Today we repacked our sea bags leaving out all flammable things. We are to make up a transport pack to hold all we can get into them. So that is my next job. We have all day, so I am not hurrying.

I feel all right physically, and my examination showed me perfect. So, therefore, I suppose I should feel good. I am not supposed to write any dope of military value. We had a whole list of things we may write about and things we cannot write about read off to us. Our mail will be censored, so all I probably will write about is the weather. We will be able to tell you whether it will be the central Pacific or the southwest Pacific. But cannot mention natives, languages, customs or terrain, etc. So you better read my letters very carefully and perhaps I can give you a rough idea of what is what. I do not want to try and slip anything over as the penalties, if caught, are very severe.

I think it will be some time yet before we see action, if we do. We may not. We may be kept as defense out on some island. One never knows. We are moving out soon, though.

One thing, darling—I'll write just as often as I can, but please be patient, as you know they hold up the mail, and it will naturally take longer to reach you. I have just time to close as it time for "chow." I tried to contact Doug [his brother, an ensign in the U.S. Navy]. He was discharged the 11th of October. I have no idea where he is. I think he must have moved out.

Kiss our little girl for me and remember, dear, I love you with all my heart, and I am always thinking of you. Keep well and wire any news about the new baby when it comes. God bless you.

Always yours,
Bill

March 15, 1945—Aboard USS Bountiful—Awake after 30 hours since injury

Data Entry: 291 days in U.S.M.C.

0630 hours wake up call. Nurses actually look real. This all seems like a dream. Here I am in the sack, a long cast on my leg, and getting further and further away from that dam island.

It is morning as I heard orders over the speaker to the crew for chow down at 0700 hours. I heard a quiet voice say "Good morning, I am certainly glad to see you are back to earth. After I clean you up and you have breakfast, I have a pleasant surprise for you." She cleaned me up and I had a real shave for the first time in many weeks. It felt so good.

She gave me some kind of medication and breakfast. I did not eat much. My mind keeps returning to the battle.

The only real good thing was the taste of the fresh coffee. The nurse came in and informed me that the doctor will see me this morning. She then handed me a package of letters. There was my small Bible, my picture of Jane and Johanna [shown on page 307], and my diary, pretty well worn. Also, several letters from Jane and Johanna. They have finally caught up to me. I began to sob and the tears came easy. She put her hand on my shoulder and said, "It's OK, marine, your combat days are over. Just relax and read your mail." I recall very clearly the first thing I did was look at the picture and, holding the Bible, gave a brief prayer of thanks to the Lord for bringing me through this terrible time. The nurse then read a letter from Jane. It was long but so warm and loving the nurse almost cried.

In midafternoon in came the doctor and my nurse. He gave me a quick overall check and told me that I was doing well but needed to get more sleep, not just rest. Tomorrow he will fill me in on what happened to me and how I got aboard this hospital ship. He said, "You've done one hell of a job, fella'. We are all proud of you and all the troops who were in combat on Iwo Jima."

(I got it on the sixteenth day. It seems that the Japs wired their caves with explosives before they retreated and waited until some of the marines were inside. Then they'd blow them up. I saw one of my buddies lose both legs that way shortly before I got it. That's what must have happened to me. I never knew what hit me. Thirty hours later I came to in a naval hospital.)

Atanacio H. Quiroga

For the family of Atanacio H. Quiroga, the only items they have of his war experiences with the 232nd Regiment of the Rainbow Division, Seventh Army are an old newspaper clipping from April 1945 and a telegram. Whenever his family would ask about his war experiences, he would say only that he fought so that his sons would not have to go and that his children (five girls and five boys) could live in a free world. Three of his brothers served in the army, as well. At each of his brothers' funerals, he would stand tall and give them a farewell salute.

WESTERN UNION
MRS FRANCES B QUIROGA=
POMONA CALIF=

THE SECRETARY OF WAR DESIRES ME TO EXPRESS HIS DEEP REGRET THAT YOUR HUSBAND PFC QUIROGA ATANACIO H WAS SLIGHTLY WOUNDED IN GERMANY 8 APR 45 CONTINUE TO ADDRESS MAIL TO HIM AS FORMERLY OR UNTIL NEW ADDRESS IS RECEIVED

=ULIO THE ADJUTANT GENERAL

(Submitted by his daughter, Sandra Mendivil)

Eugene Rochlus

May 25th, 1945
Bolbec, France

Hi brother Jack:

Just received your birthday card, thanks ever so much. It was a cute little moll you sent by jigger.

I was really sorry to hear that Charles Paash was killed in action. I suppose you've heard that Paul's brother died. I'm going to send a card to the family.

Mrs. Frankman is sending the *Sentinel* and a letter every week, so I'll have to jot down a few lines and thank her for same. It's tough to think of something to write to the old girl, though. I might put in some lovey-dovey stuff, and she might get serious, and if I would want to get married it would be over here, as the women do all the work. Ha Ha.

A Yank magazine came back, which I had sent to you. It hadn't been forwarded as you are in some remote section of the country where the mail can't catch you. We were a lost battalion for quite a while in Santa Maria, California. We were supposed to get a furlough before leaving the States. In fact our outfit was supposed to go from Ontario to Camp Haan and then to a marshaling area, but they must have got the orders mixed and we went to Santa Maria. Slept on the ground for eight months during this time. We were trained to defend an air base. I have had numerous questions from home as to which army we were in. We landed on Omaha Beach and stayed there overnight in foxholes. Pretty rugged. Then moved in with the 1st Army at St. Lô. I was on guard the night of that great breakthrough, then we moved in to St. Helair and got mixed up in the Third Army. We got strafed a couple of times until we hit Paris. There it was OK. An occasional buzz bomb or V-2 but not bad. After that to Belgium under the wing of the mighty Ninth Air Force Command. So you were right with the statement that we were with the Ninth A.A.F. strafing buzz bombs, dodging V-2s. Oy yoy, what a time in defense of Antwerp.

I sure had a good time on my birthday, was shaking everyone's hand as a farewell gesture, and of course they congratulated me, even the chaplain was looking for me, but I was out for a walk with Pulinski. I'm to see him tonight; he says he's got a little one for me. Ha Ha. The *S & S* [*Stars and Stripes*] had an article about all men over 38. Will probably get out of this army soon. Now the guys are trying to talk me into staying with them. Even the major said I should stick it out till we're through with Japan. I get an awful kick out of him. His jeep driver and I are good friends. They go to Paris quite often and bring back a couple bottles of eau de cologne or cognac de la poop. I usually get a couple of snorts from that and then fix up some wooden shoes or throw some of his laundry in with mine when I get up the ambition to do it. (Can you understand this? Ha Ha. I don't.)

Just came back from the stockade, had a detail of a hundred men to do some work, but couldn't find the captain or the job to be done, so marched them back again. The prisoners don't like that, as it seems they would rather be out in the open. A fellow sure has to keep his eyes open as all the fellows have to be accounted for when bringing them in again. How would you like to do this? One thing, though, I'll get plenty of experience in handling a large parade when we go marching with our ribbons and slick uniforms down Wisconsin Ave. (eh, what?).

Heard that Franklin is classified 1-A. I hope he doesn't get in the army, but if he does, I believe he'll get a good job. If he was over here, I know he would with the experience he has. It will be tough on Juliet and the kiddies; tough, also on his business. They haven't written me for quite some time now. I didn't think they were taking them over 30 years of age, but it's probably changed now.

I'm writing this letter in an awkward position lying out in the sun and on a blanket soaking in the sun. It's real cold here nights and hot during the day. We're situated on a very high spot here in France. There is also plenty of rain, usually once a day at least. It's been that way ever since landing here. Probably we'll get new insignias or shoulder patches as we're now attached to the Normandy Base Section. You were saying to the folks that they should let you know when I arrive in New York. When my feet touch the ground at any place in the good old U.S., I'm making tracks to the first telegraph office and sending you a wire. We're going to have an advance drinking fest together. That is, if it's possible. I'm sure anxious to see you again. I'll be glad to be with all the family, but I haven't seen you for such a long time, you probably won't know me. I don't want to have you throwing me out of the house thinking me a stranger. Ha Ha.

Do you see quite a few movies? I saw *Strike Up the Band* with Mickey Rooney, pretty good show. Also saw *A Tree Grows in Brooklyn* and a propaganda picture. The first good; the second, phooey. I guess we've gone too far to believe all that Bull S—t.

Well Jack, I hope to hear from you shortly, and let me know what your status is in the army and if you're getting out soon. The time has come for a fellow to decide which to do—get out or stay in. Of course, I'm crossing bridges before I come to them, but I never dreamed that someday I'd be debating this question. I was always of the opinion that when this was over I would be too glad to get out.

Here's wishing you good health, happiness, and the best of wishes.

Bon chance. Auf weidersehn. Good luck.

Your brother,
Gene

(Brothers Eugene and Jack Rochlus both served in the U.S. Army—Eugene in France, Jack in New Guinea. Jack had earned enough points so, at the time this letter was written after censorship rules had been lifted, he was in the army in Arkansas. Both were bachelors. Their nephew, Jack A. Draak, submitted the letter.)

Dudley Chapman

Osaka, Japan

Dear Mother, Dad and All,

Well, I guess you think I am not going to write any more. This is the first time I have stopped traveling since I left home Sept. 16th. We sailed from Seattle, Wash. on the USS *Blatchford* on October 16th at 12 o'clock noon for Nagasaki, Japan. If you remember it is one of the cities hit by the atomic bomb. We got in there on Nov. 1st. After we got there, our orders had been changed and we were supposed to go up to Nagoya, which was 900 miles from Nagasaki. We arrived in Nagoya last night about 5 o'clock and did not get off the ship till 4 o'clock this morning, then had a two-hour train ride, such as it was, to this place we are now. This is an old Jap army camp, and I mean it is old. There are about 500 of us sleeping in an old shed they threw together after they knew we were coming. There are no windows in it, and the roof is all shot full of holes. Some place. This place has been occupied about two weeks by the American troops. I do not know what we are going to do. The ones here say they do nothing but sleep and eat. They make the Japs do all the work. The government pays them 66¢ a day, and some are not worth that. This place is sure torn up by the bombs. You can't believe it till you see it. No pictures you will ever see can describe it. Down at Nagasaki where they dropped one of the atomic bombs—they did not drop but three all together in Japan—the rest of the damage was done by other bombs. When they dropped it at Nagasaki, it was a city of around 800,000 and they claim it killed 30,000 outright, and about 40,000 died in a day or so from the effects. This city was built in sorta' a valley and the railroad went up through the center of the city, and there must have been a train in the station. All you can see is some molten wheels of a train that had 30 cars on it. You can't believe it—bicycles and cars just in a molten clump. There was a big torpedo plant in the center of the city made of steel and brick about three quarters of a mile long, they told us. All you can see left is some dirt that used to be brick and some molten girders. There were four streetcars just all molten together, also. I don't think anyone will believe it unless they would see it. You never smelled such an odor in your life from the bodies under some of the wreckage. They have not cleared but about four blocks but built new roads. What it did not blow down it burned buildings in a radius of four miles. We docked about six miles from the city, and there was a big shipyard there with all the windows blown out. I have not seen any cars. Some people riding bicycles and the streetcars remind you of the Toonerville Trolley. They just have four wheels on them like a wagon and so do the train coaches. I got two letters from you this morning and one from Jim and was sure glad to hear from you all. Jim had a dollar in his letter and you had one in yours, and it sure did come in good, because I was broke. We have never been paid. I did not have but $5 when I left the States, bought five cartons of cigarettes on the boat at 50¢ a carton, so did not have much left. You won't believe me but the Jap people will pay 30 yen for a pack of cigarettes, which is $2 in American money. We have one pack issued to us a day, one bar of candy, one stick of gum, three bottles of beer a week. So you don't need much money. Hope everyone is OK. Maybe if Dad would have had one of the boats like the Japs have, he would not have been upset. They paddle them from the back.

Love, Dudley

Yoshiko's Letter

This was written to Dudley Chapman while he was in Japan during the Occupation.

Osaka, Japan November 1945

To my Lover,

I hope you have safely reached Tokyo. Weren't you tired in the trip? Since our separation Yoshiko is cheerfully working at the store every day, and I think you're working very cheerfully every day, too. It's the fifth day since we separated. And it feels as if we didn't see each other for one or two years.

I'm firmly keeping the promise I made with you. I've never thought that we had to part so soon. But to my determination, no matter how far we part, my spirit will never change. Personal characters may change, but I think love will not change according to my determination.

The way Yoshiko feels now is only longing to see you a day quicker. My mother would not allow me to go to Tokyo only by myself, but I have a happy thing here. Mother said that she has a hasty engagement and is going to Tokyo with my aunt. But Mother is so busy, so I told her that I go for her, and then on my way I could go and see my friend, which is a little story I always use.

Quickly finishing my mother's work, I can go to your place quicker, which I'm longing, even a day earlier. I thank God for making me this opportunity. It depends upon my aunt's circumstances, but I think it will be in four or five days.

Well, I think I will leave my pen here. Until we meet again I hope you will keep yourself healthy.

Yours truly, Yoshiko

Prisoners of War

Allied prisoners of war at Amoroi

Wayne W. Livesay

Descent into Captivity

Although the experience occurred over 50 years ago, it still stands out as the most vivid event in my life. As I look back in sentimental memory, I find the story sobering, quite humorous, and worth retelling.

It was August 9, 1944. The day began as just another Wednesday for me and other members of bomber crews stationed in England. We were awakened around 2:00 A.M., had breakfast about an hour later, and attended mission briefing at 4:15. Target for this was Munich, with our group scheduled to plaster Nazi airfields on the outskirts of the city. We had been to Munich before and had neutralized these targets, but the Germans rebuilt the runways, which gave us the invitation to return.

Takeoff was uneventful as the fully loaded Flying Fortress lumbered down the runway and became airborne with all four engines straining in rhythmical accord. Assembling wing formation was completed with ease, and by 7:30 A.M. we were at 8,000 feet and climbing on course toward the North Sea. Before reaching the enemy coast, all guns were tested and we were ready for what was to become my thirty-third and last time to participate in a bombing run over Hitler's Europe.

From the standpoint of enemy action, this was one of the easiest missions I experienced. As we moved inland over Holland without seeing a burst of flak, I thought of those rough days during '43 when we couldn't stick our noses across the English Channel without doing battle with the cream of the Luftwaffe based along the coast. This day was also a far cry from the missions where much flak and numerous fighters were thrown at us in strikes on Berlin, Schweinfurt, and targets in the Ruhr Valley. On this final trip to Munich I did not see a single enemy plane, and very little antiaircraft was dispatched in our direction. Our 54-plane group was just a small portion of the large armada, which left England that day to pulverize targets throughout Europe. We were virtually unopposed—the air war had been won.

It was not until we were approaching the coast of Holland on our way home that I was forced to reassess my complacent reasoning. Flying over an area where no German antiaircraft guns were plotted and with no fighters in the area, we took on an attitude of "mission completed" and were almost ready to begin our letdown from 23,000 feet before adversity took control of the mission. As I gazed down upon the scene below, I was thinking ahead to the huge steak I would receive when we arrived back at the base. Steak was a rather rare commodity for us except upon our return from a combat mission, and each of us looked forward to the routine of selecting a choice chunk of beef and having it prepared under our personal direction. The cook at the combat officer's mess never served a steak less than two inches thick, and the caliber of preparation was such as to put most top-rated restaurants to shame.

My thoughts were suddenly interrupted as I heard a loud bang, somewhat similar to the noise of an exploding firecracker. In the same instant, the plane flipped upward, and we spiraled lazily out of formation. I wasn't sure what had happened, as the physical sensation was about the same as running over a rock or metal object in an automobile and having it thump against the underside of the car.

We were able to level off at 21,000 feet and continue on course toward England. Apparently we had received a direct hit from a burst of flak knocking out two of our engines, but at our altitude this in itself presented no reason for panic. No one had been injured by the blast, and we thanked God for seeing us through the narrow chasm of disaster.

Since we were now alone without fighter escort, all gunners were cautioned to be alert for the Luftwaffe who might be in the vicinity and looking for cripples such as us. We flew along for about two minutes, and I once again started to think of the base, a shower, and, most of all, the steak. I then had my dreams destroyed as I heard 12 words that should go down as the most disruptive sentence ever put together. One of the gunners came on interphone and in a voice as calm as an experienced mortician stated, "Sir, you've got a fire on top of number three gas tank."

When I looked out the right window and saw a hole in the wing with fire coming out and the aluminum peeling backward, there was an emptiness in my stomach that defies description. The hole in the wing was rapidly increasing in size, and the escaping flame reminded me of a blacksmith's forge as it shot forth with leaping force. I knew in a glance that my bombing days were over and that I wouldn't enjoy a steak for many days to come. As the bail-out alarm was sounded, I picked up my chest chute and secured it to the harness I was wearing. There was no panic as I and other crew members seemed to move like precision robots in accordance with practiced procedure for abandoning the aircraft. Later, while lying in a cold cell during my first night as a prisoner of war, I experienced a seizure of fear as I recalled the events of the day; but while the incidents were taking place we didn't have time to be afraid.

I had never made an actual parachute jump, although all bomber crews received extensive training in both ditching and bail-out procedure. The one concern going through my mind as I prepared to exit the plane was the possibility that I might hit one of the open bomb-bay doors, which were located just a few feet to the rear of the escape hatch under the nose of the plane. We had witnessed one man meeting this fate after a B-17 had been hit by flak over Berlin; his chute seemed to open prematurely, causing him to be swept backward into the bomb-bay doors. Although I tried to think of more pleasant things, it was impossible to dismiss this adverse image from my mind.

By this time, all escape doors were open and members of the crew were bailing out. The plane had become a roaring inferno when it came my turn to crawl to the exit. Without stopping to look, I lowered my head and pushed my feet against a side bulkhead. In an instant I was clear of the aircraft and started my downward journey.

Once out of the plane I experienced a sudden sense of relaxation. There was absolute silence as the noise from the crackling flames and roaring engines was out of range. I felt no sensation of falling but seemed to be floating on a cloud. Slowly and deliberately I began to count, "One thousand one, one thousand two, one thousand three." I then pulled the ripcord and settled back to enjoy a new adventure as I thought the parachute had opened.

However, as I blinked my eyes, I began to realize that something was wrong. I was viewing the sky, then the water in a series of monotonous successions that meant that the world had either increased its pace of rotation or that I was still plummeting downward in a somersaulting motion. Although these events were taking place in a short space of time, it seemed like an eternity before I reached the conclusion that my parachute was still tucked neatly in the pack.

Glancing down at the unopened chute pack, I saw the small lead chute extended about six inches, but not out enough to deploy the main parachute. I grasped the pack with my left arm and pulled on the extended portion with my right hand. All of a sudden, I felt as if someone had struck me across the bridge of my nose with a boat paddle, and I was stunned to the point of near complete disorientation. As a navigator, I had studied celestial navigation and had learned the identity of many stars, but I had never seen this number together at one time. I do not believe the blow knocked me unconscious, but my reasoning processes were addled for several minutes and my head felt as if it were locked securely in a vise. Two days later, when I looked into a mirror, my nose and the underside of both eyes reflected the appearance of a losing participant in a bruising fistfight.

When the chute finally opened, it seemed as if I were on an elevator going upward at a fast clip. To see the opened umbrella above me was about the only point of comfort I garnered from the experience thus far, and, although more problems were still to be faced, I now had a chance. My first concern was to account for the rest of the crew as I looked around the sky and began counting the chutes. It appeared that all were safely out of the plane, and one thing was for sure—although I had been third from the last to exit the doomed aircraft, I was going to be the first one down. All the others appeared to be from 6,000 to 8,000 feet above me as the unscheduled free-fall had put me well out front in the race downward.

I then began to face the prospect of another danger. I had never been the best of swimmers, and now it appeared that I would spend a few hours in the water. I estimated my altitude at about 10,000 feet, and I was well over a mile from some islands off the Dutch coast. Under my harness I was wearing a small "Mae West"-type life jacket, and, as I descended slowly toward the water, I began to mentally rehearse the procedure of extracting myself from the harness and inflating the life jacket in a simultaneous motion as I hit the water. If I were to eventually drown, I at least wanted to get clear of the parachute and make a try at reaching land rather than perish while entangled in the lines of the chute.

I then remembered watching some movie heroes manipulate the direction of parachutes by pulling on the shroud lines, and I attempted to follow their actions in an effort to steer myself closer to the islands. About all I accomplished by doing this was to create a severe rocking of the chute, which could have led to its collapse. I soon stopped this futile effort and tried to condition myself to the prospects of a long swim.

If I had been thinking clearly, I would have realized that the wind was blowing out of the west onto the Dutch coast. On this particular day, the velocity was stronger than usual which had given us a faster ground speed on our way inland at the beginning of the mission. This fact hit me when, at about 3,000 feet above the water, I noticed that I was less than half a mile from one of the islands and that I was drifting in that direction. At about 2,000 feet, I was sure that my landing would be on terra firma, and I began making plans for my initial movements on the ground.

I took a good look at the island before me and estimated it to be from six to eight miles in length from east to west. It was shaped like a football with two very small villages visible on the western side of the island. I had heard much about the Dutch Underground and wondered if there was a possibility of getting in touch with them. Our chutes were visible for all to see, but being the first man to land might give me opportunity to hide until nightfall before the Germans got organized to search for me. Many thoughts were going through my mind, and, by the time I hit the ground, I had decided on two things: (l) hide until dark, and (2) work my way eastward toward the mainland while hoping to make contact with the Underground.

During his first parachute jump, a man is just not prepared to cope with the speed he seems to gather as he approaches the ground. At about 200 feet, I became aware that I was falling very fast, and I had little time to make adjustments to control my method of landing. Just as I was about to hit the ground, a sudden gust of wind took charge, causing my feet to swing forward and making me practically horizontal with the landscape. Then, as my body started its return in an arc to the upright position, I abruptly reached the point of touchdown. My heels hit first, then the seat of my pants, followed by the back of my head. I rolled backward two or three revolutions and found myself entangled in the shroud lines like a butterfly trapped in a net.

After getting free from my cage, I stood in utter dismay at the scene before me. Finding a place to hide was my primary concern as I found myself standing on the flattest piece of real estate in all of Hitler's Europe. My past evasion training had been based upon the premise of finding a place to hide during the initial hours in enemy territory, and here I was in a place without a tree, a haystack, a barn, or anything that could furnish temporary cover. Of all the areas I had flown over that offered a bonanza of hiding places,

I went down in freshly seeded lowland with nothing but canals crisscrossing the island.

Still hoping to find a place of safety, I moved toward the north away from the villages I had seen from the air. I ran for about two minutes, slowed to a walk, and then stopped to raise my hands into the air. Two members of the German Occupation Army intercepted my exercise in futility and made it quite clear that I had officially become a guest of the Third Reich.

Later that evening as I lay in a cold cell in the town of Flushing, I was given a small ration of cheese and two slices of bread. I tasted it but had no appetite, since my thoughts were still fixed upon the steak I would have received if some gunner's aim had been less accurate.

My Moment at the Wall

Around daylight the next morning, I was awakened by a rifle butt against my ribs, and a soldier motioned for me to go outside. He directed me to a truck in the parking lot where four other soldiers and a German officer were waiting. Not a word was spoken by any of them as I was pointed to the back of the truck and directed to climb in. Three of the soldiers then entered the truck and motioned for me to sit with my back against the cab. Each of these three was equipped with a weapon, which appeared similar to a Thompson submachine gun. The German officer and the other soldier entered the cab of the truck.

As the truck engine started and the vehicle began to move, myriad thoughts filtered through my mind. I thought of my family, my girl back home, the men at the base, and the others who had been captured along with me. Underneath these thoughts was the distinct possibility that I was making my last ride and that these silent men were intent on just one thing—to finish me off and leave me somewhere in the countryside. The three soldiers with the guns were sitting on a bench just inside the tailgate, and they kept their eyes glued on me the entire journey.

I had always pictured German soldiers as professional and neat in appearance with an inbred attitude of military discipline. The three characters I was facing were just the opposite—unshaven, with uncombed hair and dirty uniforms, which appeared to have never been cleaned. The officer and soldier who drove the truck looked somewhat better but far below what I expected.

We rode for approximately 20 minutes at speeds from 5 to 15 miles per hour. Since the truck was covered by a foul-smelling canvas, I could not see outside, but, judging from the way the truck was bouncing up and down, I was convinced that we could not be on a road but were pioneering a path through open country replete with rocks and gaping holes. We seemed to reach a downgrade, and the truck picked up speed only to come to a sudden stop as if we had struck a barricade. Two of the three German captors were thrown off their seats, and one almost dropped his weapon.

After a few seconds, the tailgate was lowered and I was motioned outside. As I jumped to the ground, my heart skipped a beat or two as a thought of utter dismay came to mind. I turned to my right and there, about 50 feet away, was a rudely constructed rock wall that appeared to me as an ideal pack ground for a firing-squad action.

The wall was about eight feet high and had been built across an open field for a distance of about 150 yards. Since it did not branch off in another direction so as to enclose a given property location, I figured it must have been a designated boundary line. Regardless of its original purpose, there appeared to be no doubt as to its present intended use.

One of the three armed soldiers indicated that I should move over to the wall. After I complied, the officer approached and without saying a word offered me a cigarette. I took a cigarette from the pack that, ironically, was the identical pack of Camels that had been taken from me when I was captured. The officer furnished me with a light, and I stood there "enjoying" what appeared to be my last cigarette.

In the meantime, the three armed soldiers positioned themselves approximately 25 yards from me and about 10 feet from each other. The officer moved to a spot on my left a few feet from them, while the truck driver stayed in the cab of the vehicle.

As I stood there looking at the scene, I started to speak but no words came out. The cigarette was almost burning my fingers, but I hesitated dropping it to the ground. My emotions at that time were a mixture of anger, prayer, and regret as I thought of many things I should have done in the past as well as numerous things I should not have done. Only one who has experienced a similar situation can truly empathize with my feelings at that moment.

Finally, I dropped the residue of the cigarette and fixed my eyes toward the weapons in the hands of my tormentors. At this point, there was no doubt in my mind as to what was about to happen, and my final decision appeared to be whether I should look or close my eyes. I thought about running but knew this would profit nothing, so I decided to assume an erect position as if someone had called me to attention.

I stood there for what seemed like minutes but, in reality, was not more than 10–15 seconds. Suddenly, the officer raised his hand and motioned for me to go back to the truck. I did not wait for a second indication as I hurried to comply with his instruction. About 20 minutes later I was placed back in my cell and given breakfast, which consisted of a slice of black bread and a cup of barley coffee.

Subsequently, I was a prisoner of war for nine months. During that time, I experienced the bitter cold in Poland, the march in the snow from Sagan to Spremberg, the three-day journey in a 40-and-8 boxcar to Moosburg, and bouts with malnutrition and pneumonia pleurisy. All of these are listed as times of suffering, but none of them approached the magnitude of what I endured during those few minutes with my back to the wall in Holland.

Joseph Millman

An Incident in a POW Hospital

On an unmarked prison train near Florence, Italy, on the way north to Germany, we were strafed by American planes. It was killing and wounding the wounded all over again, this time by our own planes. In a few seconds it was over.

It must have been about March or April 1944. Some of the cars were derailed, and by the time some semblance of order was restored we had to be taken to a hospital in Florence, which was ill-equipped to handle such an influx of wounded POWs. My stretcher, with me on it, was placed on the marble floor in the hallway near the entrance next to another man. Hour after hour this man kept complaining bitterly that if something was not done to the wound on his foot he would die. All he had to protect him from the cold floor was a skimpy blanket while I, being encased in a heavy body cast, was insulated from the cold.

I tried to get the attention of the Italians and Germans milling about, but no one would spare a minute to listen to this man's complaint. The hours slowly went by. In desperation, I finally got the attention of a German wearing a long leather coat and fur hat who had just entered through the door opposite us, and I beckoned to him with a "*Bitte, mein Herr.*" He came over with a Hitler salute and bent over to hear what I had to say. It was then I noticed the death head insignia on his hat, and my blood ran cold. He belonged to the notorious *Totenkopfverbande*, Himmler's private army of killers used to round up Jews and other "undesirables," for extermination. This time he reversed his role and listened to me about helping my companion. Within ten minutes my neighbor was carried away to an operating room at the far end of the hall.

The following day I was finally bedded down with other men in a ward. In the days that followed, my companion's foot was amputated. A few days later, another chunk of his leg was cut away and then the rest of his leg to stop the spread of gangrene.

About a week later, we were entrained again to continue our journey to Germany—everyone except this man because they felt he could not survive. As I was carried past his unconscious form, I murmured a goodbye, never expecting to see him again.

Almost a year later while standing on the deck of the SS *Gripsholm*, the ship used in a prisoner exchange, about to enter the New York harbor, a tap on my shoulder roused me from my self-absorption. I looked up at a tall man with one leg and crutches.

"Do you remember me?" he asked. I looked at him in a daze and shook my head. "You once saved my life; you got them to operate on me at the Florentine Hospital. You told them I was a very important person."

Words failed me as tears filled my eyes. Here was the man I never expected to see again thanking me for saving his life. We promised to see each other again but somehow in the confusion of our debarkation we never got to see each other. I never knew his name but have never given up hope of meeting him again. Hopefully this article will find him.

(From his memoirs titled *The Eleventh Passenger*)

William F. Larimer

Bataan Death March and Beyond

In 1941, I joined the U.S. Army after completing Shattuck Military School in Faribault, Minnesota. I asked for and received assignment to the Philippine Islands, where I arrived in July 1941 at the 12th Military Police Company, Fort William McKinley, which is about nine miles outside Manila.

From July 1941 until December 8, 1941, I performed the duties of a military policeman at Fort McKinley. On December 8, 1941, when I came downstairs for breakfast, I saw my first sergeant reading the morning paper and he stated, rather nonchalantly, that the Japanese had bombed Pearl Harbor. Needless to say, that threw us all in a turmoil. We really didn't know what to do until they told us to pack all our personal belongings for storage. Within the next couple of days everything was rather hectic in preparation for war. The Japanese came in, bombing the Philippines. To show you how ignorant we were, there was an airplane dogfight over Fort McKinley and all of us were shooting at the plane being chased! The one we were shooting at turned out to be American, and we shot it down. Fortunately, the pilot was not injured badly.

In the event of war, the defense plans of the Philippine Islands called for the immediate withdrawal of all troops to Bataan. Bataan was protected by the 16-inch guns on Corregidor Island, which was just off the tip of Bataan. The guns could fire in a 360-degree circle. After the bombing, all the troops withdrew to the Bataan peninsula. My military police company was assigned the duties of guarding General Lough; however, I was assigned to motorcycle escort and messenger duties. One day I was escorting a convoy of military trucks from Manila to Bataan when the Japanese planes came in dive-bombing us. I turned my motorcycle to avoid the strafing, and I hit a pile of sand on the side of the road. My motorcycle flipped over on top of me; my pistol fired accidentally, and the bullet grazed my knee. Another incident happened to me just before our surrender when I was carrying messages to Corregidor. I was riding down the road and passed out from malaria. When I came to, I was in the hospital; I had smashed my motorcycle and was scratched and bleeding from head to foot. The day after my accident, the Japanese bombed the hospital, and I got out of there quick and made my way back to my company.

Just to show how the Japanese were during the fighting, we strung barbed wire entanglements ahead of the front line. When the Japanese attacked us, they would form a human ladder, throwing their bodies over the barbed wire—as many as four, five, or six Japanese in a row lying over the wire so the rest of the Japanese troops could run across their bodies to get over the wire.

While we were fighting the war, we received our supplies from Corregidor Island. Corregidor had huge refrigerated storage caves where all the food was stored. We received no supplies whatsoever from any place except Corregidor. The Japanese kept a constant day and night bombardment of Corregidor and eventually were able to knock out the refrigeration; as a result, all the food spoiled. Also our ammunition was so low that it would have been useless to continue the fight; so, on April 8, 1942, General King surrendered all the American and Filipino troops on Bataan. Just prior to this, General Douglas MacArthur had left the Philippines for Australia. General Wainwright was left in command of the Philippines.

I would like to tell you that the surrender was a real nightmare. There were about 30 of us military police still guarding the general when they announced that we should lay our weapons down and the Japanese would be coming in. We were really frightened! I put a couple of guns on the ground in front of me; however, I had a submachine gun immediately behind me in back of a tree because I made up my mind that if they came in shooting, I could at least try to get a few of them.

Soon we heard a hubbub at the forward end of the line way ahead of us around the bend in the road, and we saw our first Japanese. The first ones were artillerymen carrying a mountain howitzer. They were cheerful-looking little fellows, and they smiled as they walked by. They were all covered in sweat, and we were amazed at the weight they carried. One carried a wheel, another the tube, another the trail, another the packs of the fellows carrying the pieces. They all had flies around their heads. Having been in the jungle for a while, they were filthy.

After them came the infantry, and they were a lot more vicious. They started to go through our pockets. Some knew a little English and hollered, "Go you to hell! Go you to hell!" One of the Japs went over to a colonel and showed that he wanted the colonel to take off his wedding ring. The colonel kept refusing. A Jap came up to me and cleaned me out. Then he reached in my back pocket. Suddenly he jumped back and his bayonet came up real fast between my eyes! I reached into my back pocket and found a rifle clip I'd forgotten about. Quickly I dropped it on the ground. The Jap took his rifle and cracked me across the head. I fell. My head was covered in blood. When I looked up, I saw the colonel couldn't get his wedding ring off, and the Jap was about to take his bayonet and cut it off along with the finger. The colonel saw me, and he reached over to get some of my blood, which he used to wiggle the ring off. Then he was slapped and kicked.

With the surrender of Bataan, General Homma (the Japanese commanding officer) still faced the problem of subduing the American garrison on Corregidor, a short two miles away in Manila Bay. Only when Corregidor surrendered could Japan claim her most valuable prize: the Philippines.

For the Japanese 14th Army, the campaign was not over yet. Before this decisive battle could begin, however, it was necessary for the Japanese to remove the enormous number of prisoners, whom Major General Edward P. King had just surrendered. Anticipating this problem in late March, an evacuation plan was developed by Homma's staff. The plan was simple: The captives would walk out of Bataan as far as San Fernando. There, they would be shipped by rail to a prison camp (Camp O'Donnell) in central Luzon. From Mariveles, on Bataan's southern tip, to San Fernando is almost 60 miles. Plans to feed and care for the prisoners along the road were proposed and agreed upon. Unfortunately for the men of the Luzon force, the Japanese plan for their evacuation was based on three assumptions, all of which proved to be false. The first miscalculation assumed the surrendered force to be in good physical condition. The second error was in not allowing enough time to work out all the details of a proper evacuation. Last, the Japanese made a faulty estimate in the number of troops they would have to move. They assumed the figure would be between 40 and 50 thousand men. Because of the chaos that followed the disintegration of the Luzon forces, it is impossible even today to give a precise number of the men who took part in the march out of Bataan. An educated guess, however, puts 62,000 Filipinos and 10,000 Americans on the march.

Mariveles. Now that was confusion! No one knowing where they were going, or what they should take, or how long it would take to get where they were going. Mariveles: tanks, trucks, cars, horses, artillery; like a Philippines' Times Square and everything buried in dust, horrendous amounts of dust being churned up by the tanks and trucks. You realized that Homma's shock troops were coming down Bataan on their way to taking Corregidor.

The Japanese were just in a rush to get us out of their way. Our officers were milling around, trying to find out what was going on. The Japanese officers also seemed confused as to what they were supposed to do with this pack of hungry, sick, bedraggled men they had captured. After they assembled the majority of us, they divided us into groups of 1,000, and we started what is now called the "Bataan Death March." We marched for eight days and covered between 60 and 80 miles to our first prison camp called O'Donnell. On the Death March, we received only one rice ball in the whole eight days and what water we could steal from streams or wherever. I don't believe anyone will ever know how many Americans and Filipino soldiers were killed on the Death March. If a man was sick or too weak to walk, the Japanese guard would just shoot or bayonet him.

We moved down the ridge a ways when we saw this GI. He was sick. We thought he had come out of the hospital because he was wobbling along, uneasy on his feet. There were Japanese infantry and tanks coming down the road alongside us. One of these Jap soldiers came across the road, grabbed this sick guy by the arm, and guided him out across the road. The guy hit the cobblestones about five feet in front of a tank, and the tank pulled on across him. It killed him quick. There must have been ten tanks in that column and every one of them came up there right across the body. When the last tank left, there was no way you could tell there'd ever been a man there except his uniform was embedded in the cobblestones. The man disappeared, but his uniform had been pressed until it had become part of the ground. Now we knew, if there had been any doubts before, we were in for a bad time.

One of the tricks the Japs used to play on us—they thought it was funny, too—was when they would be riding on the back of a truck, they would have these long black snake whips and they'd whip that thing out and get some poor bastard by the neck or torso and drag him behind their truck. 'Course if one of our guys was quick enough, he didn't get dragged too far. But, if the Japs got a sick guy . . .

They would halt us at these big artesian wells. There'd be a four-inch pipe coming up out of the ground, which was connected to a well, and the water would flow full force out of it. There were hundreds of these wells all over Bataan. They'd halt us intentionally in front of these wells so we could see the water, and they wouldn't let us have any. Anyone who would make a break for the water would be shot or bayoneted. Then they were left there. Finally, it got so bad farther along the road that you never got away from the stench of death. There were bodies lying all along the road in various degrees of decomposition: swollen, burst open, maggots crawling by the thousands—black, featureless corpses. And they stank!

Sometimes they'd make us stand at attention two or three hours. They'd just stop us and make us stand still. If you got caught sloughing off, shifting your weight from one foot to another, you'd get beaten. And the weather was hot, hot, hot. The sun comes up hot, and it goes down hot, and it stays hot all night. It was just plain hell hot.

We were waiting in the sun in an open rice paddy. We stayed there without water 'til half a dozen men had passed out from the heat. Then we were ripe. The guards put us on the road and double-timed us. Every kilometer they changed the guards because they could not stand to double-time in the sun either. After a couple of miles, you could hear the shooting start at the tail of the column as the cleanup squad went to work—the old Indian gauntlet with an Oriental twist.

When it came daylight, the Japanese would wake you up, make you form columns of four and stand at attention. Maybe once or twice they would allow an individual to collect a bunch of canteens, so that he could go and get water. Then again, maybe they wouldn't. It depended on the individual guard you were with.

First thing we would try to do is get all the men who were in the worst shape up to the front of the columns. That way as they got tired and the men who were helping them wore out, we could pass them slowly back through the column taking turns holding them or helping them. We knew if a man reached a point where he couldn't walk anymore, he was going to be killed. So we tried to take turns helping the sick and injured. Sometimes we would prevail upon the guards to let us regroup, and we'd be able to put the sick back up front. Sometimes we couldn't.

We could see some artillery pieces by the side of the road and some Japs taking a break in the shade. Some of them had tied a big pole onto a tree so that it could swing back and forth. With this they were taking turns raking it through the column of men. It was a big game to them, seeing how many of us they could knock down with one swoosh of this pile driver across the road. Some guys would duck or fall down, and the guy behind would stumble. It created a lot of confusion.

Of course, we had a grapevine that worked like a telephone. Word traveled pretty fast. If there was trouble up ahead, the word would come back down the columns and those who could would walk more lightly. When we saw the trucks carrying infantry, we learned to get as far off the road as we could. The Jap troops would carry bamboo sticks (rifle butts were heavy) and they'd lean out and swat you as they went by. If they didn't have sticks, they had stones or knotted ropes. They'd just swing whatever they had and see if they could hit you.

There was a big tin warehouse or granary somewhere along the march that they packed us into one night. You could sit or lie down, but there was no water and it was very hot. And it stank! The next morning across the road the Japs had dug a hole and had some Filipino soldiers burying some dead men, except not everyone was dead. One poor soul kept trying to claw his way out of the hole. The Jap guards really started giving these Filipinos a hard time, trying to get them to cover this man up faster. Finally a Jap came over, took a shovel, and beat him on the head with it. Then he had the Filipinos cover him up.

Late in the day my group had been herded into a field surrounded by three strands of barbed wire. It could have been the town square or close to it. There were a number of Filipino and American soldiers already there. We were so tired, hungry, thirsty, and so many were sick or wounded, that we didn't at first notice the condition of those that were there. We would never forget it by the time we left the next day. Fortunately, it was close to dark and we didn't have to sit under the tropical sun. It had been another long hot day without food and very little water.

Sometime after dark the Japs brought some cans of rice to the enclosure gate. A five-gallon can for each hundred men. These cans were not full. Who cared? Those close to the gate were fed. There was not enough to go around. There was no crowding or pushing. A friend helped a friend. Many didn't care. Besides being tired, many were at the last stage of malaria, just wanting to be left alone in the grass or dirt to rest, sleep, or die. To have at least one close friend, a buddy to hold you in his arms and comfort you as you died, was enough. The few that still had faith and courage would have lost it if they could have foreseen the future.

Later I talked to men at Camp O'Donnell who were behind us and arrived at San Fernando a day or two later. The dead had not been buried.

The same terrible odor had doubled, and the sick and dying almost filled the area. Shortly after noon all that could walk were lined up outside the barbed wire and marched a few blocks to the railroad station. In the months ahead, we would realize that each time we left the sick, they would never be seen again.

There was a train and a few boxcars. The Filipino trains are smaller than ours, and the boxcars about two-thirds the size we used. Our spirits rose. We were going to ride instead of march. In a few minutes we all wished we had continued to march. The boxcars had sat in the tropical sun with the doors closed.

The Japs divided us into groups of 100 men for each car. One Jap guard was assigned to a car. He pulled the door back and motioned us inside. The heat from inside hit us in the face. We stalled for time, but the Jap guard with his bayonet motioned us to climb in and he meant business. We all knew by now to openly resist them would be fatal.

We jammed in—standing room only. Into the oven we went and, protest be damned, the doors were closed. The three hours that followed are almost indescribable. Men were fainting with no place to fall. Those with dysentery had no control of themselves. It seems to me that once in a while our train would stop, and the Jap guards would open the doors so we could get some fresh air. Then is when we'd get the dead ones out. If we could, we'd lift the corpses and pass them over to the door. There was no way we could have passed them through.

We arrived at the small town of Capas. The boxcar doors were opened, and we were ordered out. Sit down and be counted. Who could have escaped from that oven? While the Japs were making sure of the count, it gave us the opportunity to take off our shoes and pour the filth on the ground.

After a brief rest, we were told to get up and line up in a column of twos. Then we started marching down a dirt road the last five or six miles to Camp O'Donnell. Some had marched all the way. A few had come by truck. Those who marched all the way suffered more. It wasn't the miles, it was the continuous delays along the march, the change of Jap command and guards, standing in place for two or three hours, waiting for the order to start marching again, the lack of food and water, the rundown condition of the men before the start. A combination of all these things would make Camp O'Donnell just one big graveyard.

We would all help each other as best we could. My malaria was still bad because we had no medicine. I can recall only about half of the Death March because I was a little out of my head even though I kept going.

There were about 27,000 American troops in the Philippines and, after our surrender, they put us all, with the Filipino troops, in Camp O'Donnell, where the conditions were deplorable. We had no sanitary conditions at all except for those we were able to implement. We had very little food and no medicine at all. We had a well for water; however, there was not enough for cleaning clothes or for bathing. We did no work at all except for work details for wood and supplies. Our people were dying like flies from dysentery, malaria, beriberi, elephantiasis, and malnutrition.

Fortunately for us we were at Camp O'Donnell only for about one month, then the Japanese moved us by rail, about 100 men per boxcar, to our next prison, Camp Cabanatuan, where they had only us American prisoners. The Japanese made us work a 2,500-acre farm, planting rice and sweet potatoes to be used for our own food.

The Japanese divided us into two groups—one the sick and the other the well group, with a separate fenced-in area for each, and the Japanese soldiers in the center. I was on the burial detail for a while, and we buried in the neighborhood of 25 to 50 or more Americans a day in mass graves.

The Japanese soldiers were pretty brutal at Camp Cabanatuan; while we were working on the farm or on any work detail, they would beat us for any reason at all. I have scars all over the lower part of my body from some of those beatings. We did get even with them once in a while. For instance, the Japanese loved cobra snake meat to eat. The cobra would take over big anthills and, when we worked the farms, we would dig out the anthills. When the cobra would start coming out, we would catch them using long nooses. We would then taunt the snakes so they would turn and bite themselves. We would then trade the snakes to the Japanese for food or cigarettes.

While at Cabanatuan, a few of us escaped. One Indian boy escaped and was caught just a little way from the camp. The Japanese took him into a field where we all could see, put him on the ground, and tied his arms and legs to posts with wet leather straps. The temperature was over 100°F, and when the sun dried the leather straps they shrank and stretched the boy to death.

The Japanese then announced that we would be divided into groups of ten men and that if any of the ten escaped, the remaining men in the group would be killed. That was a deterrent for a while. However, one night one of the men escaped. The following morning they took the remaining nine men from the group outside the prison fence and lined all of us up to watch. They made the nine men dig their own graves and kneel down in front of the graves. A Japanese officer went behind each of the nine men and shot him in the head and pushed him to his grave. Needless to say, there were no more escapes.

Around October 1942, the Japanese moved some of us prisoners by boat to Japan. There were around 700 of us in one of the holds of the ship. We could not even lie down we were so crowded, and we were not allowed on deck because they had the hold covered over. They would bring us a little food and water once a day, and the sanitary conditions were horrible. While on the 18-day trip to Japan, one of the prisoners had a bad attack of appendicitis and had to have an operation right away. One of our doctors performed the operation right there in the hold. He had no medication whatsoever. The Japanese gave him only a little catgut to sew the boy's incision.

We were all amazed that the boy recovered and walked off the ship when we docked in Japan.

There were a few Japanese ships that were carrying prisoners of war to Japan that were later bombed by our own planes. Of course, our planes did not know they were bombing prisoners.

In one instance, 1,619 American prisoners of war boarded a Japanese ship on December 15, 1944. There were also 2,000 Japanese women and children and 2,500 Japanese soldiers on board. The ship got a short distance from Manila and was repeatedly bombed by our bombers. The hold where the American prisoners were suffered a direct hit; there were only 1,200 Americans alive to leave the ship back in Manila. Later they were loaded on another ship for Japan, and their treatment was terrible. The Japanese would not feed or water them in the holds, and some of the prisoners turned to cannibalism and to drinking the blood of the dead to sustain themselves.

We stayed in Cabanatuan for about six months, and I can't tell you how many of us were sent out on a freighter to Japan. We were taken to a camp in Japan by the name of Hiro Hata. It's right on the seacoast. We worked in a steel mill, did every imaginable work to maintain that steel mill. There were 475 of us there, and we had one American officer who was a doctor. Thank gosh we had him! He was a wonderful man. My wife knew him after the war. He ended up on her ward in Fitzsimmons Army Hospital. Conditions were much, much improved in Japan. First, we got away from the army. We had Home Guard guarding us; we had only two Japanese army people in the whole camp. They gave us hot baths twice a week; sanitary conditions were much better. The daily rations were 600 grams of rice, 21 ounces of rice a day, and a green vegetable for soup. That was our rations for three and a half years. We learned to steal very well. If we were working ships, we would loot the storeroom or wherever we could find food. At that time, the Japanese food consisted of primarily the same thing we had. Of course they got much more and they would have a fish thrown in there.

The Japanese personnel we worked with were the Home Guard, who were the old, nondraftable men who guarded us. They would carry us to the steel mill where they turned us over to the steel mill personnel, who took us to our work areas. Discipline at the steel mill was rather lax; all they cared about was getting the work done, and we'd make a good show at working. We worked right alongside the Japanese and many Koreans. The Koreans were imported to do labor.

As far as mail from home or any correspondence with home was concerned, my parents did not know what had happened to me for a full year and a half. Then they received word that I was a prisoner of war, through the Red Cross, I think it was. About two years after I was captured, they finally let letters through. At maybe two and a half years, they let a box through. My parents sent me as big a box as they could that had all kinds of goodies in it. Also, at about the same time I got the box from home, we got a few Red Cross boxes. Our correspondence with our parents was only on form letters. They would fill in most of it: I am well. I am in Hiro Hata Prison Camp. Say hello to . . . and they would leave a blank spot to fill in.

Just to give you a little example: Every day, twice a day, we had roll call. This one night we had been working all day, 12 hours a day, on all shifts. We all had our own number. My number was 311. We had to count off in Japanese when you spoke to the Japanese, and while I was waiting for my number to come up, I yawned. My number came; I sounded off. After I got through, the Japanese who was in charge called me down and asked me why I yawned. I said I was tired, and he said we don't allow Japanese Army men to yawn. So he started hitting me, and for about 20 minutes he beat my face. The next day my face was swollen and black and blue. That's the way they were. One thing could be said of them, however: They were also sadists with their own people. One of the Japanese soldiers did something wrong, and an officer took out his sword and cut off the soldier's head.

As I mentioned, we had no medicine, and our doctor asked us if we were ever on any ship detail and saw any medication, we should steal it. Well, we had to steal to keep alive. On these ships we would go and loot the storerooms. I was in one of these storerooms, and I saw some medicine in vials on a shelf. I put it in my little loot bag and marched back to the camp that night. All the guards were out in front. I thought, this isn't right; they never were out in front. They would always march us into the compound, and if they wanted to shake us down it would be there. That day they made us strip right out in the road in front of God and everybody. Of course they found what they were looking for in my bag. To make a long story short, the vials that I had stolen were syphilis medicine. It did us no good, but this medicine was not allowed for anybody outside the military, and this was a civilian ship that had it from the black market. So they beat me around quite a bit, and they put me in a five-foot-deep fire bucket. This was in the middle of the winter. They broke the ice on the fire tub and put me down into the cold water and left me in it for about 45 minutes.

We had one interpreter who went to school at UCLA. He was a real nice old man; he would try to keep us abreast of the war situation, and he was as good as he could be to us. One morning we awoke and there were no guards. The interpreter came in a little bit later and said he didn't know what happened, but the Americans had dropped a bomb on Hiroshima, and he said they had just leveled the city. We couldn't imagine what had happened. After the bomb was dropped, the Japanese guards stayed away. Our prisoners caught the two Japanese Army soldiers we had; they didn't live very long. As for food drops, those we got immediately after the Japanese surrendered. First Americans came in little Grumman navy fighting planes. They were little swept-wing planes that would come in low and throw barracks bags of cigarettes and stuff down to us. Then the big planes came in and dropped all kinds of supplies. Three American Army men came in by jeep about three or four days after the surrender to liberate us. They didn't know where all the prison camps were. They said, "Look, you can stay here and we'll arrange transportation, or you can go to the nearest railroad station and commandeer a train to take you to Yokohama," which we did. We couldn't see sitting there waiting for transportation. In Yokohama they kept us there a day or two while they deloused us and prepared to send us back to the Philippines.

One little sidelight: I weighed 120 pounds when I was liberated, and there was no end of food after we were liberated. When we got to the Philippines, we had to go through medical treatment, and we were there about a week. They kept a mess hall open 24 hours a day; you could go in and eat all you wanted. I got off the plane one month later in Minneapolis, Minnesota, where my folks were meeting me, and I'd gained 100 pounds! Just bloat, I had put it on so fast.

After we went through pretty extensive medical exams at Camp Carson, Colorado, they let me go home on a 90-day furlough. I was due to go back to Camp McCoy, Wisconsin. At the end of 90 days, I decided that I'd reenlist in the army, which I did! I spent the next ten years in the military police. In turn, I volunteered to go to the Army Language School to study Chinese. I learned to read, write, and speak Chinese after one year, eight hours a day. I was then sent to the Army Counter Intelligence School at Fort Holabird, Baltimore, Maryland. After completing the school, I was a Special Agent in the Army Counter Intelligence Corps. We were then sent to Okinawa where Ruth (my wife), Connie (my daughter), and I spent two and a half years.

To anyone who doesn't know, the Army Counter Intelligence Corps is an intelligence-gathering organization, and the only thing I can liken it to is a spy outfit. We wore no uniforms; we were not allowed to tell anybody that we were in the military; we always traveled on secret orders; we were not even allowed to live among the military. Ruth, who was a civilian nurse in the army hospital, was not even allowed to tell the people she worked with where I worked. My job in Counter Intelligence was the security of our classified installations such as missile sites or any place where the military stored classified information.

At one time on Okinawa, we were on 24-hour call. My wife and I were home at 11 o'clock at night, and my commanding officer called us into a super hush-hush meeting. We weren't even told what it was. We were told to go home and get what uniforms we could rustle up. A few days later we finally got the alert. We were all called into the office; this was maybe one o'clock in the morning. At about three o'clock, we had to go down and meet a ship pulling into the harbor. We had about 30 trucks and were all armed with submachine guns and our own pistols. We escorted those trucks containing 41 huge metal boxes, maybe 10'x10' square, to a warehouse. For three months we sat (four men to a shift) around the clock on that warehouse. No one was allowed in or close to that warehouse. My organization was the only one allowed there because we were all cleared for top-secret information, which was the classification. They took half the detail away in the middle of one night, and we met an air force plane. The airplane dropped its bomb-bay doors, and we unloaded eight million dollars American money. Then we knew what was in the warehouse! The next morning we went and got these 41 crates. All told, the army had moved 50 million American dollars into Okinawa to exchange all money in the Far East. They had military scrip over there, and they exchanged all this scrip to dollars. The reason there was so much hush-hush on this whole move was to prohibit counterfeit scrip from being exchanged.

Going Home!

General Douglas MacArthur—the Japanese surrender

U.S. airmen at Bradley Field, Connecticut

Leonard Dziabas

Hayward

May 1945

I was delighted and, with a twinge of excitement, I began making plans for my trip back home to Hayward, Wisconsin. It was almost three years since I had left for war.

To go by train I would have to go to Chicago. There I would have to change to a different station and train. From there I would have to make another transfer at Eau Claire, Wisconsin. I came to the conclusion that I could travel faster and in more comfort by hitchhiking, so I purchased a suitcase at the PX, packed it, and sent it on to Hayward by way of Railway Express.

I jumped into a cab and asked him to drive me to the highway at the north end of town. He let me off at an intersection that he figured would be the best place to catch a ride. I was busy getting balanced on my crutches when a farmer stopped and told me to hop in. I never even got to put my thumb in play. The farmer was able to take me only eight miles, but here again, he took me to a point in the road and said, "This is a good place to catch a ride. Good luck and goodbye, soldier." A car was approaching right behind him. It was driven by a beautiful young lady. As I got into position along the roadside, she slowed down and I thought, by Jove, another ride already. But as she came alongside she picked up speed and went on her way.

Disappointed, I watched her progress up the nearby steep hill. When she reached the top she turned into a driveway and backed onto the highway. She turned and started to come toward me. Reaching my position she turned again and stopped. Rolling down the window she said, "Soldier, I didn't mean to pass you by, but I'm a teacher, and my school is at the top of that hill. I think you have a better chance of catching a ride down here than up there; however, if you wish to go up there, hop in." I thanked her and told her that I agreed with her. I had a better chance for a ride down here. She had no more than disappeared at the top of the hill, when the next car came and stopped. They were two salesmen on their way to Minneapolis to attend a sales meeting. They bought my lunch and treated me like royalty during the whole trip. Reaching Minneapolis, they insisted on taking me to St. Paul where I could catch a streetcar that would carry me to the outer limits of the city.

I boarded the streetcar. Sitting down, I noticed the capitol building out of the window across from me. I kept watching for a road sign for Route 63. After what seemed like a long time, I was startled to see the capitol building once again. I then approached the motorman and explained my dilemma to him. He said he would show me where to get off. As I hobbled back to my seat, a man tapped me on the shoulder. He said he overheard my conversation with the motorman and he could help me get to Hayward in good speed. He handed me a business card and said, "I will tell you when to get off, and you walk a block to this trucking company. Give this card to the dispatcher, but don't say a word; he'll see to it that you will get to Hayward fast."

I pushed the card through the slot to the dispatcher. He told me to have a cup of coffee at the grill on the corner and when a truck honked twice to hurry and get into the truck. I didn't even finish my coffee when a semi-truck was out in front and honked twice. The driver was amazed. "They even have a Bill of Lading made out for you. They are shipping you as if you are cargo."

By the time we reached Eau Claire, it was dark, and it was here that I had to transfer to another truck. While waiting for the truck, the dispatcher cleared the top of his desk and giving me a blanket, told me to get some shuteye.

The next truck dropped me off in the parking lot of the CoOp Store in Hayward. I entered the store and noticed the clock above the counter. It was 7:10 A.M. I had beaten the train by five hours.

Sunday my aunt and I went to church. As we were leaving the church, a crowd of people gathered around me. They were all so happy to see that I had made it back home. I felt a tug at my sleeve. Looking down, I saw a pretty little girl looking up at me. She must have been seven or eight years old. She said to me, "Soldier, when I was going home from church, I noticed the patch on your shoulder. It was the same as my Dad's, so I ran home and told him. He wants to know if you would come to our house and have breakfast with us. He can't get out."

We entered the living room and off to the right was an archway that led into the dining room. As I went through the archway, I saw a dining room table with a man in a wheelchair at the head of the table. The minute he saw me he raised his arm and pointed his finger at me and said. "I know you. You're the soldier who covered me with his raincoat when I was wounded!" With that I recognized him as Johnnie Dignan who worked for the *Sawyer County Record* newspaper before the war. He then added, "I know that I would have died that night if you had not covered me."

Don F. Hanlen

Coming Home

I'm an emotional guy, but most of the time I control it pretty well. Looking back on something more than 70 years, only two (very different) occasions come to mind wherein I found myself at the mercy of my emotions. One was somewhat recently, when I lost my wife. The other was my return to the United States following World War II. Both occasions can still evoke in me the deep, welling tide of emotion, and yes, even tears. This story is about the first time I discovered this overwhelming vulnerability, five days in October 1945—five mostly missing days that must have been the epitome of fulfillment, yet lost without detail, only fragmentary flashes of incident without context.

Clarity of sorts had led me aboard a troop train near Boston on that evening in early October. The train, little better than World War I rolling stock, filled two of those days and nights, of course. The trip is a blank, although I do remember laying out my Valpac to serve as a bed in otherwise very primitive accommodations. When did we eat? Was there a diner? I haven't a clue!

Those days dissolved in the flow of homewardness and were followed by two more at Camp McCoy, only slightly clearer. Tests? Examinations? Yes. I remember refusing to have a small cavity treated. That would have meant delay, so I signed a waiver.

Then a day to get home, but how I don't remember. Perhaps a train at first, then finally the local bus. I do remember getting out of the bus in front of the hotel, speaking to Jack, the hotel proprietor, who gave me my first welcome-home handshake, but that's it. I haven't thought often about those days, now fifty years past, and I guess they're lost.

But the beginning—that first day—that's another thing! A single cherished day full to overflowing with memory and incident, in context, in detail, in living, breathing, moving color. Tumbling, metallic sounds surged into my consciousness, becoming a roar as full wakefulness swiftly came. Instant comprehension presaged the emotion that welled up through my whole body, quickly choked back and swallowed in automatic protection of my masculinity, for men don't cry—not in exultation anyway—and especially not a tough artillery veteran with Sicily, Italy, France, and Germany behind him.

In the misty, dim past a furtive convoy had slipped into the Atlantic battleground to begin the saga. Twenty-eight incredible months later, the anchor chain in the next hold rattled, then roared—a triumphant crash, then was silent. Only seconds from deep sleep to profound awareness. Home. I am home. Groping for composure, then looking about, I saw that my traveling companions were grim faced, eyes cast down as they, too, slipped from the rows of six-tier bunks. "That's pretty odd," I thought. "I wonder why they don't feel as I do—this overwhelming joy, nearly out of control." Then, I realized that my eyes also weren't really looking at anyone—that my teeth were clenched in a spasm of forced control—that I too must be looking pretty grim.

"Damned anchor," someone muttered. "Can't get any sleep with that kind of racket." It was 3:30 A.M.

"Wonder where we are," queried someone uselessly, knowing full well that troop ships don't drop anchor in the North Atlantic. Our destination was Boston. We must be there.

I headed for the deck for some fresh air. However chilly it might be this early October morning, it would be better than the stuffy hold—our quarters for the past, mostly stormy eight days. The grim faces began to relax, and, when our nonchalant exodus turned into a jam at the bulkhead, somebody cracked, "Christ, do you guys need an MP to direct traffic?"

Not really funny, but it was the excuse I guess we'd been looking for to vent a pent-up emotional tide. Our laughter was loud and disproportionate—the first of many ridiculous reactions on that blessed day.

On deck there was little to see, but we watched anyway. At first there was only the looming ship under our feet and the slick water of a sheltered harbor stretching away from the sides of the ship—then the breaking dawn began to silhouette a rolling promontory of land. Home! Well, anyway, Boston, Massachusetts, U.S.A.!

I watched for an endless time of thirst for every new shadow of land and city. The holds emptied and the decks filled, but it was strangely quiet. For now, we just watched as the dawn became day and the day became beautiful.

The morning moved on. All the sundry things were done, as much to prove self-possession as anything. Some of us shaved, and most of us had breakfast because two meals a day for eight days had left even exhilarated systems hungry. We ate and washed and all those other things, and proved our composure, then returned to the now sun-drenched deck to watch "home" some more.

For a time, we mostly just drank of the harbor panorama. Portions of the city were vaguely in view, far away, and it seemed that the harbor grew quieter with the advancing day. Boston didn't seem to know or care much about our return, but after all, the war was two months ended, and for many more months than that Boston must have witnessed the turmoil of tens of thousands of returning servicemen. It didn't seem wrong to not have the parade, or the tumultuous welcome that all the movies of other wars had depicted, but it was a little disappointing, that's all.

Then the sounds of music were born, and they grew. The most beautiful of days was filled with the strains of martial, then of popular music as a boat drew close and hove to about a hundred feet off the starboard rail. It was complete with stage and people, a converted tug. Later asked, I wasn't sure what kind of people. I suppose there were probably some girls, but all I really saw were people—people who cared and took the time to come way out in this harbor to show they cared.

Time flowed by again as we watched in rapt contemplation the unexpected greeting, then our captain warned over the PA system, jokingly I guess, that if any more went to the starboard rail, we'd probably capsize. Only then did we notice the visible list caused by nearly 3,000 soldiers hanging from every vantage point starboard of ship's centerline. Maybe he was not joking. Anyway, very shortly after, the tug moved on to other ships nearby in Beantown harbor. We'd had our welcome. Let's get on with it, someone said.

Magically, the captain responded, for the anchor rattled again, more slowly to be sure, but every bit as welcome as it had been at 3:30 A.M. Once underway, we mostly all dispersed to other areas topside, and the final leg of our homeland journey unfolded. We discovered that Boston wasn't through with us, not quite yet.

As we passed them, vessel after vessel riding at anchor signaled welcome. Ships slipping by on their way to sea saluted, and our captain responded to them all, every one. As we closed on the inner harbor, the festive air seemed a continuous melody of organ-toned counterpoint. I couldn't help myself as a destroyer knifed by us on its way to some obscure duty at sea. I pointed dramatically to sea and shouted, "Go get 'em, Yank." Most of my 3,000 companions roared with laughter, as everything seemed to take on hilarious overtones, the hysteria of unbounded joy.

A tiny tug tootled joyfully at us, but got no response from our captain. From the deck rose a crescendoing "Boooooooooo," almost equaling the volume of the captain's belated, hoarse response. His hesitation was understandable, for he apparently no longer had sufficient steam to fully resonate his horn. It made only rasping, funny noises, but we gave him a mighty cheer for his effort.

Closing on the wharf, we edged past a tied-up navy transport, a complement of marines lounging on deck. "Where've you guys been?" one of them jibed. "Fighting a war, remember?" "Didn't the army tell you the war was over months ago?" "Somebody had to clean up the mess you guys left behind."

The effervescent, silly conversation died across the growing distance. In minutes we were easing into the long wharf, hawsers were tossed, and our ship, the *Montclair Victory*, snugged in and tied up.

With almost drill precision, the gangplank was placed, and shore-based military personnel boarded. Incredibly efficient, they hustled us through debarkation instructions and preparations, and in what seemed like minutes, debarkation was under way.

No one kissed the ground, or at least not that I saw, but neither did anyone look grim anymore. I started grinning the moment my foot touched Boston—just grinned—at, toward, and with everybody. There was no diffidence, there was no nonchalance. For the moment at least, the acting was over. We were really home.

A holiday aura filled the dock area. Donuts and fresh milk—wonderful, forgotten fresh milk—was distributed as we were formed up and regimented toward a waiting train. Were we there ten minutes? An hour? No one remembered later. But the train did fill and move out, and it seemed that all of Boston came to a stop for a few minutes.

The streets near the dock teemed with wildly waving and cheering people. As the train moved out and across a street viaduct, vehicles moving toward and under it stopped and the occupants got out to add their welcome. I have no words to describe my oneness with mankind at that moment—singular moments of oneness with my fellow man. I just sat and watched and lived in the warm, tumultuous scene. As the train passed through the thinning city I regained awareness and only then felt the self-consciousness of unrestrained emotion. I furtively brushed away some tears and noticed that I wasn't alone.

Somewhere near Boston, the army had thrown away the book as it set up troop debarkation and transfer points. The old standbys of hurry and wait, long lines, inefficiency, and studied indifference were gone. Camp Miles Standish existed to serve, not just to be. We were maneuvered like checkers, saw things, heard things, signed things, and did things in incredible succession! Soon the day was gone, and a new day began, and we did more things just like the day before. Following instructions, I joined a large group assembled in a small amphitheater where a droll fellow began his instructions with an apology. "Men, I know you're anxious to get out of here and on your way home, but as you can see it's already past noon. There will be some delay, which I'm sure you will understand." We all groaned. This was the army we had come to know. We'd been here 24 hours—just one day. How many more?

The droll fellow went on: "It's two-thirty now. With all that you must yet do, and all your paperwork to process for transfer with you, we can't possibly get you on your train and on your way west before—oh, before six-thirty tonight."

Incredibly, at six-thirty that evening, our train headed west, and I watched in disbelieving wonder as Camp Miles Standish passed from view.

Contributors

Contributors *continued*

Notes

A Coast Guardsmen at the grave of American servicemen

Glendale Quick Order Form

Fax orders: Fax this form toll free to 800-555-9269.

Credit card phone orders: Call Glendale toll free at 800-653-5515.

Internet orders: www.ParadeStore.com.

Postal orders: Glendale – 192 Paris Avenue – Northvale, NJ 07647-2016.

Please send ________ copies of *Theaters of War: We Remember.*

Please also send a copy of Glendale's parade equipment catalog. ______

Name: ____

Address: ____

City:________________________ State:________ Zip:________

Telephone: ____

Email address: _____________________________________

Quantity: ________ @ $19.95 each ________

Sales tax:
Please add 6% for books shipped to New Jersey addresses.
For books shipped to New York, please add applicable tax. ________

Shipping:
To U.S. zip codes: $4 for the first book; $1.50 for each
additional book. International addresses: $9 for the
first book; $5 for each additional book. **Total** ________

Payment in U.S. dollars:

Check in the amount of ______________.

Credit card: Visa MasterCard Discover Amex

Card number: _______________________________________

Name on card: _______________________ Exp. Date: ____/____

Signature: ____